Feminist Theory

Terrell Carver
Editor

Feminist Theory

Two Conversations

Previously published in *Contemporary Political Theory*
Volume 18–22, Issue 1–4, 2019–2023

Editor
Terrell Carver
School of Sociology, Politics
and International Studies
University of Bristol
Bristol BS8 1TU
United Kingdom

Spinoff from journal: "Contemporary Political Theory" Volume 18–22, Issue 1–4, 2019–2023

ISBN 978-3-031-55396-7

© The Editor(s) (if applicable) and The Author(s), under exclusive license to Springer Nature Switzerland AG 2024

This work is subject to copyright. All rights are solely and exclusively licensed by the Publisher, whether the whole or part of the material is concerned, specifically the rights of translation, reprinting, reuse of illustrations, recitation, broadcasting, reproduction on microfilms or in any other physical way, and transmission or information storage and retrieval, electronic adaptation, computer software, or by similar or dissimilar methodology now known or hereafter developed.

The use of general descriptive names, registered names, trademarks, service marks, etc. in this publication does not imply, even in the absence of a specific statement, that such names are exempt from the relevant protective laws and regulations and therefore free for general use.

The publisher, the authors and the editors are safe to assume that the advice and information in this book are believed to be true and accurate at the date of publication. Neither the publisher nor the authors or the editors give a warranty, expressed or implied, with respect to the material contained herein or for any errors or omissions that may have been made. The publisher remains neutral with regard to jurisdictional claims in published maps and institutional affiliations.

This Palgrave Macmillan imprint is published by the registered company Springer Nature Switzerland AG
The registered company address is: Gewerbestrasse 11, 6330 Cham, Switzerland

If disposing of this product, please recycle the paper.

Contents

1. Editor's Introduction 1
Terrell Carver

Conversation I: Feminist Classics, Genres, Contestations

2. The Poetics of Failure in Simone de Beauvoir's *Les bouches inutiles* 7
Ani Chen

3. On ne naît pas femme: On le devient: The life of a sentence 31
Bonnie Mann and Martina Ferrari

**4. The "Agonistic Turn"*: Political Theory and the Displacement
of Politics* in New Contexts** 35
Lida Maxwell, Cristina Beltrán, Shatema Threadcraft,
Stephen K. White, Miriam Leonard, and Bonnie Honig

5. A feminist theory of refusal 69
Bonnie Honig

6. Toni Morrison and political theory 73
Alex Zamalin, Joseph R. Winters, Alix Olson, and Wairimu Njoya

7. New forms of revolt: Essays on Kristeva's intimate politics 99
Sarah K. Hansen and Rebecca Tuvel

**8. Wayward lives, beautiful experiments: Intimate histories
of social upheaval** 103
Saidiya Hartman

9. Agonistic mourning: Political dissidence and the Women in Black 107
Athena Athanasiou

**10. The politics and gender of truth-telling in Foucault's lectures
on *parrhesia*** 111
Lida Maxwell

Conversation II: Feminist Lives, Desires, Futures

11. **Sex wars, SlutWalks, and carceral feminism** 135
    Lorna Bracewell

12. **Feminist afterlives: The defenses and dead ends of revisionist history** 157
    Lorna Bracewell and Manon Garcia

13. **Feminist sexual futures** 165
    Judith Grant, Lorna Bracewell, Lori Marso, and Jocelyn Boryczka

14. *Les Aveux de la chair*. **Vol. 4 of** *L'Histoire de la sexualité* 189
    Michel Foucault

15. **The right to sex** 195
    Amia Srinivasan

16. **Lauren Berlant's legacy in contemporary political theory** 199
    Samuel Galloway, Ali Aslam, Ashleigh Campi, and Hagar Kotef

17. **Queer Terror: Life, death, and desire in the settler colony** 225
    C. Heike Schotten

18. **Living a feminist life** 229
    Sarah Ahmed

19. **Ecology, labor, politics: Violence in Arendt's** *Vita Activa* 233
    Dawn Herrera

20. **Epilogue: On Retraining the Senses** 257
    Karen Zivi

Editor's Introduction

Terrell Carver

FEMINIST POLITICAL THEORY: TWO CONVERSATIONS

Contemporary Political Theory (*CPT*) is a journal where conversations are emergent rather than specially curated. This selection of published items includes peer-reviewed articles, Critical Exchanges—in which contributors and editors work together on a theme or issue—and reviews that are themselves more than simply "about the book." Like the authors of articles, and the contributors to Critical Exchanges, the reviewers, contributors, and authors selected here are important participants in the emerging conceptual logoscapes of political theory.

For this volume we at *CPT* have selected participants in this community whose thinking relates to feminist theory. As feminist theory emerges in this Collexion the concept is construed very broadly and imaginatively, probably more so than any individual author or reviewer here would anticipate. While there are three different genres of academic writing represented, this is not a reason to inhibit thinking across the boundaries and hierarchies of genre, but rather to celebrate the concepts and theorizations. To some extent form determines content, as Hayden White (1990 [1987]) argued many years ago, but when content matters, as it does here, we can separate the ideas out and see how they work together in this new, conversational Collexion.

As in any conversational context there is an interplay between what is said and who is saying it. So in these published items the content will shift the reader's attention from personalities—whether classical, canonical figures, not

---

T. Carver (✉)
Department of Politics, Clifton, University of Bristol, Bristol, UK
e-mail: t.carver@bris.ac.uk

© The Author(s), under exclusive license to Springer Nature Switzerland AG 2024
T. Carver (ed.), *Feminist Theory*,
https://doi.org/10.1007/978-3-031-55397-4_1

all understood within or solely within political theory—over to historical-conjunctural issues and long-standing dilemmas. While this may sound unfocused, actually—like real-life conversations—this content and these personalities will themselves speak within the reader's mind's ear, taking twists and turns of discovery and disclosure. This strategy allows readers to find their own way, and form their own judgements, to an exciting degree. Whatever the genre, *CPT* aims to help its community of readers and writers to think carefully but imaginatively about politics.

Conversation I: Feminist Classics, Genres, Contestations

The first of these Conversations explores feminist thinking in and through literary modes, featuring contributions that engage with literary classics and revered authors, and exploring quite varied genres and writers, notably Simone de Beauvoir, Toni Morrison, Julia Kristeva and Bonnie Honig. This engagement extends even to considering how a variety of feminist writers have focused on just one sentence from Beauvoir, showing how it acquired such theoretical importance and a political life of its own. Perhaps rather similarly a re-examination of a foundational book of thirty years ago—by Bonnie Honig—again demonstrates the resonance of a single descriptor, "agonistic turn," within quite different understandings of political theory itself, and feminist theory in particular.

What counts as political theory, and who counts as a political theorist, is an evolving matter of debate and discovery. Hence the position of Toni Morrison in the conversation, as it emerges here, is particularly notable, posing questions of genre-identification and -critique that are increasingly influential in feminist theory and activisms. The way that literary writing and theorizing becomes part of theoretical thinking about politics then emerges very clearly in a discussion of the way that the work of Kristeva has been made relevant to feminist theory. Proceeding the other way round, from the everyday voices and re-narrated realities of lives that are politicizing, precisely because these narrations are so personal, the examination here of Sadiya Hartman's writing practices and methodological subversions marks an important moment.

Continuing the ethnographic theme, the conversation turns to Athena Athenassiou's experiential encounter with the Women in Black of Belgrade. This is understood through the "lens" of agonistic theorization, thus turning conversationally back in that direction. And rounding off with a classically theoretical issue—"truth telling"—we find ourselves re-reading Euripides' play *Ion*.

Conversation II: Feminist Lives, Desires, Futures

The second conversation presented here explores controversial and continuing core values of feminism as a movement for women's liberation from oppression, and thus a political movement for freedom intersecting with liberalism and the state. By validating woman as a subject of knowledge and women as knowers of all things human, the conversation opens with a provocative consideration of sexual liberation and "carceral feminism," contextualized to the politics of the "sex wars" as seen in SlutWalks.

As thinkers, feminists have engaged with the danger/pleasure binary, and as a movement feminism has faced co-optation and misappropriation. Here the conversation crosses the line between feminist activisms and queer-critiques as a way to consider feminist futures, even "utopian longings." Moreover the conversation considers the local US framings through which these issues arise, in the way that they do, but taking them out into a global and thus more diverse array of contexts. Indeed, given diverse perspectives and histories, what can we know about sexuality as bodies, and societies as power, in the first place? Do recently published lectures by Michel Foucault have the answer? Or perhaps, in a more feminist way, do we simply get more questions for more people to think about? And, in the light of the foregoing feminist-queer suspicions of liberalism and the "carceral state," is there a "right to sex"?

Much of this experiential questioning can be found in the life and work of Lauren Berlant, celebrated here in this conversation, where gender-liberation as queer-idea and -practice confronts gender-oppression as a normalizing hierarchy. Is "queer terror" an appropriate and defensible response and political strategy? Does the Killjoy Manifesto, derived from reflections on "living a feminist life," qualify? This conversation arrives at very unsettling discussions of violence and politics: Are they antithetical and thus definitional erasures? Is instrumental violence politically justifiable? What happens to us all when political freedom is mistaken for the "violence of world consumption"?

Reference

White, H. (1990 [1987]). *The content of the form: Narrative discourse and historical representation*. Johns Hopkins University Press.

Conversation I: Feminist Classics, Genres, Contestations

Article

The Poetics of Failure in Simone de Beauvoir's *Les bouches inutiles*

Ani Chen
Cornell University, Ithaca, NY 14853, USA.
aac245@cornell.edu

Abstract I argue that Simone de Beauvoir's only play *Les bouches inutiles* reveals the centrality of failure in Beauvoir's feminist account of political freedom. In recent years, political theorists have mobilized failure to capture the diverse ways of being and doing that stand outside of hegemonic models of political life, with some conceiving of failure as a form of negativity. Negativity, on these accounts, captures an "antisocial" form of resistance by which subjects refuse configurations of sociality in order to achieve freedom. I argue, however, that this form of negativity runs counter to the collective conception of freedom in Beauvoir's political thought. To make this case, I interpret the play as a performance *manqué* and demonstrate that the failures that the women encounter in *Les bouches inutiles* are conditional on responses from the men. This allows me to recover a conception of failure as a form of positive negativity. What Beauvoir does in her literary theory is to conceptualize that same place of negativity, to which men have consigned women, as a place from which women might disclose themselves and their unique situations. Read in this way, failure is both the foreclosure of the space of intersubjectivity between women's appeals and men's responses, and at the same time opens ways for women to resist those failures. I then leverage Eve Sedgwick's theory of the periperformative to show how, by engaging in poetic practices, women re-signify the political meanings of their bodies and become free with and through others. I conclude by stepping outside of the frame of the play to evaluate its recent resignification by contemporary readers. Doing so underscores the point that resisting failure requires ongoing practices of contestation and disclosure by subjects and audiences across time to affirm the collective dimension of freedom in feminist political theory.
Contemporary Political Theory (2023) **22**, 506–528. https://doi.org/10.1057/s41296-023-00622-8; advance online publication 1 March 2023

Keywords: Beauvoir; Sedgwick; freedom; failure; embodiment; theater

'This was a lovely day; I hardly thought of the war…and I would like something solid to eat', wrote Simone de Beauvoir on Thursday, 21 September 1939 (Beauvoir, 2009b, p. 74). Eight months later, in May 1940, Germany would invade

France and the Low Countries, beginning a nearly 5-year occupation, which affected every aspect of daily life. Endemic food and fuel shortages, coupled with severe military and policing operations, created a situation of hunger and fear. As civilian women moved through cities to acquire food, first aid, and other supplies, they would have experienced this situation acutely. Soldiers sought to enforce order in markets and transportation centers, which were then used to deport, incarcerate, and ultimately exterminate Jewish residents (Naji and Stanley, 2011, pp. 16–20).

Against this backdrop, Beauvoir wrote and staged her first and only play, *Les bouches inutiles*, which premiered in November 1945 at the Théâtre des Carrefours in Paris. While set in the medieval town of Vaucelles, the play's premise would have been easily recognizable to its audience; Paris had been liberated only a year earlier in August 1944.[1] In *Les bouches inutiles*, the citizens have only just liberated themselves from their despotic ruler, the duke of Burgundy, and have constituted a democratic town council in his place. Awaiting assistance from the King of France, the town residents now find themselves with only six weeks supply of food left in the communal granaries. The town council, however, is composed of only the adult, able-bodied men of the town. In this situation of starvation and war, the all-male council condemns the women, children, and elderly as 'useless mouths', basing their decision on the valuation of the productive labor of able-bodied men to defend and guard the town, and on the devaluation of the reproductive labor of the useless mouths who feed and care for the town. Judged useless, the latter are sentenced to their certain deaths. The play's surprising conclusion, in which the character Jean-Pierre persuades the town council to revoke the condemnation, ultimately results in the townspeople assembling at the ramparts to fight the Burgundians together. But focusing on this ostensibly happy ending obscures the women's embodied experience of failure at making their voices and their hunger heard in the majority of the play.

In recent years, Catherine Naji's and Liz Stanley's efforts to newly translate *Les bouches inutiles* have prompted scholars to begin considering its place alongside Beauvoir's philosophy and philosophical fiction (Naji and Stanley, 2011; Beauvoir 2011). Similarly, Ashley King Scheu and Kate Kirkpatrick have recently argued that Beauvoir's fiction has value in its own right (Kirkpatrick, 2019; Scheu, 2011).Building on these important recoveries of Beauvoir's play, I focus on the play's illumination of an underexplored aspect of Beauvoir's philosophy, namely, how she thinks about the role of voice in relaying the politics of embodied experience.

To make this argument, I focus on the women's embodied experience of failure at making their voices and their hunger heard in the majority of the play. In my view, Beauvoir's play mirrors wartime material shortage in order to stage a critical examination of how the body becomes a site for voice that surmounts the failure of not being responded to. In *Les bouches inutiles*, this staging occurs in the ways women use gesture and costume to solicit audiences within the frame of the play to look upon their failed appeals to the men and to take up their appeals to freedom. More specifically, *Les bouches inutiles* communicates the conditions of that experience of failure and of the possibility of resistance, making sensible through the artifice of the stage the otherwise incommunicable work that the women of Vaucelles perform. Their labors of building and repairing, cooking and feeding allow the townspeople to endure the siege. These labors are juxtaposed to feelings of devastation and loss, when they learn that despite these efforts, they have been condemned to death. In this way, the devaluation of so many mouths and bodies, I argue, relates the materialist account of resistance that appears in *The Second Sex* to the discursive account of resistance that appears in both Beauvoir's literary writings and *Ethics of Ambiguity*.

In *The Second Sex*, Beauvoir gives an existentialist-materialist account of women's resistance, locating their becoming free in meaningful work (Garcia, 2021, p. 135; Heinämma, 2003; Bergoffen, 2003). In *Ethics of Ambiguity* and her literary works, Beauvoir gives a discursive account of resistance, premised on the notion that writing literature is a speech-act, meant to convey women's experience of the world through the disclosure of truths in their own voices (Moi, 2009; Deutscher, 2008, p. 672). What *Les bouches inutiles* adds, crucially, is the political insight that women will not be able to become creators until there is a radical, social reevaluation of women's work and women's voices.

In Beauvoir's philosophical and literary universes, the subject becomes a creator, and thereby free, by resisting failure. This facet of Beauvoir's account of political freedom is often eclipsed by the prevailing view that Beauvoir was not concerned with the possibility that one's words may not reach another (Moi, 2009) and, with respect to *Les bouches inutiles* specifically, the play's exultant resolution. I believe that such a view is incorrect. I argue that Beauvoir's concern with failure is most overt in her literary writings, especially on the theater. I demonstrate that Beauvoir in these works evinces a concern that women's appeals, whether spoken or transposed into literature, may not be responded to by men. Failures of response, in Beauvoir's schema stand as an obstruction to the movement of the subject of appeal into freedom. For this reason, I believe, Beauvoir emphasizes the importance of literary works in standing against the tides of time and space to one day be responded to.

I argue that *Les bouches inutiles* is central to understanding the role of failure in Beauvoir's explicitly feminist account of political freedom. In recent years, political theorists have mobilized failure in order to capture at once the limitations of existing institutions and power-holders to effect ideals of justice and the diverse ways of being and doing that stand outside of hegemonic models of political life (Ahmed, 2021; Dilts, 2017; Halberstam, 2011). Perhaps most influentially, Jack Halberstam has conceived of failure as a form of radical negativity. Critiquing a liberal mode of feminism he associates with Simone de Beauvoir, Halberstam theorizes a conception of "shadow feminism," in which actors engage failure as an "antisocial" form of resistance and refuse to reproduce forms of subjectivity and political relationality complicit with patriarchy. "The antisocial," Halberstam explains, "dictates an unbecoming, a cleaving to that which seems to shame or annihilate, and a radical passivity allows for the inhabitance of femininity with a difference" (2011, p. 144). Along these lines, Lori Marso argues that failure and antisociality contribute as much to Beauvoir's conception of feminist political freedom as do solidarity and allyship (2017).

In this article, I build on this significant aspect of Marso's scholarship, and I recover a conception of failure as a form of *positive* negativity.[2] My central contribution is to demonstrate that failure figures as the foreclosure of the space of intersubjectivity between women's appeals and men's responses, prompting the women to undertake poetic practices of resistance to those failures vis-à-vis their words. Resistance, in this analysis, refers to efforts by subjects, occupying the space of negation, to create meaning by disclosing their situations to others. In Beauvoir's lexicon, negation denotes the status to which patriarchal order seeks to consign women and other feminized subjects as objects, so that it can then differentiate men from them and build systems of meaning and value. And yet, Beauvoir conceptualizes the same place of negation as the space from which women can disclose themselves as subjects of appeal, who, by means of literary and ordinary language, become free.

I read failure in the play through what I call the performance *manqué*, which I define as the subject of appeal's expectations of what would have been, could have been, and ought to have been in the response. By capturing failure as a set of conditional possibilities that have to be inhabited and resisted, I mark how women's efforts at becoming free are stalled when they are not responded to by the men. As Elizabeth Wingrove has argued, one of the reasons that discursive resistance by feminized political subjects fail is because they cannot help but make claims within gendered grids of political intelligibility that secure "settled significations" of gender, equality, and difference (2016, p. 413). And yet, the women of *Les bouches inutiles* distend the gendered division within the speech situation by inviting others to look upon, contest, and judge their failures. They do so, I argue, by politically re-signifying what their bodies mean before these audiences. In this way, I argue that the women resist those failures together and become free.

Leveraging Eve Sedwick's theory of the periperformative, I claim that we can see how audiences within the play become a site of response that enables the subject of appeal to resist failure and become free. Sedgwick defines the periperformative as the space that occurs around performative speech acts. Sedgwick argues that the periperformative space shows how literary texts can conscript audiences into failed speech acts. I analyze the women's appeals against their condemnation to death as such acts. As opposed to a strictly literary genre, the theatrical form of *Les bouches inutiles* magnifies the periperformative dimensions of the women's appeals, making them physically visible to the audience of the performance, and revealing how these appeals can prompt audiences in the periperformative space to spectate upon each other's embodied experiences of failure in their appeals. The women (1) interpellate and contest each other's failures in their appeals to the men on the council, and (2) elicit imagined futures. The periperformative lens therefore shows how the women resist the failure in their appeals by soliciting audiences within the frame of the play to engage with their failures. These audiences contest the political meanings that the men assign to their bodies and affirm their appeals for freedom.

I begin by introducing my reading of Beauvoir's political thought through her literary theory, and I attend to what in her view makes literature distinct from philosophy, highlighting the centrality of disclosure and negation to communicating one's embodied experience across differences of situation. I then demonstrate the ways in which women's embodied experience, in particular, is shaped by failure and the importance of this understanding to Beauvoir's feminist account of political freedom. Next, I show that the significance of failure to political freedom is most explicit in Beauvoir's writings on the theater and in her dramatic prose. I bring these issues to bear on *Les bouches inutiles* by reading failure in the play through the lens of the performance *manqué*. By reading the play through the lens of the performance *manqué*, I bring together the material and discursive accounts of resistance by concretizing women's embodied experience of failure in the appeal. Attending to the dramaturgy of the play, I demonstrate that gesture and costuming illuminate how the women occupy the conditional possibilities of failure so as to resist. A periperformative reading of the play illuminates how different audiences within the play become sites of response that enable the subject of appeal to resist failure in the response and become free. I conclude by considering the mirroring of the women's experiences of failure in the play to Beauvoir's own experience of professional failure at the time of the play's initial performance in 1945. I argue that the play's recent reception underscores how the theatrical medium is a powerful tool for re-signifying the political meaning of women's bodies and affirming the collective character of political freedom in the feminist key.

Beauvoir's Literary Theory

Recently, Sharon Stanley has illuminated how Beauvoir's fiction rehearses many arguments that would later appear in *Ethics of Ambiguity* and *The Second Sex* (2001, p. 202). This interpretation and those like it seek to demonstrate the significance of Beauvoir's literature to her larger philosophical *oeuvre*, often viewing her literature as a container for the philosophical universe she constructed in *The Second Sex* and *Ethics of Ambiguity* (Fichera, 1986; Jones & Reinelt, 1983; Megna, 2018; Stanley, 2001). To be sure, Beauvoir states in "Literature and

Metaphysics" and "Existentialist Theater" that philosophy can provide the background conditions for literature. Indeed, she argues in her readings of Jean-Paul Sartre's *Les mouches* and Albert Camus' *Caligula* that both existentialist thinkers posed questions about ethical action and clarified the moral and psychological constraints that their characters encountered in achieving human freedom (Beauvoir, 2011, p. 145).

However, Beauvoir herself saw philosophy and literature as occupying two poles of a "hybrid aesthetic space," in which literature would enrich existentialist philosophy and vice versa (2011, p. 4). If existentialist philosophy claimed to get at human existence, then the practice of writing existentialism into literature ought to disinter the experience of subjectivity from pure understanding and to give it concrete representation in narrative. Beauvoir writes, "Existentialist thought claims to grasp the essence at the heart of existence; and if the description of essence is a matter solely for philosophy properly speaking, then the novel will permit us to evoke the original upspringing of existence in its complete, singular, and temporal truth" (Beauvoir, 2004, p. 274). For Beauvoir, philosophical writing alone cannot give an "adequate expression" of what it means to be in the world, because philosophy seeks to understand the world with "intelligence alone" (2004, p. 275). Human subjectivity precedes intelligence, understood here as philosophical reflection and contemplation. Philosophy, therefore, needs literature in order to give an account of the marvelous complexities of what it means to be human.

Literature fulfills this function through disclosure (*dévoilement*), defined in "What Can Literature Do?" as the communication across situations. In Beauvoir's vocabulary, "situation" refers to the myriad aspects of history, social status, and individuality that differentially shape one's singular relation to the world. Importantly, Beauvoir describes the situation as a "detotalized totality," open to the situations of others (Moi, 2009, p. 192). As Eva Gothlin reminds readers, the subject has the ability to disclose herself, because she begins from a place of negativity, whereby she distinguishes herself from what she is not in an effort to signify positively who and what she is (1999, p. 91).

For Beauvoir, literature empowers the writer to let the reader experience her situation as if walking in her own shoes. "I annex them to my universe, but I do not change universes…I abdicate my 'I' in favor of he who is speaking, and yet I remain myself" (Beauvoir, 2011, p. 202). A poignant example of this occurs in Beauvoir's *Wartime Diary*, throughout which she details the carnal experience of eating and reading. She observes in "What Can Literature Do?" that books were "the only form of communication capable of giving me the incommunicable—capable of giving me the taste of another life" (Beauvoir, 2011, p. 201). The reader perceives the text on the page through the sight of the words, the taste of someone else's life, and, crucially, the sound of the writer's voice. By "voice," Beauvoir refers to the unique way each writer uses language, which functions for Beauvoir as a "signifying vehicle," a medium by which subjects create relationships with others across their situations (2011, p. 199). Using informal and formal elements of this medium, the writer seeks to "speak" to the reader. Beauvoir names these elements "a style, a tone, a technique, an art, an invention" (2011, p. 199). From these building blocks, the writer constructs a portal through which readers might pass into her situation.

When we consider this account of disclosure in Beauvoir's literary theory alongside her political theory in *The Second Sex*, we begin to see what a radical act of resistance it is for a woman to engage in disclosure. In *The Second Sex*, Beauvoir argues that women "represent…[a] negation" by which men define and project their values, aspirations, and desires (2009, p. 747). What Beauvoir does in her literary theory is to conceptualize that same place of negativity, to which men have consigned women, as a place from which women might disclose themselves and their unique situations. For Beauvoir, such acts are the beginnings of "posit[ing] oneself as a freedom," where freedom is understood as engaging in creating and making meaning about who one is, what one desires, and what one hopes for (2009, p. 748). These efforts at attaining freedom require an active resistance of failure.

The Drama of Embodied Experience

One entry-point into the centrality of failure to Beauvoir's account of political freedom is through her statement at the end of *The Second Sex*, "As long as she still has to fight to become a human being, she cannot be a creator" (2009, p. 750). Beauvoir points to one of the myriad obstacles facing subjects in their efforts to become free: the human condition of ambiguity. Ambiguity allows us to grasp what failure looks like for Beauvoir and to clarify the feminist political stakes underpinning Beauvoir's conception of the subject who discloses her situation.

Marso glosses the connection in this way: "Ambiguity is for Beauvoir a kind of 'twoness'. Our lived experience is as subject and object, transcendence and immanence, freedom and body, choosing agents and trapped objects…Thus while ambiguity is ontological—we are all exposed and vulnerable to each other— ambiguity is also political: some are disproportionately vulnerable, marked as other, doomed to immanence and denied transcendence" (2017, p. 3; see also 2012). Marso helpfully captures the politicality of ambiguity vis-à-vis Beauvoir's emphasis on the embodied dimension of subjectivity. In *The Second Sex*, Beauvoir catalogues how bodies marked "woman" experience the world. Sexual differentiation at birth, coupled with social and economic structures, concretize women's lived experience of themselves and in relation to others as a "painful split." They come to see themselves as autonomous individuals and as man's Other, the object by which men, through the process of negation we saw earlier, realize their own projects, futures, and freedoms (Beauvoir, 2009a, p. 273). Beauvoir describes the phenomenology of becoming a woman in terms of the concrete or lived experience by which the female child becomes negated, objectified, and made immanent, as well as the technical conception of her relationship to the world. In some cases, women may let go of lived experience altogether, preferring submission to patriarchal oppression by "conforming to the status of the Other," as Manon Garcia puts it, over the dissatisfaction of their mal-adaptation (2021, p. 154).

Marso and Garcia are right in delineating the ways ambiguity illuminates how women's embodiment takes on political meanings. At the same time, Beauvoir also affirms the ways women can contest the political meanings that are assigned to their bodies. Beauvoir refers to this conflict that women experience as a drama of ambiguity. She writes, "Woman's drama lies in this conflict between the fundamental claim of every subject, which always posits itself as essential, and the demands of a situation that constitutes her as inessential" (Beauvoir, 2009a, p. 17). Beauvoir emphasizes that although women may submit to patriarchal order there will always remain an inner conflict or rebellion that manifests itself. Although women are free subjects and can ontologically move into transcendence, their efforts are frustrated as patriarchy seeks to consign them to negation and immanence. This sense of frustration creates a sense of rebellion and indignation within women, playing itself out in the failed efforts of women as subjects to be and do freely in the world, like the cases of young girls and women Beauvoir describes.

If *The Second Sex* addresses the case of the woman who, confronted by the possibility of failure, submits to patriarchal order, Beauvoir shows in *Ethics of Ambiguity* how the subject might resist failure and become free. In *Ethics of Ambiguity*, Beauvoir analogizes such efforts to making art. "[F]ailure and success are two aspects of reality which at the start are not perceptible…Art and science do not establish themselves despite failure but through it…[I]t has to found itself though it is prohibited from ever fulfilling itself" (Beauvoir, 1976, pp. 139–140). Here, too, Beauvoir argues that accepting ambiguity requires resistance, not acquiescence, to failure. This resistance is the condition for freedom, because it is at once the acceptance of the obstacles that lie in one's way and at the same time an exercise of the intention to confront those obstacles.

Beauvoir defines freedom as the creative act through which one becomes a subject in the world. The content of freedom's art is the disclosure of one's desire to impress some lasting trace of oneself in the world. She writes, "It is not necessary for the subject to seek to be, but it must desire that there be being. To will oneself free and to will that there be being are one and the same choice, the choice that man makes of himself as a presence in the world" (Beauvoir, 1976, p. 75). In one sense, practicing freedom for Beauvoir is discursive. When one practices freedom in the world, one makes a claim on others about who one is. At the same time, practices of freedom are also material, insofar as the creative act of freedom requires acting in the bodily presence of other people. In this way, practicing freedom is similar to what Michael Vicaro has called a "rhetoric of display," by which some/body expresses herself by means of bodily word and deed—mouths, hands, gesture (Vicaro, 2015, p. 175).In *The Second Sex*, Beauvoir acknowledges that these displays can be risky. In a world ordered by patriarchy, women are expected to "fit into a world that has doomed her to passivity," and when women seek to move into transcendence, others can endeavor to treat them as objects, rather than subjects in the world (2009, p. 724).

Where philosophers and political theorists have read in *The Second Sex* a theory of resistance that rests in women taking on meaningful projects in the world (Garcia, 2021; Heinämma, 2003; Kirkpatrick, 2019), literary theorists, as we have seen, have emphasized the discursive account of resistance whereby women's claims render them as free subjects in the world (Crawford, 2013; Moi, 2009; Scheu, 2011). To be sure, Beauvoir argues that women's emancipation lies in taking control of the means of the production of their own labor, whether through taking on their own projects or gaining control of their reproductive labor. Beauvoir also argues that the forms of women's labor most conducive to human freedom are discursive: art, literature, and philosophy (2009, p. 750). That is, women must channel the ways in which they use language in their unheeded protests to "found the world anew on a human freedom" (Beauvoir, 2009a, p. 748). In the concluding chapters of *The Second Sex*, Beauvoir argues that these paths of resistance toward emancipation will not come to fruition unless there is a complete reevaluation of women in society such that they and their work are no longer viewed as "inessential" (2009, p. 568).

What joins together these seemingly disparate arguments in *The Second Sex* and *Ethics of Ambiguity* is that the ethical response to the failure that women experience in doing freedom requires responding poetically, as creators who make or do something in the world (Beauvoir, 2009a, p. 748). In order to become a creator in the world, Beauvoir argues, women must orient themselves as subjects capable of willing freedom. Such a stance, however, is not possible without social and economic structures to support women in their endeavors and to fundamentally reevaluate their voices in society. As we shall see, theater is a unique regime of aesthetic representation that can act as a structure for making sensible women's embodied experience of failure, their acceptance of their own ambiguity, and their efforts at poetic response.

Theater: A Tangible Point of Support

Given the experience of failure that imbues the space between self and other, how can women become free if their appeals are not joined by response? Toril Moi argues that what distinguishes Beauvoir's account of the literary voice from those of prominent speech-act theorists is that she "does not appear to worry about situations in which I might utter words that completely fail to reach others, words that convince others that I am incomprehensible, a mad babbler" (2009, pp. 194—

195). I disagree. I argue that Beauvoir is highly preoccupied with the possibility that one's words may fail to reach another. In this section, I demonstrate that we can see this preoccupation unfold in the context of Beauvoir's writings on the theater, its genre-specificity, and the efforts a playwright ought to undertake for her work to be received by the audience.

If in "What Can Literature Do" and "Literature and Metaphysics" Beauvoir offered broad arguments about literature, in "The Novel and the Theater" and "Existentialist Theater" she argues that the specificity of theater as a genre lies in rendering moments when one's words fail to reach another sensible to the audience of the performance.[3] The novel and the theater require different modes of depiction to communicate to their respective audiences: the reader and the spectator. The reader, Beauvoir notes, can neither see nor hear the words of the novel's characters unless the novelist mediates those words through the page. And so, the novelist's task requires using language plausible to her readers. While the language ought to be plausible, the novelist should not create a direct copy of the real world. "If [the writer] wants to be convincing, he must not copy the real world like the naturalists wanted to, but rely upon it for support" (Beauvoir, 2011, p.104). What the novelist borrows from the real world are aspects of spoken language and feeling, embellished slightly in ways that will effectively communicate the characters' words and actions to the novel's readers (Beauvoir, 2011, p. 105).

Where the "foremost condition" of any artistic work is "communication," the ambitious scope of theatrical communication sets it apart (Beauvoir, 2011, p. 147). Beauvoir defines the content of theatrical communication thus,

> Something to say, that something is worth being said, and that something, therefore, has a value. And furthermore, there are human beings (*des hommes*) to whom it can be said, men who are capable of hearing, therefore men who are free and also capable of responding. So it is to say that there is something to express, and something to do, and something to hope for (2011, p. 149).[4]

In this passage, Beauvoir argues that art is an expression of freedom, because, despite the possibility of failure in the reception, the artist persists by creating something in the world, rather than acquiescing to failure. The artist expresses freedom through the theatrical artwork, because the theatrical artwork, too, is an assertion of value in the world. This value can be ascertained through Beauvoir's belief that theatrical artwork in particular would find an audience across differences of situation, space, and time.

The genre, nevertheless, imposes several constraints on the playwright. Because the spectator is not privy to the characters' innermost thoughts in the same way that the reader of a novel might be, the playwright relays her characters' motivations and actions so as to, as Elizabeth Fallaize writes, "bring an imaginary universe to life" (2011, p. 93). To do so, the playwright uses language to augment the costumes and props, aiding the reader with the flow of the plot and composing scenes built on the action and reaction of characters' dialogue. Above all, the language is "simple, direct, and evident" (Beauvoir, 2011, p. 103). With the "physical presence of the actors and the costumes, the stage then serves as a tangible support for the spectator's imagination" (Beauvoir, 2011, p. 105). Language would join gesture and costume to tangibly disclose the situation onstage to the audience. As I demonstrate in the following section, Beauvoir implements these dramaturgical notes to display the embodied experience of failure by the women of Vaucelles in *Les bouches inutiles*.

Les bouches intuiles, a Performance *Manqué*

In *Les bouches inutiles*, the dramaturgy helps us view the play as a performance of failure, which I call a performance *manqué*. I use the term performance *manqué* to capture the conditionality of the women's appeals. Beauvoir's protagonists lodge their appeals within a context of expectation that they will or should be responded to by the male antagonists, who consist of their fathers, brothers, lovers, and neighbors. The performance *manqué* denotes the possibility and ultimate foreclosure of a space of intersubjectivity between the women's appeals and the men's responses. I argue that, when we read the play periperformatively, we can see how the women occupy the attendant space of negation to resist the experience of failure to the men's response.

Unfolding over eight *tableaux*, the play discloses the women's embodied experience: from the open-air ramparts, where the soldiers resent sharing rations with women, elderly, and children to the floor of the town council, where the men decide to condemn the useless mouths, to the home of the D'Avesnes family, composed of the town patriarch Louis, his wife Catherine, their children Clarice and Georges, and their adoptive children Jean-Pierre and Jeanne.[5] In the town square, Clarice declares her love for Jean-Pierre and refuses her father's engagement of her to another alderman, Jacques van der Welde. At home, Jeanne and Catherine prepare food for the townspeople. In the town council, Catherine unsuccessfully protests her husband's decision. Later, Jeanne discovers Georges' conspiracy to install another alderman, François, as sole ruler and she is swiftly murdered. Her death and the threat of a new despot ultimately move Louis to reconvene the council. In the final scene, Jean-Pierre persuades the men to overturn their initial decision, and all, including the useless mouths, gather to fight the duke's army.

These various spaces pose the question of the women's status in similar ways. Even the name of the town asks after it. Many render "Vaucelles" as a play on the question "*vaut-elle?*," or "does she have worth?" (Stanley and Naji, 2011, p. 12). This translation obscures in part the plural dimension of the question. Paul Robert defines the verb *valoir* as referring to "a relationship of equality (*un rapport d'égalité*)" (1987, p. 2062), thereby supporting Virginia Fichera's view that the play interrogates the "male fiction" of equality in relationships between men and women (1986, p. 58). Moreover, the rendering of *elle* as the subject of the question individuates the subject of the play. Robert further defines *celles* as the feminine plural form of the pronoun "celui" (1987, p. 272).[6] The play's title is in the plural, and the play stages women in the plural, seeking to resist the devaluation of their mouths, the source of both their hunger and their voices.

By devaluing women's voices, the men have unilaterally made their decision about who is entitled to eat. They judge who is "useful" based on their contribution to the activities they believe sustain their vision of the town's future (Stanley, 2001, pp. 214–215). These so-called "useful" activities are: defending the town, guarding the ramparts, and building the belfry. Because only able-bodied can do these activities in Vaucelles, they are entitled to eat from the diminishing food supplies and to live. The women, along with children and the elderly, are considered "useless" because they do not contribute to these activities, although they do contribute to sustaining the siege in meaningful ways—cooking and feeding the townspeople, as Catherine later argues, when she is trying to prove that she is "useful," laying the foundation stone of the belfry and sewing the heraldry flags.[7]

In the third *tableau*, cues for silence and corresponding pauses work to expose the failure that Catherine experiences in her appeals to Louis regarding the council's decision. When Catherine learns about the council's decision, she confronts Louis. As Catherine begins to grasp that she, for all the mouths she has fed, is a useless mouth, her speech becomes interspersed with unsettling silences and pauses. She says to Louis, "You're frightening me. (She looks at him. A pause.) What has the Council decided. (Silence.) You're not surrendering the town?" Louis answers first by acknowledging that Bruges will not come to their aid and then by trying to change the subject, asking why Clarice, standing off to the side, is crying. Catherine, sensing his deflection, replies. "(To the three children) Leave us. (They go out.) Tell me the truth. (Silence.) You know full well that no help will come before spring" (Beauvoir, 2011[1945], p. 56).[8]

These pauses amplify Louis's non-answers. At each of Catherine's efforts to rebut the council's reasons, Louis demurs both by refusing to answer and by turning his eyes away from her. In a pivotal moment of their exchange, Louis abruptly tells her, "Do not ask me anything, Catherine." Catherine, however, presses further. "Has there ever been a secret between us? (Silence.) If all is lost, if we must die in a hopeless attempt to escape, don't be afraid to tell me: I'm ready" (p. 56). When Louis turns his eyes away from her and begs her to leave him alone, Catherine implores him to tell her "whatever the future will be," and that she "want[s] to face it with [him]." Catherine pleads, "Speak to me" (p. 56). When Louis finally responds, his own speech is punctuated by silence, as well. "As soon as I have spoken, we will be separated forever. (Silence.) The council has decided to get rid of the useless mouths. Tomorrow before sunset they will be driven into the ditches: the infirm, the old men, the children, and the women" (p. 56). Despite Catherine's efforts at demonstrating to Louis how useful she is by using the language of use that the council has set out, Louis dismisses her.

The performance *manqué* in this *tableau*—made salient by Beauvoir's stage directions— captures what political theorists have identified as a sense of loss when appeals to formal institutions for certain political commitments result in the narrowing of those commitments and the restriction of who is entitled to them (Dilts, 2017; Stauffer, 2015). In the *tableau*, Catherine, believing her voice to be equal to Louis's and the other men of the town council, expects that Louis will give her a fair hearing. She finds instead that she has been denied her voice, an experience performed in the play when Louis does not respond at all. These non-responses work to mark an absence in the exchange between him and his wife. The burden of this loss disproportionately falls on Catherine. When the curtain, drops on the third *tableau*. Catherine's loss of voice is reflected in the silence with which she is met from Louis and by the simultaneous falling of the stage curtain.

In a reading which captures why Catherine, in her frustration, seeks to prove her use, Judith Zykofsky Jones and Janelle Reinelt categorize Catherine as the married woman, who, in the schema Beauvoir provides in *The Second Sex*, reacts to the inessentialization of her work by submitting to the patriarchal structures that constrain her (1983, p. 532). To be sure the dramaturgical silences in the third *tableau* function as a space of double negation and mark how Catherine seems resigned to the condemnation. Louis seeks to put Catherine into her place as his wife, and while Catherine sees this place as a source of possible transformation, motivating her to speak out, Louis's silences undermine her efforts. I argue, however, when we look at the fourth *tableau*, we see a different picture of Catherine emerge.

In this instance, Catherine uses language to transform her body into a site of contestation. There she reminds Louis that her future is entwined with his and thereby Vaucelles's. "We had one future between us," she proclaims, before asking why, if the future of Vaucelles is theirs together, then she must die. She points to the bodily sacrifices that she has made for the sake of living and dying for the town, including the hunger she felt while feeding the townspeople from her own larders. Offering up her own body, Catherine suggests, "We could have thrown ourselves at the duke's army, set fire to our houses and all died together" (p. 58). Catherine's instrumentalization of her body in this way is distinct from the council's instrumentalization of her body and the bodies of the useless mouths. Throughout the play, Louis and the council instrumentalize the bodies of the useless mouths as objects over which they can exercise authority and therefore sacrifice to achieve their ends. By contrast, when Catherine speaks about her body as an instrument of sacrifice—through its labors and now through immolation—she asserts herself as a subject, who refuses to acquiesce to the terms of the decision that Louis and the council have made. As Banu Bargu has put it, such moves by political actors are meant to "transform [them] from the object of violence into the subject of resistance" (Bargu, 2016, pp. 282–283). As Louis distances himself from Catherine, he confirms the instrumentality of her body to the project he and the council envision for the town. Catherine, for her part, metamorphosizes them both into bodies to be set alight. Here, Catherine does not concede, but instead resists by exposing her own body to violent sacrifice.

Louis's response demonstrates the performance *manqué* as what could have been; that is, Catherine's expectation that Louis would heed her appeal. In his monologue of why he refuses Catherine's appeal, Louis argues that the useful mouths are engaged in an exceptional fight which they will have to carry on long after the siege. "Vaucelles must live! (A pause.) Something has been accomplished here which hasn't yet happened anywhere else. A town has overthrown its prince; men have chosen to become free and to determine their happiness for themselves" (p. 58). In making this argument, Louis appears to say that the useless mouths have to die so that Vaucelles and its struggle can live on, on the condition that the useful citizens continue to do their useful activities, unhindered by the useless mouths and their useless activities.

Wingrove (2016) offers one way to think about the failure of Louis's reception. When women's assertions of a wrong are refracted through gender and "the differences it presumes and reproduces," women's otherwise "poetically polemical" assertions risk being heard as "blah blah blah" (416-417). When Louis asserts that the useless mouths must die for Vaucelles to live, he condemns the plural subject of the question the town's name rings out—the worth of the useless mouths—but insists that the town, as singular subject, deserves to live. As Wingrove points out, this problem is primarily one of address (p. 418). When we shift our attention to who is being addressed in these scenes, then we can begin to see how Catherine, made *inutile*, may be heard by Louis as saying "blah blah blah."

At the same time, Catherine resists the failures of that reception by drawing other audiences to spectate the situation. Louis's pronouncement motivates Catherine to call on stage two other useless mouths - Jeanne and Clarice - as an audience to witness what their father Louis and the town council, which includes their brother Georges, have done. 'Come here. Look at these men. They have met with thirty other men and they have said, "We are the present and the future, we are the entire town, only we exist. We decide that the women, the old men, the children of Vaucelles are no more than useless mouths" (p. 58). Catherine draws Jeanne and Clarice as compulsory witness with the use of the imperative mood, commanding them to come [*a*]*pprochez* and to look [*r*]*egardez*.' With her use of the imperative and by a ventriloquy of the town council's performative utterance that is, "We decide... (*Nous décidons*)," she moves Jeanne and Clarice from the margins of the scene to its center.[9]

Sedgwick's theory of the periperformative reveals the potential of Catherine's ventriloquy. *In Touching Feeling*, Sedgwick draws on J.L. Austin to demonstrate that there is a spatial dimension to performative speech-acts (2003, pp. 67, 71). She argues that an illocutionary act, a speech act that does something, has perlocutionary force, effects. Sedgwick explains that in every I-You relation in the language upon some second-person singular "You," and that act conscripts a third-person plural "They" into the act. Sedgwick argues, the I invokes the They as a "compulsory witness" in order to gain the necessary consensus to authorize her action (2003, pp. 69, 71).

Here, we see the significance of rendering the subject of Vaucelles as feminine plural, for it is two women, Clarice and Jeanne, who are also deeply affected by Louis' decision and who authorize Catherine's words by remaining silent on the stage. Per the stage directions, Jeanne throws herself into Catherine's arms (p. 58). The embrace emphasizes that Louis' rebuff affects not only Catherine, his wife, but also his adoptive daughter. The togetherness of the two women's bodies functions as a kind of embodied talking-back. They appear to say to Louis that they feel the decision bodily. By seeking out in one another, they use their embodied presence to denote that, while the space of intersubjectivity has closed between Catherine, Louis, and the aldermen, another space of intersubjectivity opens in the embrace between Catherine, Jeanne, and Clarice.

As compulsory witnesses, Clarice and Jeanne occupy the periperformative space as an internal audience for Catherine's appeal. One effect is that Clarice especially acts as a subject of response for Catherine's appeal. While Jeanne remains speech-act, there is a space called the periperformative, which accounts for the third-person plural, a They, which can act as "compulsory witness." Unable to excuse themselves from the speech act, they allow themselves to be affected by it (Sedgwick, 2003, p. 69). The first-person singular "I" imposes

silent and embracing Catherine, Clarice erupts with rage at the council and to Louis. To the council, she asks, "This is what you've come up with? You are going to murder us so that you can eat your fill!" (p. 58). She then turns to Jacques, to whom her father had hoped to betroth her, and asks him, "Is this what you call love?" (p. 58). Clarice's response amplifies Catherine's appeal. Her language wrests her voice from the silence to which her father and the town council have condemned her. Her words to the town council and to Jacques call into question the authoritative weight with which the men have made their pronouncement and at the same time recite aspects of Catherine's appeal. In doing so, Clarice demonstrates that while Louis and the town council may seek to interpellate her and the other women as "useless mouths," Clarice, like Catherine, refuses their interpellation.

The Performance *Manqué* of Judgment

The failures that the women in *Les bouches inutiles* face are evidence of what Andrew Dilts has called the "tragic" aspect of Beauvoir's theory of ambiguity (Dilts, 2017, p. 187). Although these moments point to the potential of becoming free, they are overshadowed by their eventual failure. Despite the contestations of Clarice and Jeanne, Louis remains steadfast in the condemnation of his wife and two daughters to death. Recently, Kruks (2012, p. 131) and Marso (2017, p. 38) have argued that moments of failure demand modes of situated, aesthetic judgment, by which the subject makes her judgment with the acknowledgment that it might result in failure, too. Likewise, I add that the performance *manqué* of judgment illuminates how Clarice makes such a judgment by practicing freedom and desiring a world otherwise. This judgment is signified within the play and communicated to the theatrical audience through costuming.

In a photograph taken by Studio Lipnitzki/Roger Viollet of the original 1945 production, actress Olga Dominique as Clarice wears a dress with puffed sleeves. The collar is bejeweled, and the skirt appears embroidered with metallic thread. Clarice's costume contrasts sharply to other characters' costumes, shown in a separate photograph of Jacqueline Moran as Catherine, who wears a modestly-silhouetted dress with a narrow belt at the waist. Costuming sets Clarice apart from others onstage, so that her presence would have been astonishing. During the German occupation, textile production and sale were tightly regulated. Fabric was rationed, making it impossible for an ordinary person to afford basic clothing, let alone a fine dress (Veillon, 2020). Onstage, Louis admonishes Clarice for embellishing herself with jewelry in times of scarcity, and tells her that her dress is made out of enough fabric to clothe two soldiers (p. 41). Flouting her father's dressing-down, Clarice gestures to her body and suggests that fine clothes are only appropriate for corpses in Vaucelles, alluding to the death surrounding them.

A periperformative lens magnifies the temporal situatedness of Clarice's actions. When Louis scolds her, he asks why she has dressed this way, since he had forbidden her to do so. "And I have forbidden you to wear your jewels before the end of the siege" (p. 42). To this Clarice replies, "Must I wait until I am dead to be allowed to live?" (p. 42). The temporal dimension of the performative act, whereby Louis forbids Clarice to wear jewels, also signals its temporal dimension. Clarice disobeys an order that occurred in the past of the play. Louis invokes his order again in the present of the *tableau*, and Clarice rejoins with an appeal that alludes to the future, that is, the rising action that will follow. Indeed, as soon as Clarice exits the *tableau*, Louis and the aldermen, hearing the voices of the soon-to-be other useless mouths, realize that they must make their decision, another performative utterance, for the future of the town. What follows the men's realization is a procession of luxurious golden banners and the town's master-weavers. The weavers' presence draws attention back to Clarice's own luxurious clothes and her disobedience to Louis's performative utterance about what those clothes signify.

For Sedgwick, the power of the performative lies not only in the compulsory witness of the third-person plural "They," as we saw, but also in the ways that the periperformative space "can be the site of powerful energies that often warp, transform, and displace, if they do not overthrow, the supposing authorizing centrality of that same performative" (2003, p. 75). That is, the periperformative space opens up the agency of other people, temporal dimensions, and even objects. Clarice's clothes, whose luxuriousness is amplified by the golden banners, appear then to have a life of their own that brings together the past, the present, and the future temporal dimensions of the performatives they are in the vicinity of. Where Clarice's choice of clothing is an improper use of cloth according to Louis, the banners appear to be a proper use, insofar as these banners, like the belfry, are to the men symbols of a free Vaucelles. Comparing Clarice's clothing to the banners brings to light the way Clarice warps the question of proper use. The costume demonstrates how Clarice turns the way the men view the "use" of objects, and of women, on its head.

Although the costume draws the male spectators—Louis and the alderman—to view it and Clarice as a spectacle, it also draws others into a space of aesthetic judgment about the political questions that animate the play. By wearing the costume, Clarice appears to engage a bimodal form of inoperativity identified by Bonnie Honig: an arc that extends from the refusal to the intensification of use (2021, p. 16). The spectacle of something, like Clarice's dress, can work to discipline her into the standards of "patriarchal normativity," evinced by Louis (Honig 2021, p. 32). As I read it, the beauty of Clarice's dress inaugurates an arc that uses aesthetics to intensify its politics. The dress's beauty calls into question whose body is seen as useful and who gets to make such a political judgment. By wearing it, Clarice not only transgresses the town's sumptuary laws, but she also refuses the reproductive labor that her father demands of her. As the daughter of the town's most prominent alderman, Clarice is meant to engage in acts of self-denial that glorify her father's leadership and Vaucelles.

Juxtaposed to the banners, the costume invites the audience to look anew and judge Clarice's use of the cloth. Like the banners, the dress is an outcome of an embodied, coordinated action of the hands that measured, cut, and sewed the cloth. Passing through the fingers of the male weavers, onto Clarice's body, and into the purview of Louis, the costume appears to demonstrate an observation Beauvoir makes in *The Second Sex*: that clothes are meant to transform women into an object to be "judged, respected, or desired in relation to how she looks" (2009a, p. 724) And yet, the provenance and aesthetics of Clarice's costume also authorize Clarice to disclose a different possible life for herself, and transforms that disclosure before other audiences into the source of her freedom.

Thus, while Clarice's defiance looks like an individual act of defiance at first blush, she mobilizes the beauty of the dress to transform her body into a display of the situation that confines her. To stay (and to die) or to go (and to die)? Such a judgment, as Beauvoir describes it in *Ethics of Ambiguity*, is an antinomy of action, which forces us to choose between equally unbearable options (1976, pp. 121, 128). For Beauvoir, there are sacrifices that come with every choice—the choice to designate some members of a community as "useless" and the choice of those "useless" members to fight back. This answer may seem unsatisfactory, even frustrating. What Beauvoir's writing suggests is that in the choice between being a "useless" member of a community and making oneself a "useful" member of that same community, there will be failure. Consequently, the only choice—if it is a choice at all—is freedom.

Fichera has argued that Clarice questions, but ultimately does not "demand" to decide her own fate (1986, p. 64). In my view, what distinguishes Clarice's choice from a bad faith choice, is that she demands a future that is otherwise. This is evident from her invocation of "the future" as justification of her sartorial choice. For example, when Clarice decides to escape Vaucelles, she implores Catherine to do so for the sake of her future, echoing something she said to her lover and foster brother, Jean-Pierre, at the beginning of the play, when she asks Jean-Pierre why he has returned. She would have stayed far away from Vaucelles, she says, "would have forgotten everything. [She] would have lived alone and free. [She] would have *lived*" (p. 39). Through the language of the "would have," Clarice takes up the language of the "future," for the sake of which the town council had condemned the useless mouths. Indeed, the council had determined the use of the townspeople according to whether and how they would have contributed to the so-called future of Vaucelles. This future had been premised on the continuation of the siege, and so, the soldiers, the stonemasons, and the town council were deemed the most useful for securing that future, while the women, children, and elderly had been cast aside.

When Clarice speaks of the future, she projects her desire for a future that has nothing to do with Vaucelles at all. Instead, the language of the future in her exchange with Jean-Pierre points to an alternative future, in which there is no talk of use, but rather talk of how to want, how to live, and how to be free. Clarice's elicitations, which prompt both Catherine and Jean-Pierre to imagine with her what it would mean to be and to do differently, freely, illuminate how Clarice draws others with her into the space of judgment. Confronted with their tragic choice, she invites them into her imagined alternative.

That Clarice takes up the language of futurity reveals the performance *manqué* in her exercise of political freedom. In *Ethics of Ambiguity*, Beauvoir writes that acts of resistance may not always change the situation at hand. Yet, the very act of resistance may open up some other future. Beauvoir writes,

Only the future can take the present for its own and keep it alive by surpassing it. A choice will become possible in light of the future, which is the meaning of tomorrow because the present appears as the facticity which must be transcended toward freedom. No action is conceivable without this sovereign affirmation of the future (1976, p. 124).

In this passage, Beauvoir argues that the commitment to the future enables human beings to live in their present situation by illuminating the possible choices before them. That is, the commitment to the future motivates human beings to accept the obstacles that lie in their paths and at the same time to make new moves. The possibility of making such moves is another aspect captured by my reading of the play as a performance *manqué*. In my view, Beauvoir's use of costuming stages Clarice's capacity to imagine with others what a future might look like, one in which she and the other useless mouths in Vaucelles express and fulfill their desires for freedom.

Conclusion

I have read *Les bouches inutiles* as a performance *manqué* to illustrate women's embodied experiences of failure in the play. Taking up a periperformative lens, I have also shown that the women seek out audiences and elicit imagined futures. These moments show that Beauvoir's philosophical and literary theory, and. especially her dramatic prose, urgently engage with the significance of failure to her broader feminist project of political freedom.

The experiences of failure faced by the women of *Les bouches inutiles* is uncannily mirrored in the reception of the play at the time of its performance in 1945, which Beauvoir viewed later in life as a professional failure. Reflecting on that time, Beauvoir recalled the embarrassment she felt while sitting with the audience in a rehearsal performance. The existentialist playwright Jean Genet reportedly whispered in her ear, 'This isn't what theater's about! This isn't theater at all!' (Beauvoir, 1963, p. 63).

When we take the periperformative lens once more to *Les bouches inutiles*, looking offstage in our contemporary moment, we can see that the play has undergone resignification by readers, who have sought to resist the failure of its initial reception by restoring its significance for Beauvoir's body of feminist thought. The 2019 production by Antonia Mappin-Kasirer, performed at the Maison Française d'Oxford and the UK Sartre Society, seeks to recover the feminist message of the play by dramatizing how women's situation differentially shapes their experience of freedom (2019, p. 28). In her staging, Mappin-Kasirer brings to life the "visual and embodied experience" of the play in order to "appeal to the 'reader[director, performer, audience member]'s freedom" (2019, p. 17).

One way that Mappin-Kasirer does this is by redistributing the speaking roles, giving voice to the otherwise unnamed characters who comprise the mass of "useless mouths" as a choral protagonist. The chorus express their embodied experience of hunger and privation through gesture, word, and noise and features both onstage and among the spectators in the audience (2019, 33). This chorus has the effect of viscerally mediating the situation onstage to the offstage, drawing attention to the status of voicelessness to which the town aldermen seek to consign them, and uniting them into a collective with the women protagonists - notably Catherine - onstage (2019, pp. 33, 37). By bringing the women out of isolation and silence from one another, Mappin-Kasirer underscores another aspect of Beauvoir's feminist message in the play: the importance of a plural, collective subject, composed of the named D'Avesnes women and the unnamed useless mouths—to resist established heirarchies and to achieve freedom (2019, pp. 46–47).

Catherine and Clarice evince a resistance of failure in the play by seeking audiences and eliciting an imagined future where they may be free with others, so, too, does theater makes these possibilities sensible to spectators by playing on gesture and costume to open up space for aesthetic judgment about women's embodiment. Mappin-Kasirer's directorial choice with respect to the chorus of useless mouths has the effect of highlighting both the "marginalization" of the useless mouths, as well as transforming them from passive objects of the spectator's gaze into active subjects, whose actions have an impact on the audience (2019, pp. 32–33). Bringing "the praying, crying, holding" into sharp relief, her production underscores the theater's capacity to make visible dimensions of embodiment that can recede into secondary importance, when the play is read rather than performed (2019, p. 33)

What this production emphasizes for my analysis is that resisting failure requires subjects in the plural. In this play, as I argued, the D'Avesnes women seek each other's presence and response, in order to resist their failures before the men. Outside of the play, a new public has recovered Beauvoir's play, despite the initial failure of its (gendered) reception. Through her own dramaturgical choices, Mappin-Kasirer has salvaged *Les bouches inutiles* from the footnotes of Beauvoir's works and recovered its centrality to Beauvoir's political thought for new audiences. This process shows that resisting failure is an ongoing process, passing through the words and works of Beauvoir, another dramaturge, and so many actors and stage managers in between so as to convey the play's feminist message to audiences anew. This effort at re-imagining the play ultimately emancipates it from its minor place in Beauvoir's *oeuvre*. At the same time, it reveals the significance of theater as a practice for re-signifying the political meanings of women's bodies by soliciting audiences to respond to exemplified failures of intersubjectivity and to affirm their collective and plural political freedom.

Acknowledgements

My deepest thanks go to Jill Frank and Diane Rubenstein for our many conversations and for making this essay the best version possible. My gratitude goes to Alexander Livingston, Begüm Adalet, Jason Frank, Patchen Markell, Chris Way, Alexia Alkadi-Barbaro, and Sarah Greenberg for helpful comments on various drafts. I am especially indebted to Antonia Mappin-Kasirer for generously sharing her work and her time with me to talk about the process of adapting *Les bouches inutiles* "from page to stage." Earlier versions of this essay were presented at the 2020 meeting of the American Political Science Association, the 2021 Western Political Science Association, and the Cornell Political Theory Workshop; my thanks go to Robyn Marasco, Karen Zivi, my co-panelists, and the audience for their generative feedback. I also thank Benedetta Carnaghi, Mary Jane Dempsey, Aimée Plukker, Amanda Recupero, Jacob Swanson, Kelsey Utne, and Samantha Wesner for conversations about this essay from its inception to the last draft. Finally, I thank Demetra Kasimis and two anonymous reviewers at *Contemporary Political Theory* for their guidance and suggestions.

About the Author

Ani Chen is a PhD candidate in the Department of Government at Cornell University.

Notes

1. For a detailed timeline of the liberation of Paris, see Jackson (2001).
2. In *Politics with Beauvoir: Freedom in the Encounter*, Marso also considers the importance of failure to Beauvoir's of feminist political freedom. Of interest in relation to my argument on *Les bouches inutiles* are Marso's chapter "Perverse Protests from Chantal Akerman to Lars von Trier," for an alternative theorization of women's experiences of failure in their encounter with enemies, as well as "Unbecoming Women with Violette Leduc, Rahel Varnhagen, and Margarethe von Trotta" on the aesthetic portrayal of failures of intersubjectivity between women. By focusing on failure as positive negativity, I focus on how the foreclosure of intersubjective relationships between men and women can also mark an opportunity for women to cultivate and rely on relationships with other women in their actualization of freedom.
3. Writing on Beauvoir's own literature, specifically her novels, Emily Crawford has described this practice of human freedom as "performance of ambiguity" (Crawford, 2013, p. 180).
4. I follow Dilts (2017) and others in rendering "l'homme' as an unproblematic reference to "human being" despite its problematic translation as "man."
5. The technique that Beauvoir uses, the *tableaux vivants*, were popular for existentialist playwrights especially in the interwar period (Freeman, 1998, p. 78). On the role of space in Beauvoir's fiction, see Allison Fell (2003).
6. I thank Diane Rubenstein for this point.

7. Sara Ahmed has read *Les bouches inutiles* through the lens of biological use. This reading illuminates the play's wartime context and the violent use of use by the Vichy government to determine which parts of the social body were worthy of survival (Ahmed 2019, pp. 100–101).
8. Simone de Beauvoir, *"The Useless Mouths" and Other Literary Writings* (2011). Hereafter cited by page numbers from the English translation by Liz Stanley and Catherine Naji (2011 [1945], pp. 31–87).
9. I refer to the original French from Simone de Beauvoir, *Les bouches inutiles* (Mappin-Kasirer 2019; 1945).

References

Ahmed, S. (2019) *What's the Use? On the Uses of Use*. Durham: University Press.
Ahmed, S. (2021) *Complaint*. Durham: Duke University Press.
Bargu, B. (2016) *Starve and Immolate: The Politics of Human Weapons*. New York: Columbia University Press.
de Beauvoir, S. (1945) *Les Bouches Inutiles*. Paris: Éditions Gallimard.
de Beauvoir, S. (1963) *La Force des Choses*. Paris: Éditions Gallimard.
de Beauvoir, S. (1976) *The Ethics of Ambiguity*. Trans. Bernard Frechtman. New York: Open Road Integrated Media.
de Beauvoir, S. (2004) *Philosophical Writings*. Trans. Margaret A. Simons, Marybeth Timmerman, and Mary Beth Mader (eds.). Champaign University of Illinois Press.
de Beauvoir, S. (2011) *"The Useless Mouths" and Other Literary Writings*. Trans. Margaret A. Simons and Marybeth Timmerman (eds.). Champaign: University of Illinois Press.
de Beauvoir, S. (2009a) *The Second Sex*. Trans. Constance Borde and Sheila Malovany-Chevallier. New York: Vintage Books.
de Beauvoir, S. (2009b) *Wartime Diary*. Trans. Margaret A. Simons (ed.). Champaign: University of Illinois Press.
Bergoffen, D. (2003) Simone de Beauvoir: (Re)counting the sexual difference. In C. Card (ed.) *The Cambridge Companion to Simone de Beauvoir*. Cambridge University Press, pp. 248–265.
Crawford, E. (2013) *Hiding in Plain Sight: The Rhetorical Workings of Simone de Beauvoir's Feminist Language*, Ph.D. Diss., Columbia : University of South Carolina.
Deutscher, P. (2008) *The Philosophy of Simone de Beauvoir: Ambiguity, Conversion, Resistance*. Cambridge: Cambridge University Press.
Dilts, A. (2017) Justice as Failure. *Law, Culture & the Humanities* 13(2): 184–192.
Fell, A. (2003) The Perils of a Room of One's Own: Space in Simone de Beauvoir's *L'Invitee, Le Sang Des Autres* and *Les Bouches Inutiles*. *Forum for Modern Language Studies* 39(3): 267–277.
Fichera, V. (1986) Simone de Beauvoir and 'The Woman Question': *Les Bouches Inutiles*. *Yale French Studies* 72: 50–64.
Freeman, T. (1998) *Theatres of War: French Committed Theatre from the Second World War to the Cold War*. Exeter: University of Exeter Press.
Garcia, M. (2021) *We Are Not Born Submissive*. Princeton: Princeton University Press.
Gothlin, E. (1999) Simone de Beauvoir's Notions of Appeal, Desire, and Ambiguity and Their Relationship to Jean-Paul Sartre's Notions of Appeal and Desire. *Hypatia* 14(4): 83–95.
Halberstam, J. (2011) *The Queer Art of Failure*. Durham: Duke University Press.
Heinämma, S. (2003) The body as instrument and as expression. In C. Card (ed.) *The Cambridge Companion to Simone de Beauvoir*. Cambridge: Cambridge University Press, pp. 66–86.
Honig, B. (2021) *A Feminist Theory of Refusal*. Cambridge: Harvard University Press.
Jackson, J. (2001) *France: The Dark Years, 1940–1944*. Oxford: Oxford University Press.

Jones, J. and Reinelt, J. (1983) Simone de Beauvoir as Dramatist: *Les Bouches Inutiles. Modern Drama* 26(4): 528–535.
Kirkpatrick, K. (2019) *Becoming Beauvoir: A Life*. Routledge: Routledge.
Kruks, S. (2012) *Simone de Beauvoir and the Politics of Ambiguity*. New York: Oxford University Press.
Mappin-Kasirer, A. (2019) *From Page to Stage: Simone de Beauvoir's Les bouches inutiles as Femimist Theatre,* MSt. Diss, University of Oxford, Oxford
Marso, L. (2012) Simone de Beauvoir and Hannah Arendt: Judgments in Dark Times. *Political Theory* 40(2): 165–193.
Marso, L. (2017) *Politics with Beauvoir: Freedom in the Encounter*. Oxford: Duke University Press.
Megna, P. (2018) Existentialist Medievalism and Emotional Identity Politics in Simone de Beauvoir's *The Useless Mouths. Exemplaria* 30(3): 241–256.
Moi, T. (2009) What Can Literature Do? Simone de Beauvoir as Literary Theorist. *PMLA* 124(1): 189–198.
Naji, C. and Stanley, L. (2011) "Introduction." In de Beauvoir S. *'The Useless Mouths' and Other Literary Writings*. Urbana: University of Illinois Press, pp. 11–32.
Scheu, A (2011). *What Can Philosophical Literature Do? The Contribution of Simone de Beauvoir*, Ph.D. Diss, Durham: Duke University.
Sedgwick, E. (2003) *Touching Feeling: Affect, Pedagogy*. Durham: Duke University Press.
Stanley, L. (2001) A Philosopher Manqué? Simone de Beauvoir, Moral Value, and 'The Useless Mouths. *The European Journal of Women's Studies* 8(2): 201–220.
Stauffer, J. (2015) *Ethical Loneliness: The Injustice of Not Being Heard*. New York: Columbia University Press.
Veillon, D. (2020) Shortages in Paris 1940–1945: frivolous accessories become essential needs. In L. Taylor and M. McLoughlin (eds.) *Paris Fashion and World War Two: Global Diffusion and Nazi Control*. London: Bloomsbury.
Vicaro, M. (2015) Hunger for Voice: Transformative Argumentation in the 2005 Guantánamo Bay Hunger Strike. *Argumentation and Advocacy* 51: 171–184.
Wingrove, E. (2016) blah blah WOMEN blah blah EQUALITY blah blah DIFFERENCE. *Philosophy & Rhetoric* 49(4): 408–419.

Publisher's Note Springer Nature remains neutral with regard to jurisdictional claims in published maps and institutional affiliations.

Springer Nature or its licensor (e.g. a society or other partner) holds exclusive rights to this article under a publishing agreement with the author(s) or other rightsholder(s); author self-archiving of the accepted manuscript version of this article is solely governed by the terms of such publishing agreement and applicable law.

Review

On ne naît pas femme: On le devient: The life of a sentence

Bonnie Mann and Martina Ferrari (eds.)
Oxford University Press, Oxford, 2017, 362 pp.,
ISBN: 9780190608811

Contemporary Political Theory (2019) **18,** S121–S124. https://doi.org/10.1057/s41296-018-0194-7; published online 23 January 2018

Yes, this book is based upon a single sentence: Beauvoir's renowned sentence: 'one is not born: one becomes (a) woman.' Yet it manages to spawn nineteen articles that cover multiple themes from numerous perspectives and disciplinary interests. Its four sections, Intellectual History; History of Scandal; the Philosopher's Debate; the Labor of Translation, include interventions on the sex/gender debates (Karen Offen, Judith Butler, Bonnie Mann, Meagan Burke), diverse philosophical interpretations of Beauvoir, as well as concrete and convincing demonstrations of how poorly translated passages promote misunderstandings (Toril Moi, Margaret Simons, Nancy Bauer). Since it is impossible to do justice to the breadth and wealth of this text in a short review, I have chosen to focus upon a few of the articles that I found particularly interesting. The brilliance of the collection lies in its interdisciplinary and meticulous analysis of this single sentence. Needless to say, its multiple interpretations don't fit together, but provide compelling arguments that can't be easily dismissed.

The new translation of The *Second Sex* in 2011 initiated a fervent debate amongst feminists. In dropping the article 'a' from Parshley's original English translation, Constance Borde and Sheila Malovany-Chevalier believed they were honoring Beauvoir's feminist legacy. They reasoned 'this best captures women as an institution, a construct, a concept; femininity determined and defined by society, culture and history' (p. 281). The presence of the 'a' stresses the existential tradition that one is free to choose irrespective of one's situation.

Bonnie Mann's 'Beauvoir against Objectivism' provides an excellent introduction to the volume by offering a concise summary of Beauvoir's philosophic concerns, which furthers the project of thinking philosophically about the tensions arising from the translation of this sentence. Unlike Butler, whose discursive theory swings towards objectivism, Beauvoir's notion of embodied engagement avoids subjectivism and rationalism, without lapsing into objectivism or materialism. Mann brings Butler's performative theory of gender into conversation with

Beauvoir's existential treatment. While Butler analyzes how norms operate to include and exclude, 'another dimension of Beauvoir's analysis drops out, leaving us with a narrower, less politically able account' (p. 46). Mann rightly notes 'this leaves the impression that oppression is undone and equality is won through the revelation of the performative nature of gender, while the entire material apparatus of domination and subordination that is secured by the norm remains intact' (p. 49).

As a social historian, Karen Offen's archival work challenges the idea that the sex/gender distinction is Anglo-American in origin. While French feminists have preferred to use the terms (masculin/féminin or la différence sexuelle) and stubbornly resisted the sex/gender distinction as well as the term 'genre' to designate socially constructed differences, Offen offers evidence that early modern French thinkers used the term 'genre' to highlight the social constitution of gender. Her point is not to claim the French were the source of the distinction, but rather to show how tracing historical usage shows that the fluidity of gender has a long history in France, contrary to the opinion of some. To dismiss the sex/gender distinction as Cartesian, as Rosi Braidotti has done, or gender as a neologism, is shortsighted. She warns theorists to be apprised of socio/historical and cultural complexity: 'being born a woman is very different in different countries,' and to give the term meaning, theorists must consult anthropologists, sociologists, as well as historians. In the process, she takes a jab at Butler and Braidotti for having evacuated the physical maternal body by seeing the materiality of the body as a linguistic construction.

In 'The Floating "a"' Debra Bergoffen shores up the new translation, though not unqualifiedly. It is praised for drawing our attention to Beauvoir's materialist sensibility: 'her analysis of the ways that social practices produce material realities that are then ideologically naturalized' (p. 143). Nevertheless, this reading occludes the singular experience of birth and how we live our human body in historical and unpredictable ways (p. 144). In erasing the 'a' one gives too much power to the myth/concept/determinations women are subject to, thereby denying women's desire for freedom and the affirmation of subjectivity, yet the assertion of the 'a' tends to ignore how existing social relations impede women's freedom. Bergoffen proposes the excellent idea of floating the 'a,' citing Kristeva, who had spent most of her life vilifying Beauvoir as male identified, but who, after Beauvoir's death, came to appreciate her approach to singularity. Bergoffen rightly identifies the tension: 'Whether we decide for or against the "a" may depend upon the extent we accept Beauvoir's conviction that, as historical beings, we are both constrained by the concrete conditions of our life, and we are also necessarily the embodiment of a desire for freedom' (p. 157).

Burke refuses to accept that the 2011 translators committed an error: rather, they made an 'informed decision' to read Beauvoir as a social constructionist and not as a phenomenologist. Beginning with Butler's social constructivism and her reading of Beauvoir, Burke argues that the significance of the sex/gender distinction is overplayed. In the process, Butler instantiates her own approach to sex as gendered, yet wrongly attributes to Beauvoir a stable, factive body as the foundation of human existence and sexed differences. Beauvoir is not an essentialist, but maintains a socially constructed position, one informed by phenomenology rather than poststructuralism. While Beauvoir admits there are sexed differences (i.e., women have weaker bodies, much to the chagrin of some feminists), our bodies are always enveloped in a worldly situation. The body does not exist outside our social or cultural relations as the grounds for gender, but the living body involves the entanglement of both biology, culture, as well as social circumstances. Thus, Beauvoir appreciates the singularity of existence 'how one lives gender as **a** woman, in **a** given time and place' (p. 172). Burke rejects the sex/gender distinction, but on different grounds than Butler and Braidotti.

The sections on translation explore the specific challenges faced by Spanish (López Sácenz), German (Baumeister), Finnish (Ruonakoski), and Serbo-Croat (Bogiç) translators, as well as offer glimpses into the politics of the translation. Although we know intuitively how important translation is, Simons, Bauer, and Moi's concrete comparisons and parsing of passages between the Borde and Malovany-Chevalier, Parshley and original texts, provides irrefutable evidence as to how meanings get misconstrued. The first section on translation – History of a Scandal – traces the history of the first translation of *The Second Sex*. Margaret Simon's 1983 article is reprinted. Noting that 10% of the original text was deleted (specifically passages on the history of women's movements, entries acknowledging women writers and exceptional women), Simons rightly points to Parshley's sexism. Since most references to socialism and socialist feminism were excised from his 1951 translation, I would also add, his anticommunist sentiments are also evidenced. Perhaps more troubling is Parshley's failure to appreciate Beauvoir's philosophic language, hardly surprising since he was a zoologist. In translating existential and specifically Heideggerian concepts like human reality, *Dasein,* as the human condition of man, he misconstrues its meaning. Building upon Simon's and Fallaize's scrupulous comparisons of the original and translated meanings in the late 90s Toril Moi brilliantly produces even more reasons and examples as to why a re-translation was in order. Her meticulous readings reveal not only bungled philosophic meanings (hiding Hegel, mistranslating Marx's concept of alienation) but serious deletions that altered the tone of Beauvoir's text. Omitting women's voices from the section on women's lived experience and removing examples of exceptional women, Parshley fueled the now common perception that Beauvoir is male-identified and not interested in women. Moi attributes Drucilla Cornell's essentializing Beauvoir's anti-maternalist stance to Parhsley's omissions and botched translation. Moi also shares her appeal to Vintage/Knopf for a new translation (cataloguing errors and serious omissions) and their churlish response.

To the new (Borde and Malovany-Chevalier) translation, Moi and Bauer respond disapprovingly, whereas Simons and Altman are more forgiving of its errors. Sadly, an annotated edition was not produced, which would have helped readers make sense of Beauvoir's referents, often local and idiosyncratic; nor was an accomplished translator (from French to English) selected. Again, errors in translation were recorded by scholars in 2010, and corrections were made in the next edition. In preserving the original structure and literalness of meaning, Borde and Malovany-Chevalier, 'sacrifice readability and clarity in favor of a highly unidiomatic word-by-word literalism that hampers the flow of the Beauvoir's prose and often obfuscates it meaning' (Bauer, p. 116). In contrast, Altman supports the 2011 translation as reliable. 'The slight estrangement induced by the text' (p. 134), she argues, is preferable to Parshley's translation, which domesticated the foreignness to please the American audience.

All the pieces in this volume thus offer unique readings of this sentence and Beauvoir's philosophic project more generally, attesting to the significance of translation, as well as providing thoughtful interventions in feminist theory, past and present. This is a must-read for those interested in Beauvoir's ideas, in translation, as well as in a critical engagement with the various turns in feminist theory.

Elaine Stavro
Trent University, Peterborough, ON K9J 0G2, Canada
estavro@trentu.ca

Critical Exchange

The "Agonistic Turn": *Political Theory and the Displacement of Politics* in New Contexts

Lida Maxwell[a,*], Cristina Beltrán[b], Shatema Threadcraft[c], Stephen K. White[d], Miriam Leonard[e] and Bonnie Honig[f]

[a]Boston University, Boston, MA 02215, USA.
lmaxwell@bu.edu

[b]New York University, New York, NY 10012, USA.
cbeltran@nyu.edu

[c]Dartmouth College, Hanover, NH 03755, USA.
shatema.threadcraft@dartmouth.edu

[d]University of Virginia, Charlottesville, VA 22904, USA.
skw2n@virginia.edu

[e]University College London, London WC1E 6BT, UK.
m.leonard@ucl.ac.uk

[f]Cornell University Press, Ithaca, NY 14850, USA.
bonnie_honig@brown.edu

*Corresponding author.

Contemporary Political Theory (2019) **18,** 640–672. https://doi.org/10.1057/s41296-019-00346-8; published online 11 September 2019

First published in 1993, Bonnie Honig's *Political Theory and the Displacement of Politics* challenged political theorists' focus on justifying political institutions and norms, and helped to usher in what we might call an "agonistic turn" in political theory. While searching for "agonism politics" in Google Scholar brings up more than 26,000 results today, for entries prior to 1993 those same search terms number only 1300 results. As of July, there are already 2160 results for 2019 alone.

Agonism's move from a marginal to central place in contemporary political theory has a double edge. Many varieties of democratic theorists have largely adopted one of Honig's main claims – that agonistic contestation is not a regrettable feature of democracy, but a democratic good – as their own. This once-provocative claim seems now uncontroversial. The absorption of agonism into the theoretical mainstream, on the one hand, means that political theorists are much more focused on contestatory politics than they were thirty years ago (when the liberal/communitarian debate was at the fore). This is to the good, especially in a contemporary political context marked by deep division and contestation over political values, identities, and institutions. Yet this absorption of agonism into justificatory and institution-building theory, on the other hand, also means that the critical edge of Honig's agonism – her claim that *all* political arrangements (even contestatory and deliberative arrangements) will generate exclusions, injustice, and inequality – may now be blunted.

This Critical Exchange revisits *Political Theory and the Displacement of Politics* to remember that a now widely dispersed mode of political theorizing has a history, and to think about what agonism should mean *now* to political theory. Have our modes of theorizing difference, contestation, and ambivalence become overly settled parts of political theorizing, which themselves require challenge and unsettling? What is the relationship of agonism to our contemporary political moment, and to contemporary approaches to thinking about inequality and injustice, like black feminism? And perhaps more importantly: what should agonistic theory be like today? Does *PTDP* call us to a *new* agonism in the present moment?

Lida Maxwell

The virago as democratic exemplar: Honig's feminist agonism

In his germinal essay, "Political Theory as a Vocation," Sheldon Wolin argues that political theory is an activity of creative ordering, imputing meaning to human activities that might otherwise appear futile or without significance. Political theory becomes most significant in "times of crisis" (Wolin, 1969, p. 9), when our existing compass or "tradition" (in Hannah Arendt's terms) has ceased to offer sufficient guidance. The theorist diagnoses the crisis, but "also deals in possibilities" (Wolin, 1969, p. 9) by opening up new ways of understanding political organization, action, and meaning.

Political Theory and the Displacement of Politics (hereafter *PTDP*) enacts theory as Wolin describes it: showing the meaning of collective life differently and offering a different "political cosmos" to describe what otherwise might feel like "chaos." Institutions and laws that other theorists (like Rawls and Sandel) argue are sites of meaningful order, Honig shows to also be sites of political inclusion and exclusion. On Honig's reading, Rawls' and Sandel's purportedly just institutions turn out to enforce disciplinary norms of gender and sexuality, and to *produce* forms of delinquency and "oddness" that they then claim to address justly. While *PTDP* was engaged with the dominant theoretical debate of the time (the liberal/communitarian debate), the book was also reframing a concrete political situation *as* a crisis: namely, the diminution and retreat of vibrant collective

Critical Exchange

politics, especially of a vibrant *feminist* politics. Honig's political theory offers a new approach to this crisis: not more ordering, but ongoing politicization. As Honig notes, in one of many asides in the book that address feminist concerns, feminists made a mistake in thinking that Roe v. Wade represented a new, settled consensus. In democratic politics, nothing is ever fully settled; participatory, contestatory politics is needed to fight ongoing attempts to reintroduce oppressive arrangements.

I am drawing attention to the book's feminist politicizing impulse at the outset because I see this as the book's most valuable legacy, what I want to call its feminist or queer agonism. While agonism has largely been taken up in democratic theory as a formal theory of contestation of laws and norms (which deliberative democratic theorists try to absorb within their own terms), I am interested in how *PTDP* points toward a practice of theoretical politicization of what we may have understood as private, non-political, or irrelevant to the public realm. I am calling this its feminist or queer impulse, not only because it emerges from concrete encounter with feminist and queer politics in the book (as I will detail), but also because it resonates with a central principle of queer and feminist theory: that private and intimate feelings, violences, practices, forms of discipline, and norms are actually publicly constructed and have political implications and stakes. To put it in classic feminist terms, the personal is political. I want to draw on this politicizing impulse of *PTDP* and pull out a vision, in my contribution to this Critical Exchange, of agonistic democratic theory as a feminist and queer project: politicizing supposedly private or non-political forms of violence and discipline that have appeared natural or immutable, and thus out of the bounds of politics.

Indeed, returning to Honig's book, I was most struck by how her agonism emerges not out of a free-floating affirmation of contestation, but most often by engagement with the concrete problem of the public/private distinction. The book is structured by mobilizing a critical politics of *virtù* (exemplified by Nietzsche and Arendt) to identify the violent and disciplinary closures of juridical "virtue" politics (that she finds in Kant, Rawls and Sandel). Honig most often aligns virtue politics with the attempt to settle lines between public and private, whereas *virtù* politics unsettles that line. Yet Honig also asks at the very outset of the text whether the model of contestation she is invoking itself represents a form of masculine closure. If "the subject of *virtù*" is typically represented (for example, by Machiavelli) as a certain type of vigorous masculinity – "the manly male warrior of ancient Greece or Rome" – then Honig's invocation of it could appear to settle the bounds of what looks like proper politics, as a masculine form of active, loud contestation. Yet Honig argues that the character of political contestation must itself be contestable, not on formal justificatory grounds, but for the sake of concrete feminist concerns, and she invokes a figure that could allow us to imagine agonistic contestation as queer and feminist: "[w]hat if the subject of *virtú* is not the manly male warrior of ancient Greece or Rome, but the virago, a figure defined variously as a 'turbulent woman,' a 'whirlwind,' a 'woman of masculine strength or

Reprinted from the journal

spirit,' a figure who, in herself, poses a limit to the continuing possible of calling those strengths and spirits masculine? What if *virtù*, with its sensitivity to excess and remainders, turns out to be a force that disrupts and unsettles such binary categories as masculine and feminine, pointing out their inadequacies, their limits, their aporias?" (16) The figure of the virago invites us to imagine politics as an activity of challenging not just unjust or disciplinary norms and institutions, but also norms of *what* and *who* count as political. Further, however, Honig's virago invites us to see political theory as itself in tandem with, or as an adjunct of, political actors, a practice of feminist politicization.

Honig seems to diminish this early reference to the virago, saying, "[a]side from occasional ruminations like this one, I do not engage questions of gender and politics in a sustained way in this book." (16) Yet I think she is not giving full credit to the import of her own ruminations, which are a powerful way of doing theoretical politicization: that is, taking pleasure in traveling down experimental paths and lines of thought that may appear irrelevant to the "central" concerns of the field or literature. Nietzsche notes the power of rumination in the opening to *On the Genealogy of Morality*: "to practice reading as an art...one thing above all is necessary, something which these days has been unlearned better than anything else – and it will therefore be a while before my writings are 'readable' – something for which one must almost be a cow and in any case *not* a modern man: *ruminating*…" (Nietzsche, 1998, p. 7). Nietzsche's invitation to let ourselves imaginatively think like a cow – to *ruminate* – rather than adjudicate and discipline on the basis of the morality of *ressentiment*, is an invitation to take animalistic (cow-ish) pleasure in forms of thinking that may appear perverse, unimportant, or un-rigorous. If Honig's book invites us to see the virago as a figure who challenges our sense of who or what counts as political, our rumination on that virago, and other figures she presents (like the Rawlsian grass counter, which I get to below), also allows us to feel *pleasure* in theoretical politicization – or, in Nietzsche's terms, to read like a cow.

Ruminations about gender pervade the book. From Honig's connection of Kant's worry about "reason's traumatic disruption of man's natural existence" (20) to his anxious sexual politics (21), to her more extended treatment of Arendt's attempt to maintain a rigid separation between the public and private realms, Honig continually shows how the project of justifying political laws/regimes has relied on the neutralization of institutions and social boundaries (especially the public/ private divide) that depoliticize laws and norms that regulate gender and sexuality. Yet I am going to skip over Honig's well-known and important politicization of Arendt's public private distinction ("Action comes in, as it were, to the private realm," 120) to point to another rumination in the conclusion. There, Honig offers a sympathetic critique of Carol Gilligan's landmark book, *In a Different Voice*. While Gilligan usefully mobilizes a feminized ethic of care to show the problems with Kohlberg's ethic of rights, Honig argues that Gilligan ultimately "reenables"

Critical Exchange

this ethic, because she situates the ethic of care as its "nurturant support" (208). The problem with Gilligan's approach is that it attempts to assure that the *formal moral* dimensions of human life are fully accounted for rather than thinking through how to *empower* those who are inevitably left out (208). "The feminism I have in mind," Honig says, "does not embrace and repeat the constations of gendered subjectivities, it does not organize itself around them," but rather "gives voice to the dissonances experienced by men and women for whom the binaries of rights versus care, reason versus emotion, or masculine versus feminine are ill-fitting, even oppressive, constraints" (209). Celebrating a "politics that contests closure" is not about an abstract celebration of political conflict as inherently progressive, but instead about *empowering* those who are rendered marginal, odd, delinquent, or invisible by the political systems that order their lives.

Honig's engagement with Gilligan (like her engagement with Arendt) invites us to see the concrete pain and violence inflicted by the settling of lines between public and private, between what counts and does not count as political – even when Gilligan is trying to account for all the dimensions of a full moral life. Yet there is a pleasure invoked in Honig's critique of Gilligan, too: even when we believe we have understood morality and politics, there may be *more*; people's lives and experiences may show us something new, significant, or unsettling that we had not seen. The pleasure of this virago politics can be seen most clearly in Honig's discussion of the Rawlsian grass counter, a "non-deliberating subject," who is a "'fanciful case' – 'someone whose only pleasure is to count blades of grass in various geometrically shaped areas such as park squares and well-trimmed lawns. He is otherwise intelligent and actually possesses unusual skills, since he manages to survive by solving difficult mathematical problems for a fee'" (152). While Rawls says that the grass counter may exist in the society of justice and fairness and not be regulated – since he is not contravening any laws or principles – Honig argues that his existence turns his fellow citizens into "case workers" (into Nietzsche's virtuous citizens of *ressentiment*) who feel a duty to interrogate his (apparently lacking) conception of the good, or what we might call his cow-ish capacity, engrossed in the grass, for rumination. The Rawlsian grass counter, in other words, is someone who leads a life governed by an affective experience of pleasure rather than by a conception of "the good." His existence thus poses a question that no one exactly knows how to ask. He is not seeking to deliberate with them, or to contest the norms by which they live. Rather, his very existence – his pleasure – is itself a living dissonance with their regime.

The example of the grass counter shows how (*contra* Arendt) private life is not a security that paves the way for public life; rather, as Michael Warner argues in *Publics and Counterpublics* (2005), public norms dictate what *can be seen* as properly private, and what as properly public. Here, by politicizing what we assumed to be unpolitical (the ruminating grass counter), Honig opens up a terrain of political life, energy, and feeling that we neglect at our peril. *PTDP* is showing us a diminished collective politics as a crisis for feminist and queer life, and the book is arguing that a vibrant emancipatory, Left politics must look beyond the parameters of institutions, laws, and norms for its energy and animating force.

Honig's agonism may serve a useful role in pushing justificatory political theorists (like deliberative democrats) to see the importance of contestation in the public realm. But I see its more important role in its character as a feminist and queer agonism, pushing democratic theory to stay in touch with politics in a broad sense: *not* just politics that happens in institutions or recognized social movements, but also in sites of incipient politicization, whether that is a social realm, an institution, a set of feelings and affects, or ideologies (among other things). It also pushes democratic theory to look to feminist and queer politics and theory, not just as something to be accommodated into a universalist theory, but as a guide to what we should be theorizing. I see this in Honig's ongoing work, that turned from *PTDP* to the politics of immigration, emergency politics, the politics of mourning, and neoliberalism. This encourages us to have a broader view of what constitutes "democratic theory": not just theory that is explicitly concerned with the nature of democracy, but also theory that is at work ruminating on concerns, actors, and ideas that we have not yet recognized as political, and offering new visions of what this politics means for all of us.

Lida Maxwell

Extraordinary events *and* mundane maintenances: Honig on the politics of sedimentation

My first peer-reviewed publication opened with a quote from *PTDP*:

> Perhaps there is no identity so perfect, so seamless, so well-fitted to her that she could wear it, be it, perform and live it without resentment, without sadness, without yearning, without guilt, hatred and even violence (183).

Published in *Political Research Quarterly*, the article was an account of the concept of *mestizaje* in the work of Gloria Anzaldúa and Shane Phelan (Beltrán, 2004). Honig's book did not focus on the question of Chicana feminism, but her analysis regarding the nature of political subjectivity shaped my thinking about how even the most radical or satisfying identities and forms of rule produce remainders that require engagement rather than displacement. And her central claim – that political theory often displays a desire to eliminate dissonance, resistance, conflict and struggle from the political regimes being theorized – had a profound impact on my own understanding of the political (Beltrán, 2010). Indeed, Honig's insights about how virtue and *virtù* theories appear in various enactments of the political helped me think more deeply about how a variety of thinkers and movements express the desire for political closure. For me, it was Honig's claim that "most political

Critical Exchange

theorists are hostile to the disruption of politics" – alongside her analysis of the "virtue" politics of Immanuel Kant, John Rawls, and Michael Sandel – that helped me recognize similar impulses in the radical visions of Chicano and Puerto Rican scholars and activists.

In my contribution to this Critical Exchange, I would like to focus on a few elements of this text that I found particularly compelling and powerful when first reading this work in the early 1990s. In doing so, I want to consider what insights from this work have perhaps become a kind of sedimented logic within democratic theory. And finally, taking inspiration from *PTDP*, I want to conclude with Honig's insistence on disrupting her own embrace of *virtù* politics, particularly her insights regarding how we approach the politics of disruption versus the politics of maintenance and institutionalization. For it's this theoretical gesture that offers particularly valuable insights when thinking about the democratic challenges we face in the wake of 2016.

PDTP explores the opposition between virtue and *virtù* theories of politics, with Kant, Rawls, and Sandel serving as virtue theorists while Nietzsche, Arendt, and Derrida represent theorists of *virtù*. According to Honig, the desire for closure has often led virtue theorists to define and confine politics to the juridical, the administrative, and the regulative tasks of "stabilizing moral and political subjects, building consensus, maintaining agreements, or consolidating communities and identities" (27). Whether "republican, liberal, or communitarian" in orientation, Honig argues that virtue theorists often do violence to the multiplicitous, contingent, contradictory, and unstable subjectivities of citizens. Intriguingly, with her focus on desires and displacements – including the various "fears, anxieties, and needs" that emerge through their political imaginaries – Honig was already making what we now speak of as the affective turn in political theory, albeit with theorists we rarely think of when discussing the politics of affect (Rawls, Kant, Sandel).

In contrast to virtue theorists who display a tendency toward closure and repressing otherness, *virtú* theorists appreciate that world-building always involves a process of becoming. In this way, they seek to politicize rather than police, punish, or ostracize "the moments of dissonance and otherness that disrupt their orders" (10, 186). Some of the most compelling discussions that Honig develops when analyzing how *virtù* theorists approach the political involve her reading of Nietzsche on responsibility and institutions and Arendt on promising.

For Honig, "Nietzsche's recovery of responsibility is pivotal in a reconstructive project to which too many readers of Nietzsche still attend too little" (8). Going beyond his well-known disruptions of convention, Honig reveals an alternative ethos that seeks to be more generous, creative, and responsive to the impulses and desires that that characterize the human condition in modernity. In thinking about the self as "an original multiplicity," for example, Nietzsche offers a recovered

Critical Exchange

sense a responsibility whose subjectivity is not premised on the need for blameworthy agent or self-destructive *ressentiment*, moving instead toward a relationship to the past that is creative and redemptive rather than passive and fatalistic (65, 52). Here, Honig builds on the politicizing impulses of Nietzsche's thought without endorsing his vision of an aristocratic "great politics" that envisions "the herd dominated and the earth shaken by the few overmen" (74). These insights regarding a recovered sense of a "responsible subjectivity" are later amplified when Honig turns to Nietzsche's "brief endorsements" and "scattered remarks" to highlight his "reverence for institutions" (73). Underscoring this important yet underrated strand of Nietzsche's political thought, Honig notes how the "commitment to maintain institutionally a measure of stability, a measured stability…'this life which must ever surpass itself,' must also situate and maintain itself, and often it will and ought to do so institutionally" (72–73). And while Nietzsche seeks to avoid overly domesticating a world characterized by contingency, he also knows that such efforts "are our way of making the world habitable and he admires and endorses our capacity to do this" (72).

Considering the relationship between responsibility, institutions, and the ongoing existence and promise of contingency, Honig turns to Arendt and her account of action and authority, offering a particularly powerful account of the idea of promising. For Honig, "[p]romising occurs precisely in a realm where Arendt's actors are not at home, [where] there is no security, no overdetermined context to domesticate" it (93). This idea of promising as "performative action" allows us to consider not only the power of promising, but also our own fears of such an uncertain, necessary and deeply political act – and thus our desire to anchor our promises in something beyond each other. We see these tensions in Honig's magnificent discussion of the Declaration of Independence. Her reading of Arendt together with Jacques Derrida and J.L. Austin allows us to reconsider the meaning of the *we* of the declaration and the power of saying "we hold these truths to be self-evident" (99). According to Honig, Arendt wants to celebrate the American Declaration of Independence "as a purely performative speech act, but in order to do so…[s]he dismisses its constative moments and holds up the Declaration as an example of a uniquely political act…an authoritative exemplification of human power and worldliness" (101). Turning to Derrida's reading of the Declaration, Honig argues that he does not see the structural combination of a constative and performative utterance as incongruous or tainting what ought to have been a purely performative act. Indeed, for Derrida, this undecidability "is *required* to produce the sought after effect." Honig writes:

> For Derrida… "We hold" illustrates beautifully a structural feature of all language: that no signature, promise performative—no act of foundation—possesses resources adequate to guarantee itself, that each and every one necessarily needs some external, systematically illegitimate guarantee to

Critical Exchange

work.... Arendt resists this undecidability because she seeks in the American Declaration and founding a moment of perfect legitimacy.... What she does not see is that the American Declaration and founding are paradigmatic instances of politics (however impure) because of this undecidability, not in spite of it (106–107).

Honig's critique allows us to see how Arendt turns to a legitimating fable of the Declaration that seeks to "bridge the impasse of freedom...the abyss that afflicts all performative utterance, all declarations of independence, all acts of founding" (109). Again, what is powerful here is not only the ways we come to see Arendt as a *virtù* theorist but how even visions of pure performativity and worldliness can fall prey to the logic of closure that Honig identifies in virtue theorists.

Indeed, one element of *PTDP* that I've always appreciated is how Honig develops a framework that she then challenges. Rather than simply reinstall the binary of *virtù* versus virtue, Honig asks her readers to go beyond the very binary she identifies. For her, "each side of the opposition tells us only half the story." For example, toward the book's conclusion, she speaks of how Rawls and Arendt are both right about the private realm, "and that is why each of them is wrong about it" (204). Unable to see or account for what the other recognizes, Honig notes, "[o]nce any conception of politics and identity or agency begins to sediment, its usefulness as a lever of critique is diminished and its generative power becomes a force of constraint" (206). This awareness that even her own framework risks becoming "sedimented" is an authorial gesture that moved me the first time I engaged this text in graduate school. It showed a kind of scholarly bravery – an intellectual confidence rarely seen in first books – to continually question and not just *defend* the logics one has so carefully constructed. As she ultimately insists: "Politics consists of practices of settlement *and* unsettlement, of disruption *and* administration, of extraordinary events or foundings *and* mundane maintenances...to reduce politics to only one side of each of these operations...is to displace politics" (205).

Honig's closing insights led me to reconsider these binaries in light of the Trump era of American politics. Prior to 2016, it seems to me, democratic theorists aligned with the Left – as well as a certain portion of Left activists in the United States – often resisted the administrative in the service of disruption. Over the past two decades, many of us working in the field of democratic theory wrote works that celebrated various iterations of *virtù* politics – practices and movements that exceeded the institutional and the electoral. We emphasized the importance of contingency, celebrating practices of resistance, unruliness, refusal, and disruption. And much of this is to the good: Democratic theory is better for these critiques and interventions. Yet I would also argue that when it came to the institutional and electoral realms of politics, many of us on the Left ceded certain aspects of administration and maintenance to liberals and the Right. In other words, did radical democratic theorists and activists embrace the insights of the first part of Honig's text while paying too little attention to the insights that conclude the book? Did we let our celebration of *virtù* politics become a kind of sedimented identity?

A year after *PTDP* was published, Newt Gingrich and the Republican Party issued the *Contract with America*, a series of far-right policies that GOP leaders pledged to enact if elected to power. In 1994, Republicans took control of the House of Representatives for the first time in forty years, and many of those same conservatives later organized as the Tea Party and the Freedom Caucus. Again and again, the American Right has embraced administrative logics in the service of disruption, working tirelessly to institutionalize their rage. At the same time, as conservatives moved further right and institutionalized themselves within the Republican Party, neoliberal rationalities were becoming increasingly ubiquitous: For many, neoliberalized law, governance, and political practices became a form of political common sense.

During this same period, Left activists resisted this turn to the right and cultivated a far more capacious understanding of the political, turning to a wide array of protest movements and aesthetic projects that aimed to expand the terrain of our political imaginaries beyond a defensive and crouched liberalism. Again, all to the good. But did we perhaps fail to take seriously the projects of mundane maintenance that virtue theorists prioritize? Did our criticisms and critiques of the limits of liberalism and neoliberal consensus lead us to dismiss the "reverence for institutions" identified by Nietzsche (73)? In our expansion of the political, did we perhaps fail to attend to the institutional and electoral realms to which the Right so effectively laid claim?

Across the ideological divide, political actors in a post-2016 world share a frustration with the failed promises of neoliberal governance and the politics of economic stagnation and endless war. In this context, I would argue that following the election of Donald Trump, the Left is in the midst of a reevaluation, coming to value the juridical and the institutional in new and unanticipated ways. Meanwhile, it is the Right that is taking increasing pleasure in the power of their unruliness – in expressive practices that generate outrage and in the pleasures of racist and misogynist utterances. So my closing question is this: Is the Right engaged in some sort of degraded and dangerously creative form of *virtù* politics – Nietzsche without his recovery of responsibility and generosity? Arendt without the commitment to thinking and judgment? If so, then today an increasingly urgent task for progressives and leftists involves engaging with and reimagining our democratic institutions. Fighting against our own sedimented approaches to the political, *PTDP* offers a powerful reminder that refusing the logic of closure and celebrating dissonance and resistance do not require turning away from the creative work of democratic maintenance and administration. Indeed, if 2016 has taught us anything, it's that our democratic future demands we do both.

Cristina Beltrán

Critical Exchange

Black feminism and the dilemma of agonism

The following are reflections on *Political Theory and the Displacement of Politics* and the dilemma the texts illuminates for black feminists. Honig's endorsement of the Arendtian conception of power, as well as her commitment to the agon and a politics of permanent contestation are welcome among a set of black feminist thinkers, namely bell hooks and Cathy Cohen. Honig presents a vision of political world that well accommodates and would support a hooksian vision of power, seeing the world building work it has the potential to do, and that is in some ways tailor made for Cohen's deviants to become the transformative political actors that Cohen would have them become. Another set, those more closely aligned with thinkers like Juliet Hooker, would see a political world in which black women and the marginal are simply doing the maintenance work of democracy, cleaning up the remainder bins of politics, doing dangerous and often deadly work. For democracy's fugitives, democratic exemplarity only invites state repression and premature death, often not the glorious kind. Honig and Hooker both have interesting takes on politics as permanently unfinished business. For Hooker, it is the very unfinished nature of our democracy that makes democratic practice itself risky, often deadly. For Hooker, once settled status inequalities like race are acknowledged, the objects in the remainder bins pile up and the unfinishedness becomes unequal and exhausting. Hooker would remind us that even as we rightly celebrate the world Rosa Parks helped to create, we remember that she had to leave the Montgomery she created for Detroit. hooks and Cohen demonstrate that we are most likely to find our agonists among the most marginalized and we must because we should not build worlds without them; Hooker implores us to consider the ethics of doing so.

Political Theory and the Displacement of Politics is an illuminating text to read through a black feminist lens. It is illuminating, for example, to think about intersectionality through the lens of virtue vs *virtù* and with an eye toward the remainders of our politics. Honig writes:

> Whereas virtue theorists assume that their favored institutions fit and express the identities or the formations of subjects, *virtù* theorists argue that no such fit is possible, that every politics has its remainders, that resistances are engendered by every settlement, even by those that are relatively enabling or empowering. It is for the sake of those perpetually generated remainders of politics that *virtù* theorists seek to secure the perpetuity of political contest (3).

This passage is striking because what is it to live a life at the intersection of multiple identities and therefore to live a life at the intersection of multiple power formations, but to constantly be a part of the unacknowledged remainders in a

Critical Exchange

world where most are convinced that politics has generated solutions to the problems of employment discrimination, reproductive rights or violence against women? On the latter issue think of the remainders that today's abolition feminists like Beth Richie, Ruth Wilson Gilmore, Mariame Kaba and Angela Davis struggle to bring to the attention of carceral feminists. What was Kimberlé Crenshaw doing in her foundational intersectionality articles but calling attention to the egregious remainders of race and gender employment discrimination law and anti-violence work, remainders that would only be addressed by agreeing that it was necessary to multiply the sites of political contexts when others held that the matters had been closed? What is intersectionality theory if it is not an effort to get some issues and indeed people out of the remainder bins of politics and onto the main field of contestation?

Honig also presents an inspiring account of the feminist potential in the Arendtian account of power, the fact that she replaced "the male or patriarchal view of power as the ability to achieve certain outcomes with a more feminine, cooperative and practice-oriented vision of power as action in concert" (Honig, 1995, p. 2). Arendt replaces masculine power with the power generated from Rosa Parks' act. But Honig also pushes the more feminine account of power toward more explicitly feminist ends:

> If action is boundless and excessive why should it respect a public–private distinction that seeks to regulate and contain it without ever allowing itself to be engaged or contested by it?…Once reminded of the rather deep and stable settlements of the private realm, the alleged exhilarations of actions disruptions start to ring false…The disruptions of action seem to leave so much in place: god, technology, gender, race, class, ethnicity…Any reading of Arendt that takes seriously the agonistic, virtuosic and performative impulses in her politics must, for the sake of that politics, resists the a priori determination of a public/private distinction that is beyond contestation and amendment (119, 118).

The Arendtian conception of power as action in concert and specifically Honig's refusal to allow Arendtian action to be walled off in the public realm as well as Honig's call to a politics of permanent contestation can be placed in productive conversation with the conception of power bell hooks endorses and Cathy Cohen's statements on the necessity of moving from deviance to politics.

hooks takes white liberal feminists to task, as she did throughout her own classic *Feminist Theory: From Margin to Center* (2015), for being enamored with masculine accounts of power as domination. She says that in doing so they had failed to look to another conception and source of power exercised by marginalized women. The most interesting account of power she outlines she names "the power of disbelief." hooks builds on the definitions of power advanced by Grace Lee and

James Boggs and by Elizabeth Janeway. She says, "One of the most significant forms of power held by the weak" is "the refusal to accept the definitions of oneself that is put forward by the powerful." She calls this the "ordered use of the power to disbelieve." hooks says:

> Women need to know that they can reject the powerful's definition of their reality – that they can do so even if they are poor, exploited, or trapped in oppressive circumstances. They need to know that this exercise of this basic personal power is an act of resistance and strength. Many poor and exploited women, especially non-white women, would have been unable to develop positive self-concepts if they had not exercised their power to reject the powerful's definition of their reality (hooks, 2015, p. 92).

hooks asserts that women on the margins have been exercising an important and unrecognized form of power that must be given greater consideration in feminist theory. Twenty years later, Cathy Cohen would prove that: first apparently feminist classics appear in 10-year intervals, and second she would take, not liberal feminists, but middle class blacks to task for not seeing the political potential in a group exercising something similar to what hooks calls power:

> Despite feelings of some in Black communities that we have been shamed by the immoral behavior of a small subset of community members, those some would label the underclass, scholars must take up the charge to highlight and detail the agency of those on the outside, those who through their acts of nonconformity choose outsider status, at least temporarily…These individuals are not fully or completely defining themselves as outsiders nor are they satisfied with their outsider status, but they are also not willing to adapt, or to conform. The cumulative impact of such choices might be the creation of spaces or counter publics, where not only oppositional ideas and discourse happen, but lived opposition, or at least autonomy, is chosen daily. Through the repetition of deviant practices by multiple individuals, new identities, communities, and politics might emerge where seemingly deviant, unconnected behavior can be transformed into conscious acts of resistance that serve as the basis for a mobilized politics of deviance (Cohen, 2004, p. 43).

Cohen is more concerned than hooks was with how to ensure that this power is political, that it is exercised collectively and that it is transformative, as something not simply to be held by the marginal and exercised to reject the positions of those who would define them inaccurately but as a world-building resource.

Thinking of Arendt, hooks, Cohen and Honig together, one gets a truly inspiring vision of politics. In a world where capacities for action are not limited to certain groups and in a world where action itself is not walled off from the private sphere, the people best able to comprehend power as something distinct from violence and the people who have had to reject the self-definitions and norms of those who have held more masculinized forms of power over them are perhaps the most suited and amenable to a politics of permanent contestation. Their lives, their circumstances may provide the best training for agonistic politics. Honig writes that it is perhaps among the most marginalized to whom we should look to enact this politics as they have lived lives that best dispose them to the politics of permanent contestation. Perhaps Cohen's "deviants" need resources and support or simply clear routes to the agon, insurance that the agon will never be closed to their contestations. Honig, with action unbound, presents the place and the terms wherein they can best do the transformative, world-building work that Cohen would have them do.

But is this what must be done in a world in which all power formations – Arendtian, hooksian and intersectional power formations – exist and we take the multiplication of sites of contest as the good to be achieved? Honig writes, "Arendt presents the bifurcation between the determinism of the natural body (in the private realm) and the freedom of the acting self (in the public realm) as attributes of individual selves, but they actually operate to distinguish some selves from others in the ancient Greece that is her beloved model" (Honig, 1995, p. 142), and Honig would add that this is also true today. "To be a citizen is not to be wholly identified with one's embodiment: for others their identity is their embodiment." When Honig says of Arendt that her action is spontaneous, novel, creative and always-self-surprising and calls for more of it, one thinks, "How creative must action be among those whose bodies remain so strongly associated with mere process?" Power though they may well possess alongside admirably agonistic spirits, Juliet Hooker would name those of whom hooks and Cohen speak among democracy's fugitives, action's outlaws.

Once the differential stakes of differential embodiment are acknowledged it is important to consider the risks facing action's outlaws, the democratic fugitives within our democracy. Hooker's critique of Wolin is instructive here. She writes:

> Engaging with [Frederick] Douglass thus extends what it means to be a fugitive democratic thinker in Wolin's sense because Douglass moves beyond recognizing the revolutionary and unsettled character of democratic politics to demonstrating the permanently uneven reach of democracy and the rule of law, as struggles to enlarge the demos are likely to be resisted and viewed as anything but "lawful" protests. Today's fugitives are thus the DREAMers or Black Lives Matter protesters who enact exemplary democratic practices even as their status as citizens is precarious, and as their political activism renders them vulnerable to increased state reprisal (Hooker, 2017, p. 32).

What is the relationship between activism to bring about the conditions of equality Arendt sees as a precondition of action, that is Honig's action unbound, and democratic action, which for Arendt demands equality? And relatedly, or more importantly, when does it cease to be the politics of augmentation to address

Critical Exchange

remainders and become what Hooker sees as the more problematic work of sacrifice and democratic repair? Can this distinction be drawn in a world in which action is boundless and a capacity that can be exercised by all? Are all remainders simply sacrifices? Should our best agonists continue to enter the field of contest when the sacrifices pile up on their side? Should they continue when often they are the ones who are sacrificed?

In Hooker's (2016, p. 448) "Black Lives Matter and the Paradoxes of US Black Politics," she writes, "When other citizens and state institutions betray a lack of care and concern for black suffering, which in turn makes it impossible for those wrongs to be redressed, is it fair to ask blacks to enact 'appropriate' democratic politics?" Hooker suggests that there is a conceptual trap in romantic historical narratives of black activism (especially the Civil Rights Movement) that recast peaceful acquiescence to loss as a form of democratic exemplarity. Honig would respond that there is never peaceful acquiescence in her understanding of democracy. But the question about the relationship between augmentation, repair and sacrifice remains. At what point do augmentation and remainders become repair and sacrifice? Hooker might label every remainder a sacrifice and point out that those most defined by their embodiment, that is the marginal, do the most sacrificing and in the end are sacrificed to the work of democratic repair. Permanent contestation is exhausting. Permanent contestation kills. Hooker's later work better illustrates this point. In later work, Hooker raises the stakes of the dangers alongside the inequity of democratic repair, as well as the presumption that blacks exist within our democracy to perform the labor of democratic repair (and to do so "appropriately," accepting sacrifice and loss), by emphasizing the toll it takes on the bodies of those so often forced to enact it. She writes:

> The death of activist Erica Garner in 2017 at 27 from a heart attack provoked "profound sadness," "deep despair," and rage among black women. Garner was propelled into activism following the death of her father, Eric, after he was placed in a fatal chokehold by a NYC police officer...Eric Garner's death scene and Michael Brown's unattended body lying in the street for hours, became the emblematic images of racial violence and racial terror in the US in the twenty-first century. In turn, Erica Garner's death, less than four years after her father was killed, poses stark questions about the intergenerational costs of state violence, the burdens of activism and the enhanced and unrecognized vulnerabilities faced by black women (Hooker, 2018).

Hooker quotes Melissa Harris Perry, who says, "The abrupt loss of Erica Garner is more than an individual tragedy; her death, like her father's is a public lesson." Hooker says, "It is American inequality wrought on a fragile human body for all of us to see." Hooker continues, "But Erica Garner's tragic premature death, the fact that her heart literally stopped beating, also points to the urgent need to examine what it would mean to grapple fully with black loss (the loss of Erica's father) without subsuming it to the imperatives of democratic repair." Or her death helps us to tally all that we have to lose in the seemingly never-ending work of democratic repair. Hooker says, "Garner's death at such a young age raises questions about the personal and physical toll of the kind of black activism against racial injustice that is usually lauded as an exemplary democratic act" (Hooker, 2018). Are these, however, the unequally distributed, occupational hazards of democratic citizenship in our intersectional democracy, filled with fugitives? Or are they something else? Will the costs for engaging in action for those so closely associated with their bodies and mere process continue to be those very bodies?

Arendt celebrates heroic action. Blacks die doing maintenance work outside the edifice she would build to house her heroic action – some of their deaths are celebrated but what remains is a problematic division of democratic labor in a world of remainder and sacrifice. Arendt spoke of public happiness. It is also important to Honig. Many activists who Hooker would say are engaged in repair work admit to feeling what she described. But they are also plagued by exhaustion, depression and death. What does Honig thinks about the fact that Erica Garner, like her father Eric, now also can't breathe?

Shatema Threadcraft

Varieties of agonism

It has now been a quarter century since the language of agonism began its rise to prominence in political theory. In reflecting on this phenomenon, we should be quite careful about how we piece together our understanding of agonism. Why? As Lida Maxwell's original invitation to this Critical Exchange noted, agonism now holds an almost unquestioned salience in left political theory; so how precisely we understand its character is of no small significance. It is, of course, always useful to be careful about the character of our core commitments. But I want to suggest that we have an additional, specific reason to be careful, and that concerns the fact that Donald Trump presents us with a vivid and authentic exemplar of one variant of agonism. And it is striking to me how often academic references to agonism seem oblivious to the fact that they, at least tacitly, affirm what is essentially the same variant.

With that concern in mind, I want to distinguish two types of agonism. For many political theorists, the most familiar variant traces back to Carl Schmitt's 1932 essay, "The Concept of the Political," an English translation of which appeared in 1976. This perspective was brought to prominence by Chantal Mouffe's deployment of Schmitt in the 1990s to critique standard conceptions of liberalism and democracy as they appear in the work of Rawls and Habermas. Today, if there is a reference to agonism in political theory, you are likely to find it accompanied by a citation to Mouffe and/or Schmitt. We might call this Schmitt–Mouffe variant "imperializing agonism."

Bonnie Honig's work, I want to suggest, offers a different type. Here we might usefully refer to the "Hopkins School" of agonism. I am speaking of Honig, William Connolly and Richard Flathman. In their own individual ways, they all have drawn upon Nietzsche – not Schmitt – to craft distinctive accounts of the importance of agonism for political theory. The differences between these three reflect the way they were influenced by additional political thinkers: Arendt in Honig's case, Foucault in Connolly's case, and a diverse cast in Flatham's case. To my mind, this is the strand of agonism which we should embrace. Call it "tempered agonism." Lest one think that "tempered" means a "softer" version of agonism, I would point out that tempering is a process that produces a metal that is more resilient than an untempered one.

What is the central difference between the imperializing strand and the tempered one? Imperializing agonism gives us a distinctive way of categorically (in the sense of ontologically and existentially) defining politics: politics *just is* the unrelenting struggle of friends and enemies. Any other way of seeing things is simply a mischaracterization of the subject matter. For tempered agonists, however, there is simply no way of declaring the truth of the matter in such a sovereign fashion. As Honig nicely puts it, agonism and its chief opponent, let us call it consensualism, "represent not two distinct options but two impulses of political life" (14). As a consequence, we should not seek to repress one or the other by definitional fiat; rather we must continually be "negotiating" between them. The title of Honig's introduction is: "Negotiating Positions."

Why is this difference so important? One sees the reason clearly in Mouffe. She begins with a full embrace of Schmitt's definition of the political as the unrelenting struggle of friends and enemies. But she then declares famously that we should tone down this straight Schmitteanism; in short, we should affirm not "antagonism," but rather "agonism," with the latter now meaning a *respectful* contest between political adversaries who agree to wage their struggle along broadly democratic lines within the rule of law. How often have I heard that mantra repeated – "not antagonism, only agonism" – as if the mere saying of these words will transform the reality of the former into the latter?

What I want to suggest is that Mouffe's move here represents a purely verbal achievement with no real conceptual substance to give it critical force. The Schmittean existential-ontological grounding that Mouffe affirms at the start *always* reasserts an imperial domination within this framing of agonism. If I am an adherent of this position, I may behave toward you, my political opponent, in a fashion that affirms some rules of equality and democracy that restrain our contests whenever it is convenient and serves my interests; but when such constraints hinder what I and my "friends" truly desire, we will, with immaculately clear consciences, grind you into the dirt of history. When push comes to shove, then, the friend-enemy dynamic simply trumps any other norms.

As I suggested a moment ago, this is no mere academic issue, because we now have an Imperializing Agonist-in-Chief in the White House. Trump clearly sees the world in terms of fundamental, synonymous binaries: friends/enemies, winners/losers, loyal people/traitors; and his actions continually make vivid the dangers of the Schmitt-Mouffe variant. Trump will defend things like due process when they fit his strategic goals; but he enthusiastically trashes them, when he finds that they impede in any way his axis of "friends," aka his loyal base. Thus, Trump, at one point, talked about a fair resolution of the Dreamer issue – "I love the Dreamers" – yet his positions later show them to be pure pawns in his broader crackdown on immigration.

One of the real pleasures that comes with rereading Honig's book today, or the work of others in the Hopkins School, is how resistant they are to the dangers of the Schmitt–Mouffe formulation. But, in issuing this praise, one also tacitly highlights a crucial issue in tempered agonism, that I want to raise. What exactly is the ontological–ethical–political source of the "tempering" force on which Honig draws in her framing of agonism, and how does she understand its status within her work as a whole?

As I ponder this question two issues stand out for me. First, in the years since *PTDP*, the importance of Jewish thought in Honig's work has become increasingly apparent. Arendt has, of course, always been there, but she has been joined over time by various figures and stories from the Hebrew Bible and by other thinkers like Franz Rosenzweig, Emmanuel Levinas, and Judith Butler. In saying this, I do not mean that these figures constitute an exclusive group, only that they are prevalent and persistent voices.

Now simply referring to this group and Judaism as a source does not yet say much about *how* they function as a source. For some scholars, a source, especially when it is religious, is like a well from which one draws all that gives thought and action meaning. The influence largely runs in one direction. But Honig's relation to her source seems intriguingly different. And this is the second issue I wish to raise. Honig does not just draw upon her source; she continually reworks, refigures and thus recreates it. Her source might accordingly be imagined as more like a circle of deeply reflective conversation partners than a well. These voices provide Honig succor and orientation, but the conversation itself is always evolving and her voice continually "augments" it as well – to use a crucial, multidimensional term that has engaged her for many years.

Stephen K. White

Theater and the dispersal of the agon

At the start of *Political Theory and the Displacement of Politics*, Bonnie Honig tells us something about the kind of reader she is, or probably more accurately used to be. "As a child," she tells us, "I used to read the last page of mystery novels first." She then outlines the benefits and costs of such a reading strategy. While being more open to "appreciating its details [and] getting to know its characters" she was, she tells us, "less vulnerable to the text" (1). The autobiographic aperçu, ostensibly about the paradox of writing introductions, in fact foreshadows a much wider interest of Honig's in narrative or what one might call a politics of form. Honig's attention to stories and the particular form these stories takes is part of what makes her work in political theory so innovative and explains to some extent her broad and deep impact on the fields of literary studies and the humanities more generally. On re-reading this book I was struck by the extent to which narrative is repeatedly foregrounded. From the start, Honig chooses to characterize what others might see as philosophical tracts or political manifestos as fables and stories. There are in fact, no less than eight references to fables in the index. The discussion of Kant starts with a reading of his "Speculative Beginnings" and the fable returns in her accounts of Arendt's, Derrida's and Rawls' "fabulist" renderings of the American Revolution and founding.

And it is a fable, perhaps the grandest of fables – Homer's *Iliad* – which gives Honig her central term, the term we are discussing here: the *Agon*. For the term agon first appears in Honig's book in the discussion of Nietzsche's essay "Homer's Contest." It is through Nietzsche's appreciative reading of the dynamics of epic combat that the term agonism first takes shape. It is in part thanks to Honig's analyses that Nietzsche's status as a political writer, indeed as a writer who has a place in the theorization of democratic politics, has been recognized. Yet, one potential legacy of this Homeric notion of agonism could be that by focusing on the heroic and sometimes savage struggles of a band of aristocratic warriors, agonism's ability to sustain a model of democratic politics is strained. Indeed, this element of agonism is carried over into Arendt's discussion of the *polis* which she sees in profound continuity rather than rupture with Homeric society. "Speaking metaphorically and theoretically," she memorably writes, "it is as though, the men who returned from the Trojan War had wished to make permanent the space of action which had arisen from their deeds and sufferings, to prevent its perishing…The *polis* properly speaking, is not the city-state in its physical location; it is the organization of the people as it arises out of acting and speaking together" (2013, p. 198). When Arendt speaks of the *polis* as not a place but as a structure of political organization, she elides the differences between different *poleis* and erases the historical relationship to democracy.

One curious feature of Nietzsche's essay, however, and one that animates Honig's commentary, is that despite foregrounding Homer in its title, much of it centers around the dynamics of competition in democratic Athens. Honig makes this evident in her discussion of ostracism, an Athenian institution which was often seen as a way of curtailing precisely the kinds of contests between aristocratic heroes which held the *demos* to ransom. But Nietzsche offers an alternative interpretation: "The original sense of this peculiar institution however is not a safety valve but that of a stimulant....This is the kernel of the Hellenic competition-conception: it abominates autocracy, and fears its dangers; it desires the preventative against the genius – a second genius" (1911, p. 58). Honig has recourse to Nietzsche's discussion of ostracism as an illustration of his "reverence of institutions" – but one could go further noting his critique of autocracy and perhaps even underline his openness to specifically *democratic* institutions. Despite the virtuosic model implied by the attention to Homer, the essay actually advocates a more collective oriented agonism. Nietzsche writes: "To the Ancients…the aim of the agonistic education was the welfare of the whole, of the civic society. Every Athenian, for instance, was to cultivate his ego in competition, so far that it should be of the highest service to Athens and should do the least harm" (1911, p. 56). Nietzsche does not see democracy as a bar to the agonistic spirit but as a stimulant. Individual *kleos* and democratic flourishing are working hand in hand. As Christa Davis Acampora writes, "It is the *community* and not any great individual competitor that founds [the agon]" (2013, p. 17).

Nevertheless, one might worry that Nietzsche's unexpected portrayal of Athens directs our attention away from the institution which supports the competition for excellence in both Homeric and democratic arenas: the institution of slavery. Contemporaneously with "Homer's Contest," Nietzsche would write an essay called the "Greek State" which, with its forthright denunciation of the "dignity of labour," also casts a shadow over Arendt's later formulations. The core of the essay is a plea to organize society in such a way as to maximize the creation of art: "Be it then pronounced that war is just as much a necessity for the state as the slave is for society, and who can avoid this verdict if he honestly asks himself about the causes of the never-equalled Greek art-perfection?" (1911, p. 15). Nietzsche's Greeks teach us this fable: "We must accept this cruel sounding truth, that slavery is of the essence of Culture…The misery of toiling men must still increase in order to make the production of the world of art possible to a small number of Olympian men" (1911, p. 12). There has been a consensus among scholars to treat Nietzsche's statements about slavery as metaphorical and to hold him at a distance from the debates about abolitionism which preoccupied his contemporaries. But as a notebook entry on Harriet Beecher Stowe and her debt to Rousseau suggests, there is evidence that Nietzsche was himself well aware of the continuities between his arguments about ancient slavery and the emancipation movements of the nineteenth century.

Critical Exchange

The fabulous world of epic, then, may ground Honig's discussion of the agon – but its features depart in various ways from their Nietzschean genealogy. In particular, while the vocabulary of fables and epics does not disappear from Honig's book, a different genre of narrative takes on greater prominence. The agon in Greek culture simultaneously denotes military, sporting, musical, philosophical, legal, political and medical contests. In the fifth-century BCE Athens, the term agon increasingly described a formal element of Greek drama, a set piece of opposing speeches by protagonist and antagonist or protagonist and chorus. The formulaic nature of these verbal encounters as well as their specific vocabulary have been read by many literary critics as a reference to the emerging institution of the law court. Thus, debates about the nature of justice or the question of human accountability conducted on stage specifically referenced the incipient terminology of legal battles. Yet the direction of travel – legal metaphor in drama or dramatic metaphor in the law court is difficult to establish. While one of Honig's concerns in her book is the reduction of politics to law, the porosity of theater and the law in Athens are a reminder, of how politics, law, and literature remain interarticulated. In classical Athens, the law is not the stabilizing discourse which keeps the disruptive force of tragedy in check – law and tragedy irrupt simultaneously to *agonize* the category of the human.

But what interests me here is how what one might call Honig's "performative turn" in the book suggests a different form for agonism. In a brilliant move, Honig brings Arendt's discussion of the question of founding and the American Revolution into dialog with Derrida's critique of J.L. Austin's theory of performativity. On Honig's Derridean reading, Arendt's theory of action becomes "a non-sovereign performance that works to reconstitute communities and inaugurate new realities" (2013, pp. 43–44). This performative action is crucial to the model of agonism which Honig goes on to develop in *Antigone, Interrupted*. The frame of democratic institutions, the involvement of the chorus, the arguments, interruptions and conspiracies between the protagonists: all of these aspects of tragedy make it a privileged place to explore the collective dimension of agonism. But it is also by tracking the genre of tragedy that Honig can specifically make good on the promise of her first book: "the same impulse can motivate the application of performativity to Arendt's public–private distinction" (122). Honig needs an agonism grounded in tragedy – not Homeric epic – to fulfill her promise. For theater is precisely the sphere where the boundaries between public and private – the very question of what is political – "how far down does the political go?" – are so insistently debated.

Nevertheless, in *Antigone, Interrupted*, Honig shows how reading these plays *tragically* may ultimately blunt their political promise. She argues that the politics of tragedy can all too easily morph into the tragedy of politics. By revealing the covert workings of a mortalist humanism in some of the most politically minded readings of the *Antigone* she uncovers again a insidious displacement of politics.

As she does in her first book, Honig calls on us to examine and rethink our reading practices. By proposing to read the *Antigone* as melodrama rather than tragedy, she keeps the agon in play. If the epic agonism of Nietzsche should be rejected because of its anti-emancipatory politics, a tragic agonism, Honig suggests, must ultimately also be rejected because of its emancipation from politics. *Antigone,Interrupted* thus shows how we might have to give up on "the tragic" but not on tragedy as drama. In her reading of *Antigone,* Honig's agonism has found, if not strictly its genre, then its stage. Perhaps this explains why Honig is sticking with drama and offering us as her next project *theatres of refusal*. It is a cliché of Greek tragedy that the audience, familiar with the mythic stories, already knew how the plays would end before they saw them staged. Perhaps the child Honig was destined to give up mystery novels in order to discover Greek tragedy.

Miriam Leonard

What is agonism?[1]

> ...to practice reading as an art...something for which one must almost be a cow
> Nietzsche (quoted in Maxwell)

What accounts for agonism's rising prominence in the last two to three decades of political theory? What should it be enlisted to do next? Can it help us understand the race and gender politics of our moment? Or combat the current faux-populism in the U.S.?

This last, especially, is on everyone's mind now.[2] But back in the early 1990s, *PTDP* was addressed to a more achievable task, though it sure looked daunting at the time: to open up room for new political theory thinking outside the frame of then current debates about liberalism versus communitarianism, as deliberative democratic theory quickly advanced to their ranks. The frame encouraged a focus on ontological questions of subjectivity, the generation of norms for governance, and practices of justification that would seal or settle the foundations of political order. *PTDP* was a critique of such foundational visions of politics as settlement and of justification as hegemony. It promoted agonism as an alternative, disorienting perspective in political theory, highlighting its commitment to attend to the remainders of political settlement and the perpetuity of political contest.

PTDP took seriously the thinkers and texts that seemed to be the greatest obstacles to the project and found *in* them the resources out of which agonists might build alternatives. Its central aim was to dislodge the debates of the day by reorganizing them into a different, staged clash between *virtù* (disruptive) and virtue (orderly) theories of politics, highlighting the contrast between these two visions of politics as sharper and more significant than the attention-getting contrasts between (deliberative) liberalism versus communitarianism. I contrasted representatives of *virtù* theory, Machiavelli, Nietzsche and Arendt, with representatives of virtue theory, Kant, Rawls, and Sandel. Then, by highlighting elements of *virtù* in the virtue theories of Rawls and Sandel and virtue elements in the *virtù* theories of Nietzsche and Arendt, the book enacted the agonism of *virtù*, infiltrating and occupying its opponents, and not (as in the agonism of Homer's epics) nobly destroying or defeating them.

Another mark of the book was that it drew on, but did not identify the book's argument with, feminist and queer theory. I wanted to mainstream such contributions, but I think Lida Maxwell is right to point out that this elision may have suggested that agonism was a merely formal practice of contestation without essential, orienting commitments on gender and sexuality or ethnicity and race. I assumed the commitment of agonism to care for the agon (elaborated from Nietzsche's "Homer's Contest") and for the "remainders" of politics would be enough to provide agonism with its substance: a political commitment above all to equality.[3] But I take Maxwell's point that my agonism was not incidentally feminist and queer (my examples, my archive): hence my turn to the virago, the female bearer of *virtù*, as an orienting figure. And, as other contributors here point out, my agonism later drew on other sources, too: Jewish, gothic, melodramatic, (post)humanist, and classical. Twenty-five years ago, however, situating the book as feminist or queer would not only have strengthened it; it would also have marginalized it and undermined its aim: to occupy and infiltrate the mainstream.[4] That said, if there was some protection for agonism in my (openly violated) "method of avoidance," then perhaps I had a bit more in common with Rawls than I realized.

Agonism's advance since then, it seems to me, is partly evidenced in the fact that twenty-five years ago, most political theorists were not doing work like that being done now by contributors to this forum, not all of whom identify as agonists but all of whose work contributes to a politicized political theory that speaks not only to the timeless questions of the (thankfully, ever-broadening) canon but also to the pressing challenges of our day. *This* is now mainstream democratic theory: normative, critical, historical, cultural, literary, feminist, queer, environmental, interdisciplinary, engaged.[5]

The engagements with *PTDP* tendered here test, extend, and perhaps (as Stephen White says) temper the book's original vision of agonism. They challenge me to rethink some things and, after rehearsing and responding to what I take to be the essential points of critique, I turn to consider three crucial points in the book that I would today handle differently.

It is striking that some of my interlocutors see agonism as possibly too combative, others as inadequately so.

Agonism must be distinguished from antagonism, says Stephen White, who contrasts my views and those of the "Hopkins school" with Chantal Mouffe's. White argues that my own version of agonism is tempered, partly, by my Arendtianism (different from the agonism of Richard Flathman and William Connolly) and by my later turn to Judaic sources.[6] By tempering, White means not a moderating process but an enhancement of strength and resilience.[7] I appreciate his take for its cautious acceptance of the ineliminability of friend-enemy relations from politics while fending off more Schmittian assumptions (that he finds in Mouffe) that politics is, as such, always reducible to friend-enemy relations.

Agonism might want to be more like antagonism. This is a way of stating Shatema Threadcraft's question regarding what, if anything, agonism has to say about the deep and enduring racism of American politics, which assigns heroic action only to some and maintenance work to others. Agonism contests this distinction, actually. Everyday speech acts, like promising and forgiveness (J.L. Austin's performatives), can be heroic, as when Arendt in *The Human Condition* treats promising and forgiveness as inaugural, not ordinary (*PTDP*, ch. 4). Conversely, Arendt's focus on inaugural action actually commits her to practices of maintenance (113–114), a point she grants in connection with her account of augmentation in *On Revolution*. But Threadcraft is right in holding that in the U.S., the division is racial and the work of maintenance leaves black activists "plagued by exhaustion, depression and death." She has Erica Garner in mind, daughter of the murdered Eric Garner whose protestations, "I can't breathe," were ignored by the police who held him, unjustifiably, illegally, and inhumanely, in a chokehold. Garner's killing was filmed and publicized by his friend, Ramsey Orta, who was then harassed and ultimately arrested. When the police arrested his mother, too, Orta made a deal with prosecutors to secure her release and is now serving time, the detailed story of which is a record of almost every evil of the American carceral system (Jones, 2019). Erica Garner, thrust into activism by her father's case, died at 27, three years after her father. She had an enlarged heart, suffered an asthma attack, and was carrying a world of responsibility on her shoulders: "For a whole year, I've protested every Tuesday and Thursday," she said. "I feel like a representative for people throughout this whole nation because I'm doing this, I'm speaking out, me being his daughter" (Wamsley, 2017). We cannot bring her back but we can grieve her loss and take up her work, offering to lighten a bit the burdens of others like her. Agonistic actors in concert are not immune to exhaustion, depression, and death. But they are also not equally exposed to them, as Threadcraft rightly points out. Being with others strengthens and emboldens those engaged in resistance, and also offers up the pleasures of being together to offset the rest.

Agonism has to move well beyond Nietzsche, where I located it in *PTDP*, lest it retain the traces of Homeric elitism, warring conflict, and unconcern about slavery. This is the concern of Miriam Leonard, who sees my later turn to Sophocles' *Antigone* as part of an effort to temper Nietzsche's Homeric agonism by replacing epic with tragedy and even, eventually, melodrama. I have worked to pluralize the genres of political theory over the years but I think of the various genres, to which Leonard rightly calls attention for their partial perspectives and historical baggage, not as a sequence in which each one corrects for the prior ones' limitations, but rather as agonistically engaged, each offering a rival approach to the films or texts under consideration. In *Antigone, Interrupted*, for example, I do not replace tragedy with melodrama, but I do unsettle habitual interpretations of tragedy by confronting them with the powers and limits of melodrama's rather different emplotment.

Agonism could be seen as too formal, a commitment to mere contestation, as such, unless I embrace the feminist and queer politics in which my agonism was, in any case, originally wrapped. This is Lida Maxwell's claim which offers its own tempering of agonism as always already feminist and queer, well before other sources were brought to bear. I previewed her claims above and return to them in a fuller discussion below.

Cristina Beltrán finds in agonism a useful contestation of the closures of identity politics, while noting the importance of an agonism that is not only disruptive but also institutional, just as my reading of Nietzsche emphasized his Apollonian side in addition to his more often noted Dionysianism.[8] This, too, is a tempering, we might say. And, looking to the book's discussion of "remainders," Beltrán asks for agonism's guidance today, now that remaindering people has become again an essential feature of American politics. Beltrán and the others would not be surprised to hear me say we need both *virtù* and virtue in moments like this. This means we need to combine: mass mobilizations against the use of concentration camps at the border; canny electoral strategies to win power for those who will do right by those betrayed by today's faux-populism; pushing the Democratic Party to more egalitarian public policies that will deliver on the promise to do better; improving outreach to black, indigenous, Latinx, and independent voters who often sit out elections, partly because of concerted Republican efforts to suppress the vote via gerrymandering and various Jim Crow style obstacles to voting such as closing locally accessible polling stations, and instituting, too close to elections, new proof of residency and identification requirements. Prosecuting illegal voting which is rare and rarely intentional is another part of this strategy of voter intimidation.[9] Mobilizing communities so we can advance the agendas we embrace even when the national government does not is important. It will also be important to develop and refine legal strategies to nullify appointments, directives, and decisions made by an illegitimate President.* There must also be a public accounting: those who have committed or covered up crimes, profited from emoluments, or violated human rights must be publicly tried and brought to justice. Finally, as I have argued elsewhere, if our current institutional arrangements survive all this, every effort must be made politically, culturally and legally to prevent the Republican Party separating itself in the future from Trump. They will surely and shamelessly make every effort to do so by scapegoating him if they need to when the time comes. Whether or not all these things happen depends on how mobilized, organized, and agonistically engaged are the citizens and residents of this country.

Returning to the book, I would make three changes to it in light of what I have since learned and developed further in my work, informed in part by the work of the contributors to this Critical Exchange.[10]

First, I would attend to Hannah Arendt's erasure of slavery from the American founding and of racism from its history since. This is one of the glaring "remainders" of her political theory. Miriam Leonard is correct to highlight the role of fable and narrative in this book. I remain inspired by Arendt's faith in the power of stories to unsettle consensus and open room for new thinking. But some stories do the opposite. Fabulist is the term I used to describe Arendt's account of the American Revolution, which she cleanses of details she saw as extraneous to the colonists' fight for freedom (slavery, political theology) and that she thought would interfere with the potentially powerful purity of its example.[11] In my new book on the politics of refusal, I compare Arendt's fabulism to Saidiya Hartman's *fabulation,* noting that Hartman's version refuses the authority of the archive to which Arendt herself contributed when she glorified the Compact of the Mayflower but said nothing about the slave ship that Hortense Spillers rightly calls the Mayflower's twin.[12] When I followed Arendt's lead, 25 years ago, and re-theorized, as a kind of social contract, the "We hold" of the Declaration without calling attention to the holds of the slave ships and the contracts that secured them, I repeated the wrong.

I also missed an opportunity to develop then in more detail what I hope I have explored since but will say here more explicitly than before: agonism must contest not only Arendt's public/private distinction but also her rather non-genealogical commitment to new beginnings. Here I might have allowed Nietzsche to do more in *PTDP* to chasten Arendt and not just vice versa. Agonism's commitment to contestation means it cannot think of new beginning as ab initio birth.[13] Indeed, its commitment to the plurality *in* every so-called unity invites a reconsideration of Arendtian natality, which, as Adriana Cavarero argues, "is perhaps the most original category of thought that Arendt gave to the twentieth century" (cited in Marso, 2018). But, as Lori Marso points out, Cavarero adds a caveat. The scene of birth in Arendt is cleansed of the *experience* of birth and is "essentially [a] scenario," Marso says, without the mother. Without her, we miss the very first experience of plurality: the relationship between mother and child (Marso,

2018). Where there was one (Arendtian natality!), there are now two (Cavarero's and Marso's natality as plurality!), and their bond is division – a relationship of love and rage, closeness and individuation. *This* is the predicament of the new: its enmeshment in and dependence on others. Casting the new as the natal with no maternal, Arendt then has to *add* plurality to her account. But *plurality is already there in natality*; and this means the "new" is marked by agonistic struggle (what William Connolly calls identity\difference).

I pursued this notion all the way into the womb in "Difference, Dilemmas, and the Politics of Home" (1994), an essay on Bernice Johnson Reagon's brilliant "Coalition Politics" (1983). Reagon criticized feminist home-yearning as the antithesis of coalition politics: "They're looking for a bottle with some milk in it and a nipple, which does not happen in a coalition." For Reagon, coalition politics means leaving behind the dream of home because in politics you have to "team up with someone who could possibly kill you because that's the only you can figure you can stay alive" (1983, pp. 356–357). Hers is a vividly agonistic picture of political action in concert. I suggested that it ultimately depended on rethinking home, too, though, since "home" is itself a more conflictual and coalitional space than Reagon here grants and even pregnancy (which I was experiencing at the time) is an agonistic struggle.[14] I cited David Haig, an evolutionary biologist (whose name startlingly resembles my own father's!) who said "the fetus shares only half of its genes with the mother. The other half comes from the father. As a result, the evolutionary interests of a mother and her offspring can be different." (You think?) I suggested the relationship between mother and fetus, in the context of a wanted pregnancy, is best seen as "coalitional" in Reagon's sense, agonistic in mine. Thus, agonism rejects Arendt's purism (her purely performative founding *and* her purified natality) on behalf of her action in concert among equals, and it tracks how, as Beltrán points out, difference is remaindered by every effort to expunge it.

Second, I would nuance further my discussion of Arendt's turn to writing in order to escape the inescapable paradox of founding. I welcomed deconstruction's critique of the ontology of presence, which takes writing rather than orality as exemplary of language, and highlights writing's play of iteration (Derrida) rather than the stability of its "permanence" (Arendt). I preferred Derrida to Arendt on this point but still, with this argument, I participated in settler societies' historical privileging of the written over the oral, which displaces and deprivileges the indigeneity that Arendt, who otherwise follows Tocqueville, never mentions. The privileging of writing as literacy over orality as illiteracy helps support the official story of the American founding as an "In the beginning" story (like Arendt's), which Michael Oakeshott contrasts with the more British conservative option of timeless beginning: "Once upon a time." The latter, it is worth noting, is associated with oral storytelling. To these two, in any case, I would add as a further contrast the most American option of all: "And then this happened" (as in: "I wasn't there and anyway it was a long time ago").[15]

Arendt's silence on the genocidal displacements of indigenous peoples and her erasure of the impact of slavery's legacy on the American republic are enabled by her rather unagonistic embrace of the new, and this is supported by her signing on to the myth of an immigrant America, one of the carriers of the idea of natality as an "In the beginning" rebirth or new start. This was a central reason I turned in my next book, *Democracy and the Foreigner* (2001), to the politics of immigration and its intersections with gender (ch. 3) and race (ch. 4).

Third, delving further into the grass-counter example in Rawls' *A Theory of Justice* might have sharpened my account of agonism. In the context of my recent work on the politics of refusal, it has become obvious to me that the grass counter, whose uncommunicative indolence I championed in *PTDP*, is a figure of what Agamben calls inoperativity (or potentiality). The grass counter is Rancière's *farniente*, Melville's Bartleby, Thoreau's saunterer, Chaplin's tramp, the sintho-mosexual of Lee Edelman's *No Future,* and a bearer of Kevin Quashie's "quiet" all rolled into one. He is also, perhaps, neuro-atypical, as has been suggested about Bartleby, too, whose penchant for repetition, intense focus, and intractability suggest the possibility of autism (Murray, 2008). Here is Rawls:

> …imagine someone whose only pleasure is to count blades of grass in various geometrically shaped areas such as park squares and well-trimmed lawns. He is otherwise intelligent and actually possesses unusual skills, since he manages to survive by solving difficult mathematical problems for a fee. The definition of the good forces us to admit that the good for this man is indeed counting blades of grass…Naturally we would be surprised that such a person should exist…Perhaps he is peculiarly neurotic…But if we allow that his nature is to enjoy this activity and not any other…this establishes that it is good for him (1971, pp. 432–433).

Is the grass-counter's pastime a mere "pleasure" that fails to make good on the promise of justice as fairness or is it a proper "conception of the good"? This is Rawls' question.

In the book, I focused on what this example might tell us about the normalizing politics of Rawls' ideal political order and the remainders of tolerance. I would add now a focus on how Rawls' contrast between pleasure and good distracts us from inoperativity and its *power*. For Rawls, the grass counter is just privative, all pleasure, no conception of the good. But his quirky pleasurable pastime could also be seen as a refusal practice that rejects social demands for perpetual (re)productivity and the attendant norms of individual investment, achievement, progress, and ambition that, since 1971, have taken shape as a now familiar ethos of neoliberalism.

When Lida Maxwell highlights the grass-counter's cow-like capacity ("engrossed in the grass" he engages in "rumination"), she affiliates him with a form of life and not its privation, and calls to mind another possible literary partner to the

Critical Exchange

grass counter, *The Story of Ferdinand,* in which Ferdinand, an unusually peaceful bull, just

> liked to sit just quietly and smell the flowers. He had a favorite spot out in the pasture under a cork tree…and he would sit in its shade all day and smell the flowers. Sometimes his mother, who was a cow, would worry about him. She was afraid he would be lonesome all by himself. "Why don't you run and play with the other little bulls and skip and butt your head?" she would say. But Ferdinand would shake his head. "I like it better here where I can sit just quietly and smell the flowers." His mother saw that he was not lonesome, and because she was an understanding mother, even though she was a cow, she let him just sit there and be happy" (Leaf, 1936)[16]

Ferdinand's mother accepts that her son's pleasure just *is* his good. But persuasively turning pleasure into a good of its own, as Ferdinand and his mother do, and as Maxwell seems to recommend, risks concealing what may be a useful agonistic tension between them.

Pleasure has the power to disturb the scene of social (re)production, a point explored in Euripides' *Bacchae*, a focus of my current work on refusal. Euripides' bacchants are also *farnientes*. Refusing work's demands, the women leave the polis to celebrate the god, Dionysus, outside the city on Cithaeron. They may not count the grass, but the bacchants, bovine, and bullish, pleasure-seeking and empowered, loll on the ground's leaves and pine branches, commune with nature, and become animal. They contest every received idea of gender, sexuality, race, foreignness and the human and reject every habit of compliance. The whole episode on Cithaeron is partly a mother–son agon that begins when the women (including the King's mother) defy King Pentheus's order to return to their looms. Pentheus thinks Dionysus is at fault for "introducing a new complaint amongst our women, and doing outrage to the marriage tie." But the women have ideas of their own and outraging patriarchy's marriage tie is definitely one of them.

That marriage tie, a.k.a. the "monogamous family," is one of the "major social institutions" on which Rawlsian justice depends along with "competitive markets and private property in the means of production" (1971, p. 7). Rawls even casts the subjects of justice as fairness as heads of families or households. This is in order to provide the intersubjectivity and intergenerationality that liberal theorists otherwise have a hard time accounting for. But Rawls' reliance on the head of household figure also subtly displaces the agon between pleasure and the good, sublimating the former into the more predictable, less disruptive passion called a "conception of the good." It is like Hegel's transmutation, via kinship, of the unreliable eros between lovers into the adamantly non-incestuous and therefore stable affection between brother and sister (modeled, incredibly, on Antigone and Polynices (Hegel, 1977). Indeed, the Hegelian transmutation is suggested when Rawls refers to the "monogamous family" – an odd locution since it is usually the marriage and not the family that is said to be monogamous.

The grass counter, who insists on his pleasure, forcing Rawls to treat it as a conception of the good, can be seen to resist such transmutation when he is paired with Bartleby and the other farnientes. (Bartleby's proximity to grass is noted by Agamben: "…the walled courtyard is not a sad place. There is sky and there is grass. And the creature knows perfectly well where it is" [quoted in Keeling, 2019, p. 48]). Rawls' grass counter is part of a broad, queer resistance to the normalization and moralization of (re)productivity's demands. He is a spanner in the works of an otherwise "well-ordered society." This may explain why Rawls takes pains to describe the grass that grips the grass counter as "geometric" and "well-trimmed." Can the grass's adjacent straightness somehow quarantine the queerness of its (gay) blades? Even Rawls seems vulnerable to the contagion, though. "Is the family to be abolished then?" he asks later. (He is worried about how the family introduces inequality to a social order determined to lessen it [Rawls, 1971, 511]). Of course not, he replies. But by floating the idea, Rawls has put it into circulation. Think of how Bartleby's "I prefer not to" ultimately infects the whole of the office where he works. Maybe *that* is why Rawls confined the grass counter to well-trimmed spaces and the straight lines of urban geometry: it is not the first time the power of enclosure has been enlisted to contain contagion.

In *The Life and Death of Latisha King*, Gayle Salamon observes that many experience trans people's "gender expression … as a form of sexual aggression." Violence against their mere existence is heteronormatively justified by "characterizing non-normative gender as itself a violent act of aggression and reading the expression of gender identity as itself a sexual act."[17] Similarly, inoperativity is often interpreted as a form of aggression, too, a willful assault on society's (re)productive commitments.[18] In *A Theory of Justice*, Rawls' imagines the threat, and responds to it by remoralizing the social commitment to reproduction to give it more force and by insulating the good from the tumult of pleasure that is often coded female. (Just ask the bacchants.) New restrictions on abortion in the U.S. may surely be seen in this light. For anti-choice activists, life begins at conception (of the good) and pleasure is a danger to be punished.[19] It is a task of agonism to contest such enclosures and their moralizations on behalf of their remaindered forms of life and pleasures, and for the sake of the more egalitarian worlds to which they might one day give birth.

Bonnie Honig

Notes

1 Thanks to Lida Maxwell for organizing this forum and the contributors for participating in it. And I am grateful to Maxwell and Lori Marso for comments on earlier drafts.
2 Almost all the contributors want me – or agonism – to say something about Trump. I have said a lot of what I have to say in public writing, including Honig (2017a, b, 2018).

Critical Exchange

3   And not only equality but also, as I have since argued, public things (Honig, 2019).
4   Infiltration and occupation are "conspiratorial" strategies. On conspiracy, see *Antigone, Interrupted* (Honig, 2013).
5   The advances of agonism are to the credit of a wide range of scholars, followers and fellow travelers of what Stephen White here calls "the Hopkins School." William Connolly and Richard Flathman advised the dissertation that became the book under discussion. Crucial too was the parallel rise of cultural studies, black studies, and interdisciplinarity – this last a hallmark of graduate study at Hopkins early on.
6   Seyla Benhabib has recently turned to Arendt's Jewishness and argues that Arendt *cannot be* an agonist because her "much neglected *Jewish Writings*," are "hard to reconcile with the agonistic paradigm." The Jewish writings have not been "much neglected" for a while, and there is nothing inherently contradictory between agonism and the Judaic sources (Benhabib, 2018).
7   This needs to be noted lest we confuse White's claims with Dana Villa's critique, which contrasted Nietzsche's "excessive agonism" with Arendt's more "tame" variety, and produced what I took to be misleading readings of both Nietzsche and Arendt (Honig, 1993).
8   But the old readings of him as merely disruptive survive: see Benhabib (2018).
9   The prosecution and imprisonment of Crystal Mason by the State of Texas is particularly outrageous: see Pilkington (2018).
10 Others, not mentioned in this Reply, from whose work I have learned since publishing the book, include George Shulman, Juliet Hooker, Tina Campt, Kevin Bruyneel, Christina Sharpe, Jane Bennett, Glen Coulthard, Jason Frank, Melvin Rogers, Ainsley LeSure, Jarius Grove, and Kara Keeling.
11 James Martel has also recently noted Arendt's "resort to fables and distortions," which, he says, help her "to produce the kinds of resistance that are necessary for [an] anarchism" he finds invited by her work, if not necessarily approved by it (Martel, 2011, p. 154.)
12 Hortense Spillers, in a reading of *Clotel*, beautifully shows how the novel "juxtapos[es] 'one little solitary, tempest-tost and weather-beaten ship,' the Mayflower, and 'a low rakish ship hastening from the tropics, solitary and alone, to the New World,' 'on the last day of November, 1620'" (Spillers, 2011, p. 19). Thanks to Ariella Azoulay for calling my attention to Spillers' essay. Hartman's recent work of fabulation, *Wayward Lives, Beautiful Experiments* (2019), is a focus of the third lecture of my *"Give me glory!" The Bacchae's Feminist Politics of Refusal* (forthcoming, Harvard University Press: The Flexner Lectures, 2020/2021).
13 See my *Emergency Politics* (2009) for how the American new beginning succeeds, on Arendt's own account, only because it had begun long before, in colonial practices of self-governance indifferent to British sovereignty.
14 Reagon does not in fact leave intact the binary of safe, conflict-free home versus dangerous or agonistic coalition. "The irony with which she characterizes the womb or an infant's bottle unsettles her assumption that home is essentially a site of nurturance, free of difference, violence, conflict, and death" (Honig, 1994, p. 582).
15 This was Mitch McConnell's sentiment in June 2019 when, deflecting questions about reparations for slavery and its aftermath, he referred to slavery and its bloody aftermath as "something that happened 150 years ago." Ta-Nehisi Coates' magnificent response to McConnell should be the required reading material (or viewing) in every American high school as should the reading list that informed it: https://www.youtube.com/watch?time_continue=140&v=vO1yqOWfjbQ&fbclid=IwAR2Nd45Ae9FKHxJ7VkqtIv6BnYfDIm3aVU7_op9DprHGRlPDvF2S0V5-0O8. On the importance of narrative in this context, see Bryan Stevenson: "The North won the Civil War, but the South won the narrative war (Morgan, 2019).
16 The comparison to Bartleby is made by Handy (2017).
17 Thanks to Lida Maxwell for calling this book to my attention.

Reprinted from the journal

18. Rebecca Schein notes how "the removal of homeless people from public space is justified on the grounds that their presence deters shoppers and tourists" (Schein, 2012, p. 335).
19. In no way should this be taken to suggest that Rawls would endorse anti-choice legislation. Moreover, though I have here identified inoperativity with pleasure, this need not be the case; it just follows from the grass-counter example. And finally I note that developing this line of argument further would require attending to Rawls' critique of utilitarianism, that social theory that takes pleasure seriously but also renders it operative via the felicific calculus.

References

Acampora, C.D. (2013) *Contesting Nietzsche*. Chicago: The University of Chicago Press.
Arendt, H. (2013) *The Human Condition*. Chicago: The University of Chicago Press.
Beltrán, C. (2004) Patrolling borders: Hybrids, hierarchies, and the challenges of mestijae. *Political Research Quarterly* 57(4): 597–607.
Beltrán, C. (2010) *The Trouble with Unity: Latino Politics and the Creation of Identity*. New York: Oxford University Press.
Benhabib, S. (2018) Time, action and narrative in Nietzsche and Arendt. *Raisons politiques* 2(2018): 15–28.
Cohen, C. (2004) Deviance as resistance: A new research agenda for the study of black politics. *Du Bois Review: Social Science Research on Race* 1(1): 27–45.
Handy, B. (2017) How the story of ferdinand became fodder for the culture wars of its era. *The New Yorker*. 15 Dec 2017. https://www.newyorker.com/books/page-turner/how-the-story-of-ferdinand-became-fodder-for-the-culture-wars-of-its-era, accessed 12 Aug 2019.
Hartman, S. (2019) *Wayward Lives, Beautiful Experiments*. New York: Norton.
Hegel, G.F.W. (1977) *Phenomenology of Spirit*. Translated by A.V. Miller. New York: Oxford University Press.
Honig, B. (ed.). (1995) *Feminist Interpretations of Hannah Arendt*. State College: Pennsylvania State University Press.
Honig, B. (2001) *Democracy and the Foreigner*. Princeton: Princeton University Press.
Honig, B. (2009) *Emergency Politics*. Princeton: Princeton University Press.
Honig, B. (2013) *Antigone, Interrupted*. Cambridge: Cambridge University Press.
Honig, B. (2019) *12 Angry Men*: Care for the Agon and the varieties of masculinity. *Theory and Event* 22(3): 701–716.
Honig, B. (1993) The politics of agonism: A critical response to "Beyond good and evil: Arendt, Nietzsche, and the aestheticization of political action" by Dana R. Villa. *Political Theory* 21(3): 528–533.
Honig, B. (1994) Difference dilemmas, and the politics of home. *Social Research* 61(3), Liberalism [FALL 1994], pp. 563–597).
Honig, B. (2017a) (Un)reality TV: Trump, Kelly, and the revolving door of whiteness. *Politicsslashletters*, Oct 2017, http://politicsslashletters.org/features/unreality-tv-trump-kelly-and-the-revolving-door-of-whiteness/, accessed 12 Aug 2019.
Honig, B. (2017b) The president's house is empty *Boston Review,* 20 Jan 2017. http://bostonreview.net/politics/bonnie-honig-president's-house-empty, accessed 12 Aug 2019.
Honig, B. (2018) Renovating the house (and senate). *Los Angeles Review of Books Blog*. 30 Sept 2018. https://blog.lareviewofbooks.org/essays/renovating-house-senate/, accessed 12 Aug 2019.

Honig, B. (2020/2021) *'Give me glory!' Gender, The Bacchae, and the Politics of Refusal.* Cambridge, MA: Harvard University Press: The Flexner Lectures.

Hooker, J. (2016) Black lives matter and the paradoxes of US black politics: From democratic sacrifice to democratic repair. *Political Theory* 44(4): 448–469.

Hooker, J. (2017) *Theorizing Race in the Americas: Douglass, Sarmiento, Du Bois, and Vasconcelos.* New York: Oxford University Press.

Hooker, J. (2018) Grief and black politics: From black death to black life. Presented at the American Political Science Association Conference.

hooks, b. (2015) *Feminist Theory: From Margin to Center.* New York: Routledge.

Jones, C.C. (2019) Fearing for his life. *The Verge*, 13 Mar 2019, https://www.theverge.com/2019/3/13/18253848/eric-garner-footage-ramsey-orta-police-brutality-killing-safety

Keeling, K. (2019) *Queer Times, Black Futures.* New York: New York University Press.

Leaf, M. (1936) *The Story of Ferdinand*, Illus. Robert Lawson. New York: Viking Press.

Marso, L. (2018) Birthing feminist freedom, *Medium*, https://medium.com/@arendt_center/birthing-feminist-freedom-985847049ec1, and in *The Journal of the Hannah Arendt Center for Politics and Humanities at Bard College* 6: 98–106.

Martel, J. (2011) The ambivalent anarchism of Hannah Arendt. In: J.C. Klausen and J. Martel (eds.) *How Not To Be Governed.* New York: Lexington Books.

Morgan, D. (2019) Bryan Stevenson: 'The North won the Civil War, but the South won the narrative war' on history of racism. *CBS News* 24 Jun 2019, https://www.cbsnews.com/news/bryan-stevenson-we-are-all-complicit-in-our-countrys-history-of-racism/?fbclid=IwAR0oawb6Yy0ufm0dJHZGoSEQ6FLOM1QkeAgPNmTq86cyzcOqXTuSllH5RpQ), accessed 11 Aug 2019.

Murray, S. (2008) *Representing Autism: Culture, Narrative, Fascination.* Liverpool: Liverpool University Press.

Nietzsche, F. (1911) Homer's contest" & "the Greek state. In: O. Levy (ed.) *The Complete Works of Friedrich Nietzsche*, vol 2, Translated by M.E. Mügge. New York: Macmillan.

Nietzsche, F. (1998) *On the Genealogy of Morality*, Translated by M. Clark. Indianapolis: Hackett.

Pilkington (ed.). (2018) Crystal Mason begins prison sentence in Texas for crime of voting. *The Guardian*. 28 Sept 2018, https://www.theguardian.com/us-news/2018/sep/28/crystal-mason-begins-prison-sentence-in-texas-for-of-voting, accessed 11 Aug 2019.

Rawls, J. (1971) *A Theory of Justice.* Cambridge, MA: Harvard University Press.

Reagon, B. (1983) Coalition politics: Turning the century. In: B. Smith (ed.) *Home Girls.* New York: Kitchen Table Press, pp. 356–368.

Salamon, G. (2018) *The life and death of Latisha King: A critical phenomenology of transphobia*, Kindle ed.. New York: NYU Press.

Schein, R. (2012) Whose occupation? Homelessness and the politics of park encampments. *Social Movement Studies* 11(3–4): 335–341.

Spillers, H. (2011) African-American women and the republics. In: A.R. Janmohamed (ed.) *Reconsidering Social Identification: Race, Gender, Class and Caste.* New York: Routledge.

Wamsley, L. (2017) Erica Garner, who became an activist after her father's death, dies. *NPR*, 30 Dec 2017, https://www.npr.org/sections/thetwo-way/2017/12/30/574514217/erica-garner-who-became-an-activist-after-her-fathers-death-dies, accessed 11 Aug 2019.

Warner, M. (2005) *Publics and Counterpublics.* New York, NY: Zone Books.

Wolin, S. (1969) Political theory as a vocation. *The American Political Science Review* 63(4): 1062–1082.

Publisher's Note

Springer Nature remains neutral with regard to jurisdictional claims in published maps and institutional affiliations.

Review

A feminist theory of refusal

Bonnie Honig
Harvard University Press, Cambridge, 2021, xiv+194pp.,
ISBN: 9780674248496

Contemporary Political Theory (2023) **22**, S153–S156. https://doi.org/10.1057/s41296-022-00592-3; published online 28 September 2022

In *A Feminist Theory of Refusal*, Bonnie Honig provides a creative re-reading of Euripides' *Bacchae* to generate a new understanding of refusal. Against the common definition of refusal as a withdrawal from the world, Honig conceptualizes refusal as a form of world-building. 'Even when refusal *seems* to reject the world', Honig writes, 'it betrays a deep attachment to it, if not the world as it is, then surely to a more just world that is not yet' (p. 3). Tracing the bacchants' arc of refusal in the play, Honig identifies three stages: first, enchanted by Dionysus, gender-bending god of pleasure, intoxication, and the festival, the women flee the city, abandoning their work in the home; second, the bacchants establish a community on the hills of Cithaeron, where they eventually dismember the king, Pentheus; third, led by Agave, Pentheus' mother, the women return to reclaim the city, only to find the male citizens unwilling to welcome them. In the last stage especially, Honig sees the potential for world-building in the bacchants' effort to bring their alternate ways of living, developed in the heterotopia on Cithaeron, home. The bacchants' world-building, however, requires the slow regicide of Pentheus, which Honig heralds as the destruction of sovereignty, patriarchy, and even kinship. Feminist refusal as world-building, Honig suggests, requires violence.

The three chapters of the book follow the arc of refusal, with a form of refusal—inoperativity, inclination, and fabulation—mapping onto each stage. In the first chapter, Honig starts with Giorgio Agamben's (1999) notion of inoperativity, derived from Herman Melville's 'Bartleby, the Scrivener'. A central figure in the canon of refusal, famed for uttering the words 'I would prefer not to', Bartleby proves wanting because his refusal to work leads him to starvation in a jail cell, and therefore renders him isolated and worldless. For Agamben, Bartleby represents inoperativity as the suspension of use, a rejection of ends for the sake of pure means. An inoperativity reading of the *Bacchae* illuminates how the bacchants' abandonment of the loom, and retreat to the hills to rest, functions as a feminist refusal of work. A *Bacchae* reading of inoperativity, on the other hand, moves beyond the suspensive qualities of inoperativity toward the intensification of use.

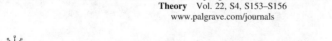

Review

On Cithaeron, the bacchants breastfeed animals and enjoy the pleasures of eating slowly. They do not just suspend use, then, but also intensify it, using their bodies for other purposes. Honig thus transforms inoperativity 'from an ethics or politics of pure means into a more worldly and impure agonistic and feminist politics of refusal' (p. 44).

The second chapter invokes Adriana Cavarero's (2016) theorization of inclination, with Honig's bacchic twist. While Cavarero treats inclination as a maternal, pacifist gesture of care, Honig brings to light its sororal and potentially violent dimensions. Attending to Pentheus' dismemberment, Honig asks: what if we read the *Bacchae* not as a cautionary tale about the need for unity within the city, but instead as a parable 'that teaches the *dangers* of unity and shows the need to dismember sovereignty or patriarchy?' (p. 58). Critics tend to assume that Agave's mourning indicates her regret for her murder of Pentheus, supposedly committed unknowingly. Honig, though, is not so sure. According to Honig, 'filicide and regicide will *always* coincide in patriarchy' (p. 59). Agave's sororal action with her fellow bacchants exposes the capacity to wound that accompanies gestures of care. She leans toward her son to dismember him and, with this violent act, cares for the city, by releasing it from patriarchal sovereignty. In this chapter, Honig draws the connection between the agonism of the bacchants' sororal action and Agave's maternal violence. For democratic theorists, her equation of agonism with violence will prove surprising and provocative.

Finally, following Saidiya Hartman (2019), Honig adopts fabulation as a method of refusal. Just as 'Hartman's fabulation rescues her wayward women from careless cruel obscurity', Honig's reading of the *Bacchae* saves the bacchants from a centuries-long interpretation of them as mad, tragic figures, under the sway of Dionysus (p. 73). Unlike Hartman's fugitive women, Agave and the bacchants return to reclaim the city. There Agave engages in an agon of fabulation with her father, Cadmus, who repatriates her into the roles of mother, daughter, and wife—importantly, Honig notes, not sister. Agave's murder of Pentheus opens up the possibility of destroying patriarchal kinship, since 'killing the king means killing patriarchy, the structure of kinship to which the position of "son" belongs'. Cadmus 'kills a world' when he robs Agave of her powers of fabulation (p. 82). To the audience, Agave appears as a mourning mother, rather than a revolutionary figure. Citing Arendt, Honig stresses the importance of the polis for remembering political action. Even though they fail, the bacchants' return represents an attempt to institute a new public, a permanent space for the exercise of freedom without patriarchy. Agave's pursuant exile paves the way for something new, 'an emancipation to waywardness', like Hartman's wayward women (p. 90).

In this third chapter, Honig could have taken Hartman's invitation a step further here by giving readers a new imagination of the play's ending. Instead, Honig reiterates the conventional belief that Agave laments her actions upon realizing that she murdered her son. Most of Agave's speech at the end of the play did not survive, however. At least fifty lines of the final scene are missing from the two preserved manuscripts. Translators reconstruct this passage speculatively, relying on references to the play in other texts. Their reconstruction typically depicts Agave's mournful, self-flagellating speech, and Dionysus' pronouncement of Agave and her sisters' exile, but what if we fabulated an alternative ending to replace the missing text? What if Agave defended her actions as democratic, even proto-feminist, rather than condemning herself? What if she appealed for her own exile, to leave a city that was not ready to receive her?

Underlying much of Honig's text is another question: What must the bacchants destroy to usher a new world into being? The king, patriarchy, and kinship, Honig answers. Critics, most notably Victoria Wohl (2005), whom Honig discusses briefly, point that the *Bacchae* also explodes the gender binary. The play begins with the return of Dionysus, an androgynous god who destabilizes gendered boundaries, and nearly every character dresses in drag at one point or another. At Dionysus' encouragement, Pentheus disguises himself as a bacchant before his murder. The bacchants themselves act like men, embodying the roles of hunter and soldier. To succeed, the play suggests, the bacchants would not only need to kill the king and kinship, but also to destroy gender itself, so that Agave might avoid repatriation into a confining version of womanhood. Honig pays little attention to this latent gender abolitionism, although she does define feminism in the introduction as 'the project of enacting sex-gender equality, which includes pluralizing sex-gender practices and identities, in the face of governing powers that insist on gender binarism' (p. 3). Such a definition plants the seeds for a challenge to the gender binary that never emerges, perhaps because of Honig's attachment to the bacchants' sorority.

Insisting that the bacchants' feminist revolution would require destruction, Honig writes against the grain of contemporary feminists and democratic theorists, who tend to assume a nonviolent approach to politics. Honig acknowledges the tension with feminist theory explicitly in her engagement with Cavarero. Yet Honig does not explore the tension that Hannah Arendt observes between violence and politics, despite her observation that 'the three refusal concepts revisit Arendtian categories and concerns' (p. 107). The Arendtian concept of world-building animates Honig's interpretation of the bacchants' refusal as more than just a turning away from the world. For Arendt, however, politics and violence are opposites: death is 'the most antipolitical experience there is', because it removes men from the common world and destroys plurality (1970, pp. 67-68). Honig's reading of the *Bacchae* suggests that removing men—at least, one man, Pentheus—from the earth is necessary for feminist revolution, though it is not clear how the actions of the bacchants translate into our political milieu. Does #MeToo count as a slow regicide, the metaphorical if not literal murder of the king, instantiated in President Donald Trump and other powerful serial sexual assailants? Or does Honig envision a feminist movement still more destructive?

Although I wished for a more explicit connection to contemporary feminist politics, Honig compellingly demonstrates the continued relevancy of ancient Greek tragedy for feminism, at a time when the role of the classics in higher education is increasingly under scrutiny. *A Feminist Theory of Refusal* will be of particular interest to democratic theorists, feminist theorists, and classicists.

References

Agamben, G. (1999) *'Bartleby; Or, on Contingency'. Potentialities.* Stanford: Stanford University Press.
Arendt, H. (1970) *On Violence.* New York: Houghton Mifflin Harcourt.
Cavarero, A. (2016) *Inclinations: A Critique of Rectitude.* Stanford: Stanford University Press.
Hartman, S. (2019) *Wayward Lives, Beautiful Experiments: Intimate Histories of Social Upheaval.* New York: Norton.
Wohl, V. (2005) *'Beyond Sexual Difference: Becoming-Woman in Euripides' Bacchae'. The Soul of Tragedy: Essays on Athenian Democracy.* Chicago: University of Chicago Press.

Publisher's Note Springer Nature remains neutral with regard to jurisdictional claims in published maps and institutional affiliations.

Rose A. Owen
University of Chicago, Chicago, IL 60637, USA
rowen@uchicago.edu

Critical Exchange

Toni Morrison and political theory

Alex Zamalin
University of Detroit Mercy, Detroit, MI 48221, USA
zamalial@udmercy.edu

Joseph R. Winters
Duke University, Durham, NC 27708, USA
joseph.winters@duke.edu

Alix Olson
Emory University, Oxford, GA 30054, USA
alix.olson@emory.edu

Wairimu Njoya
Williams College, Williamstown, MA 01267, USA
wrn1@williams.edu

Contemporary Political Theory (2020) **19,** 704–729. https://doi.org/10.1057/s41296-020-00397-2; advance online publication 27 May 2020

Before she died on 5 August 2019, the black American writer, Toni Morrison, managed to become one of the most influential writers of the past century. Her eleven novels – from *The Bluest Eye* (1970) to *God Help the Child* (2015) – interrogated the twin pillars of white supremacy and the unrelenting quest for black dignity and subjectivity in the USA. Toni Morrison was born in Lorain, Ohio, on 18 February 1931 and studied English and Classics at Howard University before receiving an MA at Cornell University, where she wrote her thesis on the theme of suicide in William Faulkner and Virginia Woolf. Morrison then took up a position as commissioning editor at Random House, with the aim of helping writers of color like Angela Davis, Toni Cade Bambara, and Gayl Jones have a platform for their creative voices. When Morrison herself took up writing, which she tried to do before and after grueling hours at work while also managing the strenuous work of a single mother, what emerged was her first novel, *The Bluest Eye*. This was a story of a young black girl, Pecola Breedlove, who desperately desires blue eyes as a way to register as white and escape the anti-black racism that structures American life. The themes that *The Bluest Eye* explored with incredible rigor and clear prose cut right into the page – alienation, melancholy, exploitation, desire, memory, hope, dreams, family, gender, masculinity, and, most consistently, love. They would be continued throughout her work. Nowhere was this clearer than in her Nobel Prize-winning novel, *Beloved* (1987). The book told the story of a black woman, Sethe, and the post-Reconstruction community in which she finds herself, grappling with the return of her child – as a ghost, named Beloved – whom she had killed in an effort to protect her from the horrors of enslavement.

When it was published in the late 1980s, *Beloved* undercut the reigning bipartisan US political consensus of the Reagan era, which stressed historical amnesia around racial violence, assumed the universality of white American experience, and upheld the virtue of unbridled individualism and free market capitalism. Yet *Beloved* refused to whitewash the violence and domination inherent in transatlantic slavery – this, at a moment when color blindness and post-racialism were the terms of the day. *Beloved* brought into relief black voices and experiences on black subjectivity and community – that weren't defined by racist images of black life. It imagined the struggle to build a democracy collectively, under the strain of racial authoritarianism, rather than assuming that personal uplift would magically overturn centuries of inequality.

This is why *Beloved* prompted serious intellectual scrutiny from scholars across disciplines – in literary studies, cultural studies, critical race theory, and black studies. And yet, despite *Beloved*'s clear exploration of themes such as power, the role of the state, justice, democracy, gender, and freedom, themes that have preoccupied political theorists for centuries, the novel didn't receive much scrutiny from political theorists. There were, of course, some notable exceptions. Scholars like George Shulman (2008), Eddie Glaude (2007), Patricia Hill Collins (2002), and Satya Mohanty (1997) would engage Morrison's work for political theory. But in the 1990s and 2000s, a survey of the field's leading journals like *Political Theory*, *Polity*, and *American Political Science Review* revealed that political theorists were busy debating the ethics of what the philosopher Jürgen Habermas (1998) called 'communicative action' against what Chantal Mouffe (2013) called agonistic democracy; the virtue of Hannah Arendt's (1998) conception of action in concert (what she called power) against John Rawls' (1971) theory of justice as fairness; the role of post-structural analysis, which assumes power is dispersed rather than exists in a top-down manner (influenced by Michel Foucault (1978)) against power being centralized and concentrated; and the political value of what Richard Rorty (1998) called pragmatic solidarity against that of political mobilization found on universal reason.

Asking these particular questions made perfect sense in a post-Cold War era when the discipline of political science was trying to justify a set of norms for a global order in which democratization seemed to be happening in many countries, capitalism seemed unquestioned, and globalization was the language of power. But what was missing from these analyses was precisely what Morrison devoted her work to exploring – racism, white supremacy, and whiteness – things that made life unlivable and progress unimaginable for many people of color. Think of the brutal beating in 1992 of the black motorist, Rodney King, by Los Angeles police officers, captured on tape and widely circulated in the media. Remember that Democrat Bill Clinton, with bipartisan political support from Republicans across the aisle, signed the Crime Bill of 1994, which gave federal money to create 100,000 police officers on city streets and continued the catastrophic rise of mass incarceration that disproportionately affected people of color: in 1980, the number of incarcerated was around 200,000 and by the 2000s it was 2 million. Then in 1996, the same bipartisan alliance eviscerated welfare for millions of people, depriving them of basic resources that, between the 1930s and 1960s, had been seen as a basic right. And of course, in 2005, after hurricane Katrina struck the black city of New Orleans, Republican George W. Bush responded apathetically. Federal resources weren't marshaled quickly to prevent unsheltered citizens dying of thirst. But Bush was enthusiastic about efforts aimed at privatizing, deregulating, and inflicting austerity measures upon post-Katrina New Orleans, which were championed by realtors, investment banks, and private equity firms.

Had political theorists been paying attention to Morrison's work during this period, they would have noticed a powerful lens through which to think about these developments in an unlikely source: fiction. Yet fiction has often been relegated to realms outside political thought because it doesn't contain the modes of structured, deductive argumentation with which political theorists are familiar. But fiction does important political theory. Consider *Beloved*'s white abolitionist, Edward Bodwin – is a paternalistic racist as well as an abolitionist – who anticipates white moderates who push forward neoliberal policies of austerity. Bodwin wants Sethe to conform to a standard of respectability, but also hires her daughter, Denver, for low-wage domestic labor, which is still not enough to keep her afloat. Denver needs to work multiple jobs to pay for basic resources to provide for her family, and her mother, Sethe, who – as the novel progresses – is consumed by grief and guilt about Beloved and is unable to work. Or notice, on the one hand, *Beloved*'s model of unconditional love evident in the philosophy of Paul D, an ex-enslaved man, who tries to make a family with Sethe despite her status as a pariah in the community. Or, the black feminism evident in Sethe's rejection of Paul D's proposal, which anticipates the arguments made recently by Black Lives Matter and #MeToo. Like these movements, Sethe's black feminism pushes back against the hegemonic status of the nuclear family, the denigration of unpaid domestic work, and the normative status of masculinity.

Morrison's work is unavoidable today. This is so especially in the aftermath of the election of Barack Obama in 2008, the increasing public attention to police brutality against people of color, the growing racial and economic equality during the neoliberal area, the public discussion of intersectionality and black feminism, and, more recently, the election of Donald Trump in 2016, whose rise was predicated on racism (the 'birther' myth that Obama wasn't a US citizen) and whose policies (the Muslim immigration ban, the separation at the border of brown refugee children from their parents) try to realize it in American life. The need to construct a form of political critique and analysis that responds to economic, racial, and gendered power has always been the impetus for much contemporary political theory. And a confrontation with the world and with history, as well as developing a vision of a horizon for the future, is absolutely necessary. This is very much the case in our time of rising nationalism, authoritarianism, violence, racism, and far-right extremism. Morrison's work is a powerful instrument for this work that political theorists cannot avoid, and must continue to read, study, and teach.

The theorists in this collection take up this challenge and do it with a theoretical clarity and political vision that follows in the spirit of Morrison's work. Joseph Winters's essay, 'Toni Morrison and the [Racial] Specters of the Political', explores the ways her novels and essays limn the limitations of any political order that promises stability and progress precisely through a process of forgetting the violence, injury, and melancholy, which is so necessary to the success of this project. In Winters's view, Morrison may not offer a theory of the state, or of justice, but her work is an account of the way stories of the racialized self and community structure the possibility of deciding whose lives matter and whose don't. Moreover, for her as for Winters, remembering and reconstituting this process is integral to challenging it.

Alix Olson takes up the question of the normative value placed on black life in a racist society and argues that Morrison's work is part of the longstanding black feminist project of refusing black surrogacy as a way to maintain the white racial order. Rather than constructing literary and political narratives that reaffirm notions of white subjectivity, Morrison's work re-centers our perspective on black women and the modes in which they resist racial capitalism.

In 'Dignity as Self-Regard: Reflections on Toni Morrison and Law', Wairimu Njoya masterfully displays the theoretical vision of dignity that underpins Morrison's political project. Morrison, in Njoya's words, refuses to be governed by a Western liberal notion of dignity that is implicitly racialized as white and gendered as male and is entrapped in possessive individualism. Instead, Morrison places self-regard – specifically, within the context of black women – as the lens through which to rethink the ideals of mutual respect and accountability found in Western liberalism. It is this idea, Njoya powerfully contends, that makes her work so necessary for black feminist movements, and all those citizens throughout the world who believe in liberation.

All told, the contributors to this issue stress that Morrison's work is indispensable not only in helping us think about racial power in all its varieties, but also the stakes of liberation. And for them, what this means is engaging with the omissions of history, the structure of domination, and the possibility of a future – and how we tell narratives about these concepts and struggle to achieve them. The task, for them, as for Morrison, is to build a world that isn't defined by violence, terror, and exclusion, but one that makes real human dignity.

Alex Zamalin

Toni Morrison and the [Racial] Specters of the Political

In his 1990 text, *The Presence of the Past*, Sheldon Wolin underscores the significance of remembrance in the process of forming citizens. For Wolin, the intersection of memory and politics is palpable during civic rituals and national celebrations. He writes, 'Civic celebration serves…to expurgate the pain and costliness of past choices so that they appear as unmitigated blessings, inevitable culminations…America's victory in World War II is remembered but not the Japanese relocation camps' (Wolin, 1990, p. 83). Celebrations like the bi-centennial in 1976 or the inauguration of Barack Obama, the first black president, reproduce triumphant accounts of US history and contribute to the making of reliable subjects, subjects attached to nation-state projects and forgetful of, or inured to, and the violence that makes these projects possible. According to the late political theorist, these public rituals 'organize forgetfulness so as to ward off the return of the repressed which…is still perceived as threatening' (p. 83). The 'return of the repressed' alludes to struggles, strivings, and losses that, if re-collected and activated differently, might generate alternatives to the current order of things. Wolin's concerns are partly directed toward strands of liberalism (Rawls, for instance) that separate principles of justice from historical losses and wounds that inform political judgments and sentiments. This is a liberalism that does not fully consider how the maintenance of order relies on narratives and rituals that corral memories, desires, and forms of grief. At the same ti
me, the endeavor to 'ward off the repressed', to keep at bay what might unsettle the congruence between subject and State, or between attachments to the past and the status quo, is never fully successful. Toni Morrison's corpus provides a witness to this failure and to the possibility of thinking, feeling, and imagining in ways that refuse to 'expurgate the pain and costliness' (Wolin, 1990, p. 83) of history.

Toni Morrison might not be the first author that comes to mind when thinking about political theory and race and politics. While Morrison wrote about an array of topics – black girlhood, black masculine intimacy, the aesthetics of anti-blackness, the afterlives of slavery, displacement and movement, conflicts and tensions within black life – it is not clear how her corpus supplements the established field of race and political theory. In other words, how do her writings pertain to matters like racial justice, recognition and rights, and state-sponsored re-distribution of

Critical Exchange

resources and goods? How does Morrison enable us to think differently about political and legal institutions or grassroots efforts to change various laws and policies that are harmful to blacks and other groups? While these are important questions to pursue, I suggest that Morrison's 'contributions' are located elsewhere, at the borders and edges of conventional political theory. In line with Wolin's reflections on memory and politics, Morrison's novels and essays direct attention to the meta-narratives, tropes, and logics (such as those of progress, linear time, US exceptionalism, settlement) that have direct and implicit effects on how people remember, mourn, hope, become attached to national undertakings, and seek alternatives to the status quo. If racial politics is always about life and death (Mbembe, 2019), or how life and death get distributed and how violence gets disproportionately directed toward populations considered not quite human, then Morrison's writings might actually get at the heart of the political. In what follows, I develop this hunch. Looking at three texts – 'The Site of Memory', *The Bluest Eye*, and *Paradise* – my aim is to show how Morrison's work responds to the guiding principles and fantasies that solidify the political order while gesturing toward the limitations of political struggles regarding the capacity to redress legacies of violence and terror.

In her essay 'The Site of Memory', Morrison revisits the significance and function of the slave narrative in the ante-bellum USA. According to Morrison, these memoirs, popularized by figures like Olaudauh Equiano, Frederick Douglass, and Harriet Jacobs, aimed to exhibit the humanity of slaves and black people more generally.So far as literacy was connected to suffrage, and writing to memory and reason, the slave memoir aspired to propel black people into the sphere of recognition, the domain of citizenship, in opposition to enlightenment-inspired racism that denied black humanity. Similarly, the slave narrative was used to 'change things' and to 'give fuel to the fire that abolitionists were setting everywhere' (Morrison, 1995, p. 87). This genre aided the goals and aspirations of abolitionists, of those attempting to dismantle a regime that reduced black people to property. Acting as patrons, abolitionists like William Lloyd Garrison guaranteed the reader that the narrative was written by the former slave, that the enslaved black had the capacity for freedom. But to pursue the abolitionist project, formerly enslaved writers had to work within writing conventions and constraints so as not to offend the sensibilities of a predominately white audience. Instructing whites and galvanizing them toward the abolitionist struggle required discussing horrifying scenes and episodes in an appropriate manner.

Consequently, writers like Jacobs and Douglass were encouraged to balance candor with propriety, to excise certain details that might be 'too much' for the reader. As Morrison writes, '[P]opular taste discouraged the writers from dwelling too long or too carefully on the sordid (violent, scatological, and excessive) details of their experience…. In shaping the experience to make it palatable to those in a position to alleviate it, they were silent about many things, and they "forgot" many other things' (p. 90). The language of 'scatological' and 'excess' indicate a surplus, or something wasteful, that threatens to upset or sicken 'those in the position to alleviate' an unjust system. The general audience did not have a taste for a black writer lingering on the sordid details of sexual violence, torture, despair, and so forth. And since the slave narrative often followed a certain linear format – from slavery to freedom, from South to North – the allusion to excess might also register aspects of these stories that elude triumphant notions of liberation, agency, and progress. As Erin Forbes (2006) suggests in her reading of Harriet Jacobs' *Incidents in the Life of a Slave Girl*, this surplus includes the specters and ghosts that haunt forward/upward movements, that remain with someone like Jacobs after she escapes to Philadelphia and New York. (Jacobs speaks of the North imitating the South: she has to confront fugitive slave laws that make her recuperable property.) Morrison is making an important intervention in 'The Site of Memory'. Her attention to the contrast between the palatable and the scatological, or what can be digested and what cannot, registers an outlet to mechanisms of assimilation and recognition. The formerly enslaved can be recognized as a human, citizen, and liberated subject only if his/her story could be fit into an often masculinized conception of freedom and agency (McDowell, 1997), a conception that must set aside the unassimilable aspects of slavery (infanticide, the unmourned millions at the bottom of the Atlantic ocean, a violent sexual economy that continues to mark black female flesh as monstrous, hypersexual, and fungible).

While 'The Site of Memory' resists tendencies to incorporate slavery and abolition into a grammar of progress, Morrison's first novel *The Bluest Eye* does something similar with respect to the black freedom struggles of the 1960s. *The Bluest Eye* is a novel about an eleven-year-old black girl named Pecola Breedlove who desires the very object (blue eyes, whiteness, ideal beauty) that is the source of her internalized contempt. Therefore, the blue eye is connected to a blues-filled I/subject. While the 1970 novel takes place in the early 1940s, the immediate historical context is the civil rights and black power struggles, projects motivated by slogans like 'black is beautiful', inspired by the relationship between politics and aesthetics. As Agnes Suranyi points out, 'Morrison worried that this slogan of racial pride would be unable to dispel the long-term psychic effects rooted in racialism and sexism' (Suranyi, 2007, p. 11). To put this differently, the cultivation of racial pride might be important to motivate struggles against anti-black and sexist arrangements, but this does not address, and may even conceal, the interminable impact of anti-black violence on the interior life of black subjects. Here, it might be helpful to broach Anne Cheng's distinction between grief and grievance (2001). For Cheng, a grievance is a wrong or injustice that can be measured and redressed through political and legal mechanisms. Grief, on the other hand, is a less determinate kind of suffering and loss 'that cannot [always] speak in the language of material grievance' (p. 4). Grief alludes to those 'long-term effects' of anti-blackness that won't necessarily be fixed by material advancements. If

Critical Exchange

politics involves the conversion of grief into a grievance, then perhaps art and literature linger within the gap between grief and grievance, a gap that does not signify an absolute distinction between the two.

Cheng relies heavily on Freud's distinction between two forms of grief – mourning and melancholy. Mourning is a psychic response to a lost object (both physical and ideal) that involves the painful labor of redirecting one's attachments to another object, a kind of substitute for the absence. Melancholy, on the other hand, fails to find a substitute object: consequently, the grieving subject incorporates the lost object in manner that blurs the line between the two. The subject is cut and emptied by the grief. Melancholy signifies an enduring wound, while mourning suggests a more teleological process in which loss can be compensated for and overcome. While Freud focuses on the individual's general response to loss, one has to think about what melancholy looks like for populations that experience incessant violence, and for communities that are constituted by ungrieved and ungrievable loss. According to Cheng, racial melancholy operates in multiple ways in the context of black strivings, including as 'a strategy in response to rejection' (p. 20). As a strategy, black melancholy has been expressed in art, music, literature, and religious practice. It has been worked through in jazz, blues, soul, reggae, and other genres. These practices of melancholy have provided ways to wrestle with (social) death and anguish while affirming the joys, pleasures, and aspirations of black life.

On this reading, *The Bluest Eye* is literary expression of this melancholic mode and an occasion for being attuned to forms of anguish that elude compensatory and teleological frameworks. Throughout the novel, the various narrators give the reader a glimpse into how the community defines itself over and against Pecola and her family. Pecola embodies the undesirable qualities associated with blackness – indigence, dirt, ugliness, and instability. As Morrison puts it in the foreword to the novel, 'I focused on how something as grotesque as the demonization of an entire race can take root inside the most delicate member of society: a child; the most vulnerable member: a female' (Morrison, 2007, p. xi). Morrison suggests that Pecola takes on the grotesque quality of anti-blackness: she gives a kind of form to the absurd process of 'demonizing an entire race'. She also comes to symbolize how black girlhood becomes subject to the internalization of aesthetic standards and protocols that rely on the expulsion of blackness, resulting in a kind of wound or tornness within black girlhood. And if this grotesque predicament takes root in Pecola, we should not allow that particular site of germination to deflect attention from the broader predicament of violence that Pecola and the other characters must navigate and endure. For instance, when her father, Cholly, brutally rapes her, the reader is encouraged to lament the conditions that have made black girls exposed to sexual violence *and* think through the forms of (sexualized) terror that have shaped and de/formed black masculinity. When Pecola's mother, Polly, slaps her for dropping the pie in the white employer's kitchen, a scene that is immediately followed by Polly coddling the startled white child, several questions emerge. For one, what is the relationship between black motherhood and the demands of black female domestic labor, especially regarding the distribution of energy, care, nourishment, and intimacy? How does Polly's need to keep her white employer's space clean and ordered, for economic and psychic reasons, require a kind of distance and separation from aspects of her life that signify disorder and instability?

Morrison's novel is read incorrectly as an expression of black cultural pathology, a view that was popularized with the 1965 publication of the Moynihan report. This would assume that one could separate the internalized violence and anguish from external conditions and circumstances – anti-black racism, racial capitalism (including the distribution and consumption of whiteness as the ideal), economic inequality, and sexism. It would also assume that the sickness is located in Pecola/ the black community rather than in the relationship between Pecola and a social world that needs certain bodies and populations to serve as receptacles of waste and surplus. As the narrator admits toward the end of the novel, 'All our waste which we dumped on her and which she absorbed...All of us felt so wholesome after we cleaned ourselves on her...We honed our egos on her, padded our characters with her frailty, and yawned in the fantasy of our strength' (Morrison, 2007, p. 205). This passage alludes to how whiteness defines itself over against blackness or how middle-class black well-being relies on comparisons and contrasts with working class and indigent black people. But perhaps Morrison is getting at something more constitutive, fundamental, and tragic. Perhaps the formation of self and collective identities will always involve excess, projection, repulsion and attraction, and exclusion. To put it differently, it could be that the general will to coherence and well-being will always involve violence, will always involve treating some set of qualities and characteristics as both a threat to, and a source of our fantasies and aspirations. And if radical political struggle is always invested in betterment, justice, and the possibility of another world, will these ideals be haunted by the kinds of existential and psychic factors that *The Bluest Eye* traces through the complexities of black girlhood? Or are these existential dilemmas the product of a particular kind of world that secures itself by foreclosing alternatives?

Morrison's (1997a, b) novel, *Paradise*, further develops the kinds of exclusions and erasures that accompany investments in progress, coherence, and settlement. The novel is about two different, yet entangled, communities. Established in 1950 by the descendants of slaves, refugees, and exiles, Ruby, Oklahoma, is a patriarchal community solidified by a certain way of remembering and celebrating the struggles and achievements of the 'Old Fathers'. These patriarchs (the Morgans) established an all-black community in the Midwest during the late nineteenth century after fleeing the white supremacist arrangements of the South. Resembling the biblical story of Exodus, these founding fathers were inspired by God and promised a better life on the other side of the trek. Just outside the town of Ruby is a convent of women who have also fled various forms of sexist and racist violence.

While the novel seems to set up a stark opposition between the normalizing practices of Ruby and the deviant (religious, sexual, sartorial) ways of the women, the novel also shows moments of overlap, affinity, and attraction. If the first scene of the novel describes the men of Ruby hunting down their 'strange neighbors' at the convent, neighbors described as 'detritus, throwaway people' (Morrison, 1997a, b, p. 4). Throughout the novel, however, the reader learns that the convent is a place where members of Ruby secretly go for healing, care, and sexual rendezvous. It is a place where what is impermissible in Ruby can be released, dumped, and relocated. So even as the community of women are described as dangerous, unstable, and monstrous (references are made to them as witches), and even as coherence and unity of Ruby is enabled through contrast and rejection, this rejection is entangled with moments of dependence and enjoyment. Freud might call this interplay between repulsion and attraction a structure of ambivalence. This ambivalence reveals the tensions and conflicts within Ruby's history that are often denied or deflected.

Paradise is in part a commentary on the logics and protocols of settlement and an allusion to the legacy of settler colonial projects. Morrison knows that black people have a complicated relationship to this legacy – kidnapped Africans replacing Native peoples as involuntary labor, slaves being used to clear territory for land speculators, slaves incorporated into Native tribes, Indians owning slaves, postbellum blacks being incorporated into schemes of Western expansion, property ownership, etc. Throughout the novel, as Morrison plays with time and temporality, we realize that the convent used to be a place where Catholic nuns schooled and trained Native American children. While this is not a central part of the story, these images interrupt linear notions of time while registering the complicated, overlapping histories and memories embedded in any place. Ruby's history of exile, wandering, settlement, and the murder of the unsettled/unsettling convent women participate in a broader history of nation-building terror and the appropriation of indigenous lands. Insofar as nation building and violence are intertwined, Morrison's novel also draws attention to the particular limitations of black nationalism. Morrison acknowledges that forms of black nationalism, especially those solidified by Exodus tropes, have empowered black communities, providing blacks with a sense of a common struggle in the face of racism. At the same time, strands of black nationalism have served as extensions of the broader nation-state (Lubiano, 2002), as ways of policing and disciplining blacks who do not conform to gender norms and expectations, like the women of the convent.

After the release of *Paradise,* Morrison revealed that she wanted to name the book *War*, but her publisher was concerned that the alternative title would be too incendiary to Morrison's audience. Knowing this, we might ask a series of questions: What is the relationship between paradise and war? How does the yearning for an ideal community rely on violent exclusions? How have nation-state borders been created, maintained, and expanded through perpetual war? Here one must pause and think about the multiple (fictional and historical) wars mentioned in the novel: the war directed at women, portrayed in the opening scenes of the novel; allusions to World War II and Vietnam; the aforementioned wars against Native people; perpetual violence against black people, which the town of Ruby attempts to protect its members against. In addition, the opening scene takes place in 1976, two centuries after the Declaration of Independence.

As discussed above, Wolin draws attention to the ways in which bicentennials and other civic rituals serve as opportunities to cultivate memories in ways that are productive and reliable for the nation-state. These rituals serve to reinforce notions of US exceptionalism and progress and diminish, or explain away, the anguish and suffering constitutive of nation building. By making the opening attack on 'strange, deviant women' which took place in 1976, alongside allusions to the earlier historical event, the novel cuts against any triumphant account of America's birth and emergence. The novel as a whole places patriarchal violence, war, anti-black racism, and settler expansion at the center of US nationhood – in a manner that dislodges desires for a coherent story. This might sound like despair. It might carry a tone of pessimism. Or it could be heard as a call to cultivate alternative ways of remembering, imagining, and tarrying with the traumatic kernel of history and political life. This is precisely Morrison's contribution to political theory during these dark times.

Joseph R. Winters

In the Wake of Morrison: Resisting Surrogacy and Black Feminist Fugitivity

Toni Morrison offers invaluable conceptual tools to contemporary political thought (and praxis) for investigating the ways in which Atlantic chattel slavery – that 'unspeakable' 300 years of U.S. history (2019, p. 107) – shapes the ongoing work of racialized exploitation and dispossession under capitalism. This recognition of what some scholars term 'slave racial capitalism', in which the 'slavebody' is preserved via transformation into the 'blackbody', poses acute problems for the meaning of freedom in political life (Morrison, 2019). But critical theorizations that explore this racialized body as the object of legal and extra-legal state violence, whether the slave, criminal, prisoner, or victim of police brutality, predominantly figure it male. In this reflection, I consider Morrison's contributions to the emerging constellation of Black feminist histories of the (racial capitalist) present that center the exploitation of Black women's (re)productive labor and dispossession of their capacity for kinship. In novels like *Beloved* and in reflections upon her political work as a writer, Morrison pursues (and resists) this notion of the Black surrogate as (re)producer of the white social order in two overlapping ways: first, Morrison is explicit about her own refusal to perform surrogate literary labor for the reproduction of the Western gaze and its stunted conception of the (always and already white) universal human. Instead, she divests from colonial artifacts and works to rememory a 'usable past' for Black world-building in the present. Secondly, it is through these imaginative historical renderings that Morrison shows Black women's surrogate labor, and concomitant 'un-mothering' through the extraction of their products/babies, as the reproductive engine of slave racial capitalism. These depictions of Black kinlessness making, and its refusal through fugitive cultivation of kinship, figure prominently in Black feminist scholarship working to theorize (and resist) the racialized violence of reproductive slavery's afterlives. After all, as Morrison reminds us, 'everything is now. It is all now' (1987, p. 41).

In *Playing in the Dark* (1992), Morrison explores the ideological work of the (white) American literary representation of Blackness and enslavement as 'surrogates' for (re)producing notions of (always and already white) American freedom, individuality, citizenship, and nationhood. It is through the literary foil of the Africanist presence, Morrison suggests, that the (white) American self has known itself as 'not enslaved, but free; not repulsive, but desirable; not helpless, but licensed and powerful; not history-less, but historical; not damned, but innocent; not a blind accident of evolution, but a progressive fulfillment of destiny' (p. 77). In other words, the American 'dream' of democratic egalitarianism is only upheld by figurations of race that conceal class struggle and rage. It is here that Morrison issues her ethical refusal to act as a literary surrogate (an 'honorary white writer') for the reproduction of this dominant White gaze and on behalf of a diminutive category of 'the human' into which black people struggle to fit with 'hyphen after hyphen after hyphen' (p. 47). Instead, she understood her historically and aesthetically rich 'word work' as a world-building project that urged readers to resist and imagine otherwise. To commit to this world required the 'freezing' of debt to the dominant Western historiography, including its sages and literary 'geniuses', since these offer little insight into the interiority of those black female subjectivities she is called to explore. It is only outside of the White gaze that Morrison can re-signify 'people' as 'black people' and in doing so 'postulate the humanity [of her characters] that writers are always being asked to enunciate' (2019, p. 297).

This ravaging critique of Western 'humanism' as a model for ethical relations paves the way for Morrison's imaginative entrance into her 'own' literary heritage of slave narratives. Morrison's critical speculative neo-slave novels are (re)memorials to chattel slavery and its psychic afterlives for Black survivors living in the wake. As bell hooks suggests, Morrison's literary gaze exemplifies the Black feminist practice of 'looking', as a critical spectator of history, and also 'looking back' from a location structured by anti-blackness and disruptive of dominant looking relations (hooks, 1992, p. 104). Her strategy is to engage in a kind of time travel in order to breathe fiction into archival shards such that THEY come to life as 'true in essence', if not as 'fact', and can enter into the present with political value. Acknowledging her place as a writer inhabiting a 'wholly racialized society', Morrison strikes out to occupy that architecture with a 'cosmology' that is 'irrevocably, indisputably black'. Morrison understands her task as *making kin* with and for black people, collecting up the members of the forgotten family, the 'population of the past' (2019, p. 481). But entering into these exquisitely rendered (re)memorials also positions us to see the ways in which the 'event' of slavery contours U.S. liberal capitalist-democracy as constitutive of black exploitation and death: from the 'extraction of (re)productive slave labor to build the nation's wealth to the ongoing erection of prison complexes to resuscitate rural economies' (Benjamin, 2018). That is, if the vitality of some (White life) continues to be predicated on what Lauren Berlant calls the 'slow death' (Berlant, 2007) of others (Black life), then Morrison's novels destabilize our cruelly optimistic attachments to ideas that U.S. democracy can ever produce racial equality. Instead, Morrison challenges us to probe what kind of polity, and what kind of a people, need to be told that the reproduction of Black Lives (and kin) Matter(s).

In *Beloved* (1987), Morrison makes plain the ways in which contemporary racial capitalism rests upon the specific exploitation and dispossession of black women's bodies that forced them to act as surrogates of the social and material (re)production of chattel slavery and white racial hegemony, while simultaneously being refused kin relations with their 'Beloved' children. *Beloved* traces the efforts of a community of African Americans to escape bondage and its after effects and foster free lives for themselves near Cincinnati. Interweaving realist, modernist and supernatural elements, Morrison focuses the novel on Sethe, a runaway slave who slits her two-year old daughter's throat when her former owners come looking for them. This inventive re-telling of the real-life story of Margaret Garner was sparked by the 1865 headline 'A Visit to the Slave Mother who Killed Her Child'. Morrison explains that she was drawn to Garner's position of 'impossible motherhood' while thinking with early 1980s (white) feminist questions surrounding motherhood as a locus of women's oppression and 'childlessness as a mark of freedom' (2019, p. 419). From the point of view of a slave woman, she realized, the capacity to *choose* motherhood would have been freedom, even anarchy: to claim maternal responsibility for her kin, to be 'not a breeder but a parent' would have signified the apex of 'intolerable female independence' under slavery (p. 419). Morrison was therefore that she was struck by the claim of Garner's supporters that Garner must have been 'insane' to murder her daughter. Instead, Morrison sets out to explore an alternative maternal logic driving the slave mother's action (p. 419).

With stunning clarity, Morrison illustrates how captivity created enslaved offspring who are owned by the master but who exist outside of the kinship system. Related neither to the 'captive female body' who birthed them nor the masters who often impregnated that body, these babies inherit what Dorothy Robert's calls their mother's non-status being (1997a, b). As Hortense Spillers reminds us, it is this dispossession of Black matrilineage and un-mothering, and the reproduction of 'fungible breeder women' in its place that structure slavery's profitability. It is in this sense that kinlessness becomes central to the 'proliferation of properties' and the surrogate (female) slave is marked as a 'prime commodity of exchange' (1987, p. 75). In *Beloved*, we see how motherhood is mediated by this 'non-being', and the loss and lamentation that is the experience of black women and children under slavery, systematically denied one another. Her own mother sent to the fields, Sethe was fed by the (Black surrogate) plantation nurse: 'The little white babies got it first and I got what was left. Or none … I know what it is to be without the milk that belongs to you…' (Morrison, 1987, p. 200). Determined to provide her own milk to her children, the substance that empowers her to nourish and claim her children as 'mine', Sethe is stricken when her milk is stolen by the white men who rape her. It is this mass-scale historical deprivation of 'milk' – emblematizing Black women as surrogates for the reproduction of human commodes and the invasion of maternal bonding and care by these property relations – that Morrison exposes as the heart of Black peoples' subjugation in the United States.

Within this context, when Schoolteacher (the slave master) and his nephews come to re-claim their property, Sethe's maternal action is instinctive and patent. The future in which Beloved grows up into slavery is one of (social) death since as property she is denied the legal and grammatical capacity to possess anything, including her own life: anti-black operations of power predicated on slavery have reduced her to 'flesh' (Spillers, 1987). It is thus *in the service of her children* and their futures that she refuses maternal disavowal and a life of endless separation from them: 'And if she thought any-thing, it was No. No. Nono. Nonono. Simple. She just flew. … collected bits of her' in order to 'drag them through the veil' where they would be safe (Morrison, 1987, p. 192). Morrison's fragmented account of Sethe's actions snapshots the lived experience of trying to make kinship out of kinlessness, exposing a milieu in which her subjectivity as a Black mother has been produced as impossible. It is a position, as James Baldwin formulates in 'Notes of a Native Son', 'of having to choose between amputation and gangrene' (1955, p. 36). But this moment is also one that lays bare a fugitive maternal logic. Through the murder of her daughter, Sethe dispenses with her own labor as a surrogate for a dehumanizing ontological order while creating the conditions for protecting her daughter from that very order. In this refusal of the white American grammar that strips her of maternal responsibility, she willfully remembers her daughter as 'Beloved' (the only name she can afford for the gravestone) and literally names her as kin.

This reading of Sethe's fugitive love as a 'gendered strike against slavery' (Weinbaum, 2019, p. 91) positions us to understand contemporary claims of black kinship – that black 'flesh and blood' matters – as resistance against racial capitalism. Indeed, Black feminist scholars have taken up the affective and political

Critical Exchange

'afterlife' of Morrison's work in developing a history of the (slave racial capitalist) present that centers the systematic denial of the ontological space of Black motherhood. Christina Sharpe's *In the Wake: On Blackness and Being* (2016), tells us to think of 'the wake'. Describing both the collective grieving of a funeral and the displacement of waves behind a slave ship, the notion of the wake signposts slavery's reproductive afterlife for those who descend from it. For Black mothers and children, Sharpe contends, living in the wake of slavery is living 'the afterlife of property' and the afterlife of *partus sequitur ventrem* (that which is brought forth follows the womb): the birth canal is transformed into 'another kind of domestic middle passage' through which black children are ushered into the mother's position of 'non/status' and 'non/being-ness' (Sharpe, 2016, p. 74). This inheritance reverberates in a twenty-first century climate of anti-blackness, in which the social, material and psychic death of Black life is (still) normative. As Sharpe points out, such 'disasters' of/for Black mother and children circulate rapidly and repetitively throughout television and social media such that Black death becomes quotidian, becomes what Sharpe coins 'the weather'. Just as we stop seeing the escalation of ecological crisis, the grammar of 'the weather' makes white domination in/visible, and 'registers and produces the conventions of anti-blackness in the present and into the future' (2016, p. 21).

This material and social abandonment of black people in slavery's aftermaths – in federal prisons, on streets and boulevards, in rising waters, and on overseas battlefields – is the insidious reproduction of Black 'un-mothering' and 'de-childing'. Claudia Rankine reminds us, for Black mothers to live in the wake is to live in the knowing that one's 'status as the mother of a living human being' remains precarious (2015). In the wake of hurricane Katrina, Black mothers in New Orleans clasped babies on rooftops or floated them away on mattresses, with dim hope of their survival; in the wake of police chokeholds, bullets and beatings, Black mothers clutched their murdered children's newspaper clippings – their corpses held as evidence or (as in the case of Trayvon Martin) left to rot on the street; in the wake of ceaseless war, Black mothers of dead soldiers hold medals and American flags; incarcerated Black mothers, often shackled throughout the birthing process, are routinely denied the ability to cradle their newborns to their chests; birthing caps continue to discipline the reproduction of mothers requiring government assistance; and, the foster care system daily rips children from their mothers' grip.

Black mothers thus remain racial capitalism's surrogates, (re)producing its products, its labor, and its racialized other, while losing these children. This dispossession of the right to motherhood, and to be mothered, as Saidiya Hartman puts it, is a pernicious 'political arithmetic' still central to maintaining the (always and already) white social order of the United States (2007). In this sense, Beloved is the ghost of the thousands of Beloveds – generations of mothers and daughters – haunted down and stolen from Africa. To 'lose' your mother (through this enduring institutionalization of kinlessness) is to be detached from your identity, to be haunted by loss and to inhabit the world as a stranger. In tracing the Atlantic trade routes in Ghana, which she details in *Lose Your Mother*, Hartman borrows Morrison's 'undisciplined modes' of entering and creatively filling in slavery's trifling archives as a way to counter the contemporary effects of this violent abstraction. Importantly, her search is not for diffuse survivors of her own genetic lineage but rather for other strangers 'obliterated in the making of human commodes' whom she might claim as ancestral kin (2007, p. 7).

Ruha Benjamin's *Black AfterLives Matter* builds upon the notion of 'kinfulness' and in particular the making of political kin with enslaved and slain ancestors – as a fugitive modality of survival and resistance in the wake of slavery. Calling upon Morrison's language in *Beloved*, Benjamin insists that speculative methods of attending to the 'needy dead' (abandoned in death as they have been in life) are central to disrupting the 'weather' of anti-Blackness. Benjamin shows how this resuscitation of black lives is at work in vivifying social movements like #SayHerName, where the 'Mothers of the Movement' call out the names of their children murdered by anti-Black racism. This naming of their flesh and blood as 'Beloved', itself a practice of resistance in an anti-Black world, is also a way to call their children's spirits into an (activist) afterlife: 'What a blessing to be here tonight, so that Sandy can still speak through her mama', said Geneva Reed-Veal (mother of Sandra Bland) at the Democratic Convention' (quoted in Benjamin, 2018). Like Sethe in *Beloved*, it is the force of these mothers' love for their 'best thing' (their dead children) that enables them to transform their reproductive labor as primary caregivers into activism and to resist the afterlife of slavery: 'I am an unwilling participant in this movement', said Sybrina Fulton, the mother of Trayvon Martin. 'I would not have signed up for this. None of us would have. But I am here today for my son, Trayvon Martin' (quoted in Benjamin, 2018).

These practices of fugitive love and assertions of maternal responsibility (as activists in the 'name' of their children) resist Black un-mothering as a constitutive part of U.S. political life. As Morrison reminds us, it is Sethe's ability to remain a mother, to hold onto the maternal control, responsibility, and voice that the ontological logic of slavery had stolen, that is central to her self-regard (1987). But these spiritual technologies of calling upon (slain) ancestors who are 'restless [for freedom] underground' can also mobilize a meta-kinship that surpasses the (impossible) biological ancestry of subjugated populations: connecting the ghost of Beloved with the spirit of Sandra Bland. These creative modes of cultivating kinship decolonize Black Afterlives and make black reproduction matter as part of ongoing futurist, feminist agendas (Benjamin, 2018). As Benjamin reminds us, 'there is a lot happening underground. Not only coffins, but seeds, roots and rhizomes. And maybe even tunnels and other lines of flight to alternative ways of life'.

In the conclusion of *Beloved*, we watch as the 'the haunting' by the vengeful child-ghost is supplanted by the 'haunting' of slavery as the total environment: 'By

Critical Exchange

and by all trace is gone, and what is forgotten is not only the footprints but the water too and what is down there. The rest is weather... Just weather. Not the *breath of the disremembered* and unaccounted for, but wind in the eaves, or spring ice thawing too quickly' (Morrison, 1987, p. 322). In the afterlife of slavery, surrounded by the 'weather' of contemporary racial capitalism, Morrison's work is a call to remember this breath of the 'disremembered' as well as the inability of some Black lives to breathe at all. Yet over melancholic remembrance, Morrison's re-memories inform a feminist-inflected positionality and praxis of Black being that teaches black life how to 'think, feel, care, ... and mother' through the wake of slavery, despite the lived relation of 'always-imminent death' (Sharpe, 2016, p. 38).

For Morrison, resistance *within* this world does not require resisting the world itself, nor does it demand transcendence beyond this world. Instead, in all of her work Morrison illustrates how to straddle the constitutive projects of refusing to perform surrogate labor for the (re)production of 'worlds we cannot live within' while imagining and laboring for those 'worlds we cannot live without' (Benjamin, 2018). The condition of black life may be, as Claudia Rankine (2015) suggests, one of abjection but it is also one of imaginatively recuperating the very fugitivity that marks black life in order to practice insurgent resistance(s): to claim kinship with black children, enslaved ancestors, spirits, ghosts, and other black feminist writers who refuse to reproduce the hegemonic white gaze is to refuse the ongoing imposition of non-being. In calling forth a haunting of the national conscience with these lost and violated kin relations, Morrison issues an ethical and political call to action for the living: 'You are BeLoved'.

Alix L. Olson

Dignity as Self-regard: Reflections on Toni Morrison and Law

Over the course of her writing career, Toni Morrison responded often and publicly to matters concerning law and justice. Her writings on legal themes include essays on the Anita Hill-Clarence Thomas hearings (1992a), the O.J. Simpson trial (1997), Bill Clinton's impeachment (1998), and early twentieth-century lynching cases (2017). There has been considerable debate among political theorists on the significance of these essays both for American politics and for our understanding of the relationship between Morrison's literary imagination and her non-fiction writings on controversial issues in the public domain. Most memorable, perhaps, was her reference to Clinton as America's 'first black President', an analogy that was widely seen as ineffective or even counter-purposive to her broader concerns for racial justice and constitutional rights (Chatman, 2000; Reinhardt, 2000; Shulman, 2000; Harris, 2019). Rather than revisiting those debates, however, I would like to suggest an alternative point of departure for an assessment of Morrison's contributions to legal criticism.

Critical Exchange

For me, the most profound commentary that Morrison wrote on a legal matter (because it speaks directly to women in that part of the world I call home) is her open letter to a Sudanese woman who was subjected to a brutal whipping at a Khartoum police station. Referring to a video of the incident that surfaced on the internet in 2010, Morrison wrote the following:

> I have seen many instances of human brutality, but this one was particularly harrowing …The lasting response I had watching that video is the most important. You did not crouch or kneel or assume a fetal position. You shouted. You fell. But you kept rising. After each cut of the lash into your flesh, you tried to stand; you raised your body up like a counter-whip. It so moved me to see your reactions; I interpreted them as glimmers of hope, of principled defiance (2011).

Newsweek published Morrison's tribute to the unnamed woman under the heading 'Dignity and Depravity'. Dalia Haj Omar, a Sudanese human rights activist, responded to Morrison's intervention soon afterwards, describing the letter as a 'direct call of solidarity with the strife of Sudanese women'. It is a reminder, she said, that 'we are not alone…' (Omar, 2011).

Morrison's passing is a loss for women around the world who, touched by her words, felt a little bit less alone. Yet we are not left without inspiration: her essays and novels remain as a potential gathering point for imagined communities of struggle. My goal in these reflections is to examine aspects of Morrison's writings that support women's fragile efforts to retain a sense of their humanity and dignity in the face of dehumanizing laws. Beginning with the novel *Beloved* (2004[1987]) and moving through a selection of her essays on American literature and law, I suggest that Morrison consciously replaced mainstream conceptions of dignity in Western political thought (based on mutual respect among subjects presumed to be white and male) with a conception of 'self-regard' that centers the black female subject as the source of her own worth. This conception of dignity as self-regard pushes critical legal theory to respond more adequately to the perspectives of marginalized women, while also helping to inform the political analysis of dignitarian ideals that guide the activism of women around the world.

As is well known, *Beloved* was inspired by the story of Margaret Garner, a nineteenth-century woman who fled from slavery in the company of other members of her family. The Garners' freedom turned out to be short-lived: they were soon recaptured under the provisions of the Fugitive Slave Act. *Beloved* creatively reimagines these events. Afraid that she and her children would be apprehended, the novel's protagonist, Sethe, kills one of her daughters as a way of protecting her from being returned to captivity. Sethe then spirals into an agonized reckoning with the murdered child and the almost unbearable trauma of racial slavery.

In several interviews and essays, Morrison discussed the dignity-based concerns that motivated her to write the novel. She was interested, she explained, in how an

Reprinted from the journal

Critical Exchange

enslaved woman would have regarded herself in that time period: 'What was her self-esteem? What value did she place on herself?' Morrison's intuition and research led her to believe that for many black women, motherhood was the principle source of self-worth (2019, p. 318). Yet the institution of slavery did not permit enslaved women to care for, protect, or parent their children in any meaningful way. A black woman was 'under the law a piece of property, as were her offspring – who in no way belonged to her – because they were stock that could be – and regularly were – sold' (Morrison, 2017, p. 90). In opposition to the law, Morrison's character Sethe claimed her children as her own and loved them powerfully. Her ethic of responsibility led her not only to kill her child, but also to hold herself so unyieldingly accountable that her own life began to slip away. It is against this background that Paul D., the man who tried to love Sethe in all her complexity, sought to reassure her that she was already fully worthy in herself. 'You your best thing, Sethe' he said (Morrison, 2004 [1987], p. 322).

Paul D.'s words are frequently quoted in commentaries on *Beloved*, and with good reason. The affirmation of dignity as self-regard is one of the most powerful elements of the novel. But there is a danger that these words will become all too familiar and lose their critical edge. In its fullest meaning, dignity as self-regard is not limited to self-affirmations: it has a political dimension that exposes and critiques a major presupposition of modern Western political thought. In the social contract tradition, dignity is based on mutual regard among citizens (presumed to be white and male), with full membership in the political community providing the guarantee that one's humanity will be recognized as such. Defining dignity as 'the publique worth of a man, which is the Value set on him by the Common-wealth', Thomas Hobbes freely acknowledged that there would be an unequal distribution of public honors and offices (1996 [1651], p. 63). Nonetheless, citizenship in his *Leviathan* functions as a floor below which one cannot sink no matter how low one is ranked in the public regard.

In seeming contrast, Immanuel Kant rejected the differential ranking of persons that Hobbes accepted as necessary. In Kant's words, dignity (*Würde*) is 'not merely a relative worth, that is, a price, but an inner worth' (1996 [1785], p. 84). This moral conception of dignity is typically understood to be universal and egalitarian. But once again, the irreducible 'inner' worth of human beings turns out to be the exclusive property of insiders. Women and people of color, who according to Kant have lower moral capacities, are not treated as persons capable of full membership in the moral community (see Sedgwick, 1997; Bernasconi, 2011).

Turning to ideologies of the American founding that also have their roots in Enlightenment philosophy, Morrison put forward a thoroughgoing critique of hierarchical relations that underpin civic dignity. 'Young America distinguished itself by, and understood itself to be, pressing toward a future of freedom, a kind of human dignity', Morrison notes (1992b, p. 33). It was not, however, a universal and equal human dignity. For European immigrants, the American dream of moving 'from social ostracism to social rank' meant, quite simply, becoming white and finding one's elevated place in a hierarchy that subordinated black people. The literature of the nineteenth and early twentieth centuries reflected these values. Reading Edgar Allan Poe, Mark Twain, Willa Cather, and other notable American novelists, Morrison observed that 'images of impenetrable whiteness...appear almost always in conjunction with representations of black or Africanist people who are dead, impotent, or under complete control' (1992b, p. 33). In other words, the dignity of the holders of the American dream was premised on the social and civic death of racially subjugated others.

Given this history, is 'dignity' really worth fighting for, or is the concept too loaded with racism and sexism? In feminist theory, the jury is still out on whether this and other 'Enlightenment concepts' (e.g., sovereignty, autonomy, progress) are salvageable. My own view is that it makes no sense to abandon concepts that have a rich history in our own traditions of thought and activism. If we look at the literary milieu in which Morrison was writing in the 1980s, we can see the theme of dignity as self-regard emerging in the work of Alice Walker, Paule Marshall, Nikki Giovanni, Audre Lorde, Maya Angelou, and many other black women who had a critical social vision. Their focus on black women's 'willful self-creation' inspired a similar line of thinking in legal studies (Roberts, 1995, p. 238). Dorothy Roberts, Angela P. Harris, and other scholars who simultaneously advanced the feminist and critical race theory movements in American law schools foregrounded the radical imagination of women of color. Mindful of the tendency of white feminists to address 'women's status under the law' only from their own location in social relations, these scholars turned to literature for a wider range of perspectives. 'In order to energize legal theory', Harris argued, 'we need to subvert it with narratives and stories, accounts of the particular, the different, and the hitherto silenced' (1990, p. 615).

Morrison's novels helped to bring attention to the hitherto silenced. In an early response to *Beloved*, Robin West (1988) argued that the novel writes into visibility the lives of African Americans who were written out of the political community through law. Noting that 'laws oppress and protect; grant and deny rights; acknowledge or repudiate one's humanity, moral worth or entitlement', West focused on images in *Beloved* that subvert the dominant political logic of the American nation (p. 154). Her reading of the novel highlighted alternative forms of sociality that emerge among the newly freed African Americans – 'communities of intimacy and respect' that come into being through tender caresses, tears, kissing, breastfeeding, dance, play, and many gestures that hold up the black body as an incomparably valuable entity (pp. 150–151).

Other feminist lawyers in the 1990s focused on identifying legal frameworks that *strain* relationships and familial bonds in African American communities. Connections were made between Sethe's struggle to be a caring mother and major public policy challenges of the late twentieth century: state regulation of sexuality

Critical Exchange

and reproductive technologies (e.g., Roberts, 1995); norms regarding motherhood and family life (e.g., Cornell, 1999); and punitive or restrictive rules attached to public assistance programs for low-income families (e.g., Roberts, 1994). Although much of this scholarship focused on critiquing existing policy and legal frameworks, the arguments were fundamentally concerned with ideas of freedom and women's rights to pursue what they hold to be valuable.

More recently, Drucilla Cornell and Sara Murphy (2008) have argued that 'the demand for freedom must be understood as the affordance of the psychic and moral space necessary for groups and individuals to engage with and re-create their multiple identifications' (pp. 175–176). Such identifications might include, for example, the decision to be or not to be a parent, to love the persons that one loves, and to form bonds of kinship and affection that express one's own notion of family life. 'The practice of literature is one place where we can see this work of re-creation, of what Toni Morrison has termed "rememory"' Cornell and Murphy contend. (p. 176). But law also has a role to play in supporting the fragile freedom Morrison writes about. Legal protection of the imaginative space for self-creation, which Cornell (1995) calls the 'imaginary domain', is needed in order to ensure that individuals can actually give their own meaning to their lives and relationships. For centuries, this protection has been denied to women, particularly women of color and low-income women. This is why we cannot simply take law as given but must re-imagine it on more ethical terms.

The conversation that began among feminist legal scholars has long since moved across disciplinary boundaries. New cross-disciplinary readings of *Beloved* have deepened the critique of family law and welfare regulations (Zamalin, 2014), while other studies have extended the discussion to address U.S.-derived legal norms that shape international human rights regimes. In Crystal Parikh's (2017) analysis of *Beloved*, Sethe's struggle to have her life and her bodily existence count as 'human' is linked to a broader, global struggle for human rights. Parikh presses us to revisit an important question: What exactly is the 'human' in human rights? In the context of the present discussion we might ask, what is the 'human' in human dignity?

Conventionally, as in Hobbes's *homo homini lupus* (man is wolf to man), humanity has been defined both in relation and in opposition to non-human animals. This opposition-relation became a favorite puzzle for race 'scientists' in the nineteenth century who cast doubt on the descent of blacks from the same origin as other human beings. While some proponents of biological racial-difference theories conceded that there was a common origin for all members of the human species, they typically placed African-descended peoples on the lower end of a spectrum, closer to animals than to other human beings (see Fredrickson, 2015). The debate on origins, which would eventually morph into eugenicist theories in the early twentieth century and the designation of certain people as genetically 'inferior', is exposed to critical scrutiny in *Beloved*.

Critical Exchange

Calling attention to passages in the novel in which the bodies of enslaved blacks are subjected to 'scientific' study and classification by slaveholders, Angela P. Harris (2009) notes:

> To be moved from the human to the non-human side of the paper is to be made a being with no moral claims, a being whose body is only flesh, vulnerable to any kind of treatment for any reason, or for no reason (p. 22).

Although nineteenth-century discourses on race and animality have long since fallen into disrepute, the afterlife of these ways of categorizing the black body continues to influence the social valuation of black lives today. This is particularly so in encounters between black people and law enforcement, where discourses on animality converge with media stereotypes of black people as dangerous, ungovernable, criminal, and automatically deserving of containment using lethal force. To set in motion this sequence of cascading judgments, one need not even say much. A single image suffices. Recalling the cultural climate surrounding the beating of Rodney King in 1991, Harris notes: 'everyone knew what it meant when officers of the Los Angeles Police Department described black suspects in that city as "gorillas in the mist"'(p. 22, citing a *New York Times* report). Never seen as quite human, the black body in the eyes of the law seems to justify the use of overwhelming force, even in advance of any encounter between a particular black individual and a particular police officer.

The force of law is overwhelming. When we take into account issues such as police killings, mass incarceration, and the school-to-prison pipeline, the idea of 'self-regard' sounds like a naïve and simplistic fix, more akin to the language of advertising than the vocabulary of serious political thinking. Morrison was well aware of the danger that her idea of dignity could be trivialized through popular culture. Her last published novel, *God Help the Child* (2015), focuses on new challenges to black women's self-regard in a neoliberal age that reduces everything to a consumer good or a transactional value. In contrast to Sethe in *Beloved*, when Bride (the protagonist in *God Help the Child*) has doubts about her worth, the initial response comes not from a loving partner but instead from corporate America's drive to tap into new markets and exploit the newest class of consumers who finally have (credit-fueled) access to the marketplace: black women. YOU-GIRL is a line of cosmetics and Bride is its face and corporate manager. The idea of being one's own best thing is treated literally as a matter of economic self-possession: taking oneself to market – not as an object of property on the auction block, but instead as a self-marketed product of the cosmetics industry, an embodied corporate brand, or a walking advertising campaign. 'You your best thing' in this context would sound like a TV commercial for a face cream or a weekend at the spa.

Without detailing the narrative twists of *God Help the Child*, I want only to suggest that Morrison understood the risks that her conception of dignity necessarily runs in the twenty-first century. As with the danger of contamination of dignity by Enlightenment racism, however, I remain convinced that feminists must not abandon the concept of self-regard to the dominant culture. Instead, we should continually seek to clarify the aspects of self-regard that resist egocentrism and commodification.

Self-regard in Morrison's novels *is* inward looking. But it has an outward component that can be foregrounded when we speak of human dignity as a core principle of social justice movements. Take, for example, Morrison's delicate rendering of an intimate scene between two lovers in *Jazz*, as recounted in her essay on 'The Source of Self-Regard'. Two black people, devalued by the larger society, turn to each other with love and mutual affirmation. In this scene, dignity appears as a turn 'inward toward the other' (2019, p. 320). But the other does not have to be a sexual partner. We can identify inwardness toward the other in other kinds of relationships, as Harris (2009) has done in defending animal rights. Acknowledging that there is an understandable impulse in communities of color to distance themselves from public discussions about animals (the failure of the animal rights movement to consistently address questions of racial justice is a contributing factor here), Harris argues, nevertheless, that anti-racism and animal rights are *internally* connected. It is in the interest of people of color to end all subordinating distinctions that are based on opposition-identifications such as human/animal or white/black (2009, p. 27). People of color are demonstrably degraded, not helped, when human dignity is premised on the abjection of non-human life or the subordination of non-human animals to the arbitrary will of human beings.

Consider that in *The Bluest Eye* (1993 [1970]), the abused and debased existence of Pecola Breedlove is mirrored through the abuse of animals – the violent killing of a cat and the poisoning of a dog in which this gentle little girl is forced to participate. Pecola's compassion for the abused animals is arguably the closest she comes to true affection and compassion for herself. It allows her to touch, tentatively, the humanity that has been denied to her. Caring for animals is a form of her own nascent self-regard. Consider also that in a number of contexts, Morrison expressed compassion for suffering humanity by linking it to suffering animal life. In her letter to the unnamed Sudanese woman, Morrison noted that 'the abused-animal life so many women are required to live is being challenged' (2011). The courage of one woman who kept rising up against the whip gave Morrison hope, and should give us confidence, that a more dignified existence is within our reach.

I have argued here that dignity as self-regard takes women who are socially devalued as the source of their own worth. It relies neither on the social contract tradition, nor on law as it currently exists, nor on a hierarchical social order with its assumptions of human dominance over non-human life. Dignity as self-regard is not a matter of egotistical self-aggrandizement that demeans somebody else. It requires us to bring all suffering life into the sphere of our care, attention, and respectful regard. It also requires that feminists continue to fight for a future in which there is legal protection of the imaginary domain – a space in which women can give shape to their own lives and identifications, including the question of what it means to be a 'woman'. Respecting women in all their shades, shapes, and ways of being is essential if we are to sustain the practice of solidarity that Morrison established in bearing witness to the dignity of a Sudanese woman who held up her own body as a counter-whip to law.

Wairimu Njoya

About the Authors

Alex Zamalin is an assistant professor of political science and director of African American Studies at University of Detroit Mercy.

Joseph R. Winters is the Alexander F. Hehmeyer Associate Professor of Religious Studies and African and American American Studies at Duke University.

Alix Olson is assistant professor of Women's, Gender, and Sexuality Studies at Emory University.

Wairimu Njoya is assistant professor of political science at Williams College.

References

Arendt, H. (1998) *The human condition* (2nd ed.). Chicago, IL: University of Chicago Press.
Baldwin, J. (1955) *Notes of a native son*. Boston, MA: Beacon Press.
Benjamin, R. (2018) Excerpt from Black afterlives matter: cultivating kinfulness as reproductive justice. In: A. Clarke and D. Haraway (eds.) *Making kin not population*. Chicago, IL: Prickly Paradigm Press. https://bostonreview.net/race/ruha-benjamin-black-afterlives-matter, accessed 9 March 2020.
Berlant, L. (2007) Slow death (sovereignty, obesity, lateral agency). *Critical Inquiry* 33(4): 754–780.
Bernasconi, R. (2011) Kant's third thoughts on race. In: S. Elden and E. Mendieta (eds.) *Reading kant's geography* (pp. 291–308). Albany: State University of New York Press.
Chatman, E.A. (2000) Clinton's black 'I': A note on public property. *Theory & Event* 4(1).
Cheng, A. (2001) *The melancholy of race: Psychoanalysis, assimilation, and hidden Grief*. New York: Oxford University Press.
Collins, P. (2002) *Black feminist thought: Knowledge, consciousness, and the politics of empowerment*. New York: Routledge.
Cornell, D. (1995) *The imaginary domain: Abortion, pornography & sexual harassment*. New York: Routledge.
Cornell, D. (1999) *Beyond accommodation: Ethical Feminism, deconstruction, and the law*. New York: Rowman & Littlefield.

Cornell, D., and Murphy, S. (2008) Anti-racism, multiculturalism, and the ethics of identification. In: R. Heberle and B. Pryor (eds.) *Imagining law: On Drucilla Cornell* (pp. 173–200). Albany: State University of New York Press.
Forbes, E. (2006) Do black ghosts matter?: Harriet Jacobs' spiritualism'. *ESQ: A Journal of Nineteenth Century American Literature and Culture* 62(3): 443–479.
Foucault, M. (1978) *The history of sexuality, introduction* (Vol. 1). New York: Pantheon.
Fredrickson, G.M. (2015) Racism, history of. In: J.D. Wright (ed.) *International encyclopedia of the social & behavioral sciences* (pp. 852–856). Amsterdam, Netherlands: Elsevier.
Glaude, E. (2007) *In a shade of blue: Pragmatism and the politics of black America*. Chicago: University of Chicago Press.
Habermas, J. (1998) *The inclusion of the other: Studies in political theory*. In: C. Cronin and P. De Greiff (eds.) Cambridge, MA: MIT Press.
Harris, A.P. (1990) Race and essentialism in feminist legal theory. *Stanford Law Review* 42(3): 581–616.
Harris, A. P. (2009) Should people of color support animal rights? *Journal of Animal Law* 5(1): 15–32.
Harris, D. (2019) *Black feminist politics from Kennedy to Trump*. Cham, Switzerland: Palgrave Macmillan.
Hartman, S. (2007) *Lose your mother: A journey along the Atlantic slave route*. New York: Farrar, Staus and Giroux.
Hobbes, T. (1996) *Leviathan*. Cambridge, UK: Cambridge University Press.
Hooks, bell. (1992) *Black Looks: Race and Representation*. South End Press.
Kant, I. (1996) Groundwork of the metaphysics of morals. In: M.J. Gregor (ed.) *Immanuel Kant: Practical philosophy* (pp. 37–108). New York: Cambridge University Press.
Lubiano, W. (2002) Standing in for the state: black nationalism and 'writing' the black subject'. In: E. Glaude (ed.) *Is it nation time: Contemporary essays on black power and black nationalism* (pp. 156–164). Chicago: University of Chicago Press.
Mbembe, A. (2019) *Necropolitics (Translated by Steven Corcoran)*. Durham: Duke University Press.
McDowell, D. (1997) In the first place: making frederick douglass and the Afro-American tradition'. In: G. Andrews and W. McFeely (eds.) *Narrative of the life of Frederick Douglass* (pp. 172–183). New York: WW Norton.
Mohanty, S. (1997) *Literary theory and the claims of history: Postmodernism, objectivity, multicultural politics*. Ithaca: Cornell University Press.
Morrison, T. (1993 [1970]) *The bluest eye*. New York: Alfred A. Knopf.
Morrison, T. (2004 [1987]) *Beloved*. New York: Vintage.
Morrison, T. (1992a) Introduction: Friday on the Potomac. In: T. Morrison (ed.) *Race-ing justice, en-gendering power: Essays on Anita Hill, Clarence Thomas, and the construction of social reality* (pp. vii–xxx). New York: Pantheon.
Morrison, T. (1992b) *Playing in the dark: Whiteness and the literary imagination*. Cambridge, MA: Harvard University Press.
Morrison, T. (1995) The site of memory. In: W. Zinsser (ed.) *Inventing the truth: The art and craft of memoir* (pp. 83–102). New York: Houghton Mifflin.
Morrison, T. (1997a) The official story: dead man golfing. In: T. Morrison and C. Brodsky (eds.) *Birth of a nation'hood: Gaze, script, and spectacle in the OJ Simpson case* (pp. 3–30). New York: Pantheon.
Morrison, T. (1997b) *Paradise*. New York: Plume.
Morrison, T. (1998) Comment. *New Yorker*. September 27, 1998. https://www.newyorker.com/magazine/1998/10/05/comment-6543, accessed 9 March 2020.
Morrison, T. (2007) *The bluest eye*. New York: Vintage.
Morrison, T. (2011) Dignity and depravity. *Newsweek*. September 26, 2011.
Morrison, T. (2015) *God help the child*. New York: Alfred A. Knopf.
Morrison, T. (2017) *The origin of others*. Cambridge, MA: Harvard University Press.
Morrison, T. (2019) *The source of self-regard: Selected essays, speeches, and meditations*. New York: Alfred A. Knopf.

Mouffe, C. (2013) *Agonistics: Thinking the world politically*. New York: Verso.
Omar, D.H. (2011) Sudan's women where are you? The world is calling. *Sudan Tribune* October 30, 2011. https://www.sudantribune.com/Sudan-s-women-where-are-you-The,40578, accessed 9 December 2019.
Parikh, C. (2017) *Writing human rights: The political imaginaries of writers of color*. Minneapolis: University of Minnesota Press.
Rankine, C. (2015) The condition of black Life is one of mourning. *The New York Times*. https://www.nytimes.com/2015/06/22/magazine/the-condition-of-black-life-is-one-of-mourning.html, accessed 9 December 2019.
Rawls, J. (1971) *A theory of justice*. Cambridge: Belknap Press of Harvard University Press.
Reinhardt, M. (2000) Constitutional sentimentality. *Theory & Event* 4(1).
Roberts, D.E. (1994) The value of black mothers' work. *Connecticut Law Review* 26(3): 871–878.
Roberts, D.E. (1995) The genetic tie. *University of Chicago Law Review* 62(1): 209–273.
Roberts, D.E. (1998) *Killing the black body: Race, reproduction, and the meaning of liberty*. New York: Vintage Books.
Rorty, R. (1998) *Achieving our country: Leftist thought in twentieth-century America*. Cambridge: Harvard University Press.
Sedgwick, S. (1997) Can Kant's ethics survive the feminist critique? In: R.M. Schott (ed.) *Feminist interpretations of Immanuel Kant* (pp. 77–100). Penn State University Press: University Park, PA.
Sharpe, C. (2016) *In the wake: On blackness and being*. Durham: Duke University Press.
Shulman, G.M. (2000) Narrating Clinton's impeachment: Race, the right, and allegories of the sixties. *Theory & Event* 4(1).
Shulman, G.M. (2008) *American prophecy: Race and redemption in American political culture*. Minneapolis: University of Minnesota Press.
Spillers, H. (1987) Mama's baby, papa's maybe: An American grammar Book. *Diacritics* 17(2): 64–81.
Suranyi, A. (2007) The bluest eye and Sula: black female experience from childhood to womanhood. In: J. Tally (ed.) *The Cambridge companion to Toni Morrison* (pp. 11–25). New York: Cambridge University Press.
Weinbaum, A. (2019) *The afterlife of slavery and the problem of reproductive freedom*. Durham: Duke University Press.
West, R. (1988) Communities, texts, and law: Reflections on the law and literature movement. *Yale Journal of Law & Humanities* 1(1): 129–156.
Wolin, S. (1990) *The presence of the past: Essays on the state and the constitution*. Baltimore, MD: Johns Hopkins Press.
Zamalin, A. (2014) Beloved citizens: Toni Morrison's 'beloved', racial inequality, and American public policy. *Women's Studies Quarterly* 42(1/2): 205–211.

Publisher's Note Springer Nature remains neutral with regard to jurisdictional claims in published maps and institutional affiliations.

Review

New forms of revolt: Essays on Kristeva's intimate politics

Sarah K. Hansen and Rebecca Tuvel (eds.)
SUNY Press, Albany, 2017, vii + 221 pp., ISBN: 978-1438465210

Contemporary Political Theory (2019) **18**, S187–S190. https://doi.org/10.1057/s41296-018-0195-6; published online 18 January 2018

New Forms of Revolt is a rewarding volume for those with a serious interest in Julia Kristeva, especially her theory of revolt. In this review, I will first name the overall strengths of the volume, then I will provide chapter summaries. Because this is a review for *Contemporary Political Theory*, I will summarize only those chapters with explicitly political themes, omitting the volume's third section, 'Language and Narrative in Kristeva.'

One strength that runs throughout the volume is the contributors' ability to relate Kristeva's thought to that of other theorists. For example, Hannah Arendt's writings are discussed by Sara Beardsworth, Elaine P. Miller, and Sarah Kathryn Marshall, but each chapter contributes something unique to Kristeva's interpretation of Arendt. And Surti Singh's chapter considers Kristeva's use of the 'society of the spectacle' as developed by Guy Debord and the ways in which their thinking converges and diverges. The second strength is the devotion of each author to reading Kristeva with a critical, yet generous eye. The editors, Sarah K. Hansen and Rebecca Tuvel, begin the volume with this careful balance. They note the increasing importance of Kristeva's understanding of revolt to our contemporary world, but they make clear the limitations caused by her failure to take histories of racism and colonialism into account. Similarly, Elena Ruiz judiciously highlights the potential of Kristeva's theory of language for understanding political art in Latin America, while also explaining how Kristeva's framework participates in a history of linguistic violence.

The editors' introduction presents a summary of Kristeva's concept of 'revolt' and then briefly summarizes the contributions that follow. In concise and clear terms, Hansen and Tuvel explain that Kristeva's understanding of revolt has changed over the decades of her authorship. Whereas her earlier work, particularly *Revolution in Poetic Language*, focused on language, there is a shift to the intimate, that is, to individual psychic life, on the one hand, and to the diffusion of power, on the other. One of the most helpful things about the introduction is that the editors show how *Powers of Horror*, *Tales of Love*, and *Black Sun* paved the way for her

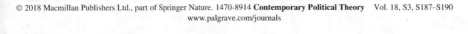

later development of intimate revolt by turning to both individual psychic processes (like abjection) and the social conditions that enable those processes. While revolt is not a central concern of this trilogy, Hansen and Tuvel make it clear that these texts are important for understanding Kristeva's later writings. The editors also explain that Kristeva is increasingly concerned with the absence of a unified authority, law, or the Symbolic, against which one can transgress. Instead, power is becoming diffuse, disciplinary, normalizing. Without a commonly understood power against which to revolt, it becomes less and less clear how one can even conceive of revolution, let alone actually revolt. This is why revolt must be intimate.

The chapters in Part I consider the theory of revolt Kristeva has developed. The first chapter is a contribution by Kristeva herself. Here, she briefly outlines her understanding of humanism, then discusses two examples: 'adolescents in want of ideals and maternal passion at the crossroads of biology and meaning' (p. 19). At barely five pages, this chapter only touches on some themes that concern Kristeva at greater length elsewhere. As such, it would not serve well as a general introduction to her thought. Instead, the chapter makes connections between her different concerns in a concise way for those already familiar with her work.

The second chapter, by Singh, has two aims: first, to interrogate the extent to which Kristeva's own psychoanalytic categories perpetuate the society of the spectacle and second, to interrogate the specifically masculine perspective of the spectacle which is neglected by Debord's analysis. Singh explains Kristeva's understanding of fantasy as occurring at different levels and across different levels of conscious awareness. Thus, whereas the Lacanian imaginary would only reinforce the society of the spectacle in which the presence of images floods our daily lives, fantasy (and the forms of art that provoke fantasy) hold the promise of encouraging revolt as questioning, as thinking and imagining ourselves and the world otherwise. Turning to Debord, Singh argues that his understanding of the society of the spectacle as constructing our subjectivities can add a social dimension to Kristevean intimate revolt. In other words, the questioning involved in intimate revolt must also be a questioning of the social conditions that give rise to particular subjectivities, namely those social conditions that hinder revolt by determining in advance what we imagine and desire.

Beardsworth's contribution is a reading of Kristeva alongside Gillian Rose. She shows how Kristeva's Freudian inheritance and Rose's Hegelian inheritance lead both authors to be critical of Arendt's dismissal of the social, but in different ways. For Kristeva, revolt involves a retrospective return to the timeless, a return in which we are pushed to the border of our speaking being, where drives meet thought and language. Rose encourages us to embrace the anxiety of beginning, the awareness that the result of our actions cannot be predicted in advance, because otherwise we fail to take political risks and fall into either a 'moral judgment that does not act' or a political idealism that acts without thinking (p. 55). In modern worlds,

Beardsworth contends, the relationship between Kristeva and Rose is a chiasmatic one: 'In the life and consciousness of action we are already strangers to ourselves; strangers to ourselves, in revolt we advance to the break of life and consciousness' (p. 60). This formulation shows how Rose's problematization of action and Kristeva's problematization of psychic life cannot be reconciled, nor are they contradictory. Instead, read together they offer two simultaneous approaches to a critique of life in modernity.

Part II contains three chapters, each of which offers an exceptionally clear application of Kristeva's theories to particular works or settings. Ruiz's chapter skillfully navigates between the promise of Kristeva's theory of language for understanding narratives of resistance in Latin American contexts and the danger of Kristeva's theory in the same contexts. Ruiz first gives a brief history of the way in which Amerindian languages that were embodied and laden with ambiguity were colonized by being forced into European grammatical strictures like the alignment of script with spoken language. She then argues that Kristeva's theory of language participates in this colonization by assuming that language is universally representational. She attributes this flaw to her commitment to psychoanalysis which leads her to make universal claims about psychic structures (and thus language). Despite this worry, Ruiz concludes by contending that Kristeva's development of the semiotic elements of language can help us understand artistic and narrative forms of resistance in Latin American contexts, precisely because of the already colonized signifying economies that threaten to erase a range of meanings and experiences.

Amy Ray Stewart's contribution analyzes the artwork of Kara Walker through a Kristevean lens. Walker's images call forth a revolt through their ambiguity, inviting the viewer's questioning and participation. Stewart borrows Lacan's term 'extimate,' understood as the Real that cuts through both the internal and external of the psyche, to describe the affect of Walker's artistic depictions of trauma as they call forth the histories of racial and sexual violence that are external to us and yet shape us deeply. But the presentation of the trauma is not just about reliving the trauma. Instead, understood as a form of intimate revolt, Walker's images call upon viewers to return to the repressed, the individual and cultural memories that are foreclosed or ignored. This offers the possibility of sublimating these traumatic memories into new forms of questioning, thinking, and response.

In the sixth chapter, Melinda C. Hall offers a model of 'patient interpretation' for medical professionals. Noting that the experience of abjection (a revulsion, for example, that I may be made sick by this patient) is a common response of medical professionals to their patients, Hall is skeptical of attempts to care for patients in which the caregiver puts herself in the shoes of the patient. Instead, she calls for a patient interpretation that listens without imposing meanings or diagnoses that allows patients to represent their own suffering, and helps them come to terms with their altered identities in their own time. In other words, patient interpretation opens up a space and time for the patient's intimate revolt. This model differs not only from the diagnostic paradigm, but also from other forms of narrative medicine, namely 'narrative phronesis,' because these medical paradigms impose narratives from the outside rather than allowing patients to develop their own self-understandings. Hall concludes by suggesting that this ethics of interaction between care-givers and patients may also become a new politics, one in which we patiently allow others to be in progress – rather than tokens of 'prefabricated images and stereotypes' – and one in which we acknowledge but refuse to be overcome by our revulsion at others' differences, illnesses, and disabilities.

In short, *New Forms of Revolt* offers multiple readings of Kristeva, each of which shows the promise of her writings while at the same time – indeed, in a Kristevean way – creating something new.

Josh Dohmen
University of West Georgia, Carrollton, GA 30118, USA
jdohmen@westga.edu

Review

Wayward lives, beautiful experiments: Intimate histories of social upheaval

Saidiya Hartman
W.W. Norton & Company, New York, 2019, xxi+441pp., ISBN: 978-0393285673

Contemporary Political Theory (2021) **20**, S176–S179. https://doi.org/10.1057/s41296-020-00411-7; published online 18 June 2020

What kinds of lives emerge in the afterlife of slavery? What is a free life? In *Wayward Lives, Beautiful Experiments,* Saidiya Hartman narrates a story of social transformation, exploring the ways young black women in the early twentieth century refused the second-class existence assigned to them. She examines alternative forms of intimacy and kinship that rejected the socially imposed standards of respectability. Hartman's work offers a powerful counter-narrative in which freedom materializes through the enactment of longing and desire in the intimate lives of these women. The protagonists move through New York City and Philadelphia, their blackness usually understood as pathological, criminal, and often subject to surveillance. Hartman, by contrast, contemplates the radical possibilities they embody. New modes of freedom find space in the wayward lives and beautiful experiments of these young black women.

Hartman's book uncovers revolutionary potential in the everyday practices that animated the lives of these women. They consistently found new ways to live, new ways to be alive, in the face of economic exclusion, material deprivation, racial enclosure, and social dispossession thrust upon black intimate life. These conditions constituted a pervasive climate of anti-blackness. And yet, in finding new ways to live against, under, and despite these modes of control, Hartman's young black female visionaries enacted their freedom as a rejoinder to anti-blackness. Some of these women lack names – Girl #1 'wanders through the streets of Philadelphia's Seventh Ward and New York's Tenderloin', and 'the Chorus' refers to 'all the unnamed women of the city trying to find a way to live and in search of beauty' (p. xvii). Other characters have names – such as Ida B. Wells, Gladys Bentley, and Jackie Mabley – and even occupy space in the official historical accounts of the period. By weaving together this cast of characters, Hartman is able to produce a narrative of rebellious practices that took shape in ghetto streets, rented rooms, and dance halls.

Review

The twenty chapters that comprise *Wayward Lives, Beautiful Experiments* are divided into three books. Book One, 'She Makes an Errant Path through the City', inaugurates the radical possibility of the ghetto, found in forms of experimentation in which young black women engaged with one another, with intimate arrangements, and with the limits of the law. The chapters in this section construct a powerful juxtaposition to W.E.B. DuBois's sociological study of 'the Negro Problem' in the seventh ward of Philadelphia. While DuBois documents deviance in black social life, Hartman celebrates the radically different forms of kinship and intimacy in the ghetto (DuBois, 2007). In Book Two, 'The Sexual Geography of the Black Belt', Hartman picks up the threads of various characters to follow the map of their desires. The result is a layered account of the choreography of black existence, where alternative intimate arrangements are constantly sidestepping and dipping out of view of the law. Book Three, 'Beautiful Experiments', begins with a discussion of wayward minor laws, legislation that aimed to curb social disorder and that ultimately marked blackness as disorderly and criminal (p. 225). This section explores the strategies that young black women undertook to cultivate and embody different kinds of freedom in the very spaces they were barred from entering as a result of such laws. Their refusal to submit to the countless forms of control imposed upon them opened new possibilities and alternative ways to live.

Hartman's text takes shape as she performs her own form of experimentation – with method, with content, and with the very rhythms and movements found in the lives of her subjects. The book begins with a note on method, which sets the tone for the work as a whole. 'The wild idea that animates this book', Hartman writes, 'is that young black women were radical thinkers who tirelessly imagined other ways to live and never failed to consider how the world might be otherwise' (p. xv). To capture the world through the eyes of her protagonists, Hartman makes use of a range of archival materials with which she engages in a mode of close narration. Reading the archival traces they have left against the grain of dominant narratives, Hartman uses the women's own voices as a window into their most intimate, quotidian, and restless moments. Because the archive is an extension of the power relations that dominate the existence of her protagonists, Hartman's method demands creative and fugitive reading practices to help recreate the lived experiences of these women. By attending to the performance of power within the archive, Hartman crafts alternative narratives and enables her readers to hear missing voices – an approach that has tremendous promise for political theorists.

Political theory is no stranger to creative reading practices that seek to unearth new modes of understanding, but these practices stop short of Hartman's approach. More than just a close reading of archival material, Hartman's narration allows the past to blossom from the pieces of her protagonists' lives recorded in the archive. From these hints – accidental pictures, mug shots, critical comments – Hartman builds a view otherwise unseen. What the dominant lens renders criminal instead emerges as a practice of freedom. Hartman's critical perspective on the archive's records as well as its gaps and silences is able to not only recreate the practices that lay hidden for so long but also transport the reader into the sensory experience of that world. This approach dares to think differently about archives and dares scholars to think differently about what it means to theorize and how to do so in creative ways. Hartman's approach grows out of attention to what is missing from the archive. In theorizing from this space, she articulates presence in empty spaces. Hartman's work engages omissions, traces patterns, and considers the structures that engender absences. Her innovative methods of narration and fabulation expand the toolbox of approaches to political thought. For political theorists, this is an invitation and, simultaneously, a challenge, to alter how one thinks and knows.

Beyond its innovative method and its challenging invitation, Hartman's book is also a rich resource through which to theorize the contours of black life in the early twentieth century. One such mode of theorizing is *refusal*. '[H]ungry for images that represented the experiments in freedom that unfolded within slavery's shadow', Hartman searches for photographs of beauty and possibility in the ordinary lives of black girls (p. 17). Hartman herself refuses other prominent representations of black life, such as family albums of black elites. These refusals propel Hartman to photographs taken by social reformers, municipal archives, and documentary surveys of the slum. Missing from all these records are the young black women at the center of her narrative. But Hartman interprets their failure to appear not as absence, but as a 'refusal of the terms of visibility imposed on them' (p. 18). Such a refusal of external standards constitutes what Fred Moten names 'fugitivity', which, for him, is central to understanding blackness (Moten, 2018). Indeed, when contemplating pictures of her protagonists, Hartman reads their slumped shoulders and radiant anger as 'fugitive gestures of refusal' (p. 19). These multiple forms of refusal facilitate Hartman's considerations of alternative ways of living and simultaneously demonstrate the way refusal captures blackness in its aesthetic, experiential, and material dimensions.

Wayward Lives, Beautiful Experiments offers a wealth of resources for theorizing, from its method to its content and its creative modes of thinking. Hartman challenges her readers to keep up and to think beyond the text, as she herself does throughout the work. The final chapter, 'The Chorus Opens the Way', returns to the 'Chorus' of all the wayward girls whose lives are chronicled in the book in an effort to highlight the ordinary character of the women Hartman has followed and assembled. It is easy for them to get lost in the crowd, enveloped by the other voices around them. Hartman's remarkable feat is to have found these women, to have made them visible, and to have narrated the significance of their practices of freedom and refusal. In Greek tragedy, the chorus mediates and directs the audience's reaction to the events on stage. Hartman's chorus does not mediate action, but facilitates it. This book dares to experiment, taking risks alongside its audacious subjects. And in doing so, Hartman invites her readers to experiment themselves, to think creatively and imaginatively about freedom, blackness, and refusal.

References

DuBois, W.E.B. (2007) *The Philadelphia Negro: A Social Study*. Oxford: Oxford University Press.
Moten, F. (2018) *Stolen Life (consent not to be a single being)*. Durham, NC: Duke University Press.

Publisher's Note Springer Nature remains neutral with regard to jurisdictional claims in published maps and institutional affiliations.

Danielle Hanley
Rutgers University, New Brunswick, NJ 08901, USA
danielle.hanley@rutgers.edu

Review

Agonistic mourning: Political dissidence and the Women in Black

Athena Athanasiou
Edinburgh University Press, Edinburgh, 2017. Xii + 348 pp. ISBN 9781474420150

Contemporary Political Theory (2019) **18,** S8–S11. https://doi.org/10.1057/s41296-017-0181-4; published online 5 December 2017

In *Agonistic Mourning*, Athena Athanasiou embeds an ethnography of the Belgrade Women in Black (*Žene u Crnom*) in a dense framework of social and political theory, not only to understand the work undertaken by the collective, but also to think about how that work can help pose broader questions regarding sovereignty, memorialization, and the possibilities of dissidence. Founded in 1991, at the beginning of the wars of succession in the former Yugoslavia, Women in Black is an antimilitarist, antinationalist, feminist group, whose distinctive mode of protest, shared with other Women in Black groups, involves silent public vigils, the participants clad in black. For seven years, Athanasiou did field work with the group, spending extended time in Belgrade, participating in street actions, gatherings, and workshops; conducting extensive interviews with both long-term members who remember the wars, and younger ones who don't; and learning from, and reflecting upon, their history and their ways of framing their praxis. This book draws from those observations and reflections to unsettle and broaden some central threads of contemporary political theory: questions of sovereign power, the modern biopolitical state, mourning and justice, and perhaps most importantly, the question of an agonistic politics.

Drawing on theorists of the political as agon from Arendt to Mouffe and Honig, Athanasiou posits that the collective practice of Women in Black constitutes an agonistic approach to the political. Rereading theorists of agonism through the group's positioning in wartime and postwar Belgrade, however, has the effect of complicating the concept. Standing in silence, engaged in what one interview subject calls 'a cruel mourning…a mourning without sentimentality' (p. 89), and what Athanasiou, after Derrida, terms 'impossible mourning,' the vigils of the Women in Black challenge what it can mean to appear in public space, to engage in the life of the polis. In her introduction, Athanasiou explains that 'I was interested in the ways in which their account of political organization and self-determination did not seem to presuppose but rather decenter the regulatory identifications and representational politics that typically sustain conceptions of political agency' (p. 21). The 'trademarks' of Women in Black's political practice, she argues, make legible this decentering: 'responsiveness, cross-border acts of grief, and becoming the enemy in the face of national mobilization' (p. 21). The stance of impossible mourning disrupts the nationalist narrative of war, by endlessly invoking without appropriating the unacknowledged and excluded others. The silence of the participants of Women in Black actions performatively underscores the limits of what can be said and heard in the public sphere, while rendering the silence articulate as such. As an avowedly feminist group that retains the word 'Women' in its name while including men, the collective insistently interrogates the militarized biopolitical state, the heteronormative gender frames of which sustain themselves in part through the mobilization of the figure of 'woman.' Refusing militarization during the war and the logic of the state grounded in ethnic distinction thereafter has frequently marked the members of the collective as traitors.

The book is divided into four chapters with an introduction and an epilogue. In the first chapter, 'Mourning Otherwise,' the author helpfully frames the political contexts of the dissolution of Yugoslavia and the emergence of Women in Black, noting the broad range of feminist organizations that preceded and continued alongside it. As her informants explain the painful quandaries of identification in the postwar context, indexing losses that are political, social, and intimate, Athanasiou outlines the themes of grievability, mourning, and testimony that will be tracked throughout her analyses. Two reigning forms of memory and memorialization characterize the postwar condition: on the one hand, a 'state-centered neoliberal governmentality of managing and normalizing the past…and the legal and traumatic realism of reconciliation' (p. 37). The Women in Black performatively enact their 'mourning otherwise' through a negotiation of and resistance to these poles: 'their enduring collective bodily presence evinces agonistic longing for a different way to inhabit and enact the political' (p. 37). That longing is bound to their practice of public mourning, a form of counter-memory that refuses allegiance to state memorialization and the logics of reconciliation alike. Athanasiou sees in the Women in Black's performance of public mourning a Derridean melancholia, keeping the other without appropriating her, keeping her an inappropriated other. The black-clad figures standing silently in the square simultaneously invoke and deconstruct the time-honored figure of the mourning mother/sister/wife and express a lack of gendered dutifulness, a disobedience to the claims of state and market. The second chapter, 'The Gendered Intimacies of the Nationalist Archive,' carries these themes forward to theorize in more depth the counter-memorializing work of the Women in Black; their form of inconsolable mourning 'works to delegitimize the monological bereavement mandated by the epistemic violence of national archiving' (p. 93). That bereavement functions to constitute a national ethno-subject, arisen from the demise of Yugoslavia; the silent mourning vigils of the Women in Black unsettle that subject, raising the specters of the losses deemed ungrievable by the official archive. It is in the third chapter, 'Spectral Spaces of Counter-Memory,' that Athanasiou unfolds the concept of agonistic mourning, drawing from her reading of Arendt, together with Derrida, to think about what it might mean to understand the activist practices of Women in Black as a form of participation in a public sphere of contention and debate that will not have them, to mark out what haunts the official public sphere, to 'carve an expansive cartography of critical memory in the polis' (p. 173), here postwar Belgrade. Standing exposed in Republic Square, the Women in Black, as Athanasiou's informants tell her, have experienced invisibility or harassment by passers-by and police. The Republic Square, a space laden with historical and political memory, is a particularly powerful location for 'unsettling…the politics of memory' (p. 173). Here, Athanasiou suggestively draws upon the ancient concept of 'stasis,' as it has been discussed by the classicist Nicole Loraux and elaborated by other theorists, to illuminate the signal characteristic of Women in Black actions, as a bodily disposition in space that is also a struggle. In Chapter 4, 'Political Languages of Responsiveness,' this question of the bodily and the vocal receives a more detailed analysis; the chapter culminates the multiple threads of the book by attending to the performative dimension of Women in Black's practice, arguing that through their silent standing, Women in Black activism 'yields an account of the political subject's social becoming and unbecoming as a performative event of responsiveness to others within a specific constellation of power' (p. 226).

This is a powerful book in many ways: Athanasiou has accomplished something that is not to be underestimated in bringing a substantial archive of political, social, and anthropological theory to bear on her ethnography of Women in Black. The risk of this kind of work is that the theory will, however ironically in this case, outweigh the voices of the informants, which are compelling and often profound in the author's presentation; at times, it can seem here that this risk has not been averted entirely. Some passages and sentences call out for the disciplining hand of an editor. However, the net effect is that, rather than being overwhelmed by Athanasiou's theoretical archive, the voices and practices of the Women in Black of Belgrade recalibrate and vivify it, causing us to reflect on the theory in new ways, and teaching us a great deal about this particular activist network. The book raises questions of nation, state, gender, and the aftermath of disaster in ways that resonate with other geopolitical locations, and especially with this moment of rising ethno-nationalisms. It offers rich resources for reflection on the ways in which the boundaries between the affective and the political are regulated – and the ways in which particular modalities of dissent might challenge and disrupt that regulation. Perhaps most vitally, the work opens up important questions regarding the possibilities and limits of agonistic politics in the modern biopolitical state. The epilogue poses this haunting question that underwrites Athanasiou's reading of Women in Black: How can those who have been 'let die' – as Foucault memorably put it – or who have been erased from public memory or rendered as less than human be made to appear? Or, to borrow from Rancière, how under these conditions can 'the part of no part' speak?

Sara Murphy
New York University, New York, NY 10003, USA
sara.murphy@nyu.edu

Article

The politics and gender of truth-telling in Foucault's lectures on *parrhesia*

Lida Maxwell
Department of Political Science, Trinity College, Hartford, CT 06106, USA.
E-mail: lida.maxwell@trincoll.edu

Abstract This essay challenges dominant interpretations of Foucault's lectures on *parrhesia* as affirming an ethical, non-political conception of truth-telling. I read the lectures instead as depicting truth-telling as an always political predicament: of having to appear distant from power (to achieve credibility), while also having to partake in some sense of political power (to render one's truth significant). Read in this way, Foucault's lectures help us to understand and address the disputed politicality of truth-telling – over who counts as a truth-teller, and what counts as the truth – that his ethical interpreters tend to neglect. Yet the essay also shows that Foucault's depiction of the predicament of truth-tellers is problematically gendered: focused on the masculine problem of moving in and out of the public sphere, rather than on the experience of the dispossessed, who are excluded from political power altogether. The essay mobilizes an alternative reading of one of Foucault's key texts – Euripides' *Ion* – to draw out an alternative, more democratic model of the predicament of truth-telling: of having to *constitute* power that can lend significant to truth-telling, while speaking from a position of powerlessness.
Contemporary Political Theory (2019) **18**, 22–42. https://doi.org/10.1057/s41296-018-0224-5; published online 27 April 2018

Keywords: Foucault; *parrhesia*; ethics; truth and politics; feminist theory; Euripides; *Ion*

I just think there's this…certain assumption that…when a man tells the truth, it's the truth. And when, as a woman, I go to tell the truth, I feel like I have to negotiate the way I'll be perceived. Like I feel like there's always the suspicion around a woman's truth, the idea that you're exaggerating…There's this whole fear that I'm gonna have finally fucking have stepped to the plate and told the truth and someone's going to say…Uh, I don't think so.

– Kathleen Hanna, in The Punk Singer.

I think it truly was a misunderstanding…I really don't think that there was any intent on your part to get this girl home so you could have sex with her whether she wanted to or not…You are kind of an open book right now…and you have been since I talked to you on [the phone four days earlier]…It says a lot for your character that you came in and sat and talked to me this morning…I really don't believe you had any intent to hurt anybody.

– A female police officer talking to a man accused of sexual assault, quoted in Jon Krakauer's Missoula.

© 2018 Macmillan Publishers Ltd., part of Springer Nature. 1470-8914 *Contemporary Political Theory* Vol. 18, 1, 22–42
www.palgrave.com/journals

111   Reprinted from the journal

While many pundits have proclaimed that the 2016 election marked the beginning of a "post-truth" era, the disputes over truthfulness, gender, race, and power in that election (and after) may also be symptomatic of a broader, longstanding political problem: the problem of a hierarchy of truth in which some people (usually white, heterosexual, cisgender men) are assumed to be truthful and others (usually women, people of color, and queer/non-gender-conforming individuals) are not. We can see this in the reluctance of many (especially prosecutors, police, judges, and juries) to believe women who claim they have been raped or sexually assaulted (cf. Krakauer, 2015; Corrigan, 2013; Hengehold, 1994). We can see it in the widespread public refusal to believe that photographic/video evidence of police killing people of color shows racially biased murder (cf. Dyson, 2016; LeBron, 2016). We can see it in the dismissive treatment of Chelsea Manning, who leaked government documents to air the truth about American operations in Iraq and Afghanistan (Maxwell, 2015). Every day, many white men are taken as real truth-tellers, and members of marginalized groups are portrayed as unreliable speakers, or as outright liars – especially when making claims that challenge the dominance of straight white men.[1]

In this political moment, many political theorists have nonetheless embraced a non-political (ethical) theory of truth-telling that they find in Michel Foucault's late lectures on *parrhesia*.[2] In those lectures – and, in particular, in his examination of Greco-Roman philosophical *parrhesia* – Foucault identifies an ethical art of the self that may, on his contemporary interpreters' accounts, release the individual from the subjection characteristic of disciplinary and bio-power. Contemporary readers argue that parrhesiastic practices of self "desubjectification" (in Dianna Taylor's words [2013, p. 89]) and/or "political subjectivation that overcomes...subjection by fully translating the truth into life itself" (as Sergei Prozorov puts it [2015, p. 7]) may allow individuals to remake themselves; moving from the heteronomy characteristic of disciplinary and bio-power to autonomous practices of self-governance (cf. Luxon, 2004, 2008, 2013; Peters, 2003; Owen and Woodford, 2012; Kim, 2015; Tamboukou, 2012; Sauter and Kendall, 2011).[3]

The idea that truth-telling is an ethical (non-political) practice of freedom that can release us from the hold of power is deeply attractive – especially, as Ella Myers (2013) has argued, in a political moment characterized by a sense of disempowerment and apathy (cf. Berlant, 2011; Cvetkovich, 2012). Yet these ethical approaches to truth-telling, so focused on individual practices of undoing and remaking the self, also stand curiously apart from political contestation over truth, and apart from the political hierarchies that structure who counts as a proper truth-teller. In other words, ethical approaches to truth-telling fail to address what I call the *disputed politicality* of truth-telling. By "disputed politicality" I mean (1) the fact that truth is disputed, contested, and sometimes dismissed in public; and (2) that the question of who is authorized to tell the truth, who *counts* as a truth-teller, is itself a site of political dispute.

In this article, I argue for a different interpretation of Foucault's lectures on *parrhesia*. Rather than offering an ethical conception of truth-telling that can reclaim the self from power, I suggest that the lectures portray truth-telling as an always politically constituted, problematized role that Foucault thematizes in terms of two distinct forms: political *parrhesia* and philosophical *parrhesia*. While political *parrhesia* in Periclean Athenian democracy is obviously political – used to achieve ascendance in the Assembly – I will suggest that the role of the philosophical *parrhesiastes* is also political insofar as it is enabled and sustained by its enmeshment in the politics of autocracy. Taken together, I argue that Foucault's theorizations of these two forms of *parrhesia*, along with his depiction of the "founding representation" of *parrhesia* in Euripides' *Ion*, depict truth-telling not as an ethical path to autonomy, but rather as a particular kind of political predicament: one that demands that the truth-teller both appear distant from political power (so as to appear credible) while also using or partaking of it (so as to have one's truth heard as significant). Read in this way, Foucault's lectures on *parrhesia* suggest that to affirm truth-telling as non-political simply obscures the inevitable imbrication of truth-telling in political contestation, political power, and hierarchy. Foucault's lectures thus draw our attention to what his readers seem to ignore: the disputed politicality of truth-telling.[4]

Yet Foucault's framing of this predicament, I will suggest, is also problematically gendered, offering an image of the truth-teller as one who *can* negotiate the tension between power and powerlessness, public and private, in his role. My claim in this article is that this image, in the end, is a fantasy that favors those who appear to have the freedom to move in and out of politics as they please – usually white, cisgender, affluent, heterosexual men – and that is sustained by the (sometimes violent) silencing or delegitimizing of those who reveal the imbrications of truth-telling and hierarchy. I make this claim through a critical examination of Foucault's reading of Euripides' *Ion*, with a special focus on Foucault's reading of Ion's mother, Creusa, whose truth-telling about her rape by Apollo is crucial to Ion's recognition as a legitimate *parrhesiastes*, even as she is ultimately silenced.

Foucault's gendered reading of truth-telling is problematic not only because it leads him to offer a typically masculine understanding of truth-telling. It is also a problem because it leads him to miss an alternative way to understand the predicament of truth-telling, which I find in the figure of Creusa in the *Ion*. As someone shut out of public discourse, Creusa's truth-telling is not caught in the problem of having to *use* power while retaining a distance from power, but rather in how to *constitute* power out of a position of powerlessness. I argue that this is what her truth-telling does, or seeks to do: namely, through engaging and helping to create a community of responsive listeners. In turn, I see this understanding of the truth-teller's predicament as equally, if not more, useful than the one Foucault offers in understanding and addressing the raced and gendered hierarchies of truth in contemporary politics.

In what follows, I first offer my distinctive reading of Foucault's lectures as revealing truth-telling as a political predicament. Then, I examine Foucault's reading of the *Ion* and argue that his gendered understanding of truth-telling hides an alternative model of its politicality from view: one in which truth-telling becomes a way of challenging hierarchy rather than negotiating one's role within it.

Parrhesia as Political Predicament in Foucault's Late Lectures

In his wide-ranging, late lectures on the Greco-Roman conception of *parrhesia* – frank or free speech – Foucault examines the problem of truth-telling from a new angle. Rather than trying to articulate criteria by which we might assess the truth of statements (what he calls the "analytics of truth"), Foucault asks why and how some come to be accepted as truth-tellers, while others are not. Foucault calls this a "critical" approach to truth-telling: an approach concerned with "truth-telling as an activity – who is able to tell the truth, about what, with what consequences, and with what relation to power" (2001, p. 170). Put differently, Foucault is not interested in asking whether a statement is true – even if that may also be an important question – but rather, "Who is able to tell the truth? What are the moral, the ethical, and the spiritual conditions which entitle someone to present himself as, and to be considered as, a truth-teller?" (p. 169) Foucault is also interested in how and why *parrhesia* becomes a problem in different social and political contexts – what he calls the "problematization" of *parrhesia*. For Foucault, if we just focus on how we know something is true (or not), we lose sight of the critical question of how and why some people and forms of truth-telling count, why those forms become a problem, and why they gain significance.

Yet if Foucault aims to reveal the political and social conditions that determine who counts as a truth-teller, most readers of Foucault's late lectures focus on, and find emancipatory promise in, one particular model of *parrhesia* that he discusses: philosophical *parrhesia*. Foucault argues that philosophical *parrhesia* presents itself as non-political: Socrates (its first practitioner) established "the foundation of *parrhesia* in the field of ethics, as opposed to political *parrhesia*, or in a founding separation from political *parrhesia*" (2012, p, 73; my emphasis,). In contrast to *parrhesia* as it was practiced in democratic Athenian politics (what Foucault calls "political *parrhesia*") – where it was vulnerable to the problem of flattery – Socrates enacts "a particular practice of truth-telling" that "is the implementation of a particular mode of veridiction *which is completely different from those which may take place on the political stage*" (p. 81; my emphasis). It is different because it focuses on individual self-care rather than the good of the demos (even if that self-care is a condition of pursuing the good of the demos) (p. 86) and because, in turn, the practices of Socratic *parrhesia* differ in kind from the practices of political *parrhesia*: they are dyadic rather than consisting in agonistic contest in front of a public (p. 149).

For Luxon, Prozorov, and Taylor (among others), philosophical *parrhesia* appears – in a world permeated by disciplinary and bio-power – as a way to condition individuals into autonomy.[5] Luxon argues, for example, that the educative practices she finds in Foucault's lectures hold out the possibility of releasing us from our continued subjection to disciplinary power by allowing us "to distinguish analytically those relations that *produce* individuals (to fit into a specific mold) from those that *educate* individuals for autonomy (such that they are the result of their own design)" (2004, pp. 464-465). For her, parrhesiastic practices initiate individuals into autonomous experiences of authorizing and being authorized that, in releasing them from the hold of authoritative (disciplinary) discourse and norms, then open onto capacities to initiate social and political change that otherwise appear out of reach. For Luxon, Foucault's *parrhesiastes* are "educators" who "teach a set of practices by which individuals can assess the claims of authoritative others who offer models for ethical living" (2004, pp. 464-465). Similarly, David Owen and Clare Woodford argue that using *parrhesia* may allow the individual to engage in a free act of self-creation or, where they may "become…(create…and discover…) what one is" (2012, p. 303). For these readers, in other words, *parrhesia* offers a way to claim the self from the disciplinary "lines of penetration" (Foucault, 1995, p. 42) that have extended into, and shaped, individual subjects – even if the practice of *parrhesia* is one of undoing and re-forming the self that is never fully finished.

These readings of Foucault's lectures display a nuanced and compelling reading of philosophical *parrhesiastes*' self-understanding. Yet they also exhibit blindness to the moments in Foucault's lectures when he reveals the politicality of philosophical *parrhesia*. While Foucault's lectures certainly show that philosophical *parrhesia* promises to rescue the individual from democracy, he also shows that it does not do so by being outside of politics altogether. Rather, Foucault portrays philosophical *parrhesia* as historically dependent on and enmeshed in another kind of politics: autocracy. Indeed, Foucault suggests that several characteristics of philosophical *parrhesia* – that it prizes the truth of the self over democratic governance, the freedom of discussion between friends over political freedom, and individual happiness over political participation – are shaped by and help to sustain autocratic governance. For example, through allowing citizens to speak freely to each other, despite differences in individual power and status, *parrhesia* helps to create an autocratic unity founded in friendship:

> *Parresia* is the most manifest form of an entire process which, according to Plato, guarantees the good functioning of the empire, namely that the hierarchical differences that may exist between the sovereign and the others,

between his entourage and the rest of the citizens, between officers and soldiers, and between victors and vanquished, are in a way attenuated or compensated for by the formation of relationships which are designated throughout the text as relationships of friendship (2011, p. 203).

Parrhesiastic non-political friendship in turn creates freedom of speech: through the uniting function of *philia*, "the entire empire will be able to function and work according to the principles of '*eleutheria*' (a freedom), not in the constitutional form of shared political rights, but in the form of freedom of speech" (204). The freedom of speech and non-political friendships created by philosophical *parrhesia* within autocracy offer solace to politically powerless subjects – that is, the solace that political powerlessness is a virtue insofar as it allows subjects to pursue the truth of themselves (pp. 204–205). To put the point differently, philosophical *parrhesia* helps to sustain autocracy by casting politics as fundamentally inhospitable to that which makes life worth living: truth. The autocrat does the dirty work of politics so that we might enjoy the pursuit of truth and happiness. It is within what I would call this "autocratic imaginary" that the work of self on self gains meaning and import.

Thus, while Foucault's readers take philosophical *parrhesia* as a model of ethical praxis that can be imitated on behalf of emancipation – and while Foucault himself sometimes seems to affirm philosophical *parrhesia* as a valuable form of "self-mastery" or "self-sovereignty" (2001, pp. 164, 162) – Foucault's account also stresses that it is shaped, enabled, and practiced through its historical enmeshment in and desire for autocratic politics. Even when philosophers risk their lives to tell the truth to kings – as when Plato tells the truth to Dionysus – their attempts to *aid* the ruler with the truth helps to sustain rather than challenge the political hierarchy that structures their speech.

Read in this way, philosophical *parrhesia* appears continuous with, while also distinct from, "political *parrhesia*," the form of *parrhesia* practiced in Periclean Athens. Philosophical *parrhesia* is distinct from political *parrhesia* in its form. Whereas philosophical *parrhesia* occurs in private or semi-private, solitary or dyadic practices, political *parrhesia* consists in an agonistic form of speech in public, between citizens, which is also a way of gaining political ascendance: the political *parrhesiastes* "maneuvers around in the city," "in this agonistic field," "in order to occupy the front rank, in this perpetual joust with his equals, in this process in which the pre-eminence of the first citizens is asserted within an agonistic field" (*GSO*, p. 157). Yet in both cases, the *parrhesiastes* gains his credibility through performing a *distance* from the political power that also shapes and enables his speech, and which his speech helps to sustain in turn. The philosophical *parrhesiastes* gains credibility through the practice of philosophy (which makes them appear removed from power), but this practice is enabled by and serves autocracy. The political *parrhesiastes* attains his credibility by virtue of lineage and birth (*GSO*, p. 162), which makes him appear impervious to political opinion, but his *parrhesia* is enabled by the democratic polis and allows him to attain ascendancy in that polis. In both philosophical and political *parrhesia*, the *parrhesiastes* thus appears as someone who is able to negotiate – rather than stand outside – the power he helps to sustain, and which enables him to count as a credible truth-teller.

Foucault offers an ideal type of this figure in his discussion of Euripides' *Ion* ("the decisive Greek parrhesiastic play" [2001, p. 38]): the figure of Ion, who can successfully partake of power *and* be distant from it. The *Ion*, Foucault says, offers a "founding representation of truth-telling" (2011, p. 106), prior to the problematization of that concept,[6] that tells the story of the "shift of the place of truth's disclosure from Delphi to Athens" – that is, the founding of the human ability to tell the truth on their own, without the help of the gods (p. 37). Raised in Apollo's temple as a slave, Ion's discovery of the truth of his birth (as a child of an Athenian mother, Creusa, who was raped by Apollo) is a parable of the origin of parrhesiastic autonomy because that truth gives him the right to *parrhesia* – a right which, in the time Euripides was writing, depended on Athenian blood descent via both the mother and father (cf. Kasimis, 2013; Lape, 2008). According to Foucault, Ion is "by nature, a parrhesiastic individual" (2001, p. 51): an "individual who is so valuable to democracy or monarchy since he is courageous enough to explain either to the *demos* or to the king just what the shortcomings of their life really are" (2001, p. 51).[7] Ion is a parrhesiastic individual, in other words, because he possesses the courageous ability to objectively analyze and speak about the shortcomings of the demos (from outside the political fray), gained from his upbringing outside the realm of power – a courageous ability he is able to put into practice within the realm of political power once he learns the secret of his birth.

By calling Ion's story a "founding representation" of truth-telling, Foucault means neither that the play is the origin of the discourse surrounding *parrhesia* in Athens, nor that Ion offers an actually achievable ideal of *parrhesia*. Rather, Foucault instead seems to be claiming that the *Ion* crystallizes an ideal understanding of truth-telling already articulated in some sense in discourse. This myth or ideal of the *parrhesiastes* is of an ideal truth-teller who is politically powerful, but also has the courageous, truthful speech of one whose natural truthfulness has not (yet) been corrupted by power (since Ion was raised as a slave of Apollo's temple). This is the myth or ideal of a *parrhesiastes* that would, in other words, come to be problematized later, in the forms of political *parrhesia* and philosophical *parrhesia*. Foucault thus draws out the image of the ideal *parrhesiastes* in the *Ion* not so as to suggest it is an actually attainable practice, but to depict the image that is being worked through in practical terms in both political and philosophical *parrhesia* – the ideal against and through which actual truth-tellers in some sense come to measure their own truth-telling, and through which they are judged and seen by others.

Taken together, Foucault's thematizations of political and philosophical *parrhesia*, and his discussion of the "founding representation" of truth-telling, point to a common predicament of the truth-teller: that truth-tellers must appear distant from and uncorrupted by the influence of power, even as they must use power in some sense to make their truth significant. Foucault's analysis of this predicament alerts us to the ways in which truth-telling is always enabled by some kind of hierarchy, even if truth-tellers must negotiate their enmeshment in that hierarchy by establishing in some sense their credibility distinct from it: the political *parrhesiastes'* aristocratic lineage, for example; or philosophical *parrhesiastes'* proclaimed position outside of politics; or Ion's secret Athenian lineage. There is a politics, in other words, to why some truth-tellers who claim to be outside of politics are recognized as proper truth-tellers, and why others are not; why some who tell the truth on the political stage are seen as credible, and others are not.

Yet if Foucault's lectures usefully illuminate the disputed politicality of truth-telling, Foucault's depiction of the truth-teller's predicament is also problematically gendered and insufficiently attentive to the violences which may enable it. I will develop this claim in the next section by showing, through discussion of feminist scholarship on the *Ion*, that the depiction of the ideal truth-teller in the *Ion* that Foucault draws out is made possible through the silencing of Ion's mother, Creusa, who tries to tell the truth about her rape by Apollo.

The Ideal Truth-Teller: Euripides' Ion

Euripides' *Ion* tells a recognition story that holds the fate of democratic Athens, and the *parrhesia* practiced there, in the balance. In the play, Creusa, the only known living Athenian, must recognize her son (Ion) who was the product of her rape by Apollo and whom she abandoned at birth. Only with this recognition will the lineage of Athenian blood, descended from Erechtheus (the son of the autochthonous Erechthonius, born of the earth (*gegein*)), continue and only then will democratic Athens exist.

The plot unfolds in the context of a visit to the oracle at Delphi by Creusa and her foreign-born husband, Xuthus (who came to the aid of Athens in war, and was given Creusa as his bride as a reward). They come to ask if they will have children, but Creusa has another objective. Raped by Apollo as a girl, and having exposed the child born of the rape in the cave where it happened, she has come to ask Apollo's oracle – the Pythia – what has happened to the child. As it turns out (and as Hermes tells the audience at the outset of the play), Apollo contrived to have the Pythia bring the child to Delphi, where he has been raised in the temple. So, Creusa's son – who will be named Ion during the course of the play – is right there in front of her, but neither of them knows it. Yet the process of discovering the truth is complicated. The Pythia first tells Xuthus that the person he will see upon exiting the temple will be his son – a person who turns out to be Ion. The potential problems arising from Xuthus bringing Ion back to Athens as his illegitimate son (conceived who knows when or where) are numerous, and lead Creusa to try to poison Ion, who then tries to kill her in return. Ultimately, however, the Pythia (spurred, she says, by Apollo) intervenes by bringing out the basket that she found Ion in as a baby, along with the things that were in it. Of course, Creusa recognizes it, and she tells Ion the truth (although she does not tell him that she was raped). While Ion does not fully believe Creusa that Apollo is his father, her story is confirmed by Athena, who then tells all of them that they must keep it a secret, and live as if Ion is Xuthus' son.

While Foucault depicts the "founding representation" of truth-telling in the *Ion* as an unproblematized ideal, feminist readers of the *Ion*, such as Nicole Loraux (1994), Arlene Saxonhouse (1986), and Nancy Sorkin Rabinowitz (1993) have pointed out that Ion's accession to parrhesiastic autonomy *does* become a problem in the play insofar as it is an illusion that gains plausibility and legitimacy only through Creusa's silence at the end of the play about her rape. At the end of the play, it is Creusa's puzzling agreement with Athena's claim that Apollo has "managed all things well" that allows for her happy reunion with Ion and his triumphant march back to Athens. As Rabinowitz says, it is the "eras[ure]" of "the violence done to Kreousa [that] makes possible the happy resolution to the *Ion*" (1993, p. 191; cf. Lape, 2008). Similarly, Saxonhouse says that the *Ion* is a story about "the exclusion of women from the foundation of cities" and "forces us to see the violence at the beginnings of cities" (1986, p. 259). These scholars thus suggest that the ending which in some sense appears happy, and which Foucault reads as happy – in which, Foucault says, Ion's new knowledge of the truth of his birth "establishes the order in which the speech which commands can become a speech of truth and justice, a free speech, a *parresia*" (2011, p. 145) – is actually tragic, producing a fantasy of self-possession through Creusa's self-silencing about the injustice at the heart of Ion's birth.[8]

Highlighting the violence (rape) and silencing (about the rape) necessary for Ion to achieve his status as *parrhesiastes*, these feminist readings show that the image of Ion *qua* truth-teller that we find in the *Ion* is deeply gendered: an image of a truth-teller whose public recognition *as* a truth-teller is premised on the silencing of those whose truth reveals the violence underlying that image. The properly public speaker (Ion) achieves his supposed autonomy in public because his mother keeps her truth in the private sphere. Yet as these readings also show, the play – intentionally or not – also productively highlights the conditions of his emergence as a truth-teller: that this emergence is achieved through violence, and through the silencing of a woman, Creusa.

These feminist readings – one of which, Loraux's, is contemporaneous with Foucault's lectures – challenge Foucault's focus on Ion as truth-teller, suggesting instead that it is Creusa who is the consummate truth-teller in the play. Here, it is not Ion who is the ideal *parrhesiastes* at the center of the play, but as Loraux especially emphasizes, Creusa, whose truth-telling about her rape and pregnancy hasten and enable Ion's recognition as a *parrhesiastes*. Indeed, in contrast to Ion's short speech that Foucault sees as exemplary of the ideal *parrhesiastes*, Creusa tells the truth at length three times in the play. First, she tells the truth to Ion in veiled terms at the outset of the play – telling him that her "friend" was raped and had a child by Apollo. Second, she confesses the truth of her rape and resulting child to her father's tutor (and her female slaves) and, finally, she tells the truth to Ion about his birth after the Pythia brings out the basket and embroidery that she left him with in the cave. Creusa's truth-telling makes Ion's recognition as *parrhesiastes* possible, while also highlighting the violence that underlies it.

Foucault acknowledges Creusa's crucial role in the play (2011, pp. 152–153) and even calls her a *parrhesiastes* at one point, but I will suggest in what follows that Foucault fails to attend to the problems her truth-telling reveals about Ion's status as a *parrhesiastes* because his reading participates in the silencing of Creusa. Foucault tends to portray Creusa's truth-telling as private (he calls her a "private *parrhesiastes*"), as opposed to Ion's public truth-telling. While Creusa attempts to reframe her truth as political, Foucault and the male characters in the play consistently reframe it as private speech. The cost of this, I suggest at the end, is that Foucault misses an alternative model and predicament of truth-telling.

Privatizing Creusa: Foucault and Ion

I argue in this section and the next that Foucault's reading of Creusa mimics the approach of two male characters in the play: Ion and Creusa's father's tutor. Like Ion and the tutor, Foucault portrays Creusa's truth-telling as not fit for the public sphere – a privatizing impulse that reflects, in the play, a desire to shore up hierarchy and a fear of democratic dispute over truth. First, I discuss Ion and Foucault, then the tutor and Foucault.

The exchange I want to focus on between Ion and Creusa occurs at the outset of the play. In her entrance onto the stage, Creusa encounters Ion (who she thinks is a slave of the temple) and tells him that she has come, on behalf of someone who was raped by Apollo, to ask Apollo what has happened to the child. Foreshadowing the end of the play, Creusa identifies Apollo's rape as symptomatic of how male and divine violence control the terms of justice and truth: "Unhappy women! What things the gods dare! And where/shall we turn for justice when we are being destroyed/by the unjust actions of those who are much stronger?" (Euripides 1958, pp. 248–254). In his response, Ion frames Creusa's public proclamation of injustice (done to all women) as private by implication when he tells her that her question is improper, not fit to the enter Apollo's temple: "No one will speak the truth on your behalf./Convicted of evil inside his own temple,/Apollo quite justly would take vengeance on/the one who told you. Think no more of it:/avoid a question which the god himself opposes" (pp. 369–380). Offering an aristocratic view of *parrhesia*, Ion claims that Creusa's truth-telling and demands for truth would unsettle the legitimate rule of those who are *truly* able to know the truth and, hence, to lead and do justice.

The broader context of this exchange points toward Creusa representing, in contrast, a democratic form of truth-telling. In response to Ion's question, "Will Phoebus tell the secret he wants to hide?" (Euripides 1958, p. 365), Creusa replies, "Yes, if his oracles are open to all Greeks" (p. 366). Creusa's claim is that the truth should be available to everyone, and that everyone should be able to demand its articulation. Her implicit claim is also that everyone should be able to *speak* the truth; she should be able to tell Apollo the truth and demand truth in return. Where Ion seeks to shore up the distinction between those able to tell the truth and rule, and those who cannot, Creusa – the progenitor of Athenian democracy – demands that everyone be able to demand and speak the truth.

When Ion tells his mother that she should "think no more" about confronting Apollo with his injustice, he not only silences Creusa, but also portrays the existence of justice and truth as dependent on elite governance and, by implication, on the silencing of those who dispute the elite capacity to do justice and tell the truth. Foucault reads the exchange as Ion does, as an intimate one between Apollo and Creusa that has no place in public (2011, pp. 86–89). Elsewhere in his reading of the text, Foucault similarly reads Creusa's truth-telling as primarily private in character – that is, as a form of speech that does not speak to issues of common concern, but that rather (through intimate confession) acquiesces in and aids her son's access to a public, political *parrhesia* from which she is naturally excluded (2001, p. 52). Foucault says, for example, that while Creusa's truth-telling "takes the form of a public reproach" (p. 53), her "truth-telling is what we could call an instance of *personal* (as opposed to political) *parrhesia*" (p. 56; cf. 2011, p. 86).[9] Her passionate truth-telling, Foucault suggests, reveals a lack of the self-control, intentionality, and rationality characteristic of the true *parrhesiastes*.[10] "[H]er bitterness," Foucault says, "her despair, and her anger bursts forth in an accusation made against Apollo: she decides to speak the truth. Truth thus comes to light as an emotional reaction to the god's injustice and his lies" (2001, p. 52). Creusa, Foucault says, "speaks in her anger" (2011, p. 108), and from "the depths of her passion" (p. 118).

Foucault, like Ion, sometimes portrays Creusa as a sympathetic private figure, but also downplays and almost buries Creusa's challenge to elite males' claim to know and tell the truth. Creusa's claim of injustice to Apollo reminds the reader, or audience, of the "self-possessed" man's inevitable dependence on the mother, the violence with which the origin of Athenian *parrhesia* was assured, and the exclusion of diverse classes of individuals (especially women) and their claims to injustice from the circle of free or frank speech, that is, of *parrhesia*. Foucault domesticates that challenge by positioning Creusa's truth-telling as merely private even as she challenges the public/private boundary by publicly confessing her rape and accusing Apollo of a wrong. Foucault domesticates Creusa, in other words, by trying to turn her into the good mother: the mother who accepts her public silence as natural and right, and who offers intimate confidences to her son only so as to further release them from dependence on her.

Domesticating Rape: Foucault and the Tutor

The event that haunts the *Ion*, and about which Creusa tells the truth at least three separate times in the play, is Apollo's rape of Creusa. In this section, I argue that Foucault's treatment of Creusa's rape in his reading of the *Ion* mimics Creusa's father's tutor's downplaying and privatization of Creusa's claim that Apollo raped her.

The scene where Creusa tells the full truth about her rape involves an exchange between her, the chorus (of female slaves), and her father's tutor. In that scene, Creusa describes her rape: "Grabbing my pale wrists/as I cried for my mother's help/you led me to bed in a cave,/a god and my lover, shamelessly/gratifying the Cyprian goddess's will./In misery I bore you/a son, whom in fear of my mother/I placed in that bed/where you cruelly forced me" (Euripides, 1958, pp. 891–900). While the chorus leader responds and reveals vulnerability to Creusa's story through tears – "O what a store of miseries is now/disclosed; who would not weep at hearing them?" (Euripides, 1958, pp. 923–924) – her father's tutor responds by asking for clarification. Indeed, he seems unable to understand what she said: "What do you say? What is your accusation/against Apollo? What child is this you claim/you bore? Where in the city did you put/this beloved corpse for beasts? Tell me again" (pp. 931–934). Through an exchange where the tutor consistently presses Creusa to reframe and re-state her accusation, the tutor ultimately turns around the story by the end of their dialogue – moving away from Apollo's rape of Creusa, and toward the exposure of the child, for which the tutor regards them both at fault: "Ah, you were harsh; Apollo harsher still" (p. 960). The tutor, like Ion, sympathizes with Creusa's pain and he says that Apollo committed a wrong. Yet rather than exposing himself to Creusa's anguish as a demand for justice, the tutor uses interrogation to portray Creusa's framing of her rape – *as* a rape – as incomprehensible and, in turn, to discipline Creusa's speech into a narrative that shields Apollo from public blame. The tutor, in turn, tells Creusa she should take private revenge on Apollo by murdering Ion (who she still does not know is her son), rather than seek public justice.

Similarly, throughout his lectures, Foucault pays little attention to how Creusa frames her rape, and seems to see the distinction between rape, seduction, and consensual sex as unimportant, as when he waffles about whether Creusa was "seduced" or "raped" by Apollo.[11] For example, when he tells the story of the *Ion*, he says that "[o]ne day, as a young girl, while picking yellow flowers by the Long Rocks, Apollo rapes or seduces her [Creusa]" – and says that the difference between rape and seduction is not as crucial for the Greeks as for us, since both acts are forceful (and perhaps even more so with seduction, since it forces the person to want something they should not want) (2001, pp. 38–39; cf. 2011, pp. 80, 117). While this is true, Foucault does not acknowledge that, as Loraux (1994, p. 228) and Lape (2008, p. 120) argue, Creusa and other characters in the play (such as Hermes) clearly indicate that Apollo forced her into intercourse. Perhaps most strangely, Foucault characterizes the rape at one point as an "exchange": "this is the exchange between the seducer god and the young girl who agrees to offer her body and who, she says, offers her 'pale wrists' to the god who summons her...This exchange, that of love and sexual union... is not accomplished in daylight and in the shining light and the sun, but in the darkness of the cave" (2011, pp. 128–129). Jarringly, Foucault also suggests that Creusa "benefited" from the rape: "And it is there, in this cave, in this night and darkness, that the child will be exposed, taken away, disappear, and consequently, as Creusa believes and thus not benefit from that daylight, that shining sun [Apollo] *that she had benefited from, or anyway by which she was seduced*" (p. 129; my emphasis).[12]

Foucault may identify with and mimic the tutor's approach to Creusa because he sees in the tutor's method of rational interrogation a figure similar to the Socratic "touchstone," or *basanos*, of philosophical *parrhesia*. On Foucault's account, interrogation by such a figure allows individuals to articulate the truth of themselves by rendering the truth subject to rational examination. This is precisely how Foucault reads the tutor's interrogation of Creusa: namely, as offering a productive form of interrogation that helps reveal the truth, which before was not fully visible: "the method of question and answer brings the obscure to light" (2001, p. 55). The tutor also, on Foucault's account, helps turn Creusa's truth-telling into something that sounds like philosophical *parrhesia*: "Creusa's parrhesiastic discourse is now no longer an accusation directed towards Apollo, i.e., is no longer the accusation of a woman towards her rapist; but takes the form of a self-accusation where she reveals her own faults, weaknesses, misdeeds (exposing the child), and so forth)" (p. 56). The tutor, on Foucault's account, is not someone who silences Creusa, but someone who helps her discover the truth – namely, by bringing her and her truth under the control and interpretive guidance of a father figure.

Both the tutor and Foucault thus portray Creusa's claim of rape, as she utters it, as essentially incomprehensible, and as standing in need of clarification (as a private, not public, wrong) through male guidance and interrogation. Creusa's public claim of injustice becomes in their hands an emotional reaction to a situation where, really, she bears some fault, as well. Creusa, dispossessed of her body by

Apollo, is portrayed as an unreliable speaker precisely because she is not fully in possession of herself. Distancing themselves from the vulnerability that Creusa reveals in her unguarded demand to be heard, Foucault and the tutor thus enact truth-telling as a practice of rendering insurgent claims of injustice legible in the language of the oppressor. Robbing Creusa of a public language of resistance in which she could be heard, Foucault and the tutor portray her speech as unintelligible, unreliable, suspect.

If Foucault's depiction of Ion highlights that he is able to move from private to public, from powerlessness to power, while combining the important traits of both spheres, I have suggested here that this depiction willfully ignores, and even participates in, the silencing of Creusa and the obfuscation of violence done to her that makes this image of truth-telling possible. Foucault thus misses that the framing of *parrhesia* he draws out – as a predicament of using while remaining distant from power – is deeply gendered, and does not address the dilemmas of truth-telling that we find in the experiences of those who are excluded from political power. In the final section, I draw out an alternative understanding of the predicament of truth-telling that I find in the example of Creusa.

Democratic Truth-Telling

In Foucault's depiction of the dilemmas of *parrhesia*, truth-tellers must negotiate between appearing as public and private figures, being distant from while capable of using political power. Yet Creusa does not have the option of simply moving into the public realm to make her truth heard. Indeed, Ion's ability to be politically recognized as a truth-teller is premised on her truth-telling being restricted to the private sphere. Creusa's truth-telling thus displays a distinct predicament, forged through experiences of exclusion: namely, of having to *create* power, which could imbue her truth with significance, from a situation of forced powerlessness. Whereas Foucault's Ion negotiates the predicament of using power while maintaining a distance from it through personal virtuosity and the favor of the gods, Creusa negotiates the predicament of powerlessness by engaging the help and sympathy of fellow outsiders, who stand even further outside the circle of power: the Chorus of female slaves. Below, I offer a reading of the final scenes of the *Ion* as staging Creusa's negotiation of this predicament, and I will argue for its import to democracy.

As I noted above, the Chorus is the only character within the play to fully acknowledge Creusa's rape by Apollo, and the suffering it has caused her. In response to Creusa's revelation of her rape, the chorus leader neither fails to understand, nor asks for clarification, but says (as I quoted above): "O what a store of miseries is now/disclosed; who would not weep at hearing them?" (Euripides, 1958, pp. 923–924). As Loraux emphasizes, the female slaves who comprise the

Chorus "share with Kreousa a particular idea of the condition of woman, who is born unfortunate; echoing the laments of their mistress, they loudly declare their hatred of perverse males" (1994, p. 191). Implicit in Loraux's comment is the fact that the Chorus of the Ion does not stand in for the community as a whole (as a Chorus of military-age men would), but rather reveals, as Donald Mastronarde notes, fractures and divisions within the community (2010, pp. 101–105). Indeed, in their first entrance, the chorus positions itself as standing apart from the Athenian community. After asking Ion if they may "pass into this sanctuary" (and being refused permission), the Chorus acquiesces to its status outside the temple: "I understand/We are not for transgressing Apollo's law./*The outside charms us enough*" (Euripides, 1958, pp. 229–231; my emphasis). Outsiders who live within, but are not fully a part of the community, they intimate that their status has its pleasures as well as its hardships. While Creusa obviously has a higher status than her slaves, the text also positions her an outsider who lacks freedom. Like the Chorus, she complies with Ion's command to not enter the temple and says that she is, like the Chorus, Xuthus' property: "[d]owry of war; the prize won with his spear" (p. 298). The text thus leads us to believe that there is an outsider sympathy between Creusa and the Chorus. The Chorus sides with her against Xuthus, stands in solidarity with her when she tries to murder Ion, and keeps her secrets for her.

Exchanges between Creusa and the Chorus tend to occur in private in the play, but the Chorus' sympathy with Creusa has public implications in the final scene: namely, in empowering her to take possession of the public language of justice that men and gods have denied her. After Creusa's plot to poison Ion is discovered, she turns to the Chorus for help: "Where can I find refuge then? For I have evaded them/by a trick, just left the house in time to save my life" (pp. 1253–1254). While both the Chorus and Creusa acquiesce in the opening scene to Ion's prohibition on entering the temple, the Chorus now urges Creusa to occupy Apollo's sacred space as a way of keeping male violence at bay. "Where," the Chorus leader says, "but at the altar?" (p. 1254) Creusa hesitates out of concern that her cause is not just: "the law condemns me" (p. 1257). Yet the Chorus suggests that the act of occupying the altar will allow Creusa, even if only temporarily, to stand as a representative of, rather than outsider to, Apollo's justice. The Chorus leader says, "Sit on the altar now. For if you die sitting there, your killers will be made/guilty of your blood" (pp. 1258–1260). On the one hand, the Chorus may be suggesting that the act of sitting at the altar will reveal that Creusa now defers to the divine law that in previous acts (such as the attempt to murder Ion), she has broken or contravened. Yet the Chorus may also be suggesting that the act of sitting at the altar viscerally displays, and perhaps creates, Creusa (and not Ion) as the voice of justice in the play. Indeed, while positioned on the altar, Creusa says in the ensuing dialogue with Ion that her "body is his [Apollo's] to save, a sacred charge" (p. 1285). Taking possession of, or occupying, the altar allows Creusa to claim that it should have been hers all along. In the absence of Apollo's appearance, the play suggests that occupying his sacred sites and symbols may work as a way for outsiders to at least temporarily transform their audience's sense of who counts as a teller of his truth and representative of his justice.

This strategy, suggested by the Chorus and carried through by Creusa, works. While Ion consistently claims that Creusa should not have the right to claim refuge at the altar – "[t]he unjust should not have the right of refuge/at altars, but be driven away" (pp. 1314–1315) – he also treats her as an equal and engages in a rational debate with her about whether he or she is in the right. Further, while Ion claimed to speak on behalf of the god in their opening meeting, Creusa now does so: "I warn you not to kill me – and I speak/not only for myself but for the god/who guards this place" (pp. 1282–1284). Framing herself in this dialogue as someone who is owed justice by the god, Creusa and the Chorus are actually the ones who – by seizing an altar they have been legally and practically denied – *take* the justice that Apollo and the men in the play have refused to give. Indeed, where Creusa claimed (unsuccessfully) in her opening exchange with Ion that the oracles should be open to all Greeks, Ion now mourns that Creusa has been able to achieve just that: "The just,/the injured party, should have this asylum./Instead both good and bad alike all come,/receiving equal treatment from the gods" (pp. 1316–1319).

The sympathetic exchange and solidarity between Creusa and the Chorus thus empower Creusa to transform Apollo's altar, previously closed to her demands for justice, into a place of refuge where she can find respite from the violence of men and speak credibly as a representative of justice and truth. Put differently, seizing the symbol of justice (the altar) works to viscerally change, even if only briefly, the discursive economy of truth and justice. Indeed, it is only after Creusa inhabits Apollo's altar that Apollo appears to acquiesce to her demands. After Ion mourns that both the good and bad can take refuge at Apollo's temple, the Pythia enters the temple at the suggestion of Apollo (she says) with the basket Ion was found in as a baby, still containing the items left in the basket with him. Seeing the basket, Creusa is further empowered – "This is no time for silence. Do not try/to check me" (pp. 1397–1398) – and tells Ion that she is his mother, and Apollo his father.

Of course, the ending to this story is not – as I have already said – happy. Leaving the altar and revealing Ion's parentage to him, Creusa compromises her truth: she omits the story of her rape and keeps the violence toward her and other women, through which the future of Athens is assured, secret. Yet what I have emphasized in this reading is that we can also read these final scenes as containing an undercurrent of outsider empowerment that allows Creusa to *survive* and tell at least part of her truth. This survival, this creation of a place within patriarchy where outsiders can find respite from its violence, and begin to transform the discursive economies of truth and justice, is not insignificant and reveals at least an outline of how powerless outsiders might constitute power out of a condition of powerlessness. Here, that constitution happens through solidaristic exchange, empathy, and strategy between outsiders that gives Creusa the courage to occupy and speak as the representative of a sacred house of justice that otherwise favors men and gods. This occupation generates a place of refuge, survival, and a certain degree of political credibility. Indeed, after witnessing the reunion between Creusa and Ion, the Chorus Leader says, "From what we have seen happen here, no man/should ever think that anything is hopeless" (pp. 1510–1511). She may be talking about Creusa's recovery of her child, but she may also be talking about Creusa's own survival. While it appeared that Creusa was going to die, the Chorus' intervention, and Creusa's truth-telling, saved her and empowered her to speak some of her story.

Earlier, I suggested that Creusa represents a democratic form of truth-telling over and against Ion's aristocratic form. Yet perhaps it is more accurate to say that Creusa and Ion represent two different democratic forms of truth-telling. As Susan Lape points out, the *Ion* dramatizes a moment of transition between an aristocratic understanding of reproduction – where the potent male or divine forebear is sufficient to assure honorable, elite status – and a democratic understanding of reproduction, where the equality of citizens is assured through equal inheritance of Athenian blood via *both* parents. As both Loraux (1994) and Lape (2008, pp. 113–119) note, the *Ion* is part of this emerging democratic understanding of reproduction insofar as it foregrounds ancestry as dependent primarily on (Creusa's) maternity. The mother of all future Athenians, the fate of Athenian democracy in the *Ion* lies in Creusa's hands or, more exactly, in her autochthonous blood. In contrast to the aristocratic view, the democratic view of reproduction reveals (even if it does not dignify) the centrality of the female body to the reproduction of citizens.

Read in terms of Lape's account, both Ion and Creusa appear as transitional figures between aristocracy and democracy. Yet they represent that transition differently. Ion's speeches and behavior reveal an aristocratic democratic Athenian coming into being: an Athenian citizen who is equal to all other citizens, but who as a citizen is a member of an elite, secured by his bloodline. He practices political *parrhesia* as Foucault describes it, as an agonistic practice through which one affirms one's "superiority" through one's capacity to tell the truth (2011, p. 156). In contrast, Creusa's speech and behavior reveal the exclusivity and violence of democratic equality: that, however valuable, democratic equality is still an exclusive status that leaves out classes of people, silences their voices, and perpetrates violence on them to maintain that status. Creusa's truth-telling is an outsider's demand, empowered and amplified through solidaristic exchange with other outsiders, that her truth and reality (violently silenced by men and gods) matter to everyone.

Foucault ignores the import of the exchanges between Creusa and the Chorus and identifies with the male characters who try to master the incomprehensible violence revealed by Creusa. The *Ion* reveals the violence implicit in Foucault's approach. Whether it reveals this violence on behalf of calling the audience to sanction or be unsettled by it (or both), the play offers an alternative exemplar of democratic truth-telling: the democratic truth-teller not as the self-possessed and self-creating *parrhesiastes*, but as the dispossessed woman who, through telling the truth to those similarly cast out of the public realm, creates the power to seize the language of justice that keeps her an outsider and demands her silence. The play also displays the felicitous audience of that truth-teller not as an elite who can approve the veracity of her statement (the tutor and Foucault), but instead a vulnerable democratic public who can (in Bonnie Honig's words) "vindicate" (2007, p. 1) Creusa's truth through their solidarity: here, the chorus of female slaves, receptive to the possibility of previously incomprehensible wrongs sanctioned by elites. These exemplars – in contrast to Foucault's Ion – reveal the democratic importance of the truth-telling of the dispossessed: truth-telling that finds vindication and empowerment not in the dominant group which refuses to hear it, but in a vulnerable, mutually dependent public of outsiders. If Foucault's elite form of *parrhesia* emerges in contrast to a raped woman as its other, that raped woman who is empowered to speak her truth publicly through synergistic exchange with other outsiders, may also serve as one exemplar of contestatory democratic truth-telling: truth-telling as a critical challenge to hierarchy and its ruse, that is, that those at the top have special access to the truth.

Acknowledgments

Thanks to Japonica Brown-Saracino, Sonali Chakravarti, Lisa Disch, Laura Ephraim, Bonnie Honig, Demetra Kasimis, Sara Kippur, Jill Locke, Lori Marso, Ella Myers, Shalini Satkunanandan, Yves Winter, and two anonymous reviewers for comments and discussions. Thanks also to Ayten Gündoğdu and the participants in the Columbia Seminar on Social and Political Thought who offered helpful comments and thoughts on an earlier version of this paper.

About the Author

Lida Maxwell is an Associate Professor of Political Science and Women and Gender Studies at Trinity College, Hartford CT, and Visiting Professor of Political Science at Boston University. She is the author of *Public Trials: Burke, Zola, Arendt, and the Politics of Lost Causes* (Oxford, 2014) and co-editor of *Second Nature: Rethinking the Natural Through Politics* (Fordham, 2013). She is currently finishing a book on Chelsea Manning and the politics of truth-telling (provisionally titled *Insurgent Truth*), and starting a new project on the politics of environmental desire. Her article from this project, "Queer/Love/Bird Extinction: Rachel Carson's *Silent Spring* as a Work of Love," was recently published in *Political Theory*.

Notes

1 I am not the first to draw attention to such hierarchies of truth. Elizabeth Markovits (2010) notes, for example, that dominant norms of truth-telling "privilege a stereotypically masculine style of talk—self-confidence, certainty, and a seemingly dispassionate tone [that] demonstrate the speaker's commitment to the discussion" (p. 34). Similarly, Utz McKnight (2013) argues that blacks are not allowed to "defin[e] the truth of racism" (p. 67), and that they must defer to dominant groups to validate their articulation of their own experience (pp. 70-72).
2 This article is less concerned with adjudicating the meaning of *parrhesia* in Athens, than in examining the theory of truth-telling that Foucault and his contemporary readers draw out of his portrayal of *parrhesia*. On *parrhesia*, see Monoson, 2000; Saxonhouse, 2005; and Markovits, 2010.
3 These authors argue that these practices have limited, and contingent, political implications. Nancy Luxon, for example, says that Foucauldian *parrhesia* offers "a model for ethical self-governance from which we can borrow and revise" (2008, p. 398). Similarly, Prozorov has argued that Cynic *parrhesia*, through "attain[ing] another life right here in *this* world" may "make it [the world] *otherwise* than it was" (Prozorov, 2015, p. 12).
4 Banu Bargu is an exception to this trend. In a recent article (2017), she builds on Foucault's "alethurgic" method in the lectures to explore precisely this disputed politicality in the context of migrant and refugee practices of self-harming. She suggests these practices may work as a form of resistance that "make[s] visible modes of counter-subjectivation" (p. 9).
5 Ella Myers (2013) offers an important, trenchant critique of this approach, arguing that "[w]hen 'action in concert' appears to be rare or unlikely, we may be attracted to the notion that democracy can be rescued by something other than itself, namely, the discovery of the proper ethics" (*Worldly Ethics*, pp. 9–10).
6 For Foucault, "there was no 'problematization' of the *parrhesiastes*" within the *Ion* because *parrhesia* is "presented as having only a positive sense or value" (2001, p. 72). Rather, we see only the "problem of gaining *access* to parrhesia in spite of the silence of god" (p. 73).
7 Foucault's framing of Ion as a natural *parrhesiastes* rests primarily on his reading of a short speech that Ion makes as a response to Xuthus' offer to bring him back to Athens as his son. In that speech, Ion classifies the people of Athens, and makes an argument about why the different groups of Athenian citizens would – if his mother were not shown to be Athenian – thwart him in his aspiration to "the city's helm." Foucault says that Ion's critical and classificatory portrayals of groups of Athenians in public life are "typical instances of parrhesiastic discourse" that you can find "later on coming from Socrates' mouth in the works of either Plato or Xenophon" (2001, p. 51).
8 Saxonhouse and Loraux see the ending as revealing the violence and exclusion at the basis of Athens and, in particular, Athenian autochthony, while Rabinowitz argues that Creusa serves as a model of sacrificial female comportment. Victoria Wohl (2015) suggests that the form of the play mobilizes a desire for a happy ending that spurs the audience, like the characters in the play, to be blind to its anti-democratic message – in particular, to the romance of elite lineage that obscures the rape in favor of focusing on the reunion. I am less interested in adjudicating the differences between these readings, and more interested in drawing attention to their agreement that the play shows the origin of *parrhesia* as dependent on silencing Creusa about her rape – a point that Foucault either completely misses or chooses to gloss over.
9 Foucault claims that her questions to Apollo, for example – "[w]hat then has become of the son you gave me, the son you made and I exposed? Is he still alive or is he dead?" (2011, p. 86) – are private

questions, in contrast to Xuthus' question ("Will I have no descendants?"), which he says is "a public question" (p. 86). Foucault claims that there is a difference here because Creusa's question relates to an intimate "question that the woman puts to the man, or rather to the god," whereas Xuthus pursues "a standard question – the consultation of the common question" (p. 86).

10 "In this struggle against the god's silence, Ion and Creusa are the two major parrhesiastic figures. But they do not play the role of the *parrhesiastes* in the same way. For as a male born of Athenian earth, Ion has the right to use *parrhesia*. Creusa, on the other hand, plays the parrhesiastic role as a woman who confesses her thoughts" (2001, p. 44).

11 Foucault's strange inattention to Creusa's language about her rape in the play has a precedent in his comments during a 1977 discussion on the law and sexuality (1988). In that conversation, he disputed the idea that we should regard rape as different from any other assault. He says, provocatively, that we could say that rape "is nothing more than an act of aggression: that there is no difference, in principle, between sticking one's fist into someone's face or one's penis into their sex" – a position that Foucault readily admits he is "not at all sure that women agree with" (p. 200). Feminist criticisms of this view can be found in Plaza, 1981; Hengehold, 1994; Cahill, 2000; and Marcus, 1992.

12 "Et c'est là, dans cet antre et dans cette caverne, dans cette nuit et cette ombre que l'enfant est exposé, et qu'il va être enlevé et qu'il va disparaître et, par consequent, comme le croit Créuse, mourir, et donc ne pas bénéficier de cette lumière du jour, de cet étincellement du soleil don't elle avait bénéficié, ou par [quoi] en tout cas elle avait été séduite." (Michel Foucault, *Le gouvernement de soi et des autres*. Paris: Gallimard, 2008, p. 120).

References

Bargu, Banu. (2017) The Silent Exception: Hunger Striking and Lip-Sewing. *Law, Culture, and Humanities*. Published online May 24, 2017. https://doi-org.ezproxy.bu.edu/10.1177%2F1743872117709684.
Berlant, Lauren. (2011) *Cruel Optimism*. Durham, NC: Duke University Press.
Cahill, Ann J. (2000) Foucault, Rape, and the Construction of the Feminine Body. *Hypatia* 15(1): 43–63.
Corrigan, Rose. (2013) *Up Against a Wall: Rape Reform and the Failure of Success*. New York: New York University Press.
Cvetkovich, Ann. (2012) *Depression: A Public Feeling*. Durham, NC: Duke University Press.
Dyson, Michael Eric. (2016) Death in Black and White. In *The New York Times*, July 6, 2016, http://www.nytimes.com/2016/07/10/opinion/sunday/what-white-america-fails-to-see.html?_r=0. Accessed July 13, 2016.
Euripides. (1958) *Ion*, trans. Ronald Frederick Willetts, in *Euripides III*, ed. David Grene and Richmond Lattimore. Chicago: University of Chicago Press
Foucault, Michel. (1995) *Discipline and Punish*, trans. Alan Sheridan. Vintage: New York.
Foucault, Michel. (2001) *Fearless Speech*. Semiotext(e): Los Angeles.
Foucault, Michel. (2011) *The Government of Self and Others*, trans. Graham Burchell. New York: Picador.
Foucault, Michel. (2012) *The Courage of Truth*, trans. Graham Burchell. New York: Picador.
Foucault, Michel. (1988) Confinement, Psychiatry, Prison. In: L.D. Kritzman (ed.)*Politics, philosophy, culture: Interviews and other writings, 1977-1984*, trans. Alan Sheridan et al. New York: Routledge.
Hengehold, Laura. (1994) An Immodest Proposal: Foucault, Hysterization, and the 'Second Rape'. *Hypatia* 9(Summer): 3, 88–107.

Honig, Bonnie. (2007) Between Decision and Deliberation: Political Paradox in Democratic Theory. *American Political Science Review* 101(1): 1–17.

Kasimis, Demetra. (2013) The Tragedy of Blood-Based Membership: Secrecy and the Politics of Immigration in Euripides' *Ion*. *Political Theory* 24(2): 231–256.

Kim, David. (2015) The Cosmopolitics of *Parrhesia*: Foucault and Truth-Telling as Human Right. In: David Kim and Susanne Kaul (eds.) *Imagining Human Rights*. Berlin: de Gruyter.

Krakauer, Jon. (2015) *Missoula: Rape and the Justice System in a College Town*. New York: Doubleday.

Lape, Susan. (2008) *Race and Citizen Identity in the Classical Athenian Democracy*. Cambridge: Cambridge University Press.

LeBron, Chris. (2016) Race, Truth, and Our Two Realities. In: *The New York Times*, July 11, 2016, http://www.nytimes.com/2016/07/11/opinion/race-truth-and-our-two-realities.html. Accessed July 13, 2016.

Loraux, Nicole. (1994) *The Children of Athena, trans. Caroline Levine*. Princeton: Princeton University Press.

Luxon, Nancy. (2004) Truthfulness, Risk, and Trust in Foucault's Late Lectures. *Inquiry* 47: 464–489.

Luxon, Nancy. (2008) Ethics and Subjectivity. *Political Theory* 36(3): 377–402.

Luxon, Nancy. (2013) *The Crisis of Authority*. Cambridge: Cambridge University Press.

Marcus, Sharon. (1992) Fighting Bodies, Fighting Words: A Theory and Politics of Rape Prevention. *Feminists Theorize the Political*. New York: Routledge.

Markovits, Elizabeth. (2010) *The Politics of Sincerity*. State College: Penn State Press.

Mastronarde, Donald. (2010) *The Art of Euripides*. Cambridge: Cambridge University Press.

Maxwell, Lida. (2015) Truth in Public: Chelsea Manning, Gender Identity, and the Politics of Truth-Telling. *Theory and Event* 18: 1, https://muse.jhu.edu/article/566093.

McKnight, Utz. (2013) *Race and the Politics of the Exception*. New York: Routledge.

Monoson, Sara. (2000) *Plato's Democratic Entanglements*. Princeton: Princeton University Press.

Myers, Ella. (2013) *Worldly Ethics: Democratic Politics and Care for the World*. Durham, NC: Duke University Press.

Owen, David and Claire Woodford. (2012) Foucault, Cavell, and the Government of Self and Others. *Iridie: filosofia e discussione pubblica* 25: 2, 299–316.

Peters, M.A. (2003) Truth-telling as an Educational Practice of the Self: Foucault, *Parrhesia* and the ethics of subjectivity. *Oxford Review of Education* 29: 2, 207–223.

Plaza, Monique. (1981) Our Damages and Their Compensation; Rape: the Will Not to Know of Michel Foucault. *Gender Issues* 1: 2, 25–35.

Prozorov, Sergei. (2015) Foucault's Affirmative Biopolitics: Cynic Parrhesia and the Biopower of the Powerless. *Political Theory*. https://doi.org/10.1177/0090591715609963.

Rabinowitz, Nancy Sorkin. (1993) *Anxiety Veiled: Euripides and the Traffic in Women*. Ithaca: Cornell University Press.

Sauter, Theresa, & Kendall, Gavin. (2011) *Parrhesia* and Democracy: Truthtelling, Wikileaks and the Arab Spring. *Social Alternatives,* 30(3): 10–14.

Saxonhouse, Arlene. (1986) Reflections on Autochthony in Euripides' *Ion*. In: Peter Euben (ed.) *Greek Tragedy and Political Theory*. Berkeley: University of California Press.

Saxonhouse, Arlene. (2005) *Free Speech and Democracy in Athens*. Cambridge: Cambridge University Press.

Tamboukou, Maria. (2012) Truth Telling in Foucault and Arendt: *Parrhesia*, the Pariah, and Academics in Dark Times. *Journal of Education Policy* 27(6): 849–865.

Taylor, Dianna. (2013) Resisting the Subject: A Feminist-Foucauldian Approach to Countering Sexual Violence. *Foucault Studies* 16: 88–103.

Wohl, Victoria. (2015) *Euripides and the Politics of Form*. Princeton: Princeton University Press.

Conversation II: Feminist Lives, Desires, Futures

Article

Sex wars, SlutWalks, and carceral feminism

Lorna Bracewell
Department of Humanities, Flagler College, St. Augustine, FL 32084, USA.
lbracewell@flagler.edu

Abstract In recent years, scholars have identified a political formation that mobilizes the emancipatory energies of feminism in the service of the expansion of the carceral state. 'Carceral feminism,' as it has come to be known, is often portrayed by these scholars as a product of feminist-conservative convergence. Here, I argue that the rise of the SlutWalk movement suggests a more complex genealogy for carceral feminism. By situating SlutWalk in the historico-theoretical context of feminism's sex wars, I reveal the carceral–feminist impulses roiling beneath its progressive 'sex-positive' surface. With its tendency to reduce sexual freedom to expressive freedom, valorize conventional forms of femininity and (hetero)sexuality, and promote a fundamentally carceral paradigm of sexual freedom, the SlutWalk movement, I argue, is descended from anti-censorship/pro-sex feminism, a liberal-feminist hybrid that emerged out of the convergence of sex-radical feminism and liberalism during the sex wars. When viewed in this light, SlutWalk no longer appears as a sign that feminism's 'pleasure' and 'danger' factions have negotiated a long-awaited 'sex-détente.' Rather, it stands as a testament to the extent to which feminism's once radical aspirations in the domain of sexual politics have been supplanted by a tepid, heteronormative, and disquietingly carceral liberal project.
Contemporary Political Theory (2020) **19**, 61–82. https://doi.org/10.1057/s41296-019-00318-y; published online 6 April 2019

Keywords: feminism; sex wars; liberalism; carceral feminism; sex-radical feminism; SlutWalk

In recent years, a body of scholarship has emerged identifying a political formation that mobilizes the emancipatory energies of feminism in the service of the expansion of the carceral state (Critical Resistance and Incite!, 2003; Gottschalk, 2006; Bernstein, 2007, 2010, 2012; Bumiller, 2008; Kim 2015; Heiner and Tyson, 2017). 'Carceral feminism,' as sociologist Elizabeth Bernstein (2010) has dubbed it, figures criminalization, policing, prosecution, and incarceration as integral to women's liberation, constructing gender justice as a matter of criminal justice. Within this scholarship, carceral feminism is portrayed as primarily a product of the confluence of feminist and conservative energies. For example, in her study of contemporary anti-trafficking activism, Bernstein associates the anti-trafficking movement's embrace of carceral paradigms of justice with 'a rightward shift' and 'feminist-conservative alliances' (formed between feminists and organizations like the Hudson Institute) (Bernstein, 2010, pp. 47, 53).[1] Similarly, Mimi Kim (2015) attributes the anti-domestic violence movement's turn toward 'punitive carceral polices' to strategic decisions made by anti-domestic violence activists to ally themselves with a conservative politics of law and order in an effort to 'feminize' and 'control' the criminal justice system (2015, p. 5). While there is no denying that the feminist-conservative convergences highlighted by this scholarship have contributed to the rise of carceral feminism, certain strands of contemporary feminist politics, particularly contemporary feminist *sexual* politics, indicate that the genealogy of feminism's carceral turn may be more complex than this narrative of feminist-conservative convergence lets on.

Consider, for example, the transnational anti-rape protest movement known as 'SlutWalk.' The SlutWalk movement began on April 3, 2011 in Toronto, Canada, when some 1,500 people, mostly women, donned miniskirts, fishnets, and other 'slutty' attire and marched to the headquarters of the Toronto Police Service. Billed by organizers as 'SlutWalk Toronto,' the purpose of the march was to protest a TPS officer's remark at a public safety forum that, in order not to be raped, women 'should avoid dressing like sluts.' Given these precipitating circumstances, one might imagine SlutWalk Toronto carried a bold anti-carceral message, highlighting instances of the criminal justice system's complicity in sexual violence and injustice such as prison rape, sexual assault by law enforcement officers, and police harassment of sex workers and sexual minorities.[2] However, this was not the case. As SlutWalk Toronto's website explains, the aim of the march was to 'call foul' on TPS for engaging in the sort of 'slut-shaming' that deters survivors from reporting their victimization and to demand that police 'take serious steps' to make survivors, 'slut or otherwise,' 'feel respected and protected' (SlutWalk, 2011). The goal, in other words, was more vigorous law enforcement on behalf of 'sluts.' Within a year, SlutWalk Toronto had inspired similar events in approximately 200 cities around the world and a global grassroots SlutWalk movement had emerged.[3]

While SlutWalk's rise from local demonstration to transnational phenomenon has elicited some criticism from feminist quarters,[4] many prominent feminists have embraced the movement. For example, according to popular author and blogger Jessica Valenti, SlutWalks 'herald a new day in feminist organizing… when women's anger begins online but takes to the street [and] when a local step makes global waves' (2011). Similarly, veteran socialist–feminist activist Selma James hails SlutWalk as 'the new women's movement…, born of student protests and Arab revolutions…, tearing up the past before our very eyes' (2011). Philosopher Judith Butler's assessment is equally sanguine. When asked about the SlutWalk marches in 2011, Butler described them as exemplifying a new kind of public assembly that harnesses 'a sense of vulnerability and injurability on the streets' to engender 'modes of solidarity' that resist the limitations of identity politics while contesting neoliberal conditions of precarity (Bella, 2011). Butler has recently reaffirmed this position, describing SlutWalks as a 'public and courageous takeover of public space' (2016, p. 227).

Perhaps the highest praise garnered by the SlutWalk movement has come from scholars who frame it as a long-awaited resolution of feminism's sex wars. The sex wars were a series of conflicts over matters pertaining to sex and sexuality that embroiled the feminist movement in the United States and Canada from the mid-1970s to the early 1990s. During the sex wars, 'sex-radical' and 'antipornography' feminists squared off over a whole range of issues, including pornography, prostitution, and S/M.[5] Despite pleas for both sides to come together to 'create a movement that speaks as powerfully in favor of sexual pleasure as it does against sexual danger,' the sex wars raged for decades, resisting any definitive resolution (Vance, 1984, p. 3). To scholars familiar with this history, the SlutWalk movement's pairing of audacious assertions of feminine sexuality with strident denunciations of gender-based violence signals a long-awaited 'sex détente' (Walters, 2016, p. 4). As legal scholar Deborah Tuerkheimer has observed, 'By taking aim at rape while expressly promoting the virtues of female sexuality, SlutWalk situates itself where anti-rape and pro-sex norms converge' (2014, pp. 1455–1456). Joetta Carr has seconded this analysis, praising 'SlutWalkers' for 'speaking in a voice that deplores sexual violence while embracing sex positivity' (2013, p. 31).

Extolled by the feminist left and lauded by scholars as a Hegelian synthesis of feminism's longstanding 'pleasure' and 'danger' antinomies, the SlutWalk movement is in no sense a product of the sort of feminist-conservative convergence scholars claim is fueling the rise of carceral feminism. In fact, conservative feminists like former British MP Louise Mensch (*née* Bagshawe) have harshly criticized SlutWalk for 'lionizing promiscuity' and making 'sluttishness a mark of feminism' (2011). Nevertheless, despite its progressive 'sex-positive' ethos, the SlutWalk movement, at least in its North American instantiations, is as steeped in a politics of carcerality as any of the conservative-feminist projects highlighted by scholars of carceral feminism.[6] My primary aim in this essay is to offer an explanation of how this came to be. How did a feminist movement that is vigorously 'sex-positive' and oriented toward the progressive left come to embrace a punitive carceral politics of law and order? How did a feminist project that takes sexual pleasure and freedom as its raisons d'être come to align itself with the carceral power of the state?

To answer these questions, I will draw on recent scholarship highlighting the role of liberalism in the feminist sex wars (Bracewell, 2016). As scholars like Duncan Bell and Judith Shklar have observed, liberalism is a 'hyper-inflated,' 'all-purpose' term that can be used to signify everything from progressivism to its opposite (Shklar, 1998, p. 3; Bell 2014, p. 691). In the present work, I use the term to denote a range of positions premised on 'the belief that the freedom of the individual is the highest political value' and that 'freedom of conscience, freedom of occupational choice, privacy and family rights all place limits on what governments may do' (Ryan, 2012, pp. 362, 377). At the heart of liberalism so conceived is a distinction between the public and the private, where the public is figured as a sphere of justice in which law serves as a neutral guarantor of liberty among free and equal individuals, while the private is figured as a sphere 'beyond justice' in which law and liberty are fundamentally at odds (Okin, 1989, p. 25).[7]

While liberals have traditionally presented the public/private distinction as a means of securing individual liberty against the encroachments of overweening governments, feminist political theorists have noted its utility for other purposes. As Carole Pateman has incisively observed, given 'the way in which women and men are differentially located within private life and the public world,' liberalism's public/private distinction 'obscures the subjection of women to men within an apparently universal, egalitarian individualist order' (1989, p. 120). It is liberalism in this sense, I argue, that played such a crucial role during the sex wars.

The earliest rumblings of the sex wars began in the latter half of the 1970s when feminists began articulating perspectives on pornography and a whole host of other matters pertaining to sex and sexuality that challenged traditional liberal perspectives. Whereas liberals had long fended off conservative calls for censorship by figuring pornography as private, apolitical, and harmless, feminists during the sex wars insisted that pornography was public, political, and potent. Antipornography feminists argued that pornography threatened women's physical, civil, and economic wellbeing, while sex-radical feminists defended pornography (and sexuality more generally) as indispensable to human freedom, community, and identity. Initially, liberals resisted these dueling feminist perspectives. They were wary of the brazen defenses of pornography and sexuality offered by sex-radical feminists, and they saw antipornography feminism as little more than old-fashioned Comstockery in new-fangled feminist drag. However, in the mid-1980s, in the midst of a robust public debate surrounding a municipal ordinance that would have made pornography actionable as a civil rights violation, all of this began to change, and liberal variants of both antipornography feminism and sex-radical feminism began taking shape.

In this article, I summarize these developments with a primary focus on the strategic appropriation of liberal 'civil liberties' and 'anti-censorship' rhetoric by sex-radical feminists in the mid-1980s.[8] While this strategy won sex-radical feminists important short-term gains, in the long run, I argue, it led to the eclipse of sex-radical feminism by a liberal-feminist hybrid discourse that I call 'anti-censorship/pro-sex feminism.' It is this liberal-feminist hybrid, I argue, that has fueled the rise of the SlutWalk movement. Despite its resemblance to the 'Take Back the Night' marches pioneered by antipornography feminists in the late 1970s, and its continuity, in at least some respects, with the playful prurience of sex-radical feminism, the SlutWalk movement, I argue, is no straightforward reconciliation of sex wars-era antinomies. Rather, with its tendency to reduce sexual freedom to expressive freedom, valorize (as opposed to problematize) conventional forms of femininity and (hetero)sexuality, and promote a fundamentally carceral paradigm of sexual freedom, the SlutWalk movement is a descendant of anti-censorship/pro-sex feminism and, thus, a product of the union of sex-radical feminism and liberalism that the sex wars occasioned. When recognized as such, the SlutWalk movement no longer appears as a sign that feminism's once bitterly divided factions have come together in some new and vital political coalition. Rather, it stands as a testament to the extent to which feminism's once radical aspirations in the domain of sexual politics have been supplanted by a tepid, heteronormative, and disquietingly carceral liberal project.[9]

The sex-radical feminist critique of liberalism

Prior to the sex wars, debates concerning sexual freedom in the United States were largely two-sided affairs centered around the topic of sexual expression. Conservatives, like 19th-century anti-vice crusader Anthony Comstock, argued that all sexual expression, from straightforwardly pornographic works to Boccaccio's *Decameron*, were 'obscene' (from the Latin for 'filthy' or 'inauspicious') and deserving of legal suppression. Liberals responded to these conservative calls for censorship by insisting that sexually explicit materials were harmless vice, deserving of moral opprobrium and some forms of governmental regulation, but not outright prohibition. John Stuart Mill's remarks in *On Liberty* concerning 'offences against decency' reflect this quintessentially liberal view. 'There are many acts,' Mill writes, 'which, being directly injurious only to the agents themselves, ought not to be legally interdicted, but which, if done publicly, are a violation of good manners, and coming thus within the category of offences against others, may rightfully be prohibited' (1989, p. 98). 'Of this kind,' Mill continues, 'are offences against decency; on which it is unnecessary to dwell, ... as they are only connected indirectly with our subject, the objection to publicity being equally strong in the case of many actions not in themselves condemnable, nor supposed to be so' (1989, p. 98).

Mill's equivocal defense of 'offences against decency' lived on well into the 20th century, shaping the thinking of some of sexual expression's most prominent liberal defenders. For instance, in an influential 1981 essay, philosopher Ronald Dworkin vindicated a 'right to pornography,' construed as a right to the voluntary consumption of 'depressingly obscene photographs and films' in private, while simultaneously defending prohibitions against the display of such photographs and films in public (1981, p. 182). Even the cadre of civil libertarian attorneys and publishers who challenged the Comstock-era regime of obscenity regulation head-on in the 1950s and 1960s embraced this ambivalent view. For instance, Charles

Rembar, the attorney who exonerated the first unexpurgated American edition of D.H. Lawrence's *Lady Chatterly's Lover* from obscenity charges in 1959 and pioneered the legal strategy that would lead to the exoneration of dozens of other sexually explicit works throughout the 1960s, lamented the more permissive sexual culture his legal victories helped bring about. 'There is an acne on our culture,' Rembar wrote in the concluding chapter of his memoir *The End of Obscenity*, pointing to a glut of books, magazines, advertisements, and films that 'play upon concupiscence' and 'peddle sex with an idiot slyness' (1968, p. 491). 'We approach,' Rembar warned, 'a *seductio ad absurdum*' (1968, p. 491).

As Rembar's reflections on 'the end of obscenity' evince, a profound ambivalence lay at the heart of mid-twentieth-century liberal opposition to obscenity regulation. While liberals defended sexually explicit expression as, for the most part, harmless, they also lamented its prevalence and denounced it as ignoble and base. Some even recommended eliminating legal restraints on obscenity as a means of eradicating it. Consider, for example, the argument Herald Price Fahringer, attorney for the publishers of *Hustler* and *Screw*, presented at a New York University School of Law colloquium in 1978. 'Obscenity,' Fahringer explained, 'breeds and multiplies in the dark crevices of a frightened society preoccupied with a sense of self-censorship' (1979, p. 253). 'Once pornography is exposed to the strong sunlight of a completely free and uninhibited people,' Fahringer predicted, 'its appeal will surely diminish' (1979, p. 253). Like John Stuart Mill, who famously argued that censorship 'robs the human race … of the opportunity of exchanging error for truth,' liberal opponents of obscenity regulation believed that the censorship of sexually explicit materials robs the human race of the opportunity of exchanging obscenity's tawdry thrill for more dignified and authentic pleasures (1989, p. 20).

During the sex wars, feminists assailed this ambivalent liberal defense of sexual expression on multiple fronts. While antipornography feminists contested liberal claims of pornography's harmlessness by insisting that pornography played an integral role in the oppression of women, sex-radical feminists challenged liberal sexual politics from another direction. Committed to a robust vision of sexual freedom that necessitated a vibrant, diverse, and *public* sexual culture, sex-radical feminists found liberals' ambivalent defenses of sexual expression inadequate and problematic.[10] Not only did they leave the stigma traditionally attached to sex and sexual expression undisputed, they evinced a deeper failure on the part of liberals to look beyond the freedom to peruse a narrow range of sexually explicit materials in private without fear of legal sanction to a broader, queerer sexual freedom. As sex-radical feminist author and activist Pat Califia[11] explained, while 'most people seem to want to visit sex as if it were a brothel or a shooting gallery, get [a fix], and then go home without getting busted,' sex-radical feminists wanted something more (1994, p. 36). 'I want the freedom to be as queer, as perverted, on the street and on the job as I am in my dungeon,' Califia, a founding member of the San

Francisco-based lesbian s/m group Samois, declared (1994, p. 36). Securing this freedom meant upending what fellow Samois member and leading sex-radical feminist theorist Gayle Rubin described as 'the system of sexual oppression,' a 'Kafkaesque nightmare' of laws, norms, and social practices designed to reward monogamous, heterosexual 'vanilla' sex and punish the rest (Vance, 1984, p. 293, 282). Such a grandiose project of sexual liberation far outstripped anything even the staunchest anti-censorship liberal ever proposed.

Liberals' failure to confront sexual oppression in all its facets and embrace a more comprehensive vision of sexual freedom made them frequent targets of sex-radical feminist criticism. For instance, in an article published in *The Advocate* in 1980, Califia criticized the testimony that attorney Heather Grant Florence offered on behalf of the ACLU at the congressional hearings for the Protection of Children Against Sexual Exploitation Act of 1977. According to Califia, Florence's 'only objection to [the bill, which made it a felony… to photograph or film a child (anyone under sixteen years of age) in the nude, engaged in sexual activity with another person or masturbating], was the threat it posed to the First Amendment' (1994, p. 45). In Califia's view, this liberal objection missed the point; what was at stake in the proposed law was not only or even primarily expressive freedom, but the sexual freedom of young people, their adult friends and lovers, and gays and lesbians and other marginalized sexual minorities who were likely to bear the brunt of any law enforcement crack down on sex crime (1994, p. 71). By failing to object 'to the committee's position that sex is bad for children and… even suggest[ing] that it would be appropriate… to increase the legal penalties for adults who have sex with minors,' Califia believed that Florence and the ACLU betrayed the cause of sexual freedom and aided in the oppression of some of the most vulnerable second-class sexual citizens (1994, p. 45).

Califia offered a similar critique of the testimony Florence and other prominent civil libertarians offered before the 1986 Attorney General's Commission on Pornography (more commonly known as the 'Meese Commission'). 'A lot of the people who turned up to testify before the commission on behalf of the First Amendment,' Califia noted, 'did not focus their testimony on the issue of pornography' and 'chose instead to speak about the dangerous impact that censorship could have on the arts, theater, and literature' (1994, p. 36). As Califia saw it, the failure of these liberals to 'stand up at the Meese Commission and say, "I want to be able to see somebody get spanked, tied up, and soundly fucked in a full-color film with a gorgeous soundtrack",' left an opening for the Justice Department to implement many of the Commission's most draconian recommendations, including cracking down on queer and s/m pornography, which were easier for authorities to cast as beyond the pale of the First Amendment than more sexually orthodox fare (1994, p. 36). By operating within rather than against the normative confines of 'the system of sexual oppression,' liberal defenders of expressive freedom failed to vindicate the sexual freedom of the most sexually vulnerable.

As this brief discussion illustrates, during the sex wars' earliest years, sex-radical feminists and anti-censorship liberals were profoundly at odds. In the face of liberal claims that sexual expression was private, apolitical, and harmless, sex-radical feminists figured the freedom of sexual expression as one integral part of a much larger sexual freedom to craft, cultivate, and live out diverse sexual desires and identities in public and in the context of erotically nurturing communities. Despite these profound differences, in the mid-1980s, as antipornography feminists championed a municipal ordinance making pornography civilly actionable as sex discrimination, tensions between sex-radical feminists and anti-censorship liberals began to ease, and an improbable liberal variant of sex-radical feminism began taking shape.

From sex-radical to sex-positive feminism

In the fall of 1983, at the request of the City of Minneapolis, Andrea Dworkin and Catharine MacKinnon drafted the first version of their pornography civil rights ordinance. Premised on antipornography feminism's defining dogma that pornography threatens women's physical, political, and economic wellbeing, the ordinance consisted of a series of amendments to Minneapolis's existing civil rights code. It singled out pornography as a form of sex discrimination and defined specific acts, including 'trafficking in pornography,' as civil rights violations (Dworkin and MacKinnon, 1988, p. 101).

The Minneapolis City Council passed what eventually came to be known as the 'Dworkin–MacKinnon ordinance' twice between December 1983 and July 1984. Both times Minneapolis mayor Don Fraser vetoed it citing First Amendment concerns. The ordinance fared better in Indianapolis where it passed into law in the spring of 1984. Over the next 2 years, versions of the Dworkin–MacKinnon ordinance were also considered in Suffolk County, New York; Madison, Wisconsin; Bellingham, Washington; Los Angeles County, California; and Cambridge, Massachusetts. In most of these cities, coordinated opposition came from antipornography feminism's long-time foes, civil libertarian opponents of obscenity regulation. However, in several instances, traditional liberal coalitions of booksellers, publishing trade associations, and state civil liberties unions were joined by sex-radical feminists acting under the aegis of a new organization, the Feminist Anti-Censorship Taskforce (FACT).

According to FACT co-founder Carole Vance, FACT was formed in the fall of 1984 in response to the introduction of a Dworkin–MacKinnon-style antipornography ordinance in Suffolk County, New York (1993). Within a year, FACT chapters had sprung up in Madison, Wisconsin, Los Angeles, California, and

Cambridge, Massachusetts 'to oppose the enactment of Indianapolis-style antipornography laws' (Duggan and Hunter, 2006, pp. 23, 242). To this end, FACT engaged in a variety of activities, including offering formal testimony at public hearings concerning the ordinance, organizing a street-theater action in protest of the 1986 Attorney General's Commission on Pornography, and publishing *Caught Looking* (1986), a tabloid-style book that paired essays criticizing antipornography feminism with sexually explicit photographs and illustrations.[12] However, FACT's most influential intervention was an *amicus curiae* brief it submitted on behalf of the plaintiffs in a legal challenge to the version of the Dworkin–MacKinnon ordinance enacted by the City of Indianapolis, *American Booksellers v. Hudnut* 771 F.2d 323 (7th Cir. 1985).

Authored by feminist legal scholars Nan Hunter and Sylvia Law and signed by what the radical feminist periodical *off our backs* described as 'an extraordinarily wide range of feminists,' from veteran sex radicals like Amber Hollibaugh and Gayle Rubin to civil libertarian attorneys like Nadine Strossen and David Richards, the FACT brief sought to persuade the Court of Appeals for the Seventh Circuit that the Indianapolis ordinance was unconstitutional (Wallsgrove, 1985, p. 12). To this end, the brief marshaled two primary arguments. First, the brief maintained, the ordinance's definition of pornography was 'unconstitutionally vague' and, when paired with the ordinance's trafficking provision, it amounted to a license to 'censor' a 'virtually limitless' number of materials, including 'experimentations in feminist art,' in violation of the First Amendment's free speech guarantee (Hunter and Sylvia, 1987, pp. 108, 89, 101). Second, the brief contended, by defining pornography in gender-specific terms as 'the graphic sexually explicit subordination of women,' the ordinance 'resonate[d] with the traditional concept that sex itself degrades women' (Hunter and Sylvia, 1987, pp. 132, 105). In FACT's view, 'sexually explicit speech [was] not per se sexist or harmful to women,' and a law designed to protect women from such a dubious harm 'perpetuate[d] central sexist stereotypes' and violated the Fourteenth Amendment's equal protection guarantee (Hunter and Sylvia, 1987, pp. 89, 130).

Judged solely on the basis of these arguments, the FACT brief appears to be a conventional liberal effort. It figures sexually explicit expression, for the most part, as harmless, and denounces attempts to regulate it as censorious encroachments on the freedom of speech. Even the FACT brief's novel deployment of the equal protection clause was in keeping with the traditional liberal claim that obscenity regulation is patronizing and paternalistic. However, despite these affinities, the FACT brief was no straightforward rehearsal of the liberal creed.[13] In fact, it flouted liberal convention in many ways. For instance, its bold vindication of 'sexual speech' as 'political' and 'highly relevant to our decision-making as citizens on a wide range of social and ethical issues' is a far cry from liberals' traditionally ambivalent defenses of sexual expression as private and, therefore, permissible in only a few discreet settings. Similarly, the FACT brief's argument that the Indianapolis ordinance would exacerbate the 'massive discrimination' endured by 'sexual minorities' by making their already marginalized 'erotica' even more susceptible to suppression was not an argument that had traditionally emanated from liberal quarters (Hunter and Sylvia, 1987, p. 109). Finally, the FACT brief's dominant theme (apart from the threat the Indianapolis ordinance posed to expressive freedom in general) was a fear that, if enacted, the Indianapolis ordinance would furnish conservatives with 'an effective tool' for the curtailment of women's 'freedom to appropriate for themselves' the 'traditionally male language' of sexuality (Hunter and Sylvia, 1987, pp. 121, 122). Such concern for women's ability to express 'unladylike, unfeminine, aggressive, power-charged, pushy, vulgar, urgent, confident, and intense' ideas about sex was a definite departure from liberal orthodoxy (Hunter and Sylvia, 1987, p. 122).

That the FACT brief both defied and reproduced the conventional liberal line on 'free speech' points to what is, in my view, the most significant aspect of FACT's intervention. Although many of FACT's founders and supporters were sex-radical feminists committed to an expansive vision of sexual freedom that exceeded conventional liberal strictures,[14] the organization was guided by a strategic vision that held that 'effective political action consists in appropriating, transforming and deploying the friendliest discourses, in order to counter the most hostile ones' (Duggan and Hunter, 2006, p. 2). In keeping with this strategy, FACT co-founder Lisa Duggan has explained, FACT 'appropriated the rhetoric of '"anti-censorship"' along with the accompanying 'framework of civil liberties' to construct what Duggan calls a 'bridge discourse' connecting the 'reform politics of liberal and progressive groups' to the more radical politics of sex-radical feminism (Duggan and Hunter, 2006, p. 2). By speaking in a liberal idiom, FACT was able to hitch sex-radical feminism's ambitious agenda, which included resisting sexual oppression in all its forms and creating a vibrant and diverse public sexual culture, to a familiar (and much less threatening) liberal politics of 'free speech' and 'civil liberties' (Duggan and Hunter, 2006, p. 7). This enabled FACT to make not only an effective case against the Dworkin–MacKinnon ordinance, but a lasting contribution to liberal thought as well. FACT's strategic deployment of liberal rhetoric led directly to the creation of a new discourse on pornography and sexual freedom that provided an alternative to the ambivalent one liberals traditionally employed. I call this new liberal-feminist hybrid discourse 'anti-censorship/pro-sex feminism.'[15]

A key figure in the articulation and popularization of anti-censorship/pro-sex feminism was Nadine Strossen.[16] As president of the ACLU from 1991 to 2008, founder of Feminists for Free Expression, and a member of the National Coalition against Censorship's Working Group on Women, Censorship, and 'Pornography,' Strossen worked to dispel what she called the 'widespread misperception' that feminists and civil libertarians were fundamentally at odds over pornography (1993, p. 1107). According to Strossen, 'feminism and civil liberties are inextricable' and the 'anti-censorship position' customarily grounded in 'free speech' and 'First Amendment principles' also found sustenance in 'feminist principles and concerns' (1987, p. 202, 1993, p. 1103). To support this claim, Strossen drew on the arguments and ideas of sex-radical feminists. Censoring pornography, Strossen insisted, would not only 'violate... cherished First Amendment freedoms,' it would hinder 'women's efforts to develop their own sexuality,' exacerbate the oppression of lesbians and other sexual minorities, 'harm women who voluntarily work in the sex industry,'[17] and undermine 'essential aspects of human freedom,' including 'sexual freedom' (1995, p. 14, 1993, pp. 1111–1112). Such contentions, originally put forward by sex-radical feminists as alternatives to the limited defenses of sexual freedom anti-censorship liberals espoused, became, in Strossen's hands, evidence of 'the falseness of the purported dichotomy between feminist and civil libertarian principles' (Strossen, 1987, p. 201). Once portrayed by sex-radical feminists as an inadequate response to a 'Kafkaesque' system of sexual oppression, liberalism's narrow sexual politics of anti-censorship and expressive freedom were now passing as a sex-radical feminist sexual politics.

Despite the willingness of anti-censorship/pro-sex feminists like Strossen to figure sexuality as an intrinsically valuable domain of human experience and to express concern for the rights of (some) sexual minorities in the course of defending traditional First Amendment liberties, this fusion of anti-censorship liberalism and sex-radical feminism did not extend liberal sexual politics beyond traditional bounds. Like their liberal forebears, anti-censorship/pro-sex feminists consistently failed to exhibit concern for sexual freedom beyond expressive freedom or to address forms of sexual oppression beyond state censorship. These failures are evident in 'Polluting the Censorship Debate,' a report issued by the ACLU in July of 1986 to criticize the findings of the Meese Commission. Although this report offers the sort of bold and unequivocal defense of sexual expression qua sexual expression that eluded even the staunchest civil libertarians for generations,[18] it stops far short of pursuing a sex-radical feminist politics of sexual freedom. For instance, the report defends 'constitutionally protected expression' like pornography by insisting on its distinctiveness from criminal conduct such as 'pandering' (i.e., pimping) and 'prostitution' (Lynn, 1986, p. 131). As the report argues, 'if producing film or pictures, not sexual gratification for money, is the primary purpose of the actors' work, then that work can in no way be called prostitution, and paying the actors' salaries can in no way be called pandering' (Lynn, 1986, p. 132). This argument for the legitimacy of pornography as constitutionally protected expression – an argument, it is worth remembering, that prior liberals had been unwilling to make – tacitly endorses the criminalization of commercial sex work like prostitution. Such an argument would have been untenable to sex-radical feminists who were concerned with a sexual freedom that far outstripped expressive freedom and encompassed the right to engage in commercial sex without fear of stigma or punishment.[19]

The stance on laws regulating child pornography and intergenerational sex adopted by the ACLU in this report is also at odds with a sex-radical feminist politics of sexual freedom. While sex-radical feminists like Gayle Rubin and Pat Califia opposed age-of-consent and child pornography laws as oppressive denials of the sexual autonomy of young people and unjust threats to the civil liberties and sexual freedom of many adults, the ACLU report shows little concern for either of these matters. In fact, the report clearly states that, while the ACLU believes that child pornography laws pose a threat to constitutionally protected speech, the organization also 'agrees with [the Meese Commission] that the vast bulk of child pornography does represent the non-consensual violation of a child's rights' and that 'the criminal law should proceed... with increased vigor against those who commit the underlying conduct which results in the sexually explicit photographs of children' (Lynn, 1986, p. 103, 105). 'There is much to be done,' the ACLU report continues, 'to reach those who finance these photographic productions; those who procure the children (with various degrees of coercion) into making the photographs; those who engage in sexual activities with children, as well as other knowing and willful participants who aid and abet in molestation' (Lynn 1986, p. 105).[20] The possibility that so-called 'child pornography' depicts benign and consensual acts or that a criminal crackdown on 'molestation' might make already stigmatized sexual minorities even more vulnerable to harassment and persecution is not entertained by the ACLU whose sole concern is expressive freedom, not sexual freedom along the lines envisioned by sex-radical feminists.

As the ACLU's official response to the findings of the Meese Commission indicates, the strategic appropriation of civil liberties rhetoric by sex-radical feminists yielded ambiguous results. While the Dworkin–MacKinnon ordinance was defeated and a space for a more robust defense of sexual expression was opened up within the conceptual confines of liberalism, these achievements came at a price. Many of sex-radical feminism's defining features – its expansive vision of sexual freedom and its concern with modes of sexual oppression beyond state censorship – did not survive liberal translation. In the end, sex-radical feminists' attempts to strategically deploy liberalism in the service of their radical ends got away from them and gave rise to the attenuated sexual politics of anti-censorship/pro-sex feminism. Adherents to this new liberal-feminist hybrid position deployed select aspects of sex-radical feminist thought to do what liberals had always done: defend the expression of sexually orthodox ideas against state censorship. Meanwhile, aspects of sex-radical feminism that were not readily assimilable to this longstanding liberal project, including its challenge to a vast sociolegal apparatus that targets dissident sexualities for regulation and punishment, fell into disuse and obscurity.

Anti-censorship/pro-sex feminism and the rise of carceral feminism

This history of the convergence of liberalism and sex-radical feminism during the sex wars bears important implications for evaluating contemporary feminist interventions like SlutWalk. In a superficial sense, at least, the SlutWalk movement shares certain affinities with feminist positions articulated on both 'sides' of the sex wars. For instance, its emphasis on the broader societal and cultural factors that produce sexual violence bears an obvious resemblance to antipornography feminism. Equally obvious is SlutWalk's continuity, in at least some respects, with the audacious spirit of public sexual assertion characteristic of sex-radical feminism. However, hailing the SlutWalk movement as a rapprochement between antipornography feminism and sex-radical feminism leaves many of its most important facets unaccounted for.

For example, in her recent study of the SlutWalk movement, Kaitlynn Mendes notes that, in addition to challenging 'rape culture,' one of the movement's central priorities has been combatting 'slut-shaming' by promoting 'respect for the individual and the variety of choices they make (including the freedom to dress how they want).' SlutWalk Toronto's co-founder, Heather Jarvis, has foregrounded this facet of the movement. When asked in an interview about SlutWalk Toronto's controversial decision to 're-appropriate' the word 'slut,' Jarvis explained that, while she 'completely respect[s]' people who have criticized her effort to 'reclaim' the charged term, using the word 'slut' in a 'positive context' is 'a choice for some people' and she 'want[s] more choice, not less' (Mistry, 2011).

This emphasis on self-expression and personal choice, especially as it pertains to the conventionally feminine and heterosexual women who bear the brunt of the 'slut' stigma, distinguishes SlutWalk rather starkly from the sexual politics of sex-radical feminism. Prior to their strategic appropriation of liberal 'anti-censorship' rhetoric in the mid-1980s, sex-radical feminists vindicated a vision of sexual freedom so expansive that it seems scandalous and utopian even today. They demanded not merely more space for individual women to enact fairly conventional forms of feminine heterosexuality, but an end to all legal and extra-legal methods of enforcing erotic conformity including statutory rape laws, child pornography laws, laws prohibiting public sex, family violence, employment and housing discrimination; and psychiatric diagnoses and hegemonic norms that punish the 'perverse' and reward the 'normal' (Rubin, 1984, pp. 294, 292, 289, 295). In stark contrast, the SlutWalk movement shows little interest in addressing these multifarious forms of sexual oppression. In fact, rather than critically interrogating the erotic conformity enacted by SlutWalkers parading around in matching bra and panty sets calling themselves 'sluts' as the ambivalent effect of a system of sexual oppression that makes alternative erotic possibilities virtually unthinkable, the SlutWalk movement valorizes these performances of a commonplace, even hackneyed, feminine (hetero)sexuality as hard-won products of individual struggle and choice.[21]

Such willful disregard for sexual oppression broadly conceived signals not only the SlutWalk movement's discontinuity with sex-radical feminism, but its continuity with anti-censorship/pro-sex feminism. For anti-censorship/pro-sex feminists like Nadine Strossen, sexual freedom was not 'the freedom to be as queer, as perverted on the street and on the job as [you are] in [your] dungeon,' but the freedom to express conventional ideas about sex and gender without being subject to state censorship. This narrow conception of sexual freedom is very much akin to the sexual freedom sought by the SlutWalk movement: the freedom to 'dress how [you] want,' 'be sexual in your own way,' and publicly perform a normative feminine (hetero)sexuality without being judged or sanctioned.

The SlutWalk movement's investment in a narrow and individualistic vision of sexual freedom fuels another aspect of the movement that marks a stark departure from sex-radical feminism. As I have already noted, the SlutWalk movement seeks not only to combat sexual assault, but to do so in a way that celebrates (rather than critically interrogates the limits of) women's freedom to express their sexuality in whatever ways they choose. Honoring these dual commitments requires the SlutWalk movement to respond to the problem of sexual violence without engaging in critiques of normative scripts of (hetero)sexuality and gender that might have a chilling effect on individual choice and expression. Faced with this quandary of resisting sexual violence while refraining from questioning norms that support it, the SlutWalk movement falls back on a strikingly carceral solution. In its rhetoric and messaging, SlutWalk places virtually all responsibility for sexual assault on individual perpetrators and figures the carceral state as the guarantor of women's sexual freedom.

As I noted in the introduction, the carceral thrust of the SlutWalk movement has been evident from its advent in Toronto. Despite the fact that the original SlutWalk was inspired by outrage at police complicity in rape culture, its primary message was an appeal to police for protection and respect. 'We want Toronto Police Services to take serious steps to regain our trust,' SlutWalk Toronto demanded via its website, 'We want to feel that we will be respected and protected should we ever need them, but more importantly be certain that those charged with our safety have a true understanding of what it is to be a survivor of sexual assault – slut or otherwise' (SlutWalk Toronto, 2011). A similar appeal emanated from a SlutWalk march in New York City in October of 2011. Despite the fact that the protest occurred only a few months after the acquittal of two NYPD officers accused of raping a woman while on duty and only one day after reports surfaced that police investigating a series of rapes in Brooklyn's Park Slope neighborhood were warning women against wearing skirts or dresses because they provide 'easy access,' SlutWalk New York figured police as agents of sexual and gender justice (Anderson, 2011). Carrying signs bearing messages like 'Punish rapists not victims!' and 'NYPD: Target Brooklyn rapist not women!!!' SlutWalk New York demonstrators called on police to use the full force of their powers on behalf of survivors to catch and punish rapists (Daily Mail Reporter, 2011; Kirschner, 2011). SlutWalk New York organizer Sammy Lifson even couched her critique of victim-blaming and slut-shaming in terms of police efficacy. 'The cops in Park Slope have really stepped up their presence and they're trying to be helpful,' Lifson told a reporter at the event, 'But to focus on women isn't going to help catch the perpetrator' (Daily Mail Reporter, 2011). As these remarks reveal, the goal of these North American SlutWalks was not to highlight police and law enforcement complicity in sexual violence and rape culture but to figure the 'slut' as a supplicant before the law deserving of its benevolent protection as any other citizen.

By framing the 'slut' as a vulnerable subject entitled to the state's protection, the SlutWalk movement employs what Iris Marion Young calls 'the logic of masculinist protection' (2003). According to this logic, men are 'gallantly masculine' protectors who '[face] the world's difficulties and dangers in order to shield women from harm,' while women are submissive 'objects of love and guardianship' who 'adore [their] protector[s] and happily defer to [their] judgment in return for the promise of security' (Young, 2003, pp. 4–5). When this gendered logic is extrapolated to the macro level of the modern state, the outcome is authoritarian. Cast in the roll of benevolent masculine protector, the state's power to surveil, police, detain, and repress in the name of the security of its feminized citizenry is virtually limitless. While the SlutWalk movement challenges the logic of masculinist protection at the micro level by repudiating 'slut-shaming' and insisting that women be treated as autonomous sexual subjects regardless of their sexual choices, its macro level demand that police respect and protect 'sluts' just as they would any other citizens bolsters the carceral state's image as masculine protector and aggrandizes its power.

The SlutWalk movement's faith in the carceral state's capacity to protect and, ultimately, liberate is not something it inherited from its sex-radical feminist forebears.[22] As I have shown, prior to the strategic alliance of sex-radical feminists with anti-censorship liberals in the mid-1980s, sex-radical feminists were ruthlessly critical of the criminal justice system. In Gayle Rubin's analysis, the carceral state was not an ally in the feminist struggle for sexual freedom, but part of a vast 'system of sexual oppression,' that 'Kafkaesque nightmare in which unlucky victims become herds of human cattle whose identification, surveillance, apprehension, treatment, incarceration, and punishment produce jobs and self-satisfaction for thousands of vice police, prison officials, psychiatrists, and social workers' (1984, p. 293).

However, as sex-radical feminism resolved into a more conventional anti-censorship politics in the late-1980s and early-1990s, its characteristic suspicion of the carceral state all but vanished. Intent on vindicating an individual's right to free expression, but wary of undermining the boundaries between the perverse and the normal that liberal defenses of expressive freedom had always bolstered and relied on, anti-censorship/pro-sex feminists defended the freedom of individuals to engage in conventional forms of sexual expression while tacitly accepting (or, in some cases, vigorously endorsing) the criminal regulation of other highly stigmatized forms of sexual conduct. One sees this carceral defense of expressive freedom at work in the ACLU's official report on the findings of the Meese Commission. While the report offers a bold defense of sexual expression qua sexual expression, it also advocates the criminalization of a variety of forms of sexual conduct, including prostitution, pandering, intergenerational sex, and 'child pornography' broadly defined.

While it may seem counterintuitive to claim that liberalism, with its emphasis on individual liberty, limited government, and a sacrosanct private realm of thought and belief, helped forge a feminist politics that aggrandizes the carceral state, this is precisely what seems to have occurred in the case of anti-censorship/pro-sex feminism. A dogged commitment on the part of anti-censorship/pro-sex feminists to expressive freedom supplanted a broader sex-radical feminist vision of sexual freedom and led to the endorsement of a variety of laws criminalizing the very marginalized sexualities that sex-radical feminists had once championed. A similar dynamic is plainly evident in North American SlutWalks. Committed to a narrow conception of sexual freedom qua expressive freedom, the SlutWalk movement holds up aggressive law enforcement as the key to securing women's freedom to look and live as 'sluts' if they so choose. Constrained by this liberal aim, the SlutWalk movement fails to address the carceral state's complicity in sexual oppression, particularly the widespread sexual abuse and harassment of prisoners, queer, trans, and gender-non-conforming people, and sex workers. Sex-radical feminists were once sharply attuned to this complicity. Recovering their analysis can help contemporary feminists look beyond a narrow liberal politics of expressive freedom and toward anti-carceral approaches to sexual liberation that center on restorative justice and community accountability.[23] A feminist movement that is serious about sexual pleasure and freedom must contest the power of the carceral state, not intensify it. A liberal politics of expressive freedom, no matter how vigorously 'sex-positive,' is simply not up to this vital task.

Acknowledgements

The author would like to thank Patrick Arnold, Cristina Beltran, Jocelyn Boryczka, Susan Burgess, Andrew Dilts, Farah Godrej, Mary Hawkesworth, Manu Samnotra, and the editors and anonymous reviewers at *Contemporary Political Theory* for their helpful feedback at various stages in this project's development.

About the Author

Lorna Bracewell is a visiting assistant professor of political science at Flagler College. Her scholarship focuses on the politics of gender and sexuality and has been published in academic journals such as *Signs: Journal of Women in Culture and Society* and popular forums such as the *Washington Post*. She earned her Ph.D. in political science from the University of Florida in 2015.

Notes

1 Bernstein also highlights several examples of 'center-left' feminists embracing the carceral politics of the anti-trafficking movement (2010, p. 54). Unfortunately, instead of asking what distinctive political commitments may be driving these liberal feminists in carceral directions, she simply describes them as 'eager partners to conservative feminist anti-trafficking campaigns' (2010, p. 54).
2 According to Bureau of Justice Statistics studies in 2011 and 2012, 3.2 per cent of all people in jail, 4 per cent of state and federal prisoners, and 9.5 per cent of those held in juvenile detention in the U.S. reported having been sexually abused in their current facility in the preceding year (Kaiser and Stannow, 2013). While data on sexual abuse in Canadian prisons are more difficult to obtain, scholars claim that rates are likely similar to U.S. rates (Ellenbogen, 2009, pp. 344–347). Regarding sexual abuse and harassment perpetrated by the carceral state beyond the walls of the prison, a 2015 report by The University of California's Williams Institute documents extensive police harassment of LGBTQ people. For example, according to a 2012 survey of more than 300 residents of Queens, New York, 54 per cent of all LGBTQ respondents reported being stopped by police, compared to 28 per cent of non-LGBTQ respondents. 'Among those individuals who reported being stopped by police,' the report explains, '51 per cent of all LGBTQ respondents and 61 per cent of just transgender respondents reported that they had been physically or verbally harassed by the police during the stop, compared with 33 per cent of non-LGBTQ respondents. Some respondents also reported 'sexual abuse perpetrated… by police officers,' including individuals who reported that they were 'forced to perform sexual acts under threat of arrest' (Mallory et al., 2015, pp. 7–8).
3 The focus of this essay are SlutWalks in the U.S. and Canada. On the movement's transnational peregrinations, see Leach (2013), Carr (2013), Lim and Fanghanel (2013), Kapur (2012), Mitra (2012), and Borah and Subhalakshmi, (2012).
4 Gail Dines and Wendy Murphy have accused SlutWalk of contributing to the 'pornification' of women and girls (2011). Bonnie Dow and Julia Wood have expressed concern that SlutWalk 'negate[s] or pathologize[s] queerness' (2014, p. 30). Kathy Miriam has criticized SlutWalk for relying on a neoliberal discourse of self-determination that willfully ignores 'the matrices of social relations through which [women's] choices are structured' (2012, p. 263). Perhaps the most influential critique of SlutWalk has been that it marginalizes women of color. See, for example, Crawford (2011) and Bogado (2011).
5 The 'sides' in feminism's sex wars have been called by many names. By 'antipornography feminism,' I mean to refer to ideas advanced by individuals like Susan Brownmiller and Andrea Dworkin and organizations like Women Against Pornography. By 'sex-radical feminism,' I mean to refer to ideas advanced by individuals like Pat Califia and Gayle Rubin and organizations like Samois.
6 SlutWalk's 'sex-positive' ethos has led at least one scholar to overlook its carceral inflection. In her introduction to a recent special issue of *Signs*, Suzanna Danuta Walters insists that 'young activists demanding changes in universities' handling of sexual assault are not simply litigious "carceral

feminists" parroting the likes of Catharine MacKinnon… but are often the same folks marching in SlutWalks and pushing for genderqueer freedom and polyamorous perversity' (2016, p. 3). Walters' implication here is clear: because SlutWalkers are 'sex-positive,' they cannot be carceral feminists. As I demonstrate in this essay, this is far from true.

7. On the centrality of the public/private distinction to liberal theory and practice, see Okin (1979, 1989), Elshtain (1981), and Pateman (1989).

8. Antipornography feminists' engagements with liberalism have been the focus of previous scholarship (Bracewell, 2016).

9. Wendy Brown has leveled similar criticisms against antipornography feminism for aggrandizing state power, juridicalizing feminist politics, and shoring up traditional norms of gender and sexuality (1995). My work supplements Brown's by demonstrating that such solecisms were perpetrated on both 'sides' of the sex wars.

10. Some particularly influential statements of sex-radical feminism include Samois (1979), Samois (1982), Vance (1984), Califia, (1994), Hollibaugh (2000), and Rubin (2011). Also, Jocelyn Boryczka's *Suspect Citizens* (2012) offers a portrait of sex-radical feminism that nicely captures its radical challenge to the dualistic logics of virtue and vice underpinning liberal defenses of sexual expression.

11. Pat Califia is now a bisexual transman who goes by Patrick. Before 1999, Califia went by 'Pat' and identified as a female lesbian.

12. For a transcript of testimony offered by FACT members at hearings for the Dworkin–MacKinnon ordinance, see MacKinnon and Dworkin (1997). For a description of FACT's protest against the 1986 Attorney General's Commission on Pornography, see English (1987).

13. It has often been mistaken for such. See, for example, Leidholdt and Raymond, (1990), Lee (2000), Larson (1993), Delgado and Stefancic (1992).

14. As Kathryn Abrams has noted, the FACT brief 'was animated by many of the concerns that inspired the sex radicals' (1995, p. 321). Carole Vance has also emphasized the continuities between FACT and sex-radical feminism more broadly (1993, p. 304).

15. My reading of FACT's strategy and its consequences differs from readings offered by other scholars. For instance, in repudiating attempts to paint FACT as an organization of 'sexual liberals,' Carole Vance makes no mention of FACT's strategic deployment of liberal rhetoric (1993, p. 304). Dierdre English, by contrast, represents FACT as a consummately liberal organization founded by women who 'didn't like having [male civil libertarians] do the fighting for them' (1995). Finally, Kathryn Abrams portrays FACT as a failed effort on the part of sex-radical feminists to influence liberal thinking (1995).

16. See also Kaminer (1980, 1992), Katz (1993), McCormack (1985), McElroy (1982, 1995), and Assiter (1989).

17. By 'women who work in the sex industry,' Strossen means 'women who pose for sexually explicit works,' not women who work in facets of the sex industry that are criminalized such as prostitutes (1993, p. 1162).

18. For example, the ACLU report describes the 'presumption that there is a difference between sexually oriented speech and all other kinds of speech' as 'completely unwarranted' and declares that 'the First Amendment should protect all sexually explicit speech' without regard to prurience, offensiveness, social value, or utility (Lynn, 1986, pp. 27–29). The report roots this sweeping defense of sexual expression in the claim that sexually explicit speech, including pornography, 'transmits ideas,' 'presents views of aesthetics and ethics about which public debate is certain and desirable,' and 'may… have as its purpose or effect the promotion of a political or ideological viewpoint' (Lynn, 1986, p. 30). To support these claims, the report cites sex-radical feminist theorist Ann Snitow.

19 As Gayle Rubin memorably states the sex-radical feminist position on the matter, 'whether sex acts are gay or straight, coupled or in groups, naked or in underwear, commercial or free, should not be ethical concerns' (1984, p. 153).
20 All in all, the ACLU report endorses 32 of the commission's recommendations pertaining to the regulation of child pornography.
21 In this respect, the SlutWalk movement is a paradigmatic example of 'choice feminism' (Kirkpatrick, 2010).
22 Nor is it something it inherited from antipornography feminism. Antipornography feminists viewed the carceral state as part of the patriarchal 'rape culture' they sought to dismantle, not its antidote. Susan Brownmiller's remarks on this score are representative: 'A police department, like a prison or an army, is by nature and structure a traditionally male, authoritarian institution ... Operating through sanctioned force, the local police precinct has always been a bastion of male attitudes and responses that are inimical to women' (1975, p. 270).
23 On these anti-carceral approaches, see Kelly (2010–2011) and Patterson (2016).

References

Abrams, K. (1995). Sex wars redux: Agency and coercion in feminist legal theory. *Columbia Law Review* 95(2): 304–376.
American Booksellers Ass'n v. Hudnut. (1986). 771 F.2d 323 (7th Cir. 1985), aff'd mem., 475 U.S. 1001.
Anderson, M. (2011). SlutWalk New York City preparing to take over union square. *Village Voice*. http://www.villagevoice.com/news/slutwalk-nyc-preparing-to-take-over-union-square-6686209, accessed 21 January 2018.
Assiter, A. (1989). *Pornography, Feminism and the Individual*. London: Pluto Press.
Bagshawe, L. (2011). Interview. *Newsnight*. http://www.youtube.com/watch?v=LytfEBYjiiQ, accessed 21 January 2018
Bell, D. (2014). What is liberalism? *Political Theory* 42(6): 682–715.
Bella, K. (2011). Bodies in alliance: Gender theorist judith butler on the occupy and SlutWalk movements. *Truthout*. http://www.truth-out.org/news/item/5588:bodies-in-alliance-gender-theorist-judith-butler-on-the-occupy-and-slutwalk-movements, accessed 21 January 2018
Bernstein, E. (2007). The sexual politics of the 'new abolitionism'. *Differences* 18(3): 129–151.
Bernstein, E. (2010). Militarized humanitarianism meets carceral feminism: The politics of sex, rights, and freedom in contemporary antitrafficking campaigns. *Signs* 36(1): 45–71.
Bernstein, E. (2012). Carceral politics as gender justice? The 'traffic in women' and neoliberal circuits of crime, sex, and rights. *Theory and Society* 41(3): 233–259.
Bogado, A. (2011) SlutWalk: A stroll through white supremacy. https://tothecurb.wordpress.com/2011/05/13/slutwalk-a-stroll-through-white-supremacy/, accessed 21 January 2018
Borah, R. and Subhalakshmi, N. (2012). Reclaiming the feminist politics of SlutWalk. *International Feminist Journal of Politics* 14(3): 415–421.
Boryczka, J. (2012). *Suspect Citizens: Women, Virtue, and Vice in Backlash Politics*. Philadelphia: Temple University Press.
Bracewell, L. (2016). Beyond barnard: Antipornography feminism, liberalism and the sex wars. *Signs* 42(1): 23–48.
Brown, W. (1995). *States of Injury: Power and Freedom in Late Modernity*. Princeton, NJ: Princeton University Press.

Brownmiller, W. (1975). *Against Our Will: Men, Women and Rape*. New York: Simon and Schuster.

Bumiller, K. (2008). *In an abusive state: How neoliberalism appropriated the feminist movement Against sexual violence*. Durham: Duke University Press.

Butler, J. (2016). *Notes Toward a Performative Theory of Assembly*. Cambridge: Harvard University Press.

Califia, P. (1994). *Public Sex: The Culture of Radical Sex* (1st ed.). Pittsburgh: Cleis Press.

Carr, J. (2013). The SlutWalk movement: A study in transnational feminist activism. *Journal of Feminist Scholarship* 4(Spring): 24–38.

Crawford, B. (2011). An open letter from Black women to the SlutWalk. http://www.feministlawprofessors.com/2011/01/open-letter-black-women-slutwalk/, accessed 21 January 2018

Critical Resistance and Incite!. (2003). Resistance-INCITE! statement on gender violence and the prison-industrial complex in the United States. *Social Justice* 30(3): 141–150.

Daily Mail Reporter. (2011) Scantily-clad 'slutwalk' women march on New York after police tell them to 'cover up' to avoid rape. http://www.dailymail.co.uk/news/article-2044213/Slutwalk-women-march-New-York-NYPD-tell-cover-avoid-rape.html, accessed 21 January 2018

Delgado, R. and Stefancic, J. (1992). Pornography and harm to women: 'No empirical evidence?'. *Ohio State Law Journal* 53(4): 1037–1056.

Dines, G. and Murphy W. (2011). SlutWalk is not sexual liberation. http://www.guardian.co.uk/commentisfree/2011/may/08/slutwalk-not-sexual-liberation, accessed 21 January 2018

Dow, B. and Wood, J. (2014). Repeating history and learning from it: What can slutwalks teach us about feminism? *Women's Studies in Communication*, 37: 22–43.

Duggan, L. and Hunter N. (2006). *Sex War: Sexual Dissent and Political Culture*. 10th Anniversary Ed. New York, Routledge.

Dworkin, R. (1981). Do we have a right to pornography? *Oxford Journal of Legal Studies* 1(2): 177–212.

Dworkin, A. and MacKinnon C. (1988). *Pornography and Civil Rights: A New Day for Women's Equality*. Minneapolis, Minn. (734 E. Lake St., Minneapolis 55407): Organizing Against Pornography.

Ellenbogen, P. (2009). Beyond the border: A comparative look at prison rape in the United States and Canada. *Columbia Journal of Law and Social Problems* 42: 335–372.

Ellis, K., et al. (1986). *Caught Looking*. South San Francisco: Longriver Books.

Elshtain, J. (1981). *Public Man, Private Woman: Women in Social and Political Thought*. Princeton, NJ: Princeton University Press.

English, D. (1987). Did porn destroy Pompeii? *Mother Jones* 12(6): 49–50.

Fahringer, H. (1979). If the trumpet sounds an uncertain note.... *New York University Review of Law and Social Change* 8: 251–253.

Gottschalk, M. (2006). *The Prison and the Gallows: The Politics of Mass Incarceration in America*. New York: Cambridge University Press.

Heiner, B. and Tyson, S. (2017). Feminism and the Carceral State: gender-responsive justice, community accountability, and the epistemology of antiviolence. *Feminist Philosophy Quarterly* 3(1): Article 3.

Hollibaugh, A. (2000). *My Dangerous Desires: A Queer Girl Dreaming Her Way Home*. Durham: Duke University Press.

Hunter, N. and Sylvia, A. (1987). Law. "Brief Amici Curiae of Feminist Anti-Censorship Taskforce, et. al." *American Booksellers v. Hudnut*. University of Michigan Journal of Law Reform 21: 69–136.

James, S. (2011). My placard read 'Pensioner Slut' and I was proud of it. https://www.theguardian.com/commentisfree/2011/jun/19/slutwalk-new-womens-movements, accessed 21 January 2018.

Kaiser, D. and Stannow, L. (2013). The shame of our prisons: New evidence. http://www.nybooks.com/articles/2013/10/24/shame-our-prisons-new-evidence/?pagination=false, accessed 21 January 2018.

Kaminer, W. (1980). A woman's guide to pornography and the law. *The Nation* 1980 (June 21).

Kaminer, W. (1992). Feminists against the first amendment. *The Atlantic* 1992 (November).

Kapur, R. (2012). Pink Chaddis and SlutWalk couture: The postcolonial politics of feminism lite. *Feminist Legal Studies* 20(1): 1–20.

Katz, L. (1993). Introduction: Women, censorship, and 'pornography'. *New York Law School Law Review* 38(1).

Kelly, E. (2010–2011). Philly stands up: Inside the politics and poetics of transformative justice and community accountability in sexual assault situations. *Social Justice* 37(4): 44–57

Kim, M. (2015). Dancing the carceral creep: The anti-domestic violence movement and the paradoxical pursuit of criminalization, 1973-1986. http://escholarship.org/uc/item/804227k6, accessed 21 January 2018

Kirkpatrick, J. (2010). Introduction: Selling out?: Solidarity and choice in the American Feminist movement. *Perspectives on Politics* 8(1): 241–245.

Kirschner, M. (2011). A 17-year-old does SlutWalk. http://msmagazine.com/blog/2011/10/04/a-17-year-old-does-slutwalk/, accessed 21 January 2018.

Larson, J. (1993). 'Women understand so little, they call my good nature 'deceit'': A feminist rethinking of seduction. *Columbia Law Review* 93(2): 374–472.

Leach, B. (2013). Slutwalk and sovereignty: Transnational protest as emergent global democracy. https://ssrn.com/abstract=2300699, accessed 21 January 2018.

Lee, L. (2000). Fact's fantasies and Feminism's future: An analysis of the fact brief's treatment of pornography victims. *Chicago-Kent Law Review* 75(3): 785–804.

Leidholdt, D. and Raymond, J. (1990). *The Sexual Liberals and the Attack on Feminism. The Athene series* (1st ed.). New York: Pergamon Press.

Lim, J. and Fanghanel, A. (2013). 'Hijabs, hoodies, and hotpants:' Negotiating the 'Slut' in SlutWalk. *Geoforum* 48: 207–215.

Lynn, B. (1986). Polluting the Censorship Debate: A Summary and Critique of the Final Report of the Attorney General's Commission on Pornography. Washington, DC: *American Civil Liberties Union*.

MacKinnon, C. and Dworkin, A. (1997). *In Harm's Way: The Pornography Civil Rights Hearings*. Cambridge: Harvard University Press.

Mallory, C., Hasenbush, A. and Sears, B. (2015). Discrimination and harassment by law enforcement officers in the LGBT Community. http://williamsinstitute.law.ucla.edu/research/violence-crime/discrimination-and-harassment-by-law-enforcement-officers-in-the-lgbt-community/, accessed 21 January 2018

McCormack, T. (1985). Feminism and the first amendment. *Justice Quarterly* 2(2).

McElroy, W. (1982). *Freedom, Feminism, and the State: An Overview of Individualist Feminism*. Washington, DC: Cato Institute.

McElroy, W. (1995). *XXX: A Woman's Right to Pornography*. New York, St: Martin's Press.

Mill, J.S. (1989). *On Liberty and Other Writings*. Cambridge: Cambridge University Press.

Miriam, K. (2012). Feminism, neoliberalism, and SlutWalk. *Feminist Studies* 38(1): 262–266.

Mistry, A. (2011). Slut-shaming begone: An interview with heather Jarvis, cofounder of SlutWalk. http://www.alternet.org/story/151025/slut-shaming_begone%3A_an_interview_with_heather_jarvis,_cofounder_of_slutwalk, accessed 21 January 2018.

Mitra, D. (2012). Critical perspectives on SlutWalks in India. *Feminist Studies* 38(1): 254–261.

Okin, S. (1989). *Justice, Gender, and the Family*. New York: Basic.

Pateman, C. (1989). Feminist critiques of the public/private dichotomy. *The Disorder of Women: Democracy, Feminism, and Political Theory*. Stanford: Stanford University Press, pp. 118–140.

Patterson, J. (ed.) (2016). *Queering Sexual Violence: Radical Voices from Within the Anti- violence Movement*. Riverdale: Riverdale Avenue Books.

Rembar, C. (1968). *The End of Obscenity; the Trials of Lady Chatterley, Tropic of Cancer, and Fanny Hill*. New York: Random House.

Rubin, G. (1984). Thinking sex: Notes for a radical theory of the politics of sexuality. In: C. Vance (ed.) *Pleasure and Danger: Exploring Female Sexuality*. New York: Routledge.

Rubin, G. (2011). *Deviations: A Gayle Rubin Reader*. Durham: Duke University Press.

Ryan, A. (2012). Liberalism. In: R.E. Goodin, P. Pettit, and T. Pogge (eds.) *A Companion to Contemporary Political Philosophy*. West Sussex: Wiley-Blackwell, pp. 360–382.

Samois, (Ed.). (1979). *What Color is Your Handkerchief?: A Lesbian S/M Sexuality Reader*. Samois: Berkeley.

Samois, (Ed.). (1982). *Coming to Power: Writings and Graphics on Lesbian S-M*. Boston: Alyson.

Shklar, J. (1998). The liberalism of fear. *Political Thought and Political Thinkers*. Chicago: University of Chicago Press, pp. 3–21.

SlutWalk Toronto. (2011). Why? Because we've had enough! http://www.SlutWalkToronto.com/about/why, accessed 21 January 2018

Strossen, N. (1987). The convergence of feminist and civil liberties principles in the pornography debate. *New York University Law Review* 62: 201–235.

Strossen, N. (1993). Preface: Fighting big sister for liberty and equality. *New York Law School Review* 37: 1–8.

Strossen, N. (1995). *Defending Pornography: Free Speech, Sex, and the Fight for Women's Rights*. New York: Scribner.

Tuerkheimer, D. (2014). Slutwalking in the shadow of the law. *Minnesota Law Review* 98(4): 1453–1511.

Valenti, J. (2011). SlutWalks and the future of feminism. http://articles.washingtonpost.com/2011-06-03/opinions/35235904_1_successful-feminist-action-slutwalks-young-women, accessed 21 January 2018.

Vance, C. (1984). *Pleasure and Danger: Exploring Female Sexuality*. Boston: Routledge & K. Paul.

Vance, C. (1993). More danger, more pleasure: A decade after the barnard sexuality conference. *New York Law School Law Review* 38: 289–315.

Wallsgrove, R. (1985). Feminist anti-censorship taskforce: The case against Indianapolis. *Off Our Backs* 15(6): 12–13.

Walters, S. (2016). Introduction: The dangers of a metaphor— Beyond the battlefield in the sex wars. *Signs* 42(1): 1–9.

Young, I. (2003). The logic of masculinist protection: Reflections on the current security state. *Signs* 29(1): 1–25.

Publisher's Note Springer Nature remains neutral with regard to jurisdictional claims in published maps and institutional affiliations.

Review Essay

Feminist afterlives: The defenses and dead ends of revisionist history

Contemporary Political Theory (2022) **21**, S95–S101. https://doi.org/10.1057/s41296-021-00524-7; published online 22 September 2021

Why we lost the sex wars: Sexual freedom in the #MeToo era
Lorna Bracewell
Minneapolis, University of Minnesota Press, 2021, 277 pp., ISBN: 798-1-5179-0674-0

We are not born submissive: How patriarchy shapes women's lives
Manon Garcia
Princeton, Princeton University Press, 2021, 234 pp., ISBN: 978-0-691-20182-5

Of the many vexing political questions that haunt feminists in the twenty-first century, one of the most difficult is also one of the most persistent: why are feminist theory and activism so susceptible to the appropriative co-optation of its best ideas? The question has undeniably contemporary motivations, given that in the last several years alone, feminist vocabularies have been deployed, very much against their own grain, to defend policing in the face of an abolitionist uprising, to denigrate and delegitimize trans women and their political claims, to explain away careening economic inequality, and to justify the extension of religious freedoms that dramatically undermine fragile gains for sexual freedom. As Lorna Bracewell and Manon Garcia show in a pair of books that return to previous moments in feminist theory and activism, uncertainty about how best to defend feminism against its would-be co-opters has been a perennial problem: from anti-feminist women and midcentury reactionary conservatives during the post-war era to liberal legal scholars in the 1980s, Bracewell and Garcia reveal a wide range of strategies that have threatened to appropriate feminist concerns for their own ends.

But these books waste no time bemoaning co-optation as evidence of feminists', or feminism's, political ineffectuality. As Bracewell rightly argues in her introduction, perennial hand wringing about how feminism has failed to live up to its promises has led more than one generation of scholars to adopt reductive narratives – such as the 'catfight' narrative that often frames the so-called sex wars of the 1980s – that both fail to take seriously the political arguments that feminists have developed and, worse still, underestimate the perniciously misogynistic ways that mainstream audiences misappropriate feminist claims in order to make them

Review Essay

amenable to existing structures and hierarchies. In refocusing our attention on the complexity of co-optation, these are books that seek to set the record straight about the range of feminist defenses that are available to us today. Where Bracewell turns to the sex wars of the 1980s to explore how both antipornography and sex-radical feminists interacted with liberal interlocutors who fundamentally undermined feminist claims about sexual freedom, Garcia returns to Simone de Beauvoir to explore how she upended the durable perception of women as passively submissive. In turning to these disparate political and disciplinary moments in feminist history, the books suggest that the contexts in which our ideas circulate can complicate – and sometimes altogether undermine – feminist efforts to realize women's liberation.

Where the books differ is in their view of what these questions mean for politics, which is in some ways as telling as the questions themselves. For her part, Garcia argues that the durability of women's oppression is an effect not only of men's domination, but also in no small part of women's submission. To understand the concept 'submission' with the kind of philosophical rigor she argues it deserves, Garcia frames the book in terms of an impasse between philosophers of the essentialist 'eternal feminine,' who argue that submission is an inherently feminine trait, on the one hand, and philosophers who see submission as a moral vice, on the other. For Garcia, these two strands of philosophical thinking pose a formidable problem for understanding women's freedom, since their actions are both circumscribed by assumptions about their inherently submissive nature and excluded from power on those same grounds. At the same time, however, Garcia is not satisfied with the idea that women's submission is wholly a social construct: women *do* submit, she argues, either to individual men in asymmetrical sexual and emotional relationships, or by failing or refusing to become feminists.

In the midst of this impasse enters Garcia's Beauvoir, who gives us the tools to understand the seeming paradox of women's submission by adapting the phenomenological method to feminist ends. In standard phenomenological accounts of power, and especially those developed by existentialists like Jean-Paul Sartre, submission – the willing relinquishing of one's freedom – is a paradigmatic form of bad faith that tempts all subjects at one time or another. However, Garcia shows that for Beauvoir, women encounter a unique situation: not only are they tempted in the usual ways to abdicate their freedom, but their whole experience of the world teaches, even *demands,* that they accede to these temptations. Thus, in Garcia's words,

> Like men, women are torn between the will to project themselves onto the world and the temptation to abdicate. Unlike men, however, submission is socially prescribed to women. There are therefore possible advantages for them in submitting … In the patriarchal context, woman's situation thus

alters the equilibrium between costs and benefits of freedom and makes freedom much more costly for women than for men. (p. 193)

Garcia's Beauvoir, thus, reveals that the challenges for an emancipatory feminist politics are steeper than we often imagine. In a world structured to offer women pleasure, love, and praise in return for their submission, women's very desire for freedom is truncated, co-opted, and narrowed in ways that sustain the status quo. Emancipation will require both confronting this reality and nonetheless persisting in the task of choosing freedom, as Garcia argues Beauvoir herself did: 'In writing *The Second Sex*,' she argues, 'Beauvoir manifests the possibility for a woman to throw herself into such and ambitious project, in this autonomous work that guarantees freedom. In that regard, she breaks the vicious cycle of women's oppression' (p. 203).

Puzzlingly, though, Garcia stops short of putting Beauvoir's analysis in any sort of conversation with the complex history of feminist politics and theory after 1949. In this way, *We are Not Born Submissive* sidesteps the very questions that give rise to the contemporary study of submission in the first place: nowhere does the book address feminists' remarkable attempts to undertake 'autonomous work that guarantees freedom' and to inaugurate political communities that ensure the possibility of women's *collective* freedom, which largely occurred, of course, after *The Second Sex* appeared. And nowhere does it address the co-optation, appropriation, and narrowing of those very projects of freedom, including a vast conservative backlash against feminist claims and their appropriation by neoliberal narratives of inclusion that would contextualize a contemporary interest in how and why submission interacts with today's world. Indeed, Garcia seems to suggest that if only feminists had more fully digested Beauvoir's philosophy in 1949, we would not have struggled so deeply with the political problems of enacting freedom from 1968 to the present.

Perhaps this is not Garcia's intention. But if she (and Beauvoir) is right that an adequate understanding of power would involve how the world militates against women's freedom in a structured way over time, then it seems an incredible overstatement to suggest that Beauvoir, in writing a single intervention into western philosophy in 1949, 'manifests' a model of freedom that can shape an emancipatory feminism in the present. Beauvoir understood that submission is something accomplished through repeated, consistent, and collective undermining of women's autonomous choices over the course of both a women's own lifetime and across generations; its power is in the granular refusals and misappropriations of women's actions over time, creating a 'situation' in which undertaking freedom becomes not only less successful but less imaginable. Without taking into account the afterlives of *The Second Sex* – or any other feminist manifestations of freedom – in the deeply divisive decades since its publication, Garcia misses perhaps the most important insight of Beauvoir's writing: that women's oppression is not

Review Essay

characterized by a dearth of free actions on the part individual women but by the exhaustion and frustration that comes with the world's constant undermining of their free actions.

By contrast, it is on precisely these grounds – the careful analysis of how feminist 'manifestations' of freedom have been frustrated by complex forces that exceed the failures of individual women – that Bracewell stakes her intervention. In her analysis of the so-called 'sex wars' of the 1980s, Bracewell takes up the afterlife of a period of feminist freedom seeking that has not only been subjected to a massive conservative backlash but also to more complex forms of undermining that even feminists themselves have largely failed to fully digest. The sex wars, Bracewell argues, 'tend to be remembered as a straightforward clash between sex-negative feminists concerned primarily with danger on one side and sex-positive feminists concerned primarily with sexual pleasure on the other' (p. 5). Bracewell's task is to expand our thinking about the range of arguments on offer by these feminists, as well as the political responses that have accompanied them over the course of decades. In pursuing this task, she shows that *both* projects, while importantly distinct and, at times, incompatible with one another, were pitched against the utter incapacity of liberal political thinking to adequately conceptualize the range of harms – and, critically for Bracewell, the possibilities for freedom – that lay just under the surface of mainstream, liberal sexual politics.

The book is an invitation to revisit ideas that, for reasons that are historical rather than conceptual, have been 'left behind' in feminist politics, and to think critically about the ways that the sex wars were 'won' on strategic alliances rather than on moral correctness. Bracewell gives a particularly generous historical reading, for example, to Catherine MacKinnon and Andrea Dworkin, whose work on notorious antipornography statutes has rendered them unwelcome interlocutors in most contemporary feminist debates. Critically, though, even as she calls for renewed attention to the range of thinkers involved in the sex wars, Bracewell claims neither to defend particular feminists on either side of the 'pleasure/danger' binary nor to offer a 'solution' to the political ambivalences that a careful analysis of the period opens up. Instead, she turns toward the question of co-optation and misappropriation much more directly than Garcia by turning attention to the responses that both antipornography and sex-radical feminists elicited in their liberal interlocutors. While she offers a range of ways that feminists have attempted to 'manifest' models for sexual freedom, she is attentive to the fact that such claims are always contested, both by other feminists and – more importantly – by those whose investments in the status quo drive them to willfully misconstrue, narrow, or undermine sexual freedom.

For Bracewell, liberalism was far from merely a backdrop for the sex wars; liberal legal scholars were not only active participants in these debates (Bracewell vividly describes encounters between liberals, antipornography feminists, and sex-radical feminists at legal conferences over two decades) but were also deeply concerned with winnowing both sets of feminist investments – so much so that both antipornography and sex-radical feminisms by the late 1980s had come to look like 'species of liberalism rather than ... [critical engagements] with it' (p. 27). This story of co-optation is more than a straightforward 'revisionist history'; it tells us something profoundly important about the intractability of gender and sex hierarchy as well as the seeming incapacity of feminist theories of liberation to remain committed to their more politically expansive impulses. Bracewell shifts responsibility for these failures away from feminists themselves and instead towards the 'situation' in which feminists found themselves in the 1980s; namely, in relation to liberal thinkers who were either unwilling or unable to recognize feminist arguments about sexual freedom as politically transformative, and whose 'tepid' engagements with feminist ideas reduced them to narrow legalistic notions like private expression and criminal violence.

Bracewell's writing is at its strongest when she underlines the gulf between these liberal legal notions and the feminist ideas they undermined and rewrote. On the one hand, she details how liberal conceptions of harm, which criminalize direct violence, diverged sharply from antipornography feminists' attempts to conceptualize sexual objectification as a new category of harm and to 'secure for it legal recognition and redress' (p. 84). Quite unlike the notion that pornography is criminally dangerous when it incites direct violence (an argument Bracewell attributes to liberal jurist Cass Sunstein rather than to feminists themselves), antipornography feminists sought to define pornography 'not by its prurience or its morally deleterious effects, but by its politics – that is, its contribution to the subordination of women' (p. 36). That Sunstein's antipornography liberalism 'conforms to, as opposed to defies or confounds, conventional liberal notions of harm, liberty, and the public and the private' (p. 46) by supporting the criminalization and punishment of violent sexual harms is a radical revision of the antipornography line, which in Bracewell's telling 'tended to view the carceral state as an extension of the patriarchal rape culture they sought to dismantle' (p. 182). Similarly, Bracewell's sex-radical feminists – Gayle Rubin, Patrick Califia, Amber Hollibaugh, and others – 'believed that the abstract liberal language of "civil rights"... hindered the cause of sexual liberation' (p. 113). In their pursuit of a radically expanded framework in which to give meaning to erotic life beyond free speech concerns, the freedom that sex-radical feminists sought 'vastly exceeded the freedom sought by midcentury civil libertarians' (p. 116). Indeed, despite their many differences, sex-radical feminists, like antipornography feminists, 'condemned defenses of sexual behavior rooted in appeals to privacy, rejected individualistic conceptions of sexual identity and freedom, questioned portrayals of (hetero)sexual desire as natural or innate, channeled significant effort into cultivating diverse sexual identities and erotic communities, and demanded a sexual freedom that entailed the destruction of what they theorized as a system of sexual oppression' (pp. 116–117).

Review Essay

Nevertheless, these models for sexual freedom, which sought to transcend a situation in which gendered and sexual hierarchies were politically obscured by liberalism's founding assumptions, were met with a range of appropriative responses that rendered their frameworks compatible with, rather than transformative of, liberalism itself. For Bracewell, feminism's failure to fundamentally transform the underlying conceptual framework of liberal democracy in the late twentieth century is not as much a feminist problem as it is a *liberal* problem, in that it reveals the granular and iterative ways that liberalism undermines feminist ideas:

> [The] feminist critique of pornography, which had emphasized the political character of pornography's harms and pursued remedies that flouted the bounds of traditional First Amendment jurisprudence, was supplanted by a much narrower liberal critique that represented pornography's harms in more conventional terms like 'violence' and 'crime', and pursued remedies that could be obtained within the bounds of long-standing liberal constitutional interpretation. In the case of sex-radical feminism, a project that began as an audacious demand for sexual freedom, which far outstripped anything even the most daring anticensorship liberals had ever envisaged, culminated in a moderately expanded liberal politics of expressive freedom (p. 127).

Ultimately, Bracewell concludes that liberals' failure to conceive of either sexual freedom or sexual harm outside of the narrow constraints of individual expression and criminal harm – and the strategic alliances that some (white) feminists made with liberals – is to blame for the paradoxical participation of feminist ideas in decidedly non-liberatory projects like the carceral state.

How different an account, then, than the one on offer by Garcia in *We are Not Born Submissive,* which poses the problem of anti-feminism as a philosophical rather than a historical question. Part of this vast gulf between the books is disciplinary; where Bracewell's aim is quite clearly to explain how seemingly feminist ideas have come to be included in an oppressive apparatus like the carceral state, Garcia's object is not so much to highlight how feminist ideas, like women themselves, are 'made' to submit to a world that militates against women's freedom as it is to elevate Beauvoir's philosophical interventions in the western canon. Nowhere are these disciplinary differences more apparent than in their treatment of the complex relationship between feminism and racial hierarchy. For example, Garcia devotes only a few short pages to the idea of intersectionality and then sidesteps the framework altogether by claiming that '*The Second Sex* has provided women from around the world a description of womanhood with which they could identify' (p. 108). By contrast, Bracewell concludes *Why We Lost the Sex Wars* by arguing that the 'failures of both white antipornography and white sex-radical feminists to take seriously the challenges offered by their Black and third world feminist allies during the sex wars … prepared the way for the liberal appropriations and attenuations' of both critiques of liberalism (p. 128).

This difference is not at all a trivial one. Indeed, Bracewell's argument that a 'monistic focus on the sexual needs, experiences, and desires of white women may have blunted the radicalism of both antipornography feminism and sex-radical feminism, leaving them more vulnerable to liberal co-optation than they otherwise would have been' (p. 178), offers a pointed rebuke to Garcia, who nowhere deals with how race or, for that matter, non-normative sexualities interact with how submission is lived or how we understand it conceptually. As Bracewell so compellingly shows, much of what has happened in feminist theory and politics since *The Second Sex* was published could be viewed as a lesson in the risks feminists incur when they fail to adequately grapple with intersectional realities. Denying or even bracketing these complexities risks the kinds of co-optations that lead, ultimately, to an even more ambivalent form of feminist submission to the liberal status quo – the deployment of feminist ideas in the service of a carceral state – in which feminism's 'ability to address sexual injustice is severely curtailed' at best, and radically rewritten, at worst (p. 198). If we are to resist such co-optations of feminism, Bracewell argues, we 'must look … toward alternatives in which potent, public, political, and most importantly, anticarceral responses to sexual injustice are at least conceivable' (p. 199). As Bracewell argues, those alternatives, at present, are largely the province of intersectional feminisms; returning to those manifestations of sexual freedom that remind us of our best, most intersectional defenses – rather than to origin stories that stake their claims in philosophical rigor – is the single most valuable weapon in the feminist arsenal.

Publisher's Note Springer Nature remains neutral with regard to jurisdictional claims in published maps and institutional affiliations.

Elena Gambino
Rutgers University, New Brunswick, NJ 08901, USA
elena.gambino@rutgers.edu

Critical Exchange

Feminist sexual futures

Judith Grant
Ohio University, Athens, OH 45701, USA
grantj1@ohio.edu

Lorna Bracewell
Flagler College, St. Augustine, FL 32084, USA
lbracewell@flagler.edu

Lori Marso
Union College, Schenectady, NY 12308, USA
marsol@union.edu

Jocelyn Boryczka
University of Detroit Mercy, Detroit, MI 48221, USA
boryczjm@udmercy.edu

Contemporary Political Theory (2023) **22,** 94–117. https://doi.org/10.1057/s41296-022-00589-y; advance online publication 26 October 2022

Lorna Bracewell, *Why We Lost the Sex Wars* (Minneapolis: Minnesota University Press, 2021).

I wrote my revisionist history of the feminist sexuality debates of the 1970s, 80s, and 90s as a ground clearing exercise. Surveying the panic over civil liberties, due process, and normative heterosexual courtship and mating rituals that the #MeToo movement inspired across the ideological spectrum from Margaret Atwood to David French, I began to experience what Eve Kosofsky Sedgwick calls 'Christmas Effects'. When all the institutions are perfectly aligned and speaking with one voice, as they tend to be during the Christmas season, the queer critic, on Sedgwick's account, is called to the work of disarticulation and disengagement. My primary goal in *Why We Lost the Sex Wars* was not so much to get the history of the sex wars right, although I haven't strayed so far from my training in the Cambridge School approach to intellectual history to repudiate that goal entirely, as it was to explode the reductive and politically debilitating myths behind which so much of that history has been concealed. As I write in the book's conclusion, 'the history of the feminist sex wars is brimming with alternatives' to a thoroughly liberalized feminist sexual politics that reduces sexual freedom to expressive freedom and

Critical Exchange

personal privacy, while framing the carceral state as a potential means to feminist ends (p. 199). My hope was that by bringing some of this history to light, I might disrupt the 'Christmas Effects' produced by liberal hegemony and create a space for fresh and historically informed feminist thinking about sexual freedom and sexual justice. This Critical Exchange on feminist sexual futures is a sign that my hope was not in vain.

Judith Grant's contribution helps us move beyond the caricatures and distortions of the 'catfight narrative' version of the history of the sex wars by recasting the debate between sex-radical feminist Gayle Rubin and antipornography feminists Andrea Dworkin and Catharine MacKinnon as a debate among structuralists and poststructuralists over the nature of the structure feminists should be contesting in their struggle for sexual liberation. For Dworkin and MacKinnon, Grant argues, the relevant structure is patriarchy, which they conceptualize as a 'simple/monolithic structure' that ties maleness to sadism and femaleness to masochism in a bipolar heterosexual system. For Rubin, by contrast, the structure of primary feminist concern is a more multifaceted and complex 'system of sexual oppression', 'a Kafkaesque nightmare' of laws and norms instantiating monogamous, vanilla, procreative heterosexual sex at the center of a "charmed circle" while relegating all other forms of sex to the reviled "outer limits" of sexual normativity' (Rubin, 1984, p. 293).

The hierarchical gender binary emphasized by Dworkin and MacKinnon certainly has a role to play in this structure, insofar as part of what makes monogamous, vanilla, procreative heterosexual sex the privileged form of sexuality is its compatibility with ideals of masculine dominance and feminine submissiveness. However, gender is not the only criterion by which sexual practices are judged and ranked in the system of sexual oppression Rubin theorizes. The question of whether a particular sexual practice supports or subverts the kinship structure of the traditional family is also brought to bear in constructing the multi-dimensional hierarchies of the charmed circle. While many scholars (including Rubin herself) have read Rubin's conceptualization of the charmed circle as marking a break with what Grant aptly describes as 'the latent structuralism of feminist theory' and the inauguration of a new poststructuralist queer theory, Grant amends this interpretation. According to Grant, 'Rubin does not dispute the structuralist idea of patriarchy, she strengthens it' by linking patriarchy to the kinship structure of the family rather than simply the gender categories male/female. Rubin, writing in the earliest phase of U.S. engagement with poststructuralism, relies on the transitional figure of Michel Foucault. She calls herself a poststructuralist, but, Grant argues, in retrospect her thinking is continuous with the structuralist strain in Foucault's thought insofar as it retains foundations. This recasting of Dworkin, MacKinnon, and Rubin as not simply bitter rivals in a sorocidal war over pornography and S/M, but as agonistic interlocutors in a shared theoretical project aimed at delineating the precise structure of patriarchal oppression, is just the sort of generative

Critical Exchange

reengagement with the sex wars that I hoped my book would incite. The choices between Dworkin/MacKinnon and Rubin, feminism and queer theory, danger and pleasure, sexual justice and sexual freedom have always been false ones. Reterritorializing the debate between Rubin and Dworkin/MacKinnon onto the history of the development of a structuralist feminist theory of patriarchy, as Grant does, strikes me as one promising way of moving beyond them.

In her contribution, Lori Marso mines recent explorations of the 'deep, lasting effects of sexual trauma' in feminist television and film for radical, intersectional, and anti-carceral insights into 'how patriarchy, racism, and capitalism shape our sexual experiences'. Marso's invitation to look to feminist cultural production as a site in which alternative routes out of the impasses of the 'catfight narrative' are being mapped is as smart as it is welcome. Reading Marso's politically and theoretically astute analyses of *The Assistant*, *I May Destroy You*, and *Promising Young Woman*, I was reminded that some of the most resonant and provocative interventions in the sex wars of the 1970s, 80s, and 90s were not the speeches, tracts, academic essays, and legal briefs that constitute the bulk of the source-base for my work, but artistic and literary productions like Alice Walker's 'Coming Apart', Pat (now Patrick) Califia's *Macho Sluts*, and the illustrations, photographs, short-stories, and poems included in Samois's *Coming to Power*. As Marso observes, the complex and ambivalent 'spectator feelings' evoked by feminist art can trigger 'difficult memories and experiences' while simultaneously troubling 'patriarchal and racialized habits' and 'suggesting possibilities for differently understanding our experiences of sex under racialized, capitalist patriarchy'. Like Beauvoir before them, feminists on all sides during the sex wars, including the antipornography feminists so unjustly maligned by their opponents as censorious enemies of culture, understood the power of feminist art to interrogate and transform sexual identities and desires. Andrea Dworkin's *Mercy*, an autobiographical novel that wounds the reader from one moment to the next with its searing horror and lyrical beauty is, perhaps, a better primer on antipornography feminist sexual politics than, say, the model antipornography civil rights ordinance which Dworkin co-authored with Catharine MacKinnon. This extraordinary and underappreciated work of feminist literature doesn't simply provide a critique of sex under conditions of mid-twentieth century white-supremacist, capitalist patriarchy; it gives voice to a wild and wanton feminist wish for sex beyond those conditions; for sex that, in Dworkin's words, isn't 'this one genital act, in out in out, that someone could package and sell' or 'some imitation of something you saw somewhere, in porn or your favorite movie star saying how he did it', but 'something vast, filled with risk and feeling' (Dworkin, 1990, pp. 171–172). In this poetic register of utopian longing, the affinities between Dworkin and the leather dykes of Samois are what strike you, not their differences.

Jocelyn Boryczka's contribution takes us still further afield from the politically debilitating confines of the 'catfight narrative'. By putting the sex wars, both past

 167 Reprinted from the journal

Critical Exchange

and present, into a broader global political context and persuasively elucidating the connections between 'the perennial ebb and flow of culture war politics' in the United States and the ideology of American exceptionalism, Boryczka connects what she calls 'an infectious liberalism' to a 'monism of the individual' that keeps feminist campaigns like #MeToo insular and beholden to domestic political institutions, especially the carceral state. As Boryczka aptly puts it, 'Liberalism in the US context pulls toward the monism of the individual in a way that delimits the possibilities of radicalism as it decouples connections across a range of groups much less nation-states, erecting obstacles to developing collectives or transnational movements'. While Boryczka graciously credits my treatments of the contributions of Black and Third World feminists like Audre Lorde and Cherríe Moraga to the sex wars debates with pushing analysis of feminist sexual politics in the more global and transnational directions that she believes are essential, I am the first to acknowledge the limitations of my work in this respect. Early in the process of writing and researching *Why We Lost the Sex Wars*, I made the decision to limit the scope of the project to debates about sex and sexuality undertaken by U.S. feminists in the 1970s, 80s, and 90s. This choice was driven, in part, by my own personal limitations. I am an American political scientist, trained at a U.S. university in the fields of political theory and American politics, who is fluent in only one language, English. Whatever there is of value to say about the sex wars of, say, Australia, India, or France, I am simply not equipped to say. I sincerely hope that those scholars who are, will.

Another factor influencing my decision to focus exclusively on the American iteration of the feminist sexuality debates was my keen interest in the equal parts maddening and astonishing capacity of liberalism to maintain itself as the horizon of all legitimate political discourse by assimilating and absorbing radical critiques and challenges. For theorists interested in this problem, the United States is one of the best petri dishes around. I hope my efforts, limited though they may be, have at least shed a glimmer of new light on these dynamics and processes.

Since I submitted the final manuscript for *Why We Lost the Sex Wars* in the summer of 2020, the radical, intersectional, and anti-carceral visions of sexual freedom it excavates have only become more vital. While it was a 'Christmas effects' feeling of boredom-tinged frustration with the narrow and unambitious sexual politics of liberalism that prompted me to begin my work on the sex wars, it is panic, fear, and horror at the fascist forces rapidly engulfing my home state of Florida, my home country of the United States, and substantial swaths of the globe right now that persuade me of its enduring value. We are living in a moment of intense heteropatriarchal white-supremacist backlash. The meager ground gained by the #MeToo movement in the generations-long struggle to render visible the normalized quotidian sexual abuse inflicted by the relatively powerful on their subordinates is being lost once again as defenders of patriarchal prerogative weaponize defamation laws to punish survivors who dare speak out about the harms and injustices they have

Critical Exchange

suffered. Abortion is also likely to be banned in over half of U.S. states, and even criminalized in some, now that the Supreme Court has issued its final decision in *Dobbs v. Women's Health Organization* and officially overturned *Roe v. Wade*. The *Dobbs* ruling has also thrown into fresh legal jeopardy other constitutionally protected substantive due process rights like the right to contraception, the right to same-sex marriage, and a right to sexual privacy which makes criminalizing gay sex unconstitutional. Meanwhile, state legislatures throughout the country are outlawing gender-affirming healthcare for trans people, banning critical race theory, restricting public schools from providing information about LGBTQ+ history and people, and enacting voter suppression measures so stringent that they recall the disfranchisement schemes of the post-Reconstruction era.

As my book is at continual pains to demonstrate, a liberal sexual politics oriented around individual rights, expressive freedom, and personal privacy is ill-equipped to secure sexual justice and freedom in even the best of times; in the face of a reactionary wave the size and scope of the one we are presently facing, it simply will not do. Women, especially those who find themselves at the intersections of multiple systems of oppression like poor women, trans women, queer women, and women of color, have virtually nothing to lose and everything to gain by embracing bold, transformative, and adamantly anti-carceral visions of sexual freedom such as those articulated by feminists on all sides during the sex wars. It is my hope that the work I have done in 'bringing these buried intellectual treasure[s] back to the surface, dusting [them] down, and enabling us to reconsider what we think of [them]' can be an impetus in these dark times against compromise, conciliation, despondency, and despair (Skinner, 1998, p. 112).

Lorna Bracewell

Structuralism, Humanism, and the Sex Wars

Lorna Bracewell wrote a terrific intervention into an important moment in feminist theory, the feminist sex wars of the 1980s. In her book, *Why We Lost the Sex Wars*, Bracewell claims that both sex-positive and sex-negative feminists devolved toward liberalism because of the interpretive context in which the sex wars took place. However, Bracewell shows that the sex wars were 'brimming with alternatives' that exceeded liberalism. Here, I want to raise one of the non-liberal debates that was also taking place in the 1980s, when the field of Women's Studies was undergoing at least three radical changes involving debates about identity/non-identity. These debates centered around what was then called 'postmodernism', multiculturalism espoused by women-of-color feminisms, and several authors writing in an emergent field of queer studies, one of whom was the pivotal figure Gayle Rubin. What I would like to suggest here is that all these approaches were reflected in the sex wars and, in a sense, part of the same debate.

Critical Exchange

In *Fundamental Feminism* ([1993] 2020) I argued that there was a feminist epistemology built around the category of experience. I used the sex wars as a kind of case study, arguing that it proved that women's experiences were so varied that the experiential epistemology could no longer hold together the category *woman* (e.g., some women participated in or otherwise claimed to enjoy pornography while others did not). I wrote that the idea of a universal female experience, however, was important as it was being used to hold the category 'Woman' together. Woman was being deconstructed from the points of view of poststructuralism, which argued against epistemology and the Subject, as well as multiculturalism, which argued that the experiences of women of color challenged the idea of a universal experience of all women. Because of the innumerable problems with experiential epistemologies, I ended by calling for feminism to abandon discourses of epistemology and move toward ontology. I argued for a structuralist theory that would leave the concept of patriarchy intact, as opposed to the various anti-foundationalist strands of poststructuralisms that talked about power as such, removed from any notion of patriarchy. The sex wars played an important role in these debates.

Andrea Dworkin and Catharine MacKinnon criticized pornography in theory and in law by arguing that it harmed women. They attempted to use civil law to empower women to sue pornographers and booksellers based on the argument that they were harmed by pornography. On a theoretical level, the claim was that gender was a hierarchy, with men representing the sadistic pole and women the masochistic one, a claim made repeatedly by Dworkin. As such, patriarchy was a structure of dominance wherein women, children, and animals could take the structural positions of masculine and feminine modeled by heterosexual sado-masochistic relations. MacKinnon, for her part, argued in a famous two-part *Signs* article that women could be turned into feminists by feminist consciousness-raising, which she regarded as the method of radical feminism. I should add, as an aside, that the Supreme Court did not address these fascinating arguments in finding the antipornography civil rights ordinance unconstitutional, but rather dismissed the laws on the basis of the relatively boring first amendment claim that they restricted the freedom of speech (and this goes to the point of Bracewell's book). Mackinnon in fact was using a critical legal studies approach to expand the doctrine of harm in a way that was consistent with Dworkin's and MacKinnon's structuralist theory of patriarchy, namely by holding that pornography harmed women as a group.

My claim is that Dworkin and MacKinnon's work was structuralist in that it relied on an idea of gender as a hierarchy connected to power (i.e., patriarchy). It was a simple, monolithic structure as it relied on a male/female dichotomy uniformly understood to be sadistic and masochistic and figured, in the first instance, as heterosexual. The idea accommodated other sexualities but only in relation to heterosexuality, i.e., in terms of the alleged sadomasochism of what they believed was the *Ur*-male/female relationship. This was codified in the ordinance proposed by Dworkin and Mackinnon in that, for example, lesbian porn continued to harm women insofar as it existed inside the structure of patriarchy and thus enacted and reproduced its heterosexual male-over-female model of domination.

Their work was noticed by west coast queer theorist Gayle Rubin, who, as it turned out, was a consumer of pornography and practitioner of S/M. Addressing MacKinnon directly, Rubin (1984) wrote about what she called 'the charmed circle'. For Rubin, the central category ought not to be gender—or not *only* gender, as Rubin later clarified—but rather should be sexuality. The argument of the charmed circle is that the more benign and reproductive sexuality is, the more it is affirmed by social custom and law, whereas the more esoteric it is, the more it tends to cast practitioners as an outgroup or 'other'. Rubin's work here was one of the pieces that initiated queer theory, and it is important that it was written explicitly in reaction to Dworkin and MacKinnon. Significantly, it suggested that sexuality determined gender, rather than that gender created sexuality, as the Dworkin/MacKinnon model contended—a claim that would become central to the queer theory of others such as Judith Butler. Further, Rubin's model proposed studying sexuality as its own model of power. While both Rubin, and Dworkin and MacKinnon, argued that heterosexuality was at the center of this power structure, Rubin did not link the existence of the charmed circle of sexualities to male power. Her text turns away from the structuralism of second-wave feminism that linked maleness to patriarchy and toward what Rubin terms poststructuralism. And while both Rubin and Dworkin/MacKinnon place heterosexuality at the center of their theories, Rubin moves away from epistemology (the use of women's experiences) toward ontology (that we all exist in a muddle of sexualities connected to power with heterosexuality at the center). Finally and crucially, Dworkin and MacKinnon view gender as creating sexuality, while Rubin argues that sexual practices create gender.

While Rubin understood her argument to be poststructural, her principal sources (Foucault and Levi-Strauss) are structuralists. It is important to recall that at this point in the U.S. there were very few texts of actual poststructuralism published in English. And Foucault himself was a transitional figure between structuralism and poststructuralism. Thus, the distinction between structuralist and poststructuralist theorists was glossed over in the 1980s in the United States. A key moment was Derrida's lecture, 'Structure, Sign and Play in Human Sciences', written in 1966, in which he argued that the difference between poststructuralism and structuralism was the removal of foundations, or to put the matter in Foucault's terms, the author. But this discussion had yet to make its way to Anglo-American feminist theory, and Foucault and Lacan were commonly and unproblematically referred to as poststructuralists in the United States. As a social scientist Rubin's work was taken up with gusto by poststructuralists working in the humanities who were talking about desire and esthetic judgements. What was missed, then, was that this feminist debate, which linked the sex wars to the debates about identity politics and poststructuralism, mirrored the one taking place between Foucault and Habermas.

Habermas had accused Foucault of destroying agency when he announced the death of the author and of applying a Nietzschean aestheticization of politics in place of the epistemological rational-justice model favored by Habermas. That is, feminist disagreements reflected a more general theoretical debate about the subject and the status of epistemology. Rubin, who had worked with Foucault, removed the subject (woman and man) when she moved the discussion to sexuality as an ontological discourse. Sexuality was the ontological soup into which we all entered, and it had no foundation in a structure of male domination, i.e., patriarchy.

Before Rubin wrote 'Thinking Sex', her 1975 essay, 'The Traffic in Women', had used Levi-Strauss to attack essentialism, arguing instead for an historicized notion of female subordination that takes both sex and gender into account. In 'Traffic', Rubin draws on the structuralism of Levi-Strauss's notion of kinship to argue that the concept of a sex/gender system was a better alternative to patriarchy for feminism because the term collapsed the normative and the empirical. Rubin's use of Levi-Strauss, therefore. was essentially methodological. Rubin was interested in generating a social scientific, mid-range theoretical concept that would be useful for empirical research, and she saw Levi-Strauss's insights about kinship as useful for this purpose. Kinship used the exchange of women to talk about the exchange of sexual access and status in a system where women themselves do not have power over the conditions of their own exchange Rubin goes on to say that gender is a socially imposed division of humanity that is an outcome of sexuality. It is the invention of kinship systems that changes males and females into men and women, i.e., what Levi-Strauss had described as the change from nature to culture. It also creates heteronormativity, insofar as it requires that sexual desire be directed toward the opposite sex.

But in 1984, Rubin wrote 'Thinking Sex: Notes for a Radical Theory of Sexuality', the essay that has been interpreted as a refutation of 'The Traffic in Women'. What happened between 1975 and 1984 has everything to do with feminism's overall shift away from structuralism. First, if we think of the second wave, including Dworkin and MacKinnon, as structuralist, then we can see that structuralism was being replaced by Rubin's poststructuralism. The debate about structuralism and poststructuralism was a debate about foundations. Under contention was whether one had to dispense with them entirely, as Derrida had argued in his attack on structuralism. It was also a debate about the subject in its role in power structures. Thus, as one of the formative texts that emerged from the sexuality debates and one of the original texts of queer theory, 'Thinking Sex' makes a strong move toward the poststructural in that it dispenses with the subject.

Rubin's argument that sexuality needed its own history came in the context of the sexuality debates and in the context of claims that, if not defending porn and S/M, showed that there were marginal sexualities which needed to be reclaimed and foregrounded. Rubin's desire to defend S/M led her to disagree with MacKinnon on the question of the foundational role of female experience and presumably also about epistemology. While both agreed that there was a structure in place, Rubin explicitly delinked sexuality from gender, while maintaining that heterosexuality was at the center of the system. Dworkin and MacKinnon, on the one hand, and Rubin, on the other, therefore offer two different ways to look at sexuality. The rhetoric of Dworkin and MacKinnon was to attach violence to the male in a simple structure, while Rubin detached gender from sexuality and made the structure more complicated.

Rubin was already talking about the themes of sex and the importance of sexual freedom and pluralism as it relates to gender in 'Traffic'. She says that she turned away from structuralism to 'discursive models of later Poststructuralism or postmodernism' but also that 'Traffic' is evidence of the increasing influence of Foucault on her work. In reflecting on the 1984 essay, Rubin said she was enormously influenced by the 1978 English translation of Foucault's *La volonté de savoir* (translated as *The History of Sexuality: Volume 1*). Her own 1984 essay marks her move from structuralism to poststructuralism and discourse theory. Foucault, however, is often considered to be one of the first generation of structuralists, and his *bona fide* membership in the poststructuralist club is disputed.

'Thinking Sex' is an argument that sexuality should be studied on its own terms as a social construct with its own history, and this argument is derived explicitly from the sex wars. Rubin not only argues that sex changes over time but also concludes with a call for a radical theory of sexuality and against sexual persecution, stigmatization, and sex negativity. Rubin (1984) directly attacks feminist anti-porn activists for their concerted attacks on sadomasochism as a sexual practice and charges the activists with being conceptually linked to right-wing sexual panics. She writes:

> In contrast to my perspective in 'Traffic in Women', I am now arguing that it is essential to separate gender and sexuality analytically to more accurately reflect their separate social existence. This goes against the grain of much contemporary feminist thought, which treats sexuality as a derivation of gender (p. 308).

The arguments of 'Thinking Sex' do not erase the structuralist claims of 'Traffic' but rather deepen its historicism in the important claim about how the patriarchal family structure is the foundational signifier against which all other sexual practices attain meaning. This is to say that perversion is judged as it stands against the measuring stick of the family, heterosexuality in its relationship to the family, and an extremely restrictive politics and disciplining of desire. In the end, I would claim that Rubin's poststructuralism does not dispute the structuralist idea of patriarchy but strengthens it, while linking it to kinship structure and the family rather than to the simpler male/female model proposed by Dworkin and Mackinnon.

Critical Exchange

This put Rubin in direct opposition to the rising tide of feminist antipornography activism. 'Thinking Sex' was in part a reaction against anti-porn activism, but it also marks an important theoretical turn as one of the key indicators of the origins of queer studies and feminist sexuality debates. It is also important for its important intervention in the latent structuralism of feminist theory. In particular, Rubin was reacting against MacKinnon who, Rubin argued, 'wanted to make feminism the privileged site for analyzing sexuality, and to subordinate sexual politics not only to feminism, but to a particular type of feminism'.

What are we to make of the tangled conversation about sexuality, gender, and theory? On the one hand, we are presented with Dworkin and MacKinnon, who make a fairly straightforward structuralist argument about power in its connection to maleness. On the other hand, Rubin's use of Foucault and Levi-Straus complicates the matter by discussing power as it relates to the sexual and by claiming poststructuralism despite retaining the family as a foundation. Further, heterosexuality is centered as the lynchpin of the normal, and other sexualities circle out from it in increasingly esoteric configurations. While 'Thinking Sex' is usually considered a repudiation of Rubin's earlier work in 'Traffic' it can be read as a parallel argument about sexuality, which also makes a structuralist argument that it mistakes for a poststructuralist one. Rubin took on Dworkin's and MacKinnon's claim that maleness is linked to sadism by delinking it from patriarchy and arguing instead that sexuality creates gender. She further detached pornography from patriarchy, arguing that it is not an ideological representation of patriarchy but can be a source of pleasure and desire. Here she provides a link to poststructuralist esthetics of desire, which analyzes sexuality as though it existed on its own, floating above gender and indeed generative of it.

Forty years hence, we remain stuck. Does pornography always and everywhere reproduce gendered patriarchy, or does it provide a way for marginalized (and perhaps also non-marginalized?) groups to engage in playful desire? Similarly, is the practice of sadomasochism the drama of patriarchy being played out in its most explicit form, or is it a way to engage, in a relatively safe space, with the power dynamics of all the (social, political, economic, and gendered) structures in which we exist?

Rather than pretending to answer these questions, I hope to add another layer to the sexuality debates by arguing that they are also the beginning of the 'postmodernism' debates. Rubin participated in the move away from discussions of patriarchy and introduces the idea of sexuality. While she did not intend to pose feminism against queer studies in so doing, she nevertheless displaces patriarchy and maleness as the targets against which feminism ought to rally, suggesting heteronormativity as a new target instead.

While I agree with Rubin about the hegemony of the 'plain vanilla' model of heterosexuality and its dire consequences for marginalized sexualities, I am still struck by Dworkin's and MacKinnon's argument. It seems to me that the enjoyment

Critical Exchange

and pleasure one can derive from both pornography and sadomasochistic sexual practices may be explained by the fact that they ratify and reproduce the reality of what is: patriarchy. They feel good because they are designed to feel good. However, Dworkin makes the same point about femininity itself, arguing that stereotypical behaviors act in conjunction with masculinity to form patriarchy. If women are socialized into these behaviors, it makes sense that they feel good. But the alternative from the point of view of patriarchy is masculinity, which is not good either. Dworkin and MacKinnon, as well as many other early radical feminists, suggest a utopian world where all these human characteristics are not systematically divided across gender but rather taken up by choice and individual desire.

Judith Grant

Winning the Sex Wars in Feminist Cinema and Media

In *Why We Lost the Sex Wars*, Lorna Bracewell reframes the so-called sex wars as pitting the 'feminist' side, which included 'antipornography feminists, sex-radical feminists, and Black and Third World feminists', against the 'liberal' side, which perceived 'feminist incursion into the domain of sexual politics' as either a 'threat or extension of core liberal values' (p. 28). Bracewell is especially interested in why and how the radical, world-changing visions of the feminists on the feminist side got narrowed and instrumentalized into talking points about free speech and the appropriate reach of the state. Bracewell says we 'lost' the sex wars in part because liberals were so good at appropriating feminist discourse, in part because carceral solutions became the go-to position, and in part because the dominant white feminist 'sides' ignored the experiences and perspectives of Black and Third World women who were much better at articulating how structural forces of race and capital, and not just patriarchy and gender, shape sexual experience.

I am interested in the multiple radical visions on the 'losing' feminist side as they are represented in recent feminist cinema and television. My hope is that we can claim a 'win' when, as viewers of feminist art, we are invited to encounter how the ambiguity of sex is shaped by women's individual and collective experiences of intersecting structures of capitalism, racism, and patriarchy. To think with feminist cinema in this way, Simone de Beauvoir's writing, in particular *The Second Sex* ([1949] 2011), is my touchstone. I use Beauvoir's language of ambiguity where appropriate and extend her insights in my characterization of Beauvoir's method and ontology as best captured by the language of encounter (Marso, 2017). The word 'ambiguity' refers to Beauvoir's insistence that we are always simultaneously subjects for ourselves and objects for others, and that this is nowhere *more*, but also *first*, apparent in the sex act. My language of 'encounter' builds on Beauvoir's idea that ambiguity is always situated (by structure, society, politics) to capture the

Critical Exchange

dynamism and agonism of the shifting and intersecting situations in which we find ourselves.

Beauvoir's language of ambiguity and my language of encounter help us see that sex acts are always intersectional in multiple ways. Sex as an encounter with an 'other' or 'others' might be experienced as pleasurable, violent, dangerous, shameful, empowering, belittling, rebellious, angry, or something else, all feelings that seem to occur in isolation from the larger worlds we inhabit. But every sexual act and its meanings are deeply informed by our encounters with structures of patriarchy, race, and capital. These encounters with seemingly distant, larger, circulating, permeating forces do not just 'situate' us materially: they also are embedded in our psyches; they influence the ways we carry our bodies; they orient our sexual desires—to whom and what our desire responds and how; and these ways of being in the world shapeshift as we move through different spaces, as we age, as we encounter different people, places, and things.

The undisputed ontological fact of ambiguity—that we are never alone, we are always entangled with others, we are always subject and object at once, and we can only seek but never guarantee freedom in encounter rather than alone—is sometimes inconvenient or frustrating, sometimes mortally dangerous, sometimes the source of great pleasure, but *always especially obvious in sex*, the meaning(s) of which feminists have long debated and which here I consider in the form of the 'sex wars'. These 'wars' include fights over how to define, regulate, participate in, and feel sex and sexual desire, as well as how to categorize sexual orientation; debating whether it is sex (sexual practices and orientation) or gender (masculine/feminine) that is more fundamental in solidifying patriarchal rule; arguing about what it is that the gendered and racialized imagery that circulates in a capitalist economy teaches youth about sexual pleasure and danger; determining when such imagery is pornographic and deciding if porn is damaging or freeing; asking whether carceral responses to sexual harassment, abuse, rape, and other forms of violation and unwanted advances are effective or desirable; and determining whether sexual practices and sexual desire are an effect of power, a natural impulse, a repetition of trauma, a source of resistance, or some combination of these.

Beauvoir's insistence on the ontological fact of ambiguity is a phenomenological claim that prioritizes subjective bodily experience, but with the language of encounter we can also see how theorizing the experience of ambiguity for Beauvoir is also a *critical* phenomenological claim. Bodies and feelings, selves and others, are not identical and available in the same ways for all, and our bodies and feelings are never ours alone. Bodily experience, and the feelings that arise from experience, are shaped by how our bodies are viewed, valued, or devalued and how they are interpreted and interpellated by a political and social world. Even our feelings which seem to be 'ours' alone, or our claiming of sexual desire, which, as Lady Gaga sings, is available at birth ('born that way!'), are actually the products of encounter between nature and culture, biological 'facts' and the framing of these facts. In other words, sex is a primary experience that is almost always an experience of hierarchy between masculine and feminine that is not only structured, but gets circulated and reinforced by gendered, raced, and ageist images and sounds, the repetition and rewarding of hierarchies and circulations of power, and our accommodating orientations to geographies that are set up to benefit maleness, bourgeois values, and whiteness.

Beauvoir's critical phenomenology, a method which captures the diversity and intensities of the lived experiences of girls and women under these circumstances, is available to us in the second volume of *The Second Sex*. She directs our attention to the way that patriarchy invades the senses, ordering and disciplining the sense perception and bodily comportment of young girls and women. In a typical passage, Beauvoir remarks that a young girl feels the encroachment of patriarchy 'in her flesh' (p. 335). In childhood, the young girl is often 'bullied and mutilated', but her future passivity is not *fully* embodied. Upon puberty, 'the future not only moves closer; it settles into her body; it becomes the most concrete reality' (p. 342). This invasion reads like horror: 'the hand that takes and that touches has an even more imperious presence than do eyes' (p. 335). Invaded, ordered, and having to breathe, hear, see, smell, and feel, the experiences of women and girls are vibrantly and vividly recounted throughout this volume and captured under Beauvoir's umbrella category of lived experience. The young girl's senses are all structured around the 'imperious presence'. 'There is this knee in the cinema pressed against the girl's, this hand at night in the train, sliding along her leg, these boys who sniggered when she passed, these men who followed her in the street, these embraces, these furtive touches' (p. 332). 'She cannot prevent his presence from haunting her'. At first, she revolts: 'She begins to feel a certain disgust for her father; she can no longer stand the smell of his tobacco, she detests going into the bathroom after him; even if she continues to cherish him, this physical revulsion is frequent'. She both wants to be desired *and* revolts against it; conflicted and confusing desires 'come from this very complexity the girl feels in her flesh' (p. 334). What is especially appealing about Beauvoir's work is that she attends to the interactions of biology, myth, history, and accumulated habits, and the culling of expected and normalized emotional responses to these habits, to show how experience is always materially shaped by situation in its manifestation as the perception of the senses.

The Beauvoirian account of sexual ambiguity, and my account of encounter. are also available to us in recent feminist film and media represented as concrete, everyday, ordinary instances of metaphysical, political, and structural dynamics. Film and television are uniquely able to bring to our attention things we might not otherwise acknowledge or want to think about. As spectators 'experiencing the experiences' of characters on screen, as Vivian Sobchack (1992, p. 3) puts it, we might newly identify how patriarchy, racism, and capitalism shapes our sexual experiences. We might even come to viscerally understand that our most ordinary experiences are impacted by power that is structural, hierarchical, affective, and what Davide Panagia calls 'dispositional', meaning circulating and enveloping as opposed to just dominating (Panagia, 2019). Beauvoir thought extensively about the role of concrete representations of metaphysical realities in literature, and she used multiple examples from literature, autobiographies, and films in the second volume of *The Second Sex* as she piles up examples of women's lived experiences. She is particularly attentive to images and sound (or we might say, our encounter with the partition of the sensible) in the process of becoming 'Woman', and she also helps us see that attention to alternate images and sounds might be a source of resistance to this same process.

Mining literature and film for exemplary details of this becoming and how to resist it, Beauvoir lauds the formal and narrative strategies of art as the 'only form of communication capable of giving me the incommunicable—capable of giving me the taste of another life' ([1965] 2015, p. 201). Feminist historian Judith Coffin characterizes the effects of Beauvoir's method as it reverberates with readers in an 'exceptionally interesting author-reader intimacy ... made intimate by the subjects discussed and the dense exchange of ideas, feelings, fantasies, and experiences' (Coffin, 2020, p. 2). Because our senses are indivisible from patriarchy's ordering of them, getting a 'taste' of the lives of others helps us feel reverberations, make comparisons, and build an alternative common sense. An individual's experience is often disjointed or jarring, and it is always, by definition, partial: as Beauvoir puts it, we each experience the world as a 'detotalized totality' ([1965] 2015). But these experiences are also always oriented in relationship to the structural architectures that shape the bodies and partition the sensible (and not just the visual) for all of us. In this in-between space that straddles agency and structure, Beauvoir leaves open the possibility to orient ourselves otherwise, hear and see new things, play discordant tunes. I see this critical phenomenology of experience utilized in recent feminist cinema and television as an invitation to spectator feeling. These feelings can trouble patriarchal and racialized habits and familiar (patriarchal family) ways of experiencing the world.

In my remaining space, I briefly point to a few key aspects of three recent examples of feminist cinema and media that depict young women (and feminized men) who experience sexual harassment, abuse, and trauma: Kitty Green's 2019 *The Assistant*, a low budget independent film about a recent college graduate (Jane, played by Julia Garner) who aspires to be a film producer in a starting position working for a Harvey Weinstein type media mogul; Emerald Ferrell's 2020 *Promising Young Woman*, a slick Hollywood film about Cassie (Casey Mulligan), herself not the victim of rape but avenging her best friend Nina's rape by luring men into sexual situations and reversing the gaze; and Michaela Coel's 2020 *I May Destroy You*, an HBO Max sponsored series about Arabella (played by Coel herself), an aspiring Black writer experiencing twinned traumas of writer's block and sexual assault. I highlight these particular examples because they are directed

Critical Exchange

by feminists; they are recent and much discussed; they represent the experiences of a diverse range of women and, in Coel's vision, a gay Black man; and in *Promising Young Woman* and *I May Destroy You*, carceral solutions to sexual offences are explored thematically. Carceral solutions also haunt *The Assistant*, as Harvey Weinstein's lawyers dealt with several criminal indictments in New York state (and later in California) just as the film was released.

The narrative focus on carceral solutions in these films—whether they work, how they impact the characters, and how they themselves are framed by racial, patriarchal, and capitalist dynamics—puts them in direct conversation with Bracewell's critique of the carceral solutions that were the seemingly inevitable outcome of pitting feminists against liberals in the sex wars. The ending of *The Assistant* is wildly anti-climactic. Jane sits in a coffee shop dejectedly eating a muffin as she wishes her father a belated happy birthday over the phone. This, after ninety minutes of the week's moments where, with Jane, spectators cannot help but notice the deep *wrongness* of office dynamics and Jane's own complicity in them. A trip to Human Resources, where Jane is gaslighted by the HR officer and told she won't have to 'worry about herself' because she is 'not his [the boss's] type' is one of the most disturbing moments. But what can she do? *Promising Young Woman* ends with Cassie's violent murder, but are spectators meant to be buoyed by her getting the last laugh when post-mortem texts she has arranged to go out arrive, seemingly from the grave, on the phones of the key players on the day of her killer's wedding? The police arrive to make the arrest, but can this be a happy ending, given we have seen earlier in the film how the dean of the medical school covered up Nina's rape and how the lawyer for that rapist got him off without reprimand? As Bonnie Honig notes, the incarceration debate in *Promising Young Women Woman* plays out as a debate about pedagogy, how to change the world 'one man at a time' (Honig, 2021) But is this a viable solution? It seems particularly doomed because Cassie is alone in her efforts. In *I May Destroy You*, we have the benefit of three potential endings that seek some form of justice for Arabella's rape by a white man: one is a scene of vigilante violence as revenge and reversal; in another, the rapist is arrested and taken away by the police after the rapist reveals his own sexual victimhood; and in the last one, because Arabella sees her rapist as a person with his own trauma, she is released from the traumatic repetition of having to watch the bar every night trying to remember what happened. This last ending is beautiful but also, in important ways, profoundly unsatisfying as the racial dynamics seem to recede in favor of a solution of individual working-through, in this case made possible because of Black sociality and networks of friendship. Regardless, in each of these films, carceral solutions are partial and imperfect at best, both for healing and for obtaining any form of justice. Perhaps what *I May Destroy You* does best is to offer all three outcomes, each a critique and supplement of the others.

Each of these pieces is also successful in subverting the male gaze (Mulvey, [1975] 1989) by using camerawork that situates viewers in an active feminine position to reorient spectator relationship to what is shown (or hidden) by the camera. In early work, Mulvey had identified the three gazes of cinema: the characters looking at each other; the spectators watching the film; and the gaze of the camera. For successful pleasure in narrative cinema, Mulvey says spectators must get caught up in the fantasy in the first dynamic—the characters looking at each other with the male active and the female passive—and forget about their own spectatorship and the framing of the camera. *The Assistant*'s slow and deliberate pace, its focus on Jane seeing her male coworkers *see* her (as inferior, as in charge of the grunt work and care-work of the office, which includes the cleaning of semen from the couch in the boss's office, fielding calls from the wife who asks about her husband's whereabouts, and delivering the new assistant to a hotel for a sexual visit from the boss) all serve to invite spectators to view the dynamics from Jane's perspective, feel the slow pace of the day, and see that Jane, from the perspective of her coworkers and boss, is an object among other objects in the office. In *Promising Young Woman*, another gaze is added to Mulvey's list as male characters (and potentially male viewers as well) are suddenly able to *see themselves as they see women* as sexual objects. When Cassie pretends to be drunk and accompanies men to their apartments only to look straight back at them when they begin having sex with her without consent, the male gaze is reversed and destroyed. *I May Destroy You* is the most *avant-garde* in its methods, employing flashbacks of sexual trauma which are presented as partial memories or fantasies that mix the gaze of young Black writer Arabella with a gaze that *includes* Arabella, thus undermining/contaminating the subject/object binary altogether. By the last episode of the series, spectators are denied the comfort of narrative cohesion when the three different potential endings fail to provide full narrative closure.

Each of these examples also uses sound in effective ways that, as I argue elsewhere, show how the 'white noise' of patriarchy invades the senses of promising young women, orienting us away from freedom (Marso, 2021). The sounds of the office telephone, xerox machine, typing, humming lights, and the coffee maker comprise the entire score of *The Assistant* (other than opening and closing credits). Director Kitty Green says of the soundtrack, 'It's about all the things that are going unsaid rather than are being said. There's barely any dialogue, but there's lots of tense sound work' (Shaffer, 2020), which alerts us to the sound of work. In addition to its bright colors and neon visual palate, *Promising Young Woman* employs a score of pop songs with names such as 'I was busy thinking 'bout boys' by Charli XCX and a remix of Brittney Spears's 'Toxic' as we see disgusting images of the gyrating male hips of aging fraternity boys who view the (pretend) drunkenness (is she lulled to sleep by the white noise of patriarchy?) of Cassie as an easy invitation to sex, and Cassie pretending to be a stripper as she approaches the bachelor party where she will be killed. The soundtrack suggests how promising young women are lured into their roles, failing to study what's beneath the lyrics, the promise or, what Emma Goldman calls the shiny bars of women's cages. And in *I May Destroy You*, we hear the noises of trauma—the thumping of the rape, the confusing hum of traffic, men's voices of excitement in the bar, and the silence of the bathroom stall where the rape occurs.

Together, the narrative arcs of these films and their technical/formal choices intentionally appeal to spectator feelings, potentially triggering difficult memories and experiences but at the same time suggesting possibilities for differently understanding experiences of sex under racialized, capitalist patriarchy. Sorority in the films, or the lack of it, is another factor to consider as we feminists propose alternatives to carceral solutions. We see no evidence of female friendship in *The Assistant*, although Jane initially goes to the Human Resources officer to try to protect the *new* assistant but is shut down. In *Promising Young Woman*, Cassie is moved by her friendship with Nina to risk her life multiple times and loses her life because of it but partly out of guilt for not being present when Nina was raped. In *I May Destroy You*, there is sorority *and* solidarity, which sometimes as a surprise when loyalties of race versus gender need to be negotiated, and historical wrongs cannot fully be righted, between white and Black women, gay men and straight women, and between friends who have personally failed each other. To see these repeated attempts in the wake of multiple failures on screen reminds us that we can continue to make promises *to each other*, and to promising young women, as an alternative to the carceral state. We might together think and act to create better sex and better conditions for more and better life. As spectators, moved by feeling these experiences vicariously, we too might make promises and *make moves*—not those of heroic action or fantastic revenge, but smaller, stealthier, pleasure-seeking, reparative moves—toward changing these experiences and rerouting the capillaries of power that undergird them.

Lori Marso

Seeing the Global Horizons of an Intersectional Feminist Future

On 24 May 2022, Salvador Rolando Ramos, who had just purchased two semi-automatic rifles and 375 rounds of ammunition on his eighteenth birthday, went to Robb Elementary School in Uvalde, Texas, after killing his grandmother. He killed nineteen school children and two teachers, wounding seventeen others before police shot Ramos to death. In the wake of this school shooting, the twenty-seventh in the United States in 2022 alone, Texas Representative Bryan Slaton proposed a law against drag shows to protect children from 'perverted adults obsessed with sexualizing young children' (Scharfetter, 2022). This occurred in a state that banned K-12 public school educators from teaching critical race theory and introduced the Texas-style ban on abortions allowing anyone to sue anyone who helps a person obtain an abortion. Texas is a pathbreaker, rather than an outlier, in terms of such legislation. Sixteen states have signed into law bans on teaching critical race theory, with nineteen considering passing similar laws (Alfonseca, 2022). Two states have enacted the Texas-style ban, with nineteen others having introduced such legislation (Nash et al., 2022). Fifteen states have passed or are considering laws restricting access to gender-affirming care for transgender youth (Freedom for All Americans, 2022). The backlash against Black Lives Matter, #MeToo, and March for Our Lives is, yet again, in full swing.

Reinvigorated culture wars such as this reaffirm Lorna Bracewell's claim in *Why We Lost the Sex Wars* that an infectious liberalism had much more to do with that loss than previously recognized—a loss that is, thus, deeply entwined with our current moment. Left political pundits refer to a readily available playbook that outlines how the current culture wars will play out. Trump Republicans, as conservatives did before them, deploy diversionary tactics by turning attention away from the 6 January 2021 insurrection at the Capitol and the intensifying number of mass and school shootings nationally to restricting and banning critical race theory, abortion, and care for LGBTQI+ youth. Progressives hold televised national hearings, organize March for Our Lives, Black Lives Matter, and pro-choice marches, and pass legislation in blue states supporting abortion, LGBTQI+, and rights for persons of color. This perennial ebb and flow of culture war politics, now a well known feature of our popular discourse, signals a much deeper, more insidious logic of liberalism that identifies its infectious nature, given its defining role in the U.S. political script.

The Sexual Revolution, lasting from the mid-1960s into the 1990s, frames Bracewell's theorizing about the sex wars which focused national dialogue on pornography. Among second-wave feminists, a 'catfight narrative' emerged that, following the 1982 Barnard conference on sexuality, broke feminists down into the pleasure versus danger camps. Bracewell successfully disrupts this narrative through a more complete reading that accounts for the tenacious force of liberalism and marginalized voices of Black and Third World feminism. Barbara Smith, Cheryl Clarke, Audre Lorde, and the Combahee River Collective members, among others, saw a more nuanced intersectional path forward—one informed, I will argue, by a global view of revolutions against colonialism from Southeast Asia to Africa and Central and South America—that went largely unseen by white liberal and radical feminists at the time. American exceptionalism, an ideological strand often lost in contemporary discourse, continues, I find, to prevent us from seeing political discourse and mobilization within a broader global context and perpetuates another monism, which I explore further here—one that must be overcome, should we hope to win the sex wars, much less the battle against white nationalism.

Biblicalism and republicanism, the two less visible ideological strands eclipsed by liberalism in American political discourse, create the groundwork for American exceptionalism. Standing aboard the *Arbella* as it sailed to Salem in 1629, future governor of the Massachusetts Bay Colony John Winthrop, drawing upon Matthew 5:14, proclaimed to his fledgling Puritan community that 'we must Consider that we shall be as a City upon a Hill. The Eyes of all people are upon us' (Levy' 1992). This biblical tradition positions America as always confronting the moral choice to either follow the path of righteousness and earn God's favor or fail to do so and fall into the decay experienced by most nations (Abbott, 1991). The 'City upon a Hill' evolves into American exceptionalism, which gained great momentum during the Industrial Revolution, resonated throughout the Cold War, and appears regularly in speeches by Presidents Ronald Reagan and George W. Bush, as a belief that God elevates the United States above all other nations as a beacon of virtue and goodness. Religious meets political morality through republicanism that identifies the community or common good, rather than the liberal individual, as the measure of national success which requires virtue of its citizens who must sacrifice the self for the good of others. The biblical and republican storylines combine to frame white women as either explicit or implicit threats to the nation's moral and political status since, as the daughters of Eve, they remain responsible for the Fall of humankind and, as such, the keepers of vice. Yet, white women reached for virtue, as the daughters of Zion, and became Republican Mothers and Wives by the mid-nineteenth century, serving as moral guardians, raising sons and daughters as virtuous citizens. Black women generally disappear from this early storyline, though they provided a moral and racial counterpoint to establishing Traditional Womanhood as white in contrast to vice-ridden Black women, often constructed as the Jezebel (Collins, 1991). Moving women between virtue and vice, in response to shifting political circumstances and calibrated according to different races, ethnicities, sexualities, and classes, exposes a societal doubt about their capacity to fulfill their civic duty, since their original moral position of vice perpetually casts them as potential disruptors of behaviors, norms, and even laws merely by their political presence, ultimately as suspect citizens.

In *Suspect Citizens: Women, Virtue, and Vice in Backlash Politics* (Boryczka, 2012), I argued that this dynamic creates a paradox in which women play a critical part in determining American democracy's fate, while simultaneously lacking the political power to participate fully in the processes that actually determine the nation's course. The New, later becoming the Christian, Right galvanized, after the 1973 *Roe vs. Wade* Supreme Court decision, around reestablishing the moral belief system and traditional institutions of heterosexual marriage and the family abandoned by women who exercised sexual freedom, demanded full political rights, and fought for equality in the workplace during the Sexual Revolution.

A dualistic logic drives the dynamics of backlash, whether in the 1970s or today. Dualism, defined as oppositional categories that never overlap, pulls toward the dominant category as determining the standards of excellence or virtue in a community. The male subject, as Simone de Beauvoir establishes in *The Second Sex*, defines history and the female object or Other. Dualisms, even if we think of a

Critical Exchange

dialectic with thesis and antithesis becoming synthesis, trend toward a monism, a view of oneness, that aligns with liberal individualism and a focus on the self over other people and community. Early second-wave radical feminists followed the essentialist path of monism by identifying 'sex' in terms of biological femaleness as the sole cause of all oppression that, once overthrown, would liberate all people. Liberalism in the U.S. context pulls toward the monism of the individual in a way that delimits the possibilities of radicalism as it decouples connections between a range of groups and nation-states, erecting obstacles to developing collectives or transnational movements. This particular brand of conservatism embedded within U.S. liberalism perpetuates a *status quo* reliant on a monism of the individual, which remains a bulwark against radical bursts of collective political mobilization for progressive change from the Sexual Revolution to the #MeToo movement.

Challenging this dominant culture involves breaking through this monism, usually by groups whose identities put them in borderlands, in in-between spaces and places. 'A borderland', as Gloria Anzaldúa explains, 'is a vague and undetermined place created by the emotional residue of an unnatural boundary. It is in a constant state of transition. The prohibited and forbidden are its inhabitants' (1987, p. 25). These 'Shadow-Beasts', as Anzaldúa described these inhabitants, clearly see the structures of oppression that shape their everyday ways of being, empowering them to reject the logics that operate to define them (1987, p. 38).

During the sex wars, a critical, though generally underexamined, internal culture war broke out among radical lesbian feminists, who had already been marginalized in the second-wave movement dominated by liberal feminists such as Betty Friedan, who proclaimed lesbians the 'lavender menace' at a 1969 National Organization for Women (NOW) conference. These radical lesbian feminists took opposing stands on sadomasochism (S/M). Pro-S/M lesbian feminists saw this sexual practice as one of many ways that women might explore desire in a conception of sex and sexuality liberated from patriarchy. Anti-S/M lesbian feminists asserted that this practice reenacted patriarchal power dynamics of domination and subordination that undermined lesbian struggles for equality and freedom. They redeployed the dualistic moral and political logic of guardianship, claiming their virtuous status to identify pro-S/M lesbians as so vice-ridden as to be outside the bounds of lesbianism and feminism. Pro-S/M lesbian feminists embraced their Shadow-Beast role and turned critical attention to fantasies as an essential component in S/M role-playing that offers a point of departure for examining moral imagination in a democratic feminist ethics. Marginalized within the lesbian and feminist movements, which was itself already located on the margins of politics and society, these suspect citizens became 'innovating ideologists' (Farr', 1989) with a particular capacity to see: to have vision beyond an immediate reality to imagine the horizon of possible futures and ways to attain them.

During the sex wars, Black and Third World feminists also occupied the borderlands between the civil rights and feminist movements, while often

Critical Exchange

remaining unseen by either. The gender monism of the Sexual Revolution failed to capture the multiple variables of race, class, sex, sexuality, and gender that shaped the lives of Black and Third World feminists. Intersectionality, now a well-established methodology and epistemology in feminist political theory, began to emerge as a result. The Combahee River Collective (1977), constituted by Black and lesbian feminists, conveyed the impulse of intersectionality:

> We are actively committed to struggling against racial, sexual, heterosexual, and class oppression and see as our particular task the development of integrated analysis and practice based upon the fact that the major systems of oppression are interlocking. The synthesis of these oppressions creates the conditions of our lives (Combahee River Collective, 1977).

Intersectionality forces a break with the dualistic logic buttressing the monism necessary for liberal individualism. Perhaps more significantly, Black and Third World feminism drew upon revolutionary struggles against colonization in Southeast Asia, where the Vietnam War raged, and across the African continent from Algeria to Kenya. White radical feminists recognized this broader global context. In 'The Fourth World Manifesto' (1970), for instance, Barbara Burris stated that 'we identify with all women of all races, classes, and countries all over the world. The female culture is the Fourth World' (2000, 251). Burris continued to identify *all* women as the most oppressed as the 'colonized group who have never—anywhere—been allowed self-determination' (2000, p. 238). Gender monism clearly functions here to establish a claim of oneness in which all women, everywhere, are the same in their oppression as biologically determined females. This position effectively erases intersectional variables in a way that flattens differentials of power and levels hierarchical structures of oppression. Global variations disappear as colonizing peoples claim to be colonized. Liberalism in this space triumphs through its dualistic logic which functions to flatten differences between cultures, peoples, histories, and geographies into one monistic worldview, one that operates in the United States to perpetuate American exceptionalism.

Radicalism in this context pulls more toward its Latin meaning of *radix* or 'the root' to identify the biological essentialism and determinism aligned with liberal individualism and away from overthrowing the national and global political, social, and economic structures required for true revolutionary change. Just a few months after the first Women's March Global in January 2017, #MeToo, initially launched by Tarana Burke in 2006, morphed quickly into a global movement by blending grassroots organizing with digital community building. Over 24 million impressions using #MeToo registered on Twitter from October 2017 to December 2019, traversing every region of the globe. #MeToo became #QuellaVoltaChe (That Time) in Italy, #Nopiwouma (I Will Not Shut Up) in Senegal, #asdas in South Korea, and #AnaKaman in Egypt. This social media-based movement continued the global momentum galvanized by the 2017 Women's March Global, when approximately five million women and their allies mobilized in eighty-two countries across all seven continents to form the single largest protest in world history (Office of Purna Sen, 2020). Black women and women of color played central roles in critiquing and organizing both of these movements, which retained a global outlook aligned with the global perspective of Black, Third World, and radical feminists of the 1980s' sex wars. And yet, the impulse in the United States toward liberal individualism pulls #MeToo toward women speaking out as individuals against sexual assault and harassment in order to share personal stories that converge in a utilitarian calculus to collective understanding. This individualism aligns with a carceral feminism according to which each person or group exercises hard-won legal rights to fight in the courts for protection. Depending on the laws and policies of the U.S. government in this way signals the undercurrent of American exceptionalism, which assumes that the nation-state will respond to preserve the female body and reproductive rights—a response that is increasingly implausible in many states of the Union. Though one of the first countries to liberalize abortion laws after the 1973 *Roe* decision, the United States now bucks a global trend toward less restrictive abortion laws (Women & Foreign Policy Program Staff, 2022). Indeed, most nation-states that today push back against expanding women's and reproductive rights identify as autocracies that often advance forms of white nationalism.

Moreover, American exceptionalism feeds into nationalist calls for isolationism and protectionism illustrated by the 'America First' and 'Build The Wall' chants at Trump rallies or the 'Make America Great Again' caps worn by Trump's supporters. Underneath these calls lingers the belief that women's role is to give birth to future citizens of the dominant white settler national identity. For white nationalists, nation-building involves limiting outsiders from entering the country and controlling women's biological capacity to reproduce children as essential to ensuring a 'pure' white bloodline. On this view, severe limitations, up to abolition of abortion and other reproductive rights; same-sex marriages and families; and protections against domestic violence, sexual harassment, and sexual assault scaffold white nationalism. Sex and race intersect in the white woman's body as her purported female biological capacity to reproduce white children equates with preserving the white nation-state from shifting sex roles, racial power dynamics, and migrating peoples. Protecting white women is integral to defending the borders of the homeland by defending the home, traditionally secured by men who exercise and represent a masculine protectionism (Young, 2005) essential to the sexism underlying the white nationalist commitment to anti-globalization. Consider as an example a demography summit held by Hungary's far-right nationalist prime minister Viktor Orbán in 2019, where he advanced the conspiracy theory that non-Europeans, mostly from Africa and Asia, will replace Europeans in the future (Walker, 2019). In the same vein, Serbia's president Aleksandar Vučić calls these declining birthrates the 'white plague', and Russian president Vladimir Putin announced 'maternity capital' paid to families with more than one child.

These efforts to increase white birth rates specify women's continued importance in the maternal production of future generations of white children through their biological reproductive capacity. Looking past the narrow boundaries erected by liberalism and American exceptionalism puts the current sex wars into a global context of rising white nationalism and autocracy, personified in leaders from Putin to Trump. This perspective also empowers us to see globalization as a means toward building the transnational feminist movements envisioned by early radical, Black, Third World, and Marxist feminists of the second wave. From this vantage point, ending the endless sex wars becomes possible through a renewed opportunity to leverage the radicalism necessary to do so: a radicalism that is both intersectional and global.

Jocelyn Boryczka

References

Abbott, P. (1991) *Political Thought in America: Conversations and Debates*. Itasca, IL: F.E. Peacock.
Alfonseca, K. (24 March, 2022) Map Where Anti-Critical Race Theory Efforts Have Reached. ABC News. https://abcnews.go.com/Politics/map-anti-critical-race-theory-efforts-reached/story?id=83619715.
Anzaldúa, G. (1987) *Borderlands/La Frontera: The New Mestiza*. San Francisco, CA: Aunt Lute Books.
Boryczka, J. (2012) *Suspect Citizens: Women, Virtue, and Vice in Backlash Politics*. Philadelphia: Temple University Press.
Bracewell, L.N. (2021) *Why We Lost the Sex Wars: Sexual Freedom in the #Metoo Era*. Minneapolis: University of Minnesota Press.
Burris, B. ([1970] 2000) The Fourth World Manifesto. In: B.A. Crow (ed.) *Radical Feminism: A Documentary Reader*. New York: New York University Press.
Califia, P. (1988) *Macho Sluts*. Boston: Alyson.
Coffin, J.G. (2020) *Writing Simone de Beauvoir: Sex, Love, and Letters*. Ithaca, NY: Cornell University Press.
Collins, P.H. (1991) *Black Feminist Thought: Knowledge, Consciousness, and the Politics of Empowerment*. New York: Routledge.
Combahee River Collective. ([1977] 2000) The Combahee River Collective Statement. In: B. Smith (ed.) *Home Girls: A Black Feminist Anthology*. New Brunswick: Rutgers University Press, pp. 264–274.
de Beauvoir, S. ([1949] 2011) *The Second Sex*. Translated by Constance Borde and Sheila Malovany-Chevallier. New York: Vintage.
de Beauvoir, S. ([1965] 2011) *What Can Literature Do?* Translated and included in *Simone de Beauvoir: "The Useless Mouths" and Other Literary Writings*, Ed. Margaret A. Simons and Marybeth Timmermann. Urbana: University of Illinois Press, pp. 197–209.
Dworkin, A. (1990) *Mercy*. New York: Four Walls Eight Windows.
Dworkin, A. and MacKinnon, C. (1988) *Pornography and Civil Rights: A New Day for Women's Equality*. Minneapolis: Organizing against Pornography.
Farr, J. (1989) Understanding Conceptual Change Politically. In: T. Ball, J. Farr and R.L. Hanson (eds.) *Political Innovation and Conceptual Change*. New York: Cambridge University Press, pp. 24–49.

Freedom for All Americans. (2022) Legislative Tracker: Youth Healthcare Bans. https://freedomforallamericans.org/legislative-tracker/medical-care-bans/.
Grant, J. (2020 [1993]) *Fundamental Feminism*, 2nd edn. New York: Routledge.
Honig, B. (2021) On Promising Young Woman. https://www.fordhampress.com/2021/04/24/bonnie-honig-on-promising-young-woman-warning-spoilers/.
Habermas, J. (1990) *The Philosophical Discourse of Modernity: Twelve Lectures, MIT Press*.
Levy, M.B. (ed.) (1992) A Modell of Christian Charity. In: *Political thought in America: An Anthology*. 2nd ed. Prospect Heights, IL: Waveland Press, pp. 6–14.
Marso, L.J. (2017) *Politics with Beauvoir: Freedom in the Encounter*. Durham, NC: Duke University Press.
Marso, L.J. (2021) Promising Young Women and the White Noise of Patriarchy, Presented at the 2021 Association for Political Theory Conference, Amherst, MA, November, and forthcoming in *Simone de Beauvoir Studies*.
Mulvey, L. (1989) *Visual and Other Pleasures*. Bloomington, IN: Indiana University Press.
Nash, E., Cross, L., and Dreweke, J. (March 2022) 2022 State Legislative Sessions: Abortion Bans and Restrictions on Medication Abortion Dominate, Guttmacher Institute. https://www.guttmacher.org/article/2022/03/2022-state-legislative-sessions-abortion-bans-and-restrictions-medication-abortion?gclid=EAIaIQobChMItdrh__yl-AIVZAaICR0PkQGhEAAYASAAEgKOLfD_BwE.
Office of Purna Sen. (August 2020) Headlines from a Global Movement, (UN Women), brief-metoo-headlines-from-a-global-movement-en(2).pdf.
Panagia, D. (2019) On the political ontology of the dispositif. *Critical Inquiry* 45(3): 714–746.
Rubin, G. (1975) The Traffic in Women: Notes on the Political Economy of Sex. In: R. Reiter (ed.) *Toward an Anthropology of Women*. New York: Monthly Review, pp. 157–210.
Rubin, G. (1984) Thinking Sex: Notes for a Radical Theory of the Politics of Sexuality. In: C.S. Vance (ed.) *Pleasure and Danger: Exploring Female Sexuality*. Boston: Routledge & K. Paul, pp. 267–319
Samois (ed.) (1981) *Coming to Power: Writings and Graphics on Lesbian S-M*. Boston: Alyson.
Scharfetter, R. (8, June, 2022) Texas Rep. Bryan Slaton Pushes to Ban Children from Drag Shows. CBS News. https://www.cbsnews.com/dfw/news/texas-rep-bryan-slaton-pushes-ban-children-drag-shows/.
Sedgwick, E. (1993) *Tendencies*. Durham, NC: Duke University Press.
Shaffer, M. (14 February 2020) The Assistant Director Kitty Green on the Banality of Evil in #Metoo Workplace Drama [Interview]: https://www.slashfilm.com/572297/the-assistant-director-interview/.
Skinner, Q. (1998) *Liberty Before Liberalism*. Cambridge, UK: Cambridge University Press.
Sobchack, V. (1992) *The Address of the Eye: A Phenomenology of Film Experience*. Princeton, NJ: Princeton U Press.
Walker, A. (1980) Coming Apart. In: L. Lederer (ed.) *Take Back the Night: Women on Pornography*. New York: William Morrow, pp. 95–104.
Walker, S. (6 Sept. 2019) Viktor Orbán trumpets Hungary's 'procreation, not immigration' policy, *The Guardian*. https://www.theguardian.com/world/2019/sep/06/viktor-orban-trumpets-far-right-procreation-anti-immigration-policy.
Women and Foreign Policy Program Staff. (5 May 2022) Abortion Law: Global Comparisons, Council on Foreign Relations, https://www.cfr.org/article/abortion-law-global-comparisons.
Young, I.M. (2005) The Logic of Masculinist Protectionism. In: M. Friedman (ed.) *Women and Citizenship*. New York, NY: Oxford University Press.

Publisher's Note Springer Nature remains neutral with regard to jurisdictional claims in published maps and institutional affiliations.

Review

Les Aveux de la chair. Vol. 4 of *L'Histoire de la sexualité*

Michel Foucault
Éditions Gallimard, Paris, 2018, 426 pp.
ISBN: 9782072700347

Contemporary Political Theory (2020) **19**, S192–S196. https://doi.org/10.1057/s41296-019-00333-z; Published online 11 July 2019

Michel Foucault's *History of Sexuality* series has long perplexed readers with the Greco-Roman detour that comes after the first volume. By contrast, his interviews on sexuality from the same period on are remarkably direct. In a 1982 interview, Michel Foucault asks, 'How can a relational system be reached through sexual practices? Will it require the introduction of a diversification different from the ones due to social class, differences in profession and culture, a diversification that would also be a form of relationship and would be a "way of life"?' (1997a, pp. 137–138). Other interviews from this period likewise experiment with the language of seeking new 'relational modes' that would back away from the nineteenth century's institutionalized model of heterosexuality that is held in place through the institutions of family, marriage, medicine, and law. The posthumously published *Aveux de la chair* effectively takes up these questions and queries: How have sexuality, power, and identity become entwined in the modern desiring subject – and with what limits to sexual relations, broadly speaking?

These preoccupations with historicizing the subject frame Foucault's *Aveux de la chair*, the long-awaited unpublished fourth volume of the *History of Sexuality* series. The title, which translates as *Confessions of the Flesh*, intimates something of the discursive stakes of the argument: the book surveys the practices that slowly bind what come to be confessional speech practices to earlier Christian preoccupations with flesh and concupiscence. *Aveux* thus sits at the crux of Foucault's concerns with sexuality and truth-telling in the ancient world. The text proceeds genealogically through dusty texts of the early Church fathers, including Clement of Alexandria, Cassian, John Chrysostom, Tertullian, and Augustine of Hippo. Its substantive focus is not yet that of sexuality (a term that Foucault usually reserves for the nineteenth century junction of confession and medicine that focus on an objectified self). Instead, Foucault analyzes the conjoinment of truth-telling practices and sexual relations in the Christian problem of concupiscence. Significantly, *aveu* can be translated as either 'confession' or 'avowal', depending

© 2019 Springer Nature Limited. 1470-8914 **Contemporary Political Theory** Vol. 19, S3, S192–S196
www.palgrave.com/journals

on context. Foucault seeks no less than to investigate how the spiritual subject of veridiction became connected to the juridical subject of law.

Sexuality thus conceived requires a genealogy of desire and the desiring subject that could explain the junction of subjectivity and truth-telling. In *Aveux*, the reigning concept is flesh and the accompanying problems of concupiscence, or the inclination towards sin (and especially sensual desire) that is the residue of original sin. Spanning the second to the fifth centuries, *Aveux* seeks to trace two crucial changes: first, changes in modes of truth-telling that permit a subject of desirous knowledge to appear later in the nineteenth century; and the second, the attachment of this truth-telling to increasingly social questions refracted onto flesh and sexuality. The book is divided into three parts (titled by the volume's editor): first, the 'formation of a new experience'; second, the experience of 'being virgin'; and finally, the experience of 'being married'.

Within the first section, Foucault bridges to his earlier work on ancient truth-telling practices. Moving from Seneca to Cassian to John Chrysostom, he tells of the emergence of an expressive performance of baptism and penitence, their entwinement, and their absorption into what will much later become recognizable as confessional speech. Organized around three moments of evaluation – interrogatory inquiry (*enquête*), exorcism and its tests (*épreuves*), and a confession of sins – baptism offers an expressive truth of one's relationship to God (p. 57), and is more demonstrative than verbal (p. 67). It is part of a larger 'spiritual combat' understood as a preparation against the Enemy, or Satan (pp. 75–77), and the penitential rites of *exomologesis* are more a '*faire vrai*' (making-true) than a '*dire-vrai*' or truth-telling (p. 105). Adopted from the ancient Greeks, the examination of conscience, or *exagoreusis,* gradually comes to offer a new relation to the self, and a new form of truth-telling. *Exagoreusis* moves away from self-mastery, but is not yet the confession of failed responsibilities or transgressive acts. Instead, it works to discover truths for oneself, by steadying the inconstancies of shadowy illusion and false appearances. Foucault clarifies that with such confessions, 'We're in the realm not of the jurisdiction of acts for which one takes responsibility, but the veridiction of secrets within oneself of which one is ignorant' (p. 144). Although confession has its roots in monasticism, the real question it raises is how its practices of mortification – this new 'form of experience' – come to spread beyond those already devoted to regulating desire broadly understood.

To answer this question, in the second and third sections of *Aveux* Foucault turns to practices of virginity and marriage, both of which become extensions of this ceaseless work of mortification in contexts beyond the monastery. In the first two centuries of Christianity, virginity was less a principle of abstention or taboo than an ascetic practice of sexual renunciation. Virginity becomes defined as a spiritual movement; it organizes as a type of relation to self, one that opens onto a domain of internal knowledge, and inscribes itself in a relation of power with another (p. 215). Flesh becomes infused with spirit, and a new kind of subjectivation is born (p. 213).

Drawing largely on John Chrysostom, Foucault argues against the common association of Christian marriage with the injunction to procreate. If virginity was a fleshy, expressive form of veridiction, then matrimonial practices are jurisdictional. They regulate the economy of concupiscence, and thus marriage must help both parties temper their desires for other ways of life. Somewhat surprisingly, Foucault argues that, '[T]he obligations that [John Chrysostom] stipulates for spouses constitutes a sort of political equality when it comes to sexual relations; the rights of one stipulate the duties (*devoirs*) of the other' (p. 275). This system of obligations is not founded on symmetry in decision-making or a community of the will: 'Its form is that of a political equality. Its foundation is that of propriety' (p. 275). Both spouses appropriate the other, an appropriation that either creates (metaphorical) slavery or reframes spousal duty as debt. It will take Augustine to articulate more clearly what desires and consumptions fuel this economy, and so to outline a subject of desire defined by a libido in need of regulation.[1]

Readers who turn to *Aveux* hoping to find an 'answer' to questions of agency (raised in *Discipline and Punish*) or an alternate theory of desire (to that critiqued in *History of Sexuality* vol. 1) will likely be disappointed. Much as *Care of the Self* (1988) and *The Use of Pleasures* (1990) contained long discussions of *aphrodisia* and *gnōthi seauton*, with little hint of how to carry these readings forward, *Aveux* gives no explicit direction for how to interpret or work with the text. One possibility is to use it to explore those bonds that imperfectly overlap with legal relationships. After all, in interviews, Foucault argues that gay rights owe more to 'attitudes and patterns of behavior than to legal formulations' and that its practice needs to be one of 'constructing cultural forms' and '[fighting] against the impoverishment of the relational fabric' (1997b: pp. 157–158). Such relationships would need to amplify that expressive, veridictional self that 'particular form of subject that the law, that juridical thought, that judicial practice has never been able to assimilate' (2014, p. 152). Some passages in *Aveux* could be read so as to imagine contemporary forms of commitment not contained within existing legal relationships of marriage.

The stakes of *Aveux* change, however, when it is read as a genealogy rather than a prescriptive solution. Such a reading makes *Aveux* the hinge between an ancient Greek self-governance through relational practices, and the sixteenth century appropriation of sexuality as a site for governance. In doing so, it opens up (for a readerly audience if not those of early Christianity) the space of a spiritual subject not yet soldered to a juridical one – a claim radical in its time, but now more familiar from the intervening years of speculation.

Perhaps more ground is to be gained by thinking about the uneasy overlap forged between body and society, and the psychosocial relations on which it rests. Two points are striking. First, much like Freud, Foucault relies on desire and family structure to offer an account of what Leo Bersani has termed a 'promiscuous curiosity' (1995) that otherwise attaches wantonly and erratically. For Freud and

Foucault, that promiscuous curiosity leads people out of themselves and into the world, and in Foucault's case, leaves readers wanting a stronger account of the psychic life of power, and what structures beyond those of religion, family and marriage might contain it. Indeed, and second, Foucault's emphasis on *dispositifs* of sexuality rather than sex covers over something quite different: namely, the fantasy of a different self as a desirable object. For Freud, the ahistorical presence of the id becomes part of a refusal to succumb to such narrativizing impulse; the id, and sexual impulses broadly, come to disorient and disrupt any effort to constitute the self. On this account, the process of self-constitution is inherently unstable and constantly undermined by its own desire to be otherwise. Foucault's move to situate the Christian libido genealogically challenges the shattering aspect of the psyche by stabilizing the libido through its historical emergence. However, by leaving unexplored those other relational modes hinted at earlier in this review, Foucault leaves the structure of desire itself intact. Yet such structures are not so easily abandoned or invented: they must contend with the aggression and destruction that attends any change in structuring order. New relational modes would require more than a different performativity – they would require a form of desire not premised on lack.

Unavoidably, *Aveux* must be read in a twenty-first century context very different from that of a France that refused to acknowledge Foucault's own death from AIDS, much less to condone homosexual relationships in his lifetime. In this sense, perhaps the clearest target of the volume is a Catholic, petit-bourgeois France still accustomed to think of sexuality as individualistic, marriage as rooted in procreation, and the repression of desire as natural to politics. Challenging these terms is indeed to seek out 'another form of life'.

Note

1 See Brown (1988).

References

Bersani, L. (1995) *Is the Rectum a Grave?* Chicago: University of Chicago Press.
Brown, P. (1988) *The Body and Society: Men, Women, and Sexual Renunciation in Early Christianity*. New York: Columbia University Press.
Foucault, M. (1988) *The Care of the Self*. vol. 3, trans. R. Hurley, New York: Vintage Books.
Foucault, M. (1990) *The Use of Pleasures*. vol. 2, trans. R. Hurley, New York: Vintage Books.
Foucault, M. (1997a) Friendship as a Way of Life. In *The Essential Works of Foucault: Ethics*. vol. 1, trans. P, Rabinow, R. Hurley, (eds.) New York: New Press.

Foucault, M. (1997b) Sex, Power, and the Politics of Identity. In *The Essential Works of Foucault: Ethics*. vol. 1, trans. P, Rabinow, R. Hurley, (eds.) New York: New Press.

Foucault, M. (2014) *Wrong-Doing, Truth-Telling: The Function of Avowal in Justice*, trans. F. Bion, B. Harcourt, S. W. Sawyer, Chicago: University of Chicago Press.

Publisher's Note Springer Nature remains neutral with regard to jurisdictional claims in published maps and institutional affiliations.

Nancy Luxon
University of Minnesota-Twin Cities, Minneapolis, MN 55455, USA
luxon@umn.edu

Review

The right to sex

Amia Srinivasan
(Ed.), Bloomsbury, London, 2021, xvi+276 pp.,
ISBN: HB978-1-5266-1253-3

Contemporary Political Theory (2023) **22,** S63–S66. https://doi.org/10.1057/s41296-022-00554-9; Published online 1 March 2022

What would it take to end the political, social, sexual, economic, psychological, and physical subordination of women? And: what would it take for sex to be free? These are fundamental, thorny questions. They are, according to Amia Srinivasan, the questions that lead feminism not so much as a theoretical endeavor, but first and foremost as a political movement. Although *The Right to Sex* announces that it is going to address these questions in its preface, Srinivasan admits that she does not know how to answer them – 'let's try and see' (p. xiii). The hesitation is not merely rhetorical. It also means that, as societies and communities, we still have to think, to discuss, but, mostly, to struggle and to conduct 'experiments of living' (p. 102) in order to realize desirable and plausible answers.

Srinivasan's questions are quite different from those currently animating academic theoretical discourses in the field. For example, they do not look for a conceptualization of what oppression is. They do not delve into the shortcomings of intersectionalist approaches either. The first question is a practical one: it looks for strategies to effectively achieve emancipatory social change. The second question seems to additionally require some form of utopian thinking. If 'freedom is a constant struggle' (Angela Davis), some conditions, figures, images and models of what we are struggling for are needed.

Srinivasan's debut has been promptly celebrated as an essential reading for our post-#MeToo moment. The six essays put together in *The Right to Sex* span a vast range of controversial issues (various forms of sexual harassment and violence, pornography, the phenomenon of so-called incels, sex education), deal with them by relying upon a rich mix of resources (from personal anecdotes to philosophical arguments, from journalistic reports to historical overviews), and provide refined analyses and diagnoses. In trying to delineate responses to her two initial questions, however, Srinivasan loses courage, gets back into line. She does not dare to experiment. Let's consider the two orders of issues separately.

© 2022 The Author(s), under exclusive licence to Springer Nature Limited. 1470-8914 **Contemporary Political Theory** Vol. 22, S2, S63–S66
www.palgrave.com/journals

Review

Liberation from oppression

Srinivasan's central thesis consists in a problematization of consent. No means no, but yes is not always yes. Sexual and intimate practices may be deeply problematic and damaging even if they are based on the explicit free and autonomous agreement of all participants. We can say yes to certain things because we enjoy and strive for them; our preferences and desires, however, are often built on sexist, heteronormative, racist, ableist deeply engrained structures and habits.

Srinivasan avoids the trap of a critique of false consciousness, as well as the unpleasantness of moralizations. She does not say that desires and preferences entangled with problematic structures and habits are not authentic or wrong. Rather, she encourages us to ask ourselves uncomfortable questions – what are the underlying conditions, motives, origins of what we like and want? The aim is not to discipline desire, but to push against the ways in which we have been disciplined, since birth, to regard only certain types of bodies as worthy, beautiful, 'fuckable' (p. 103).

The problematization of a consent-based feminist critical theory is also the basis, as I read it, of Srinivasan's second major point, which corresponds to her conviction that the law and the judicial system are not the right medium for solving the most controversial problems faced by feminism today – especially from the perspectives of women of color, or of queer and non-cis persons. Note that Srinivasan's theorization of liberation from oppression is essentially negative: consent is not enough, the law is not enough (sometimes, both are part of the problem). But the question of emancipatory transformation would require at least a few positive indications as well.

Is normative theory right for the job though, as Sally Haslanger (2021) suggests in her review? Many critical theorists have shown that normative prescriptions about what has to be done, if not already at play in current objective social dynamics and movements, are merely naïve and ultimately empty operations. A discourse on emancipation also needs descriptive, ontological conceptualizations, e.g., of how moral, political, and social progress might occur. Many proposals have been elaborated to explain emancipatory social movements (e.g., those based on notions of recognition, habit, affects). Alas, Srinivasan does not mention any of them.

However, there is a passage in *The Right to Sex*, dedicated to the practice and ethics of teaching, that exceeds negativism: this happens when Srinivasan gives her own personal example as a teacher. The move deserves philosophical attention, as it goes beyond both normative theorizing and critical social ontology. Her point here is that teachers who sleep with their students fail, as teachers, for they do not give them what they really want and need, which is an education, and not sexual thrill or romance. And the real reason why teachers are tempted to initiate, or give in to sexual or romantic escapades, is the desire for retrieving an intensity and adventurousness of life they feel they have lost. (There is an argumentative last step that Srinivasan fails to take: for her reasoning to hold, she should have shown why the education that still may happen between teachers and students who become lovers is a damaged and damaging one.) As in many other passages of the book, Srinivasan convincingly explains power on the basis of desire, and not vice versa. In this case, this is not just a theoretical point. As such, it shakes the reader: it might set in motion processes of (self-)questioning, have a therapeutical effect, shed a new light on past traumatic experiences.

We surely need more positive examples of this sort. But I wonder whether this radiant positivity alone would not risk becoming overwhelming, thus discouraging, widening the gap between ideal role models and the majority of us, imperfect, confused, 'bad' feminists (Roxane Gay). Feminist movements, it seems to me, unfold through personal examples of another sort as well. There are indeed thinkers and activists – I am thinking of Virginie Despentes or Rebecca Solnit for example – who have most effectively taught us through what can be called 'negative exemplarity': not by showing how to be good, but by exposing the mistakes, failed experiments, self-doubts, bewilderments they have gone through to become who they are.

After liberation, freedom

How to imagine and desire free-desire? Can we figure out sexual practices that are at the same time delightful, enjoyable, and free from oppression? This is hard. Srinivasan ends up dashing any enthusiasm when discussing the legacy of the sexual revolution, which has left almost everything 'unchanged' (p. 121). 'We have never yet been free' (p. 122). Never?! The problem with this pessimist claim is twofold.

The first one is highlighted by Maggie Nelson in her *Ballad of Sexual Optimism*, an essay that shares many of Srinivasan's concerns, but stands out in the end as much messier, queerer, and hence more experimental: freedom is a chiaroscuro and is itself a process of change. Phases of liberation give rise to new forms of oppression, liberties are gained and lost, what appears as freedom at a certain moment in time, and from the perspective of a certain social group, does sometimes shade or even hinder the freedom of others. This is particularly true for the realm of sex (Nelson, 2021, p. 78), full of 'gray areas' (Nelson, 2021, p. 80). Trying to conceptually go through them does not mean we have to give up critical work or justify the status quo. On the contrary, emancipatory change works better if we give up on the pernicious dualism freedom vs. unfreedom. When liberated from the obsession of perfect, full freedom, we might become able to spell out some of the things that would indeed make us free.

In principle, Srinivasan shares this view (p. xv). But she tends to dispel the ambiguity by predominantly concentrating on the negative sides of sex and desire. For example, the major part of her essay on pornography consists of criticisms of the mainstream porn industry, picking up arguments presented in the 70s and 80s. In the end, alternatives are sketched, but only very briefly and weakly. This is a pity: the chapter misses an opportunity to outline a model of 'sex education' by getting into what I believe are the most interesting debates on the topic. There are many practices that claim to be ethical, e.g., feminist, lesbian, queer pornography. And as such, they open up many important questions, for instance: what does it take for pornography in order for it to be not just ethical, but critical and emancipatory? Can heteronormative problematic forms of desire be really changed through nonmainstream pornography? What about the relationship between pornography and art?

The second problem is Srinivasan's only negative, and thus limited view of freedom. As Judith Butler (2021) points out, a shortcoming of *The Right to Sex* is that it does not consider 'the right to have sex claimed by those,' namely by LGBTQI people, 'who have been illegitimately denied that right.' This is due to the fact that Srinivasan sees freedom as mostly a masculine, white supremacist, market-driven endeavor. But freedom can and should be more than that. To understand the ways in which we are (becoming) free by participating in the (ambivalent, conflictual) processes of freedom, we need an enlarged conception: to think of freedom in collective terms, in terms of the possible alternatives that we can and must build up together.

References

Butler, J. 2021. Whose freedom? *The New Statesman*.
Haslanger, S. 2021. Feminism and the Question of Theory. *The Raven*.
Nelson, M. (2021) *On Freedom. Four Songs of Care and Constraint*. Penguin.

Publisher's Note Springer Nature remains neutral with regard to jurisdictional claims in published maps and institutional affiliations.

Federica Gregoratto
University of St. Gallen, 9000 St. Gallen, Switzerland
federica.gregoratto@unisg.ch

Critical Exchange

Lauren Berlant's legacy in contemporary political theory

Samuel Galloway
Purchase College, State University of New York, Purchase, NY 10577, USA
samuel.galloway@purchase.edu

Ali Aslam
Mount Holyoke College, South Hadley, MA 01075, USA
aaslam@mtholyoke.edu

Ashleigh Campi
Pomona College, Claremont, CA 91711, USA
ashleigh.campi@pamona.edu

Hagar Kotef
SOAS University of London, London WC1H 0XG, UK
hk11@soas.ac.uk

Keywords: Lauren Berlant; Affect theory; Critique; Fantasy; Intimacy; Political theory

Contemporary Political Theory (2023) **22**, 118–142. https://doi.org/10.1057/s41296-022-00584-3; Published online 22 August 2022

Losing Lauren Berlant in 2021 was depressing. For weeks I would wake abruptly in the early morning only to cry: my world—our world—had become profoundly impoverished with Lauren's passing. Mourning with friends from the University of Chicago, where Berlant was the George M. Pullman Distinguished Service Professor of English, helped to communalize the experience. So did returning to their vast archive of work, which spans eight books (two co-authored), dozens of articles and chapters, and many interviews and recorded lectures over more than

Critical Exchange

thirty years. To differing degrees, for all the contributors to this Critical Exchange, working through Berlant's ideas and concepts was also a way of working through their loss and what it means for our discipline, especially as political theorists were becoming more aware of Berlant's scholarship following the prescient intervention of *Cruel Optimism* (2011).

It is hard to overstate the impact Berlant's thinking was beginning to have on political theory, where so many of us have been gnawing on the limits of deliberation, persuasion, and critique with increasingly bitter returns. The political world around us is noisy, chaotic, and contradictory—shot through with fantasy, ambivalent attachment, and the aggressive desire for paralytic institutions to redress our sense of dislocation. Berlant, as Hagar Kotef writes below, was a keen critic of fantasy in public life, though they never sought a world without illusions. To see the role of fantasy in political life though, Ali Aslam notes, we need to loosen our hold on the political as statist, rational, and deliberative to see it operate in more minor registers and, as Ashleigh Campi reminds us, in politically unconventional spaces, such as the family and the schoolhouse.

As a political theorist, Berlant appreciated that the sublime object of politics in America is the nation, which "is not a thing, but a cluster of fantasmic investments in a scene that represents itself as offering some traction, not a solution to the irreparable contradictions of desire" (Berlant, 2012, p. 76). Exemplary among these investments, all the more pointedly in our current political moment, is the attachment to the fetus, the "virtual citizen," whose politics of reproductive futurity creates what Berlant theorizes as the "intimate public sphere" of mass or democratic mediation (Berlant, 1997, p. 6). The politics of infantile citizenship is utopian in casting a vision of the future, even as this future "stands for a crisis in the present" (Berlant, 1997, p. 6).

Crisis is managed, in both *The Queen of America Goes to Washington City* (1997) and *Cruel Optimism*, by "technologies of patience" (Berlant, 1997, p. 222):

> How can U.S. "minorities" abide, just one more day, the ease with which their bodies—their social labor and their sexuality—are exploited, violated, and saturated by normalizing law, capitalist prerogative, and official national culture? Mass violence by subordinate groups must seem an ongoing possibility to anyone who knows U.S. history, anyone who has seen occasional moments of violence flash up only to be snuffed out in a mist of hegemonic handwringing, suppression, neglect, and amnesia. What are the *technologies of patience* that enable subaltern people to seem to consent to, or take responsibility for, their painful contexts? What are national subjects taught that causes them to channel the energy of collective distress into the work of deferring a demanding response to it?

Published more than twenty years ago, Berlant skirts a provocative conclusion with questions that could just as easily be raised in the wake of the 2020 uprisings against the impunity of the police vanguard of the white state.

Deleuze and Guattari unsettled us by asking after the desire *for* fascism. For Berlant, however, desire is less straightforward. With their concept of cruel optimism, Berlant shows how what we take to be what we want is often a way of keeping us in proximity, not to the object of our desire or its attainment, but to some sense of comfort and normalcy—an "ordinariness" that is anything but for being purchased at the expense of others, no less than in its attrition against the self. Take the perverse insistence that *more* guns will make us safer as indexing an attachment of cruel optimism no less than the imperative to "vote harder." Such investments in the "national-symbolic" (Berlant, 1997, p. 103) keep us stuck in the impasse of our compounding crises. This impasse is lived as the glitchy two-step of progress and reaction that, with each jagged oscillation, intensifies the social antagonisms that animate a diverse nation where nationality is the prerogative of white, cisgendered, and increasingly armed men.

The contributions to this Critical Exchange dwell within the crises of our distended present to analyze its contours, contradictions, and necessary identifications, but also to scrounge for ways of collectively exercising "lateral agency" (Berlant, 2011) in ways that do not flatten or thin under the catastrophic pressures of market competition, national security, and social division. In this, we are students of Berlant's own appreciation for the propensity of attachment to ambivalence, some of which you will see at work in this Critical Exchange: on the one hand, Berlant can be read—rightly—as a fierce critic of the attrition of locating politics in feelings of trauma, pain, grief, and harm; and yet, on the other hand, one can simultaneously draw from the same critical repertoire to understand how minoritarian formations of resistance and survival integrate affect into their politics in ways that build power, grow community, and foster relations of intimacy.

All this is lesson enough, but it must be noted that we have, collectively and unconsciously, coalesced around a cluster of concepts in Berlant's oeuvre—the intimate public, the limits of ideology critique, the ambivalent political uses of affect, and the role of fantasy in forestalling and fomenting justly reparative futures—to the neglect of much else in their work that merits attention from interested political theorists. For instance, their long and sustained engagement with the law, especially the jurisprudence of the Supreme Court, remains uncannily prescient to our moment. And their later turn to comedy should be required reading for a subfield otherwise transfixed by the tragic.

We hope to introduce some of Berlant's rich, complex, and original thinking while also sharing a sense of them as a person. One of the pleasures of this project was its collaborative nature, which in its very structure honored Berlant's own commitments to thinking *with* others, out loud, vividly, in ways that render theory "live." In this, we invite you to join us.

Samuel Galloway

Lessons learned: in gratitude to Berlant

News of Lauren Berlant's death last summer reached me suddenly and unexpectedly. I did not know Berlant other than through their writing, so I returned to their work and what I learned from it as a way of processing this loss. While I was drawn to and immediately persuaded by Berlant's description of cruel optimism when I first encountered it as a graduate student, I struggled to comprehend the alternatives they laid out because they struck me as so far outside what I knew or could comprehend, at the time, as democratic politics outside of the state. There was no galvanizing event, no mobilizing, or organizing. Berlant seemed to describe silent retreat into the self, observation and pause, or even walking away, all of which I interpreted as fatalistic resignation, failure, and a falling away from each other. Berlant helped me pinpoint how much of democratic theory remains tethered to the state. Even those theorists who argue for democracy outside its statist forms—whether in local or transnational assemblies or movement spaces—imagine that these bodies address the state, contest its authority, or act in reference to state actions. Berlant, by contrast, was for walking away and leaving the state behind.

On further consideration, Berlant was pointing to another form of politics—or more precisely, another form of initiating politics—for those worn down by its conventional grammars. That other politics began with individual and collective self-preservation as a matter of survival. Berlant started with concerns and experiences that fell outside the acceptable boundaries of politics, because they worked with and from an archive of stories composed by groups who were denied full political membership and targeted by state-sanctioned violence. Berlant's attention to affect and the body, informed by the experiences of queer communities in particular, put their scholarship in conversation with political theory, even as Berlant sounded discordant notes about the role and direction of critique, recognition, progress, agency, and fantasy in public life.

For me, Berlant's conceptual starting points—impasse, exhaustion, affect, desire, and the mundane demands of survival— suggest how flight, as it relates to these concepts, can be not only reparative but also transformative of subjects, norms, and institutions. Central to my ability to grasp this transformative potential was learning from Berlant how to read actions against the grain, beginning with an appreciation of the deeper reservoir of non-political experience from which they sprang. In my case, this meant loosening my own attachments to politics as a cherished activity and line of inquiry. Additionally, it required acknowledging how my self-understanding as a being committed to "politics" was a marker of my standing, even if, as a Muslim male, I was presumed suspect after 9/11. Berlant connected me to groups that were, in effect, homeless after being turned out and denied the same standing. Their lessons of survival and resistance are, I believe, instructive for all of us who feel bound by our despair for the world at this moment in history.

As a literary theorist, Berlant approached politics in terms of genre, sensitive to the affordances of particular genres and when they appear to break down. It is this awareness of genre that helped Berlant also grasp the limits of genre (Berlant, 2011, p. 6). Can we see ourselves in this story? is the question Berlant imagines subjects ask about what they read as well as the narratives of belonging to which they are attached or wish to attach. When subjects can no longer see themselves in the story of which they aspire to be a part—because they realize it did not include people like them or it remains persistently and exhaustingly out of reach—they must invent something else to survive, to connect with others, or to find themselves. How Berlant revalued political impasse and the resulting lateral agency as starting points for another form of politics places them in the company of Nietzsche, even if his influence is never explicit.

Berlant's insight into "waning genres (Berlant, 2011, p. 7) can be traced back to the influence of Eve Sedgewick's observations on the limits of critical theory, specifically its "paranoid" style. Sedgewick attributes her doubts about the performative aspects of knowledge—that is, what knowledge *does* or makes possible once it becomes known—to conversations during the late 1980s with HIV-activist and scholar Cindy Patton about the origins of the virus. Patton's response was to ask what difference knowing whether or not HIV was engineered by the U.S. military would make for those living with HIV/AIDS. What would change? Patton asked. If anything, Patton suggested that putting energy toward determining the virus's origins would come at the cost of much needed care and support for survivors, given conditions of finitude (Sedgwick, 2002, pp. 123-124). To Sedgewick, the promise of critical theory's paranoid style, that action would promptly follow discovery and exposure, presumed not just a naïve public, but one that was unified in its commitment to righting moral wrongs and the use of reasoned argument. Critical theory's assumptions appeared gossamer thin, even fanciful, in the light cast by Patton's response (Sedgwick, 2002, pp. 139-140). Sedgwick suggests that to cling to paranoia, indeed, to tighten the grip of paranoia in meeting the world, given its failures to motivate action, is to court exhaustion and cynicism. Doing so, furthermore, shields from view how people learn to live with knowledge of systemic oppression and injustice without being flattened by it (Sedgwick, 2002, p. 144).

Berlant's scholarship is animated by and deepens Sedgewick's insights into the limits of critical theory. Refusing critics who framed these alternatives as retreat, resignation, or fatalism, Berlant and Sedgewick view these activities as explorations that might provide repair for traumatized subjects. For Berlant, the severed link between knowledge and action resulting in repetitive cycles of notification and exhaustion signifies a flattening of the "event" that crystalizes action as the crux of critical theory.

In *Cruel Optimism*, Berlant translates the flattening of the event into a theory of "crisis ordinary," which inverts the conventional structure of trauma. Crisis ordinary prolongs the period of trauma, stretching it to acknowledge that trauma is not an interruption of ordinary life that is steady and uneventful but constitutive of its background conditions. Crisis ordinary responds to the traumatic afterlives of violence, which reproduce intergenerationally (Berlant, 2011, pp. 9-10). This trauma lives in the body; its gestures, showing up as stress, fatigue, impassivity; and the need to survive. How do damaged lives persist? Departing from Adorno's framing, Berlant's scholarship is more closely in dialogue with Foucault and might be understood as a response to a question that is a minor chord in the history of political thought.

Sensitive to the need to recover from the violence of historical progress, Berlant keeps company with and contributes to a tradition that is pessimistic about modernity. Like Nietzsche, Foucault, and more recently Fred Moten and Frank B. Wilderson, Berlant illuminates how liberal statehood, political membership, and the political epistemologies that justified their dominance, fell and continue to fall short of their self-representations. To call these orders civil, enlightened, or to see them as harbingers of progress, is to testify to the role of fantasy in structuring reality. Associating one way of living with the "good" is not only another way of seeking pleasure, but it is a pleasure linked to the disavowed knowledge of one's shameful complicity in the violence that makes such pleasure possible. Whether this complicity materializes in the advantages of white supremacy, gender and sexual normativity, or the environmental costs and labor exploitation connected to consumer capitalism, Berlant highlights both the pleasure of possession and domination, on one side, and the shame and pleasure sought by those who do not meet those standards, on the other.

In each case, Berlant's focus on affect cautions against straightforward claims about subjects or their responses. Like Nietzsche's (1969) indictment of philosophers, empowered by their claims to the truth and a tradition of deep thinking ("We Knowers"), Berlant challenges a history of political thinking that identifies politics with decisive, demonstrable, and public action, not abjection, subjugation, or the concealed. One part of the difficulty is the "tone of voice problem" that labels many persons or their affects non-normative. Gender, sexual, and racial minorities are often misheard or interpreted as accusatory or threatening dominant social positions; the perceptions and fantasies of those judging at the top of the social ladder are not open to self-reflection or interrogation. Unacknowledged is how those hierarchies depend on misrecognition to sustain the "normalcy" of their self-image (Berlant & Warner, 2002, p. 205).

Emotions, Berlant argues, do not work in one way; they are not stable or singular. They can partially surface in the subject's response, while what lies beneath is only partially known or understood. Berlant suggests how this other activity can reflect desire for individual and collective agency that has either been actively thwarted or suppressed thanks to the depoliticized rituals of national belonging. When public identity is reduced to surface rituals, like rote proclamations about the "tragic loss of life" after each mass shooting, politics becomes a sphere of togetherness unable to bear conflict or difference. Under these conditions, a reservoir of emotions, like anger and resentment, that have no public outlet take root in "non-political" spaces and associations.

That which cannot be expressed outwardly turns inward or against others, Berlant observes. Shame at not having agency, mixed with a desperate desire for what cannot be had, can take the form of binge-eating, followed by a cycle of dieting, eating, dieting, eating. Such cycling is one route lateral agency can take. This an attack on the self, while self-organized border militias and the pleasure taken in verbal attacks on migrants, Muslims, and Black public officials are attempts to recover norms of white masculinity and domination through controlling the movement and agency of others (Beltrán, 2021, pp. 93-95, 106-107).

Berlant had been tracking how the cruel paradoxes of public life had diminished and transformed political agency from nearly the start of their career and anticipated its reactionary politics (Berlant, 2016a, b). Reactionary politics was not Berlant's central concern, however. Berlant instead explored how to live free of reactionary cycles, understanding how this comes down to how people negotiate their relations in the process of going on together.

Very often, persisting starts in silence, picking up the pieces that can be salvaged and repurposed. In Liza Johnson's *South of Ten* documentary, Berlant observes post-Katrina survivors moving in silence amidst the storm debris, with only the ambient sounds of ongoing life. The failure of the government's response formalized a long pattern of state abandonment; now released, Berlant suggests that survivors do not want to return. Though it may not look like anything is happening, Berlant interprets their movement differently. They write, "People are tending, tending to things, having tendencies to go in this, then that direction." Each person, Berlant proposes, is like the tip of a rhizome, inaugurating connections that constitute the conditions of solidarity. This movement is not purposeful, but it is an act of recovery (Berlant, 2011, p. 255). This is the core of the optimism that Berlant wishes to preserve. But how does one learn to tend to this particular form of optimism and detach from its crueler variants?

The answer lies with what Berlant terms the "esthetic education" of the senses (Berlant, 2011, p. x). Dulled by the sheen of the familiar and routine, Berlant suggests the senses must be retrained to see what lies hidden in plain sight. Berlant's writing with Kathleen Stewart, entitled *The Hundreds*, models this esthetic education for the reader. "Anything can start to act as a hinge, activating something suddenly somehow at hand," they write in one of the entries, "Weight of the World." *The Hundreds* scenically catalogues mundane moments at the convenience store, walking the dog,

Critical Exchange

with the handyman, where conversations can veer into something more than the utilitarian exchange of information. "A stranger exchange is a flickering resource," they continue, before observing the geographic variability that invites such exchanges. According to Berlant and Stewart, in Texas, unlike in New England, putting free items on the curb is an invitation for someone to ask about the condition of what has been offered or why it has been let go— to create friction in a transaction that might be void of it. And while this might be enough to dissuade one from opening oneself up to these social exchanges, Berlant and Stewart conclude, "We need the weight of the world we fear" (Berlant and Stewart, 2019, p. 22).

The Hundred exemplifies this kind of receptivity, as its narrators discover moods that do not square with their expectations about the content and pacing of the world. What they encounter instead are unexpected folds and swerves that tarry and even glue them for moments of confession, exhalation, and reprieve from routines that have left them harried, attention spans frayed. Together they suggest that social repair might start not in "humanistic critique" which "just keeps snapping at the world as if the whole point of being and thinking is to catch it in a lie" but rather:

> all the extensions of ways of being touched, what feels like to be carried along by something on the move, the widespread joking, the voicing, the dark wakefulness, the sonorousness, how managing a life views with an unwitting ungluing, how things get started, how people try to bring things to an end, like the day, through things that slam or slide down their throats, why thought becomes an add-on or take the form of a speed list, or why it matters that attention sometimes slows down to a halt waiting for something to take shape (Berlant and Stewart, 2019, p. 42).

What they suggest is that the possibility of world-making relationships, even the idea of utopia, might lie in something that starts as an interruption or distraction. A conversation overheard or a viewer comment addressed to the Fox News anchor whose words scroll across the mute television set in the hospital emergency room waiting area, can inaugurate new ways of relating to the self and others. Another kind of politics can be witnessed here on a small scale which, if taken up in larger numbers, would abolish politics as it has been commonly known. Berlant and Stewart intimate that the seed of this resistance is already present but that its growth requires new habits of attention to the ordinary. These moments are recuperative, if we learn to recognize them for what they are and can be: opportunities to speak and be heard, not dismissed or silenced. They represent forms of living that can put hurt and injured people back together by helping them to learn to trust themselves and others again.

This was the lesson of queer world-making for Berlant, in particular the invention of "safe sex," against the backdrop of the HIV/AIDS epidemic, when sexual norms and pleasure were rapidly transformed in intimate relationships. This sexual intimacy was not private or personal but profoundly political. As Berlant writes with Michael Warner, sexual relationships were transformed into spaces that

Critical Exchange

made possible the creation of "a common language of self-cultivation, shared knowledge, and the exchange of inwardness" (Berlant & Warner, 2002, p. 202). The challenge then, as it is now, was how to create and care for those relationships and practices, to recognize their latent possibilities for the self and those with whom we share the world. For a glimpse into those worlds and our capacities to nurture them, we have Lauren Berlant to thank.

Ali Aslam

May the lover's tools repair the houses that America built

Lauren Berlant leaves us a life of examples of how to practice gender liberation as a writer, teacher, scholar, and friend. I came to know Berlant by co-teaching a seminar at the Center for the Study of Gender and Sexuality (CSGS) at the University of Chicago, which they helped found and sustain during their long career at the university. Berlant became famous for their distinctive forms of communicating on the page and in person. In my view, this distinctiveness grew in part from their attempt to wield theory as an aid to compassion. To cultivate compassion as "suffering with" oneself and another as practiced by traditions including Buddhism and Christianity (Dalai Lama, Tutu, and Abrams, 2016), is a practice with which gender theory is profoundly aligned.Spiritual traditions teach that compassion is linked to wisdom—compassion is a spiritually wise way of relating to self and others that has the power to transform suffering. The rich and precise descriptions Berlant offers of the common contours of subjective experience allow us to see and feel one another more clearly, and in this their work carries a transformative force.

Berlant's body of work addresses subjects of femininity—women, queer, trans, and gender non-conforming persons whose subjectivity exists in relation to dominant hetero-masculinity. They read and taught a wide archive of American culture, both middlebrow and pop, and paid attention to the desires and disappointments registered there. The subjects in these stories are wounded, and Berlant used theory as a tool of thick description to give an account of how these wounds bridged interior and exterior worlds. Innovating in affect theory, Berlant tracks how subjects' activities and attentions stretch out over structures of racial and gender norms and economies, falling short of flourishing in ways that are patterned and predictable. Structural harms are scarcely less tractable for being predictable. For these subjects hold on to worlds shaped by convention and the desires offered therein to, as Berlant would say, "stay in the room with desire" and be "held in a scene."

Work on identity and belonging pushes us to grapple with how to give an account of wounds that are personal but have a common shape. We are asked to bring ourselves into the room, but not as detached observers or confessional subjects. At its best, gender theory is an emancipatory tradition that fosters compassion because it asks us to come to consciousness of the constraints on our freedom and to recognize the shared structures of these constraints. Lauren contributed to emancipatory traditions in political and gender theory in two ways, I suggest, that are well worth remembering today. First, their work on "intimate publics," as distinguished from the mass-media "intimate public sphere" brought about by "the right-wing cultural agenda of the Reagan revolution" which, Lauren argues, fixates on "traditional" sexuality and family life in order to stigmatize those who diverge from white heteropatriarchal norms and provide moral cover for their increasing economic deprivation (Berlant, 1997, p. 7). By contrast, in cultivating an intimate public, they modeled how we can come from our own experience to receive, interpret, and relate to stories of others, including those differently positioned than us. Second, they committed to interpreting how trauma shapes subjective and collective worlds, and in so doing gave us tools to work through our most difficult stories.

Introducing the concept of an "intimate public," Berlant documented the creative and life-sustaining subcultural spaces where personal story, fantasy, and complaint circulate (Berlant, 2008). Berlant's catalog of public complaints about, and affronts to, normativity (as opposed to *Cruel Optimism*'s impasses in normativity) is a catalog of liberatory praxis, from the radical to the modest. Sometimes these publics helped loosen the hold of sex/gender normativity and other unfreedoms, as in the queer subcultural work of "Sex in Public" (Berlant & Warner, 2002). Others, such as the contributors to nineteenth- and twentieth-century women's culture in *The Female Complaint*, performed the work of consciousness-raising. Lauren documented both with great care.

The Female Complaint (2008) is a book-length meditation on the insight that moving beyond the self to locate oneself in a common experience is a step toward agency. This central axiom of feminism is messy in practice. How do we come to recognize an experience as common? Berlant teaches that public help us to do this, and therein lies their transformative potential. When addressing a public, quasi-anonymity cushions the vulnerability of personal disclosure. A public is intimate when narrative structures and desires are shared, and this intimacy provides more cushion for more disclosure. Yet these disclosures don't look or feel like confessions. In intimate publics, Berlant argued, "the personal is the general," "the autobiographical isn't the personal," and narratives can be read as "autobiographies of collective experience" (Berlant, 2008, p. vii). Taking part in intimate publics, we recount stories that are, and are not, our own.

The feminist author Dorothy Parker attests to this when, in an interview Berlant cites, she refuses to reduce the story of a woman she authored to an account of incidental experience.

Interviewer: What about "Big Blonde?" Where did the idea for that come from?
Parker: I knew a lady-friend of mine who went through holy hell. Just say I knew a woman once. The purpose of a writer is to say what he [*sic*] feels and sees. To those who write fantasies—the Misses Baldwin, Ferber, Norris—I am not at home (Berlant, 2008, p. 217).

Parker, Berlant insists, is an expert. She demonstrates "expertise" by knowing that the story about her friend is exemplary, and that she can tell it without divulging all the gory details of her friend's particular experience. This is expressed in the terse phrase, "'Just say I knew a woman once.'" Berlant writes of Parker, "Her demurral derives from a sisterly ethics, an ethics of friendship: by not revealing the map from real life to fiction, while saying that a map could be easily drawn, she solicits curiosity about it while blocking traffic in in the epistemological pleasures of misogynist and sentimental schadenfreude" (Berlant, 2008, p. 217).

Parker's demurral is an act of gentleness toward her friend, herself, and anyone else who might seek a space to share such a story. There is tenderness in this expert wielding of knowledge, even if the emotions that accompany it are not. Berlant observes that Parker "emit[s] empathy, bitterness, and sadism toward her friend, the story about her friend, the scene of solicited storytelling, and her own mixed feelings," and attributes this complex reaction to "the flood of emotional exposure the person who engages in feminine transactions will inevitably undergo (Berlant, 2008, p. 218).

Parker knows stories about women, and she wagers that we know them, too. The female complaint Berlant tracks in the book by that name focuses on middlebrow, midcentury, normative femininity. But the contours of the complaint are recognizable to subjects of femininity in historically and socially more and less proximate positions. There is a collective experience of the bargains "a woman" makes with femininity, "which is to measure out in a life in the capital of intimacy, opening herself to a risky series of sexual and emotional transactions that intensify her vulnerability on behalf of securing value, a world and 'a life' that are financially, spatially, and environmentally stable and predictable enough." Berlant and the authors in their archive make these bargains visible (Berlant, 2008, p. 217).

Berlant's catalog of liberatory praxis includes the scholarly and artistic work they curated as a teacher and collaborator at the Center for the Study of Gender and Sexuality over the thirty-plus years they were deeply involved there. In the space of the Center, Berlant championed queer and feminist studies, queer of-color critique, and Black feminism, because these literatures talk about sex/gender as it is lived. They tell stories about relationships, intergenerational trauma, sexual trauma, body image, racial/gender identity, and struggles with mental health. I began my teaching career as a graduate student intern with Berlant in 2015 at the height of campus sexual assault activism, in the wake of the murder of Michael Brown by police in Ferguson, Missouri, and on the eve of #MeToo. I drafted a syllabus for our course on "Advanced Theories of Gender and Sexuality" that did not include sexual violence, and Berlant pushed back. I revised the syllabus to include political accounts of sexual violence, and Berlant shared with me their folders of materials and asked me to try again. They pointed me to accounts of sexual violence that are "autobiographies of collective experience," including Patricia Lockwood's poem, "Rape Joke," and Latoya Peterson's essay, "The 'Not Rape' Epidemic." They gave me Black feminist accounts of anti-Black sexual violence and intergenerational trauma including Patricia Williams' "On Being an Object of Property" and Hortense Spillers' "Mama's Baby, Papa's Maybe."

Teaching "autobiographies of collective experience" of sex, gender, and race with Berlant and in my own courses, I have learned how knowledge and theory practices can help repair wounds by addressing them. This learning came both from the texts themselves and from observing their impact on students.

Berlant's repertoire of course texts taught me the following:

- The personal is the general. Personal stories are stories about structures (of institutions, ideologies, and attachments).
- The family, i.e., inherited structures of desires and intergenerational trauma, is the stuff of which sex/gender normativity is made. The family in the U.S. is always a racialized construct.
- Trauma impacts subjective experience in ways that are patterned and recognizable in personal stories, including a shattering of sense of self and attendant depression, hypervigilance, compensatory behaviors, and withdrawal.
- Trauma stories in the U.S. often come from common conditions and patterns of experience: sexual and racial coercion, stigmatization, and violence; and economic deprivation.
- Identity-based trauma in the U.S. is omnipresent and deserves our deepest care as political theorists. If we are not talking about how trauma impacts our political culture and agency, our accounts of democracy risk losing purchase on reality. Accounts of how our democracy might work that are framed as critical but detached from reality are in themselves a form of ideology and domination. (I take this as a subtextual argument of *The Queen of America* and *Cruel Optimism*).

I witness the impact that personal stories of collective experience have on students in classroom discussion and through two assignments that Berlant taught me, which I continue to use. The first is a creative project accompanied by an artist statement which Berlant offered as an alternative format to a final research paper for students to explore course themes. The second is an autobiographical essay, which I have adapted as a political autobiography for introductory courses in

Critical Exchange

political theory. By creating an experimental and open space for student reflection in assignments and in the classroom, I've observed:

- The personal is the general. Teaching texts grounded in personal stories is an effective way to teach about structures (of institutions, ideologies, and attachments). Doing so gives students an entry way into texts; they relate to personal stories, even if this relation is one of distance. I can then help them see how the author builds concepts and knowledge claims from these stories.
- Stories about family and intimate relationships are effective entryways into teaching about sex/gender and racial politics and identity.
- In writing, students are eager to reflect on their parents' views, the social and family environment they grew up in, and how these relate to their politics. Undergraduate students have often learned to recognize shared social structures before they have worked through how their own ideas, experiences, and aspirations relate to them.
- Students get traction and motivation to think critically about our culture and politics when that learning is couched in relatable stories about family, identity, and education.
- A small but significant number of students take up course concepts, frameworks, and examples to help them write and/or create creative work around traumas they have experienced. In these essays and projects (zines, photo projects, animated short videos, poems, podcasts) students practice healing self-authorization by sharing their take on the personal as the general as it relates to abuse and violence.

Berlant provided an example of a gender theory pedagogy that is challenging because it asks us to root our knowledge in self-reflection, and to gain knowledge of the self while gaining knowledge of our culture and politics. This is an example of critical and interpretive knowledge practice with deep roots in the humanities and humanist social sciences. It is distinct from the boogeyman of the professor-as-therapist cited by some defenders of scholarly expertise, and the boogeyman of professor-as-vengeance/sympathy-seeking-minority cited by right-wing activists parading as defenders of scholarly expertise. Interpretive practices help students to recognize and evaluate the styles and epistemic frameworks through which authors craft stories and frame knowledge claims. With these tools, students learn how to how to link personal experience to shared questions, archives, and knowledge traditions.

These are valuable tools for students today. Humanist education helps students develop critical distance from the confessional disclosures and tabloid exposés so prevalent in the media landscape of their daily lives. Furthermore, it counters the knowledge-undermining effect of media that blurs opinion and fact. In their final projects and subsequent careers, students draw on these lessons in order to communicate knowledge, theory, and personal story through media, exemplifying how the humanities can contribute to raising the level of our discourse, and our relationships.

I picture the weary and joyful smile this work brings to Berlant's face, and it makes me smile, too.

Ashleigh Campi

Coaxing ideology critique toward a pedagogy of unlearning: a reparative approach to a paranoid practice

Lauren Berlant defied easy cataloguing—queer, feminist, Marxist, anarchist, vegan, critic, pedagogue—and it is outside the scope of this setting to attempt an adequate accounting. I will therefore limit myself to the modest proposal that Berlant exemplified "queer critical theory" forged in the AIDS crisis and finely attuned to the affective dimensions of power and resistance. Rather than standard ideology critique, Berlant elaborated a pedagogy of unlearning those attachments to the good life that are killing us. Among the subtle implications of their queer pedagogy is unlearning expectations of the emancipatory power of critique, not to neglect its perennial exigency but to endeavor a deflationary relationship to its necessity. While ultimately resisting a full embrace of the reparative turn recently criticized by Patricia Stuelke (2021) as a "ruse" of neoliberalism, Berlant participated in the millenarian critique of critique, especially as articulated by Bruno Latour, Wendy Brown, and Eve Kosofsky Sedgwick, contributing with their pedagogy of unlearning a reparative approach to a paranoid practice.

Through etymologies of assembly, psychoanalytic theories of loss, and a deconstruction of the paranoid genre of critical theory, Berlant's contemporaries sought to shift critical energy away from asking *what* is to be done? to *how* is it to be done? For Latour, the emergence of the "thing" as an assembly of critical attention and enthusiasm on an object as a matter of concern renders critique less a subtractive or divisive operation than a critical massing (Latour, 2004; cf. Myers, 2013). Wendy Brown's (1999) diagnosis of a self-destructive "left melancholy" as the structure of political desire organized around "an unavowed loss—the promise that left analysis and left commitment would supply its adherents a clear and certain path toward the good, the right, and the true"—positions critique as a self-reflexive scrutiny of the potentially conservative tendencies that form in reaction to fragmentation, diminution, and "broken promises" (p. 22). Sedgwick (2003) helps us understand melancholy leftism as the paranoid desire to defeat surprise, gesturing instead to the reparative energies of the Kleinian depressive position for its uniquely unguarded propensity to endeavor new beginnings in the wake of loss through democratic vernaculars of the "additive and accretive" (p. 149). In all three articulations, disappointment with critique prompts a shift of focus from

Critical Exchange

divisive matters of theory (tiresome sniping about what to do) to praxis (collective attempts at how to do it) in ways that incite multiplicative "things" to happen.

If Lauren was ever disappointed in critique, it never showed, even as they responded to this intellectual mood by proposing a pedagogy of unlearning that resisted conservative nostalgia for reconciliation, integration, and wholeness. Throughout their work, the emphasis is on a critical capacity to open practical relations oriented to the challenges and pleasures of world-building with fuzzy boundaries (Berlant & Warner, 1995). Attentive to Marx's (1978, p. 51) provocations that any "call to abandon [our] illusions about [our] condition is a call *to abandon a condition which requires illusions,*" Berlant trusted critique to a relational, material practice of what they called "revisceralization."

Here they parted from their friend and collaborator, Lee Edelman (2017), for whom queerness is a relentless and unyielding exercise in "learning nothing," or rather in learning that "jouissance [is] the undoing, the zeroing out, of the (constitutively divided) subject as the subject succumbs to the negativity, the contentless energy of pure division" (p. 163). By contrast, for Berlant the mettle of queer critique is its capacity to induce and sustain an "active retraining of the senses" that, at the material level of embodied affectivity, attempts to unlearn the habits, intuitions, and aspirations of neoliberalized possessive individualism. Keen to loosen the hold that the fantasy of sovereignty exerts, they were emphatic that "whatever makes it possible to bear each other will not come from belief in an abstraction," but must instead be cultivated intramurally in relations of care and contestation (Berlant, 2016a, p. 413).

The classic text where Berlant develops an account of unlearning is the essay "The Theory of Infantile Citizenship," in *The Queen of America Goes to Washington City*, where they set their sights early on to an episode in the young life of Audre Lorde. They write (1993, p. 396; my emphasis):

> Lorde's "education" in national culture provoked a nauseated *unlearning* of her patriotism—"Hadn't I written poems about Bataan?" she complains, while resolving, again, to write [to] the president, to give the nation another chance to not betray her desire for it—and this *unlearning*, which is never complete, as it involves leaving behind the political faith of childhood, cleaves her permanently from and to the nation whose promises drew her parents to immigrate there and drew herself to identify as a child with a horizon of national identity she was sure she would fulfill as an adult citizen.

I see two distinct "unlearnings" occurring in this passage. The first is the unlearning of a naïve patriotism, one that faces up to the fractures of the nation by race, gender, sexuality, and capital, and sees Lorde recognizing her exclusion from the bounds of citizenship. And yet, this "nauseated" lesson is itself promptly unlearned in the resolution to write to President Truman to give the nation another

Reprinted from the journal

chance, a resolution that dissolves the tension produced by the lesson of American undemocracy experienced in segregated Washington, DC.

What is learned in the first unlearning of patriotism—i.e., Lorde's embodied disjuncture from the nation—is, in turn, unlearned in the resolute reassertion of growing into citizenship. This second unlearning is a "disavowal," or an "act of optimistic forgetting," one that "is neither simple nor easy: it takes the legitimating force of institutions." This account prefigures Berlant's popular concept of "cruel optimism," while also illuminating something crucial about its vicissitudes, namely that it is "never complete" as it "cleaves permanently from and to the nation" and its promises of "adult citizenship" (1993, p. 396.) In *Cruel Optimism* (2011), Berlant will again signal that "What we are talking about here is the hardest problem: understanding the difficulty of unlearning attachments to regimes of injustice," a pedagogy all the more complicated by the fact that "Justice itself is a technology of deferral or patience that keeps people engrossed politically, when they are, in the ongoing drama of optimism and disappointment" (p. 184).

Immersed in the drama, one lives in the key of the "as if," what Sloterdijk (1987) termed the cynical reason of an "enlightened false-consciousness," which Berlant thickens in their account of the "juxta-political" (Berlant, 2008). The juxta-political is experienced as "relief" from the political, even as it is enjoyed through a certain proximity to it—that is, to the disturbing facts that arise to matters of concern in what they term "intimate publics" (Berlant, 2008, p. 9). *Pace* Latour, with the concept of the "intimate public," Berlant attends to how matters of care and investments in repair can sustain conditions that should otherwise be contested, modified, even abolished. This occurs because "the sense that changes in feeling, even on a mass scale, amount to substantial social change" is a "confusion" made "credible" by the hegemony of a mass "sentimental politics" that renders "these violences bearable, as its cultural power confirms the centrality of interpersonal identification and empathy to the vitality and viability of collective life" (Berlant, 1999, p. 54).

Unlike the post-Habermasian counter-public developed, respectively, by Nancy Fraser and Michael Warner, and often the subject of political theorizing, the intimate public indexes a para-democratic siphon for the "desire to be in proximity to okayness, without passing some test to prove it" (Berlant, 2008, p. 9). In the bounds of belonging held open by public intimacy, *feeling* political is what happens when a "capitalist culture effectively markets conventionality as the source and solution to the problem of living in worlds that are economically, legally, and normatively not on the side of almost anyone's survival, let alone flourishing" (Berlant, 2008, p. 31; Anker, 2014).

Berlant's sharp sense of the traps posed by sentimentality also meant that they were attuned to the volatility, or ambivalence, of this medium of mass politics. Thus, as much as they critique a certain political sentimentality hegemonic in the

Critical Exchange

vernaculars of reactionaries and liberals alike, they also insist that "nonetheless, flourishing happens." Trained to this dissonance, they consistently sought out what they later would term "a concrete utopian," or modes of "inducing better relations and potentials from within the cracks of the present" (Berlant & Stein, 2015, p. 19).

Unlearning, then, as much as it is a process of divesting ourselves from putatively unreflective attachments, intuitions, habits, idioms, priorities, and fantasies in sustainable ways, is effective insofar as it also proposes fashioning relational terms that, at least provisionally, offer a basis for reconfiguring conceptions of the good life when that promise is thrown into crisis. Berlant gives us a sense of what such a pedagogy of unlearning might look like in their late theorizing on the commons concept, to which they turn for its "power to retrain affective practical being, and in particular in its power to dishabituate through unlearning the overskilled sensorium that is so quick to adapt to damaged life with a straight, and not a queer, face" (Berlant, 2016a, p. 399). In the form of unlearning elaborated out of the commons concept, the senses are queered in a way that makes resistance to resiliency and repair on the terms of neoliberalism an embodied lesson in feeling out new relations to precarity, trauma, and proximity to others, in part by learning how to refuse some demands to make room for others.

Berlant gestures to the unfinished business of a counter-hegemonic sentimental politics, arguing that "what remains for our pedagogy of unlearning is to build affective infrastructures that admit the work of desire as the work of an aspirational ambivalence" (Berlant, 2016a p. 414). For Berlant, rather than a "failure of a relation, the opposite of happiness," ambivalence is "an inevitable condition of intimate attachment and a pleasure in its own right" (Berlant, 2008, p. 2). To begin imagining and creating relational forms able to absorb aggression, retrain appetite, and nurture a taste for living differently, Berlant (2016a) looks, in part, to Liza Johnson's magical realist film, *In the Air*, which presents a kinetic circus routine set to the dance-club banger, "Better Off Alone" (1999), as an image of what it might look like to common sites of destitution into spaces of renewed assembly and bearable proximity. Something of a cross between squatting and a rave, the scene enjoys an easy execution of an affective choreography that is utopian in its indeterminacy—things are "in the air."

Resistance to fascist decisionism tilts the political idiom toward collaborative experimentation and provisional configurations of already ambivalent relations. Throwing things in the air can be freeing, when it is, but it can also arouse feelings of suspense and nausea that yearn for steady ground—to return us to our opening scene with the young Lorde, who swallows her lesson in undemocracy by affirming her commitment to something like participation in the fantasy of democratic citizenship practiced through private entreaty to figures of power in the humanist tradition of a conversation through letters (Sloterdijk, 2009). As Lorde would discover and teach in her own way, stomaching instead the shiftiness of unlearning calls for revisceralization, which in turn calls for some collective act of commoning that, if not exactly furnishing a *ground*, nevertheless provides a holding environment wherein transitioning to a more loose and freeform comportment is not compromising and nauseating, but can become a venue for developing dexterity, savvy, and a counter-commonsense.

The dynamic I am gesturing toward is usefully illuminated by a scene from the film, *The East* (dir. Batmanglij, 2013). Whereas in *In the Air* nausea might come from the leaps to and falls from great heights, in *The East* nausea is the effect of an affect, made plain in a scene wherein a young, undercover corporate counterinsurgency (co-COIN) operative (Brit Marling) is taught how to eat with her hands tied behind her back as part of her induction into the titular eco-activist commune, The East. After a few clumsy and failed attempts to feed herself with the clunky wooden spoon she is provided with, her comrades—all in like restraints—demonstrate how it is to be done: by using their spoon, gripped in their teeth, to feed the person to their right, while being fed in turn by the person to their left in like manner.

It is a disarming scene of slow food (Honig, 2015; Martel, 2015), for the rhythms of feeding and being fed do more than merely care for a physical need. The proximity to other people is intimate for an act like eating; the comrades make eye contact as food passes between their lips. In becoming plugged into an "annular" relational circuit (Hocquenghem, 1993), the body is revisceralized in its interruption of the exchange model of reciprocity, possession, and exclusivity: the one you feed is not the one who feeds you; you don't eat from your bowl, it is what you use to feed the person beside you, that is, a person besides you; the annular circuit is non-exclusive, you give and receive from different partners, commoning care without collapsing individuality into sameness (as made plain in a later, further immersive scene of spin-the-bottle, where the individual form surfaces as an interface negotiating proximity and contact in what is a sexy even if somewhat awkward scene of group affirmative consent). Mindful of Berlant and Warner's (2002) queering of "sex in public," this scene of intimate feeding gives an admittedly romantic, but still evocative glimpse of what elsewhere Berlant (2016a, p. 403) theorizes as a "positive version of dispossession," where the experience of non-sovereignty does not denote domination, but distributed insecurity and mutual aid.

It is a characteristic trope of Hollywood filmmaking to present a problem that cannot be resolved on the terms within which it is framed, and *The East* is no different. Whereas initially Brit rejects the lesson, the shared meal provides a scene of unlearning the securitized self-reliance of sovereignty that allows our protagonist to feel out different relations with her comrades, and the rectitude of their retaliatory "jams" against corporate polluters. However, the solution with which the film ends completely fails to incorporate the pedagogy of unlearning into its critical practice—a failure that, in presenting its absence, makes it all the more pressing. As the credits roll, our operative goes rogue, only it is to track down other

Critical Exchange

co-COIN agents to persuade them through rational debate and facts, with her personal narrative peppered-in, perhaps, to similarly defect to the very causes they were dispatched to undermine. By the logic of the film, such appeals are doomed, and rightly so: without unlearning the sensibility of security, calls for insecurity will be predictably greeted as unsound and suspect.

Too much critique fancies itself the final scene set to the end credits of *The East*: a rational and deliberative accounting of the wrongness of a given reality, paired with a rolling list of authoritative citations, something conclusive. By contrast, in condescending to the visceral, a pedagogy of unlearning cultivates a critical practice of inaugurating new beginnings, which "after being for so long and so deeply at best a stereotype is to take on the project of acting in excess to the forms of distortion you normally inhabit" (Berlant, 1997, p. 93). Countering conditions of catastrophe will take solidarity, cooperation, risk—all of which entails retraining our taste for living a different life in a differently constituted world. For that, projects of contention and care that presently nurture the "concrete utopian"—squatting, raving, protesting, feeding each other—provide tangible, even if shifty and tentative, common infrastructures for unlearning cruel optimism in projects of world-making.

Samuel Galloway

Reading political fantasies with Berlant: Some reflections

Fantasy is an opening and a defense (Berlant, 2011, p. 49).

Even though not officially "in" political theory, Berlant's work offers some of the deepest and most productive insights to understanding our political reality. I never knew Berlant, and was asked to contribute to this conversation based on my relation to their work. But what would it mean to eulogize from this place? How does one capture a debt—to one's own personal thought, to a discipline, as a form of eulogy? I tried and failed several times to write this text. Partly, I failed because Berlant's contribution to political theory is not simply wide and does not simply span over so many different domains. I have a sense that much of it operates beneath the surface and is therefore difficult to capture. Berlant's writing infiltrates so deeply into the mind, the soul, or the fibers of one's being that it is difficult to think without them once one has thought with them. So many of us have begun to read so much of the world through their words. I therefore decided to engage in a small gesture of reading with Berlant, in recognition of a debt in a different way, if you will. It is a very local reading of the role of fantasies in political lives.

One of Berlant's main contributions to the understanding of politics has to do with their practice of taking fantasies seriously. Rather than an image of the world as governed by rational decision-making and structures, Berlant shows that so many of our political relations, institutions, and ideologies are based in fantasies, in a mode of existence that resides somewhere between the real and the imagined. These are not grand fantasies, but small, ordinary ones. These fantasies help us deal with a world that is no longer fully bearable: through fantasies we can continue being in the world despite and amidst the continuous betrayals of the world (and more concretely, of so many of those around us) in its/their promises. Fantasy is thus the defense that makes life possible. But this means that how we see the world and give it meaning, as well as how we construct our relations to others, is often at least partially given within the realm of the imaginary. If "fantasy is the means by which people hoard idealizing theories and tableaux about how they and the world 'add up to something'" (Berlant, 2011, p. 2), then these meanings are often far from being rational or calculated.

This mode of being-in-the-imaginary can be an "opening", a "projected possibility" (Berlant, 2011, p 25): it can create spaces of hope and action, but it can also end up destroying us. This is not just because the content of our fantasies is part of the impasse that has forced us to the phantasmatic domain to begin with (it is shaped by the same order and ideology that has created the unbearability of the world—shaped by the desire to accumulate, for example, or by similar visions of "the good life"), and therefore they are almost bound to fail to provide the expectations and fulfill the desires they create in us. It is also because ultimately, something about the attachments these fantasies form betrays the structure of attachment itself: they keep turning inward or meeting empty objects, dropping dead on empty floors, as it were (the neighbors are never there when one visits, the lover or child turns out to be imaginary, the other citizens with whose suffering we identify do not need or want our sympathy, or we sympathize with a wrong cause). When I teach Berlant, students often report being "shattered" by their texts. I think partly this is an outcome of this sense that even our hopes, our projections to the future, end up undermining our possibility to thrive.

But as mentioned, I limit myself here to a reading in one such fantasy, inspired by Berlant's ways of thinking along an extended archive: the fantasy portrayed in *Frozen II* (2019, dir. Lee and Buck). I read this film, first, alongside Berlant's cruel optimism, as a fantasy that reproduces the conditions of the very *impasse* it seeks to overcome. Second, I read it as providing a defense by opening a route for self-exoneration and perhaps also offering a political opening. I end with some more general reflections can hopefully help to move beyond this reading to a more systematic inquiry.

At its core, *Frozen II* presents one of the most difficult political questions for the west. Indeed, it may not be accidental that the film opens with existential reflections on the meaning of transformation, the ephemeral nature of life, the fear of getting old, but also the fear of childhood itself. These are all represented by Olaf, the snowman created by Elsa, whom we meet at the beginning of the film as he fulfills the main fantasy he had in *Frozen I*: enjoying the sun without melting. *Frozen II*, then, seems to begin with a slightly less pessimistic point of departure than its prequel. Whereas *Frozen I* recognized that the content of our fantasies is often self-destructive and ends up betraying not just its own promises, and with it our wellbeing, but also our very ability to survive (Olaf simply melts in the sun until Elsa's magic saves him), *Frozen II* seems to allow Olaf to enjoy the content of the good life, as he sees it, without having his very survival threatened.

Yet, the presumed material stability that Olaf obtains does not do away with the fear of change, which he comes to understand is inevitable and probably unpleasant. Being a childhood fantasy—a playful animated object—Olaf embodies the eroding conditions of life, if not the impossibility of living in the world, and certainly the impossibility of living our desires. This playfulness is itself a defense, yet one that allows us to get closer to what often remains buried in us.

Frozen is a fantasy, and in what follows I will read it as representing a particular fantasy that shapes life within settler colonialism by drawing on and expanding on Berlant's analysis of life within or under late capitalism. *Frozen* is also one of the many materials from which fantasies are made, and the fear of change that Olaf's erosion both incarnates and phantasmatically overcomes, is not just the fear of death or growing up, but also the fear of coming to terms with one's place in history—a fear of a political world that is changing, in which "the bastards changed the rules" and accountability for ones' positionality becomes necessary. This fear concerning shifting positions and identities prepares us for the big question that drives the plot: how should one deal with the discovery that one is one of the bad guys? How can one deal with their own role in history as a dispossessor?

The movie tells the story of Queen Elsa and Princess Anna from Arendelle, who discover that they were raised on false historical narrations. In these narrations, their grandparents' generation was engaged in a defensive war against untrustworthy people from a nearby magical forest. Those people bear the iconography of Indigenous people (based, according to Disney, on the Sámi people of northern Europe, but to an untrained eye they can easily seem to represent Indigenous Americans): they have a tribal name (the Northuldra people) and are placed in a particular historical setting that resonates with a history of colonization (the opening song presents a Thanksgiving-like celebration, commemorating the settlers' placement). In what is being told to the young girls as the story of a brutal attack, the Northuldra killed Elsa and Anna's grandfather, started a war, and were punished by magical forces that sealed them in their forest. The truth, however, is that Arendelle's people, led by Elsa and Anna's grandfather, were the attackers and destroyers of both a peaceful tribe and nature itself. They built a dam that destroyed the Northuldras' livelihood and refused to demolish it. Echoing histories of settler colonialism replete with gestures of "peace" that are really self-interested acts which bring much destruction (cf. Idris, 2018), this dam is presumably a token of peace and friendship but was really necessary to protect

Arendelle from flooding. Now, Elsa and Anna must confront history, and both are willing to do anything within their power to right past wrongs.

As a movie, *Frozen II* is a familiar fantasy for those who inherited the role of dispossessors or have various privileges that come from past atrocities. It is a fantasy concerning one's own position in relation to the past, and hence about the possibility of enjoying the fruits of past violence without being complicit in it. It is the fantasy that one never knew, and that the truth is a powerful political engine of change. I argue (2020), along with Gil Hochberg (2020) and Bruce Robince (2017), that the discovery of the truth is not a sufficient condition to promote egalitarian, progressive or of-the-left political change, and may even facilitate entrenchment of conservative political projects. In Berlant's terms, *Frozen II* represents an attachment of cruel optimism since such narratives affix us to a (phantasmatic) image of a future that can be opened by the power of truth. Anna says, for instance, that "Arendelle has no future until we make this right," and the trolls also comment that "the truth must be found; without it, [there is] no future." This presumes that the discovery of the truth will indeed set us free, correct the wrongs of the past, or lead to some reconciliation—as if one could really live without knowing (see Kotef, 2020). But this fantasy is linked to a more fundamental form of cruel optimism concerning the question of justice.

Elsewhere I read Lorraine Hansberry's *Les Blancs* as offering two answers to the question of postcolonial justice when it is posed from the point of view of the colonizer or the settler. One could either leave or die (Kotef, 2020, p. 131): die because, Hansberry and Fanon tell us, the fight for decolonization must take a violent form if justice is to be achieved; or leave because, as Albert Memmi (2016) contends, once they understand the price that others pay for their very presence on the land, the only coherent possibility of refusing the structure of colonization available for the colonizer is leaving. Any other form of refusal ends up being either paradoxical or itself a form of self-negation. Indeed, Anna and Elsa each inhabit one of these two possibilities. Elsa dies in her effort to discover the truth. Anna understands that the dam must be demolished and that therefore she—and the people of Arendelle—must leave.

But as is often the case in fairytales, Elsa eventually comes back to life and a miracle stops the water just before it floods the kingdom. Moreover, we discover that Elsa and Anna do not belong to the "bad guys" but rather embody reconciliation, as it turns out that they are the offspring of a union between the two peoples—their dad an Arendellian, their mom a Northuldras. Everyone lives happily ever after.

Yet precisely in this resolution lies the fundamental political impasse. The opening it presents is but a reproduction of a fantasy of justice in which the correction of past wrongs and violence does not really come at the expense of the wrongdoer. It stokes a fantasy of justice with no real price, which is also a fantasy about ourselves as people who can be invested in justice-making without undermining the very grounds of our (unjust) existence.Such phantasmatic "openings" of shared life and even shared indigeneity entrench attachments to the present and are hence part of the present impasse itself. They foster the sense that we can keep on holding to the present conditions of life when we project ourselves into the future. Moreover, *Frozen* offers us the ultimate settler-colonial fantasy of indigenization, wherein Elsa and Anna can ultimately emerge as part-natives themselves, never fully colonizers, always of-the-land. There is a fantasy here of self-transformation that is but a return to a presumably pure past. One does not need to abandon who one is, only rediscover it. As such, it is a political fantasy of justice which cannot fulfill its promise and itself becomes an obstacle to justice.

Yet perhaps *Frozen II* offers us a different ending. The rapture between Elsa's death and her resurrection, accompanied by the rapture between Anna's reckoning that Arendelle must be destroyed (or at least evicted) and the last-minute magical saving of the kingdom, haunts this good ending, as if questioning its very possibility. Moreover, this image of self-transformation as ultimately harmonious and peaceful is questioned by Olaf's fear of change that frames the adventure. I therefore suggest we read this ending alongside the endings of movies such as Spike Lee's *The 25th Hour*, Tony Scott's *True Romance*, or, differently so, Tarantino's *Once Upon a Time in Hollywood*: an ending in which cinema presents what it explicitly recognizes to be an impossible fantasy; a good ending that can never take place in real life.

In this very recognition of its impossibility, the ending moves from being "a defense" to being a real "opening." Or perhaps this rupture within the fantasy allows *Frozen II* to be both: a defense against an unbearable reality in which one must die or leave their home for justice to be made, but also a small aperture wherein what may seem like the ultimate impasse (death) is also a springboard to re-imagining an alternative politics. Could we think of such alternatives not through physical deaths and projects of mass-destruction but through figures of social dis-existence that can open new modes of being in the world that are themselves less destructive? Could "death" be symbolic or otherwise not final—indeed a transformation, as the film keeps reminding us, rather than an end? Can it show that eventually people may find ways of sharing the land, even if at a particular historical moment this seems impossible? Or does the film merely show the phantasmatic nature of the image of priceless justice? Even if *Frozen* only does the latter, it thereby nevertheless urges us to see the need for crafting other visions.

Part of the power of Berlant's work is that they refused to settle questions of interpretation and instead called us to inhabit the unsettled. In a way, if one thinks of undoing settler colonialism, this is precisely the mode of inhabitation at stake.

Berlant's *Cruel Optimism* to a great degree is about the erosion of collective fantasies. It is about fantasies that can no longer fulfill their function: they can no longer provide the comfort that the world indeed "add[s] up to something" (Berlant, 2011, p. 2). Elsa and Anna's world no longer makes any sense. Ever since

Olaf stated at the beginning of the film that "nothing is permanent" and shedding leaves marks the change of seasons, *Frozen II* is also about erosion. The good life with which it opens is clearly and explicitly ephemeral.

But *Frozen II* is not just *about* eroding fantasies: it is also a symptom of such erosion. A fantasy in and of itself, the movie addresses a certain erosion of the fantasy of enlightened colonization—the fantasy that settler societies can just push away the reality of settlement. *Frozen II* is the outcome of a colonial society whose collective fantasy about its own self-identity is no longer sustainable and must come to terms with its violent past. Yet its way of coming to terms with this past is a replication of its phantasmatic self-image. The question of justice can thus be reconstructed in relation to both past (Did we know? Did we not know? rather than: Did we commit a genocide? Is this land stolen?) and future (How can I transform myself to become a better person? rather than: What is the material future of this land?), in ways that enable one to take responsibility, albeit in incredibly convenient terms (not unlike land-acknowledgments at the beginning of well-funded academic conferences, for example).

Berlant calls us to see ideological, material, and affective frameworks that attach us to the idea that we can thrive to preserve a system in which we can barely survive. We become attached to objects and ideological schemes that can never deliver on their promises and that we can never fully obtain or inhabit. I am not sure this carries well from the analysis of modern capitalism to that of settler colonialism, although elsewhere I tried to propose that in some way it does. But at the very least, what is at stake in both cases is a set of impasses that betray both our image of the good life and the set of relations between us and others—a system (material and ideological) that holds us captive by continuously attaching us to a future that can never come. At stake is a trajectory toward the future (in capitalism it is the promise of accumulation, here it is the promise embedded in self-transformation) that ultimately hinders change in the present.

Hagar Kotef

References

Adorno, T. (2005) *Minima moralia: Reflections from damaged life*. Verso.
Anker, E.R. (2014) *Orgies of Feeling*. Durham: Duke University Press.
Beltrán, C. (2021) *Cruelty as Citizenship: How Migrant Suffering Sustains White Democracy*. University of Minnesota Press.
Berlant, L. (1993) The theory of infantile citizenship. *Public Culture* 5(3): 395–410.
Berlant, L. (1997) *The queen of America goes to Washington city: essays on sex and citizenship*. Duke University Press.
Berlant, L. (2001) 6. The Subject of True Feeling: Pain, Privacy, and Politics. In *Feminist Consequences* (pp. 126-160). Columbia University Press.

Berlant, L. (2008) *The female complaint: the unfinished business of sentimentality in American culture*. Duke University Press.
Berlant, L. (2011) *Cruel Optimism*. Durham: Duke Univeristy Press.
Berlant, L. (2016a) The commons: Infrastructures for troubling times. *Environment and Planning d: Society and Space* 34(3): 393–419.
Berlant, L. (2016b) Trump, or political emotions, *The New Inquiry*. https://thenewinquiry.com/trump-or-political-emotions/. (Accessed 15 Feb 2022).
Berlant, L. and Stein, J.A. (2015) Cruising Veganism. *GLQ: A Journal of Lesbian and Gay Studies* 21(1): 18–23.
Berlant, L. and Stewart, K. (2019) *The Hundreds*. Duke University Press.
Berlant, L. and Warner, M. (1995) Guest column: What does queer theory teach us about X? *PMLA* 110(3): 343–349.
Berlant, L. and Warner, M. (2002) *Publics and Counterpublics*. Zone Books.
Brown, W. (1999) Resisting left melancholy. *Boundary* 26(3): 19–27.
Buck, C. and Lee, J. (2018) *Frozen*. Walt Disney Studios Motion Pictures.
Lama, D., Tutu, D. and Abrams, D. (2016) *The book of joy: lasting happiness in a changing world*. New York: Penguin Random House.
Edelman, L. (2017) Learning nothing: bad education. *Differences* 28(1): 124–173.
Hocquenghem, G. (1993) *Homosexual desire*. Durham: Duke University Press.
Honig, B. (2015) Public things: Jonathan Lear's Radical Hope, Lars von Trier's Melancholia, and the democratic need. *Political Research Quarterly* 68(3): 623–636.
Hochberg, G. (2020) *Becoming Palestine*. Duke University Press.
Idris, M. (2018) *War for Peace: Genealogies of a Violent Ideal in Western and Islamic Thought*. Oxford: Oxford University Press.
Kotef, H. (2020) *The Colonizing Self, or: Home and Homelessness in Israel/Palestine*. Durham: Duke University Press.
Latour, B. (2004) Why has critique run out of steam? From matters of fact to matters of concern. *Critical Inquiry* 30(2): 225–248.
Lorde, A. (2012) *Sister outsider: Essays and speeches*. Trumansburg: Crossing Press.
Luibhéid, E. (2022) Sexual citizenship, pride parades, and queer migrant Im/Mobilities. *Ethnic and Racial Studies*. https://doi.org/10.1080/01419870.2022.2046842.
Martel, J. (2015) Against thinning and teleology: Politics and objects in the face of catastrophe in Lear and von Trier. *Political Research Quarterly* 68(3): 642–646.
Marx, K. (1978) Contribution to the Critique of Hegel's *Philosophy of Right*: Introduction. In *The Marx-Engels Reader*, 2nd Ed. W.W. Norton & Co.
Memmi, A. (2016) *Colonizer and the Colonized*. Souvenir Press.
Myers, E. (2013) *Worldly Ethics*. Durham: Duke University Press.
Nietzsche, F. (1969) On a Genealogy of Morals (W. Kaufman, Trans.) New York.
Robince, B. (2017) *The Beneficiary*. Durham: Duke University Press.
Sedgwick, E.K. (2003) *Touching feeling*. Duke University Press.
Sloterdijk, P. (1987) *The Critique of Cynical Reason*. Minnesota: University of Minnesota Press.
Sloterdijk, P. (2009) Rules for the Human Zoo: A Response to the Letter on Humanism. *Environment and Planning d: Society and Space* 27(1): 12–28. https://doi.org/10.1068/dst3.
Stuelke, P. (2021) *The Ruse of Repair: US Neoliberal Empire and the Turn from Critique*. Durham: Duke University Press.

Publisher's Note Springer Nature remains neutral with regard to jurisdictional claims in published maps and institutional affiliations.

Review

Queer Terror: Life, death, and desire in the settler colony

C. Heike Schotten
Columbia University Press, New York, 2018, 272pp.,
ISBN: 9780231187473

Contemporary Political Theory (2021) **20,** S49–S52. https://doi.org/10.1057/s41296-020-00389-2; published online 17 March 2020

C. Heike Schotten's *Queer Terror: Life, Death, and Desire in the Settler Colony* brings together conversations in political theory, native studies, queer theory, and biopolitics to offer a stunningly original theory of the temporality of settler sovereignty. Trenchant, polemical, and committed to a revolutionary politics against settler sovereignty, *Queer Terror* nonetheless seeks to conscript its reader to a seemingly untenable position. Schotten closes the book with the memorable and apparently indefensible declaration, 'We choose to stand on the side of "terrorism"' (168). *Queer Terror* builds a solid theoretical armature for why standing on the side of 'terrorism' is a queer and decolonial position.

The core of the book is chapter 2, in which Schotten conducts a highly original reading of Hobbes's *Leviathan* in order to theorize settler sovereignty as driven by futural, expansionist desire. For Hobbes, what is desired is possession, and possession is a temporal affair. In the state of nature, there is no hope of securing the object of one's desire from all those who would seek to take it from you. Hence, there can be no temporal continuity of desire into a future of guaranteed satisfaction. Thus, the state of nature is characterized by hopelessness and emotional stasis. The stable order of the commonwealth, by contrast, is supposed to guarantee a future of satisfied and protected possession. But in Hobbes's theory of desire, possession is never enough, as desire seeks to constantly renew itself, as well as the experience of satisfaction, by turning from one object to another. For Schotten, the expansionist character of desire within the settler commonwealth is one driving engine of imperialism. The disavowed violence of settler sovereignty – in actual settler states as in Hobbes's myth of the founding of the commonwealth out of the state of nature – is its other engine. Because the violence of native dispossession and would-be genocide cannot be acknowledged by the settler state, and because the continuing existence of native peoples threatens this disavowal, imperialism emerges with deadly force: 'Empire functions as a kind of substitutive satisfaction to compensate for the failure of settler sovereignty to finally and fully exterminate indigenous peoples' (59). Schotten's critique of the temporality of settler colonial desire in chapter 2 thus offers shared ground for native studies and (post)colonial studies – two fields that are often seen as in tension with one another.

The second pillar of Schotten's argument is an astonishing reading of Lee Edelman's *No Future: Queer Theory and the Death Drive* as a politically revolutionary text in favor of native life and native resistance. This flies in the face of the well-established reading of *No Future* as an a- or even anti-political text. Indeed, Edelman famously critiques all politics as based on a futural temporality that must repudiate the meaninglessness and a-temporality of the death drive, which, for Edelman, is socially represented by queers. In Schotten's reading, however, *No Future*'s project of saying no to the futurism of politics 'is not equivalent to abolishing politics as such and could only mean as much if every modernity were European modernity, if every politics were a sovereign biopolitics, and if every temporality were futurist' (109). Instead, she reframes Edelman as an advocate of the opposition to the futurism of settler sovereignty developed in chapter 2 – a settler sovereignty that, much like the death drive itself, posits all resistance to it as irrational ('terrorism') and/or a-temporal ('savage'). Hence, in Schotten's rereading, Edelman's project is 'wedded to life, albeit a life that is unlivable as life, which is the status of native life within settler colonial regimes' (110). To be sure, Schotten concedes that Edelman universalizes the futurism of the settler state as the futurism of *all* politics, just as he universalizes the hetero-reproductive futurity symbolized by the white child as that of *all* children. Hers is therefore less a reading of Edelman than an adventurous and compelling appropriation – for the most part, that is. For to say that native life is not recognized as life, that native futures are not recognized as futures, and thus that native life occupies the structural position of the queer, of death, and of anti-futurity, is to concede the symbolic order – the order of representation and meaning – to settler sovereignty. As Schotten acknowledges, 'it seems particularly cruel and benighted to dismiss futurist movements and political struggles when they are so often waged precisely by those who were never meant to survive' (112). Edelman would surely respond that indigenous political movements, like all political movements, are versions of futurism that queers must oppose, because every futural politics, even that of the most disenfranchised, necessarily repudiates the a-temporality of the drives. Beyond the Edelmanian frame, we might wonder whether a truly decolonial politics and theory would *decolonize futurity*, rather than conceding it to the settler state, while refuting the meanings of death, a-temporality, and structural queerness that settler sovereignty assigns to native resistance. But Schotten's faithfulness to the Edelmanian frame – and to 'high' theory itself – prevents her from articulating the alternative terms of native and decolonial futurity. Though she helps us to see how settler sovereignty falsely universalizes its own futurity, ultimately, like Edelman, she concedes the terms of political discourse to settler sovereignty, granting it an absolute chokehold on representation itself.

In the final chapter, Schotten constructs an illuminating genealogy of 'terrorism' that will not only be highly teachable but also useful to scholars of the Global War on Terror, Palestinian resistance, and contemporary anti-Muslim sentiment. Throughout the chapter, Schotten puts 'terrorism' in scare quotes to signal that the term, on her view, functions as a moral epithet rather than a description of any particular form of political violence. 'Terrorism's' sole function is to designate a political threat as evil, making outraged condemnation and military violence the only possible responses to it. Schotten demonstrates how, during the Cold War, Western states sought to use the language of 'terrorism' to delegitimate 'totalitarianism,' whether it be Nazi fascism or Soviet Stalinism. During the same period, the Soviets sided with anti-colonial movements to brand colonial violence as 'terrorism.' The Global War on Terror effectively wrested the term 'terrorism' away from its anti-colonial usage, while adding Islam to its existing genealogies. Schotten tracks how U.S. and Israeli architects of contemporary 'terrorism' discourse conflated radical Islam, Nazism, Marxism, and fascism in order to delegitimate 'terrorism' as a threat to civilization and democracy. 'Emptying oppositional politics of any content whatsoever,' Schotten writes, '"terrorism" becomes another word for savagery and nihilism, for the negation of the West and everything it ostensibly stands for: freedom, democracy, and the American way' (141). In a reading of two scenes in which right-wing conservative pundits face off with defenders of Palestinian resistance, Schotten demonstrates how 'terrorism' discourse leaves no room for dialogue or retort. Rhetorically, defenders of Palestinian resistance, particularly when they are Muslim, cannot respond to 'terrorism' discourse without either condemning Palestinians as 'terrorists' or being themselves branded as 'terrorists.' For those in solidarity with Palestinian resistance, the choice, in fact, is no choice at all. In a compelling use of the Edelmanian model, Schotten concludes: 'Let's declare that we, too, are queers, bent on the annihilation of the social order and its ceaseless reproduction of specters of nihilism and death. We choose *not* to choose empire or the endless futurism of colonial domination. We choose to stand on the side of "terrorism"' (168).

Queer Terror is a polemical must-read for scholars of biopolitics, native studies, queer theory, and the Global War on Terror. Few readers will agree with all of Schotten's claims, but the work of a polemic is to generate disagreement, controversy, and conversation as much as it is to convince its readers. *Queer Terror* is sure to do all of the above. Structurally, *Queer Terror* is built around a series of highly original, illuminating, and, at times, counterintuitive readings of canonical political and queer theorists. This means that, paradoxically, *Queer Terror* seeks to contribute to native studies by building an original theory of the temporality of settler desire from the works of canonical, white settler theorists. *Queer Terror* is thus not a book about decolonial tactics or imaginaries, and it does not engage the alternative temporalities, futurities, or cosmologies of native life. Readers interested in concrete political praxis and modes of native resistance will therefore be left with questions that go beyond the book's abstract theoretical framing. What does the praxis of resistance to settler sovereignty consist of, beyond performatively declaring oneself to stand on the side of 'terrorists'? Is the choice to declare oneself on the side of 'terrorists' as available to Muslims, Palestinians, and indigenous water protectors, who are already likely to be targeted as 'terrorists,' as is it to white settler queers? Is there a danger in taking 'queer' and 'terrorist' to be structural markers of everything that settler sovereignty deems threatening, given the way these terms bundle together vastly divergent peoples, politics, practices, imaginaries, and yes, uses of violence? These and other questions of concrete praxis are the stuff of another project. *Queer Terror* is best read as an anatomy of the settler symbolic order and the impossible position in which it places native and decolonial resistance – a position, as Schotten compellingly if controversially argues, of death, 'terrorism,' and queerness.

Publisher's Note Springer Nature remains neutral with regard to jurisdictional claims in published maps and institutional affiliations.

Kadji Amin
Emory University, Atlanta, GA 30322, USA
kadji.amin@emory.edu

Review

Living a feminist life

Sarah Ahmed Duke University Press, January 2017, ix+299 pp.,
ISBN: 9780822363194

Contemporary Political Theory (2019) **18**, S125–S128. https://doi.org/10.1057/s41296-018-0199-2; published online 13 February 2018

Sarah Ahmed's *Living a Feminist Life* is much more than a farewell to her institutional academic life in the wake of her highly publicized resignation from Goldsmiths, the University of London, in protest of the university's handling of sexual harassment. Her latest work retains a fierce grip on the spirit of feminist critical theory, while avowing that it is possible and even powerful to 'leave a life' that is not feminist.

It is customary to begin studying feminism by defining it as a 'life question'. For educators, such discussions flow into rewarding 'clicks' of transformative political consciousness when students re-examine their own experiences in the light of feminist theory. Ahmed, writing explicitly for students, begins by considering what it means 'to make everything into something that is questionable' (p. 2), recounting her own 'clicking' moments: 'I began to realize what I already knew: that patriarchal reasoning goes all the way down, to the letter, to the bone' (p. 4). In laying out a foundational self-reflexivity, constantly connecting her background in philosophy (the letter) with her life (bone) as a brown lesbian feminist of mixed heritage, Ahmed shows us how to re-politicize the personal: 'I began to appreciate that theory can do more the closer it gets to the skin' (p. 10).

In urging feminists, 'do not become the master's tool!' (p. 160), Ahmed invokes Audre Lorde's well-known concept of the master's house: 'I had to find ways not to reproduce its grammar in what I said, in what I wrote, in what I did, in who I was' (p. 4). Her own refusal to be a master's tool crops up in, for example, Ahmed's policy of citing feminists of colour rather than white men, because citations 'are the materials through which, from which, we create our dwellings' (p. 16). Feminism's fault lines (such as excluding trans women) show us the cracks in dogmatic certainty: Ahmed argues that a 'feminist tendency … does not give us a stable ground' (p. 7). Stability mires feminisms in injustice. Instead we must learn to reject what Alexis Shotwell (2016) describes as a politics of 'purity', and instead embrace the idea that feminism's houses may be reconstructed and deconstructed on shifting terrain.

Review

Ahmed freely acknowledges the difficulty of such work. For her, 'intersectionality is messy and embodied' (p. 119), and feminism creates difficult, 'sweaty concepts' (p. 12). These concepts are expressed with Ahmed's characteristic style of 'turning them this way and that, like an object that catches a different light every time it is turned' (p. 12), producing prismatic rainbows of meaning. In so doing, Ahmed also refuses to separate poetry from politics, affirming, 'I think of feminism as poetry' (p. 12). Language, in order not to become the master's tool, must be recuperated through close scrutiny, through loving litany, through rippling repetitions. Thus, Ahmed repeatedly circles back to her theoretical and literary foremothers – to bell hooks, Audre Lorde, Virginia Woolf, Rita Mae Brown, George Eliot, Toni Morrison, Chandra Talpade Mohanty and Gloria Anzaldúa, to name only a few. In her words, we hear their voices; in her voice, we hear their words – the direct, accessible rigour of hooks, the flowing stream of consciousness of Woolf. In summoning this circle, Ahmed displays the collective power informing her singular voice.

In her classic essay, *The Laugh of the Medusa*, Hélène Cixous called for an *écriture feminine* in: 'Write your self. The body must be heard' (Cixous, 1976, p. 880). Now, with growing numbers of women coming forward (#metoo) to say that their bodies are not being heard, Ahmed's *écriture feministe* (my twist) takes on even greater relevance. Her writing insists upon embodiment as epistemology: 'feminism begins with sensation', is 'sensible' (p. 21), 'a body that is not at ease in the world; a body that fidgets and moves around' (p. 22). She recalls painful experiences of violence and sexual assault that result in trauma lodged deep in the body. For Ahmed, this violence accompanies every process of gendered assignment, constricting a body that's expected to appear, speak, move and behave in specific ways.

Feminist 'noticing becomes a form of political labour' (p. 32). It is for that reason that the 'feminist killjoy', the one who notices and who names, interrupting the smooth flow of normative traffic, becomes such a central figure. The feminist killjoy must resist the 'promise of happiness' because 'inequality is preserved through the appeal of happiness, the appeal to happiness. It is as if the response to power and violence is or should be to simply adjust or modify how we feel' (p. 60). Ahmed's sister concept of the 'willful subject' is similarly persistent, embodied in the stubbornly raised arm of the 'Willful Child', a grim folktale. The violence that greets any exercise of will necessitates 'a call of arms' (p. 87), the refusal of silence and complicity within the master's house.

Ahmed then invites us to explore diversity work within the master's house of the academy, where the diversity workers themselves often embody lip service paid to policies of inclusion that do not lead to action: 'diversity work is the work we do when we are attempting to transform an institution; and second, diversity work is the work we do when we do not quite inhabit the norms of an institution' (p. 91). Diversity workers are 'institutional killjoys' facing a 'brick wall': 'indeed the wall might become all the more apparent, all the more a sign of immobility, the more the institution presents itself as being opened up' (p. 96). To gain any real transformation, Ahmed argues, feminists everywhere must be willful, must push. Again, she acknowledges how exhausting such work can be; how 'institutional passing' (p. 127) may be a survival strategy: 'For those who are not white, whiteness can be experienced as wall: something solid, a body with mass that stops you from getting through ... **Heavy, slow, down, brown**' (p. 146). To combat such exhaustion, Ahmed calls for solidarity 'to give support to those who are willing to expose the will of the institution as violence; we need to become our own support system ... so that when she speaks up, when she is, as she is, quickly represented as the willful child who deserves her fate, who is beaten because her will is immature and impoverished, she will not be an arm coming up alone; she will not be an arm all on her own' (p. 159).

The anguish that pervades *Living a Feminist Life* is excruciating; the sorrow and frustration of a woman patiently and gently articulating what it is like to be left all on her own. Perhaps that is why the book is such an intense read – the writer Carin Beilin described her reading as 'like gasping in nettles' (Beilin, 2017). And yet, out of the consequences of being a feminist killjoy, from the pain of leaving a life, comes a moment of 'feminist snap' that Ahmed describes as 'how we collectively acquire tendencies that can allow us to break ties that are damaging as well as to invest in new possibilities' (p. 162). Again, one thinks of the #metoo movement, the snap of speaking out in multitudes. Movements that only venerate 'strong women' leave little room for the bodies that shatter, the idea that one has been or can be broken. Yet, for Ahmed, there is much to be gained from fragility, 'learn[ing] making from breaking' (p. 169). This is one of her most powerful concepts: that great strength can be derived from shattering experiences: 'From a shattering, a story can be told, one that finds in fragility the source of a connection ... A break can offer another claim to being, being in question as a break in being, recognizing breaking as making a difference in the present, shaping the present' (p. 183). For Ahmed, 'life unfolds from such points' (p. 192). A snap can be an enormous 'relief from [the] pressure' of normative expectations (p. 194). Following her 'snap' from Goldsmiths, Ahmed writes, she has recreated 'feminist hope' and a 'feminist communication system' (p. 211) – *Living a Feminist Life* appears alongside her blog feministkilljoys.com.

The feminist hope of *Living a Feminist Life* rests on the power of assembling collectivities, affinities, shelters and survival kits as a 'shared feminist project' (p. 236). Ahmed's 'Killjoy Manifesto' (an instant classic for feminist survival kits everywhere) concludes that 'we must stay unhappy with this world' (p. 254) if we want to change it, must honour our killjoys, our broken spirits and fragile communities if we want to stay strong.

References

Beilin, C. (2017) *Full Stop*. http://www.full-stop.net/2017/02/28/reviews/caren-beilin/living-a-feminist-life-sara-ahmed/.

Cixous, H. (1976) *The Laugh of the Medusa*. Trans. Keith Cohen and Paula Cohen. University of Chicago Press, *Signs*, vol. 1, no. 4 (summer 1976), pp. 875–893.

Shotwell, A. (2016). *Against Purity: Living Ethically in Compromised Times*. Minneapolis: University of Minnesota Press.

Aalya Ahmad
Carleton University, Ottawa, ON K1S 5B6, Canada
aalya.ahmad@carleton.ca

Article

Ecology, labor, politics: Violence in Arendt's *Vita Activa*

Dawn Herrera
Oregon Institute for Creative Research: E4, Portland, OR 97215, USA.
dherrera@oicr-e4.org

Abstract Hannah Arendt famously argued that acts of violence are corrosive to a free and plural politics. However, the broader implications of her critique of violence are less well known. Reading her concept of violence comprehensively, with regard to (ostensibly non-political) labor and work as well as action, this article reveals its broader relevance for contemporary political thought: the political question of violence lies at the heart of our ecological crisis and is crucial for the social structure of labor domination. While Arendtian politics is without normative guarantees, the conceptual distinction between instrumental violence and free politics is crucial, because it renders the political judgment of violence possible. In every realm of human activity, the refusal to acknowledge violence stunts our capacity to care for the world.
Contemporary Political Theory (2023) **22,** 460–482. https://doi.org/10.1057/s41296-022-00612-2; advance online publication 18 January 2023

Keywords: Hannah Arendt; violence; power; ecology; labor; domination

---

In political theory, as in political life, violence is a perennial question. Perhaps due to the phenomenal clout of its basic example, studies of violence tend to interrogate its necessity, legitimacy, or desirability, for purposes of justification or critique; it is less common to linger over the somewhat vexed question of what violence is. Accordingly, the concept of violence remains theoretically murky (Duong, 2022).

Nevertheless, the assumption that violence lies at the root of politics persists. In *On Violence*, Hannah Arendt observed 'a consensus among political theorists from Left to Right to the effect that violence is nothing more than the most flagrant manifestation of power' (1969, p. 35). As representatives of the penchant to ground politics in violence, she names Weber, Marx, Voltaire, and Bodin; today, we might include Agamben, Mouffe, and Žižek.[1] Despite appearing to draw a strong distinction between them (Frazer & Hutchings, 2008), contractarianism in the liberal tradition locates violence at the ground of politics in a different way: because the presumed violence of ante-political life necessitates the formation of the social order, political relations are motivated by relations of immediate domination.

Arendt's treatment of violence famously diverges from this tradition. Even as she acknowledges that violence can be justified for political ends, she insists on a thoroughgoing conceptual separation between them. Thus, many have read Arendt as inviting us, in Caroline Ashcroft's words, 'to simply ignore the existence of violence in politics,' 'a potentially catastrophic omission' (2021, p. 6). Ashcroft responds with a careful study of Arendt's judgments of political usages of violence in their historical contexts, underscoring the complexity of Arendt's thinking about the instrumental value violence can have for politics, and the importance of context for political judgments of this kind.

In this article, I employ a heuristic frame similar to Ashcroft's, reading violence through the *vita activa*'s domains of labor, work, and action. However, I argue that it is precisely due to the 'intimacy' between power and violence (Breen, 2007, p. 363) that Arendt posits a strong conceptual distinction between them, insisting on the contingency of their relation. The common view of politics as violent and violence as political – a view closely linked to the political philosophy of the will (Zerilli, 2016, pp. 186–197) – obscures violence as a political question, at the margin of politics rather than its center (Arendt, 1963, p. 9).

As is well known, Arendt's critique of violence anchors her vision of politics. Here, I will show how it also elucidates the political meaning of work and labor (domains she is sometimes thought to regard as extrinsic to politics) in surprising and strikingly relevant ways. Arendt's critique reveals violence against nature as both an irreducible prerequisite to the work of fabrication, *and* as an urgent threat. In accord with the growing literature on Arendtian environmental politics, this analysis identifies the constraint of violence against nature as a fundamental political imperative.

Regarding labor, the relation of violence to the 'realm of necessity' in Arendt's work is more nuanced than it is often taken to be. While she does not consider bodily necessity a species of violence, her complex interpretation of Marx suggests that violence structures the experience of poverty and, thus, subtends the 'social question.' Like the catastrophic ravishment of the earth, modern structures of socioeconomic inequality are attributed, in her analysis, to the violence concealed within the process logic of necessity that drives capital accumulation. Ecological violence and the phenomenon I term 'labor domination' are parallel examples of the political meaning of violence in ostensibly non-political domains.

The penultimate section of the article returns to politics proper, revisiting Arendt's controversial applications of the violence-politics distinction to critically assess the sum of its implications. Arendt rejects standard views of violence as either too 'irrational' to be studied seriously, or as a quasi-natural reality that we must simply accept (Zerilli, 2016, p. 186; Arendt, 1969, pp. 35; 75). Naturalized as an element of politics, violence is an answer given in advance—a foregone conclusion which Arendt refuses. While this has given rise to accusations of utopianism, my reading underscores the lack of normative guarantees within this paradigm, insofar as the free political action of a given community does not preclude (and may facilitate) the domination of the politically excluded.

Given the frequency of their coincidence, the temptation to a political paradigm of violence is understandable. Nevertheless, the possibility and the principle of non-instrumental political relationality may depend on a capacity and willingness to distinguish between violence and politics. In any realm of human activity, the refusal to acknowledge violence – the denial of its phenomenal weight, historical wake, and processual tendencies – precludes an adequate political response. This expanded reading clarifies certain elements of our escalating ecological catastrophe as well as the inveterate problem of labor exploitation. I submit that Arendt's conceptual paradigm, as well as her own failures of acknowledgement, might help us come to grips with the political questions of violence we face today.

The Phenomenology of Violence

Ordinarily, violence indicates the threat or causation of physical harm. While her conceptualization encompasses this everyday sense of the word, Arendt grasps that violence names a relation (Duong, 2022); she places primary emphasis on the phenomenal structure of violence, the distinctive intentionality toward an object entailed by a violent act.[2] As a concept, violence receives its first explicit treatment in *The Human Condition* (1958). Notwithstanding two subtle shifts (addressed below) the same schematic exposition appears basically unchanged in *On Violence* (1969). In these works, Arendt consistently adopts Walter Benjamin's understanding of violence as instrumentality; as early as 1953, she, like him, counterposes violence to speech (Arendt, 2002, p. 291; see Finlay, 2009, pp. 38–39, Birmingham, 2010).

Provisionally, we can take the instrumentality of violence to consist in the usage of a harmful act as a means to an end. In Benjamin's 'Critique of Violence' (2019 [1920/1921]), violence is a means to the end of law – violence is law-constituting or law-preserving. Arendt adopts Benjamin's basic understanding but radically alters his critique. Rather than root law in violence, she critiques the western tradition's tendency to posit violence as the ground of politics. Politics, she argues, grounds itself in human beings' particular capacity for free action, which enables the coordination of life in common by means other than force through the medium of speech; thus, *arché* can be understood in terms of an initiative carried out among equals, rather than rule by command (Markell, 2006). For Benjamin, language constitutes a 'sphere of human agreement that is nonviolent to the extent that it is wholly inaccessible to violence' (2019, p. 304; see Swift, 2013). Arendt, thus,

Ecology, labor, politics

remains closely aligned with Benjamin's 'Critique of Violence,' even as she departs from it.

However, this well-known distinction between violence and politics does not give us the whole story, but must be viewed in its phenomenological context, against the backdrop of the *vita activa*.[3] Arendt's typology of the modes and motives of human activity should not be understood as an effort to draw 'territorial' distinctions that can be applied as if they were rules (Markell, 2011, 2015); more meaningfully, it can be read as an effort to foster a finer-grained understanding of how the factical 'conditions' of human being give rise to and constrain the practices and concepts that constitute our way of life, and how historical developments have been shaped by particular modes of attunement or inattention to these given conditions. Arendt's analysis of violence, thus, reflects her broader attempt to understand how material being conditions human life. Her distinction between violence and power as modes of agency must be considered in terms of this orienting inquiry. The significance of the power–violence distinction cannot be adequately assessed absent discussion of the other conceptual divisions bound up with it: not just power and violence, but also strength and force.

Force describes the basic experience of being compelled to activity. Eschewing the use of the word 'force' to denote coercive violence, Arendt associates it with those compulsions that are independent of and impervious to individual human agency – the force of nature and the force of history, i.e., of events in motion (1969, pp. 44–45).[4] We are most intimately acquainted with the force of necessity exerted by the metabolic requirements of our bodies. Individuals may be strong enough to withstand greater or lesser degrees of physical hardship, but all embodied beings are ultimately subject to this basic force. It compels continuous interaction with nature in the production of 'necessities,' perishable goods fit for consumption, and is met and matched by fertility, the superabundant life force exerted by the laboring body. The fertility of labor enables production of more than we can consume, and generation of new life (1958, p. 112).

Force, then, primarily describes the imperative motive of biological embodiment; bodily necessity 'possesses a driving force whose urgency is unmatched by the so-called higher desires and aspirations of man' (1958, p. 70). Arendt compares the urgency of necessity's drive to torture, likening it to helplessness before the concerted application of violence (p. 129). This equation also tells us something important about violence: the experience of violence is an experience of being compelled, one that reduces the human being to a *body* in the moment of subjection to physical necessity. Violence and the force of necessity have similar leveling effects.

In contrast to the impersonal tide of force stands the individual's quantum of strength. Strength describes the capacity for independent activity; it is 'nature's gift to the individual' and maintains them apart from others (1958, p. 103). As 'the property inherent in an object or person… which may prove itself in relation to other things or persons, but is essentially independent of them' (p. 45), strength can be possessed or held in reserve, indicating that unlike power, it may exist independent of its exercise. However, it cannot be shared or divided, but seems to depend on the individual's physical vitality, mental acuity, and the quality of their self-relation – what Arendt calls 'character' (1969, p. 44).

Arendt emphasizes that strength is optimally effective in isolation, highlighting strength's affinity with work. As she understands it, work is the activity of fabrication or making, the concrete reification of an ideal. As distinct from cyclical labor and boundless action, work is an individual enterprise.[5] Arendt specifically associates strength with the ability to fabricate durable goods: worldly solidity that will persist over time is not a given, but is the result of human strength (1958, pp. 140; 161). This link between individual strength and fabrication is important because, in Arendt's diagnosis, the problem of modern politics it its valuation of strength over and against collective power – the idea of politics as making.

The distinction between force and strength reveals violence as experientially akin to force but more like strength in its enactment. As noted, the most important feature of violence is its instrumental character.[6] This does not mean, however, that all instrumentality is violence – a caveat which marks a divergence between Arendt's position and that of the Frankfurt School. In Arendt's reading, the 'instrumentality' of violence has a double meaning. First, violence is instrumental because it tends to use instruments to multiply strength: violence is 'the multiplied strength of the one' (Arendt, 1963, p. 142). It is phenomenologically close to strength, the enacted material intensification of this natural capacity (1969, p. 46).[7] Second, echoing Benjamin, Arendt also understands violence as instrumental because it can only function as a means to an end.[8] Often dependent on implements, violence is also an implement itself.

Violence always needs some external purpose, meaning, or justification (Arendt, 1969, pp. 51, 79; 1963, p. 9). This accounts for Arendt's distinction between a violent act and properly political action: even as it pursues an objective, action constitutes its own end by generating power – an end in itself. Violence's need for external justification foregrounds its muteness, another basic quality. As pure means and purely material, enacted violence is incapable of the speech by which shared ends are articulated (1963, p. 9; 1958, p. 26). Violence is 'a marginal phenomenon in the political realm' because politics is a mode of relation in speech (1963, p. 9).

Work: Violence as Predicate of Mastery

Violence, then, is material instrumentality that casts its object as means to an end. For Arendt, perhaps surprisingly, the basic experience of violence is not interpersonal, but rather characterizes the relation of human beings to nature in fabricating a world of objects. The work of fabrication produces the human 'world of things' by reifying natural materials as worldly goods. They become use objects, 'there in their own durability,' and so obtain an objective reality outside the household of nature; the world itself has an objective character (1958, pp. 94, 138). Work consolidates the produce of nature according to an image, a model of utility (or, in the case of art, beauty) conceived by the human mind. The solid object produced by work activity constitutes its 'objective,' its determinate end. The durability of the use object as end distinguishes the product of work from that of life-sustaining labor. Products of labor are destined for consumption and are, therefore, ephemeral, linked to the inexorable process of life in a way that makes the determinacy of an 'end' unthinkable (1958, pp. 143–144). In a quite literal sense, the products of labor can only provisionally be thought of as ends.

Arendt posits that fabrication's violence is not in the reification of natural materials into durable objects, but rather in the initial procurement of the materials themselves. The material of labor is given in such a way that it can, in a quasi-Lockean imaginary, be gathered 'without changing the household of nature' (1958, p. 136). This is not the case with material to be worked:

> Material is already a product of human hands which have removed it from its natural location, either by killing a life process, as in the case of the tree which must be destroyed in order to provide wood, or interrupting one of nature's slower processes, as in the case of iron stone or marble, torn out of the womb of the earth. This element of violation and violence is present in all fabrication, and *homo faber*, the creator of the human artifice, has always been a destroyer of nature (p. 139).

In this passage, violence is qualified not only by the destructive quality of the activity – the killing, destroying, and (unsettlingly gendered) tearing which accord with the sense of the term's Latinate etymology – but also by the fact of interference into a natural process that would otherwise be ongoing. Thus, the extractive violence of procuring material for fabrication interferes with nature both spatially and temporally, as material is removed from its natural location and introduced into a different order of time.

Arendt writes, 'The experience of this violence [of fabrication] is the most elemental experience of human strength and therefore, the very opposite of the painful, exhausting effort experienced in sheer labor' (p. 140). In the human condition of worldliness, our habitation of a built environment, strength is bound up with the exercise of violence. It is more palpable as such because in its accomplishment of a chosen and determinate end, it differs from cyclical, processual, indeterminate labor. Unlike the objective end of work, the 'end' of labor can neither be chosen nor accomplished – it is the ongoing maintenance of life itself.

The construction of the human artifice has been enabled by material violence against the natural world. In this accomplishment, *homo faber* (the human being as maker) assumes another order of mastery: he [sic] 'conducts himself as lord and master of the whole earth' (1958, p. 139). *Homo faber*'s strength, then, is primarily identified with the capacity for production of material objects (p. 207). It rests on a foundation of violence and specifies a distinction between fabrication and the nonviolent but distinctive activities of labor and political action. The latter two share an inherent process character which tends to indefinite ongoingness (Hyvönen, 2016). Consequently, to engage in these activities is always in a sense to be subject to their continual unfolding, regardless of the immediate accomplishments (the full belly, the consensus) they may entail. Arendt's association of fabrication with mastery turns on this distinction between processual and ends-oriented activities. Neither the life process that conditions labor nor the plural others who condition action can be objectified and remain what they are. By contrast, the bringing into being of things with an object character, whose durability *qua* stasis can be counted upon, is the essential purpose of fabrication, which entails a corresponding form of reason: the reckoning of means and ends (1958, p. 144). Taking violence against nature as a point of departure, it becomes possible to see that Arendt's violence is neither abstract nor disembodied (Frazer & Hutchings, 2008); rather, it is fundamental to life as we live it.

Critique of (Ecological) Violence

Violence, then, has a primary phenomenal affinity with the human condition of worldliness. It pertains fundamentally to *homo faber* and the basic activity of fabrication because the realization of an objective end entails the appropriation of material to be worked and, generally, the instrumental amplification of individual strength (1958, p. 7). Violence against nature both proceeds from and enables the human condition of worldliness, the 'unnaturalness of human existence' according to which life transpires within a human-made artifice (p. 7), by virtue of which hiddenness and visibility are made possible. From this perspective, violence acquires a disconcerting normative neutrality, or at least asks to be considered in an ambivalent and perhaps even tragic register (Cannavò, 2014), for it is difficult to defend a political project that would eschew the built environment in its entirety.

However, it is precisely at this juncture where we may locate the resources for an Arendtian ecological critique (Whiteside, 1994). Through the development of industrial capitalism, the work of fabrication – making durable goods for continuous use over time – acquired the *processual* character of labor and its counterpart, consumption (Hyvönen, 2016, 2020). Manufactured goods take on the ephemeral quality of labor's perishable products: we trea[t] all use objects as though they were consumer goods, so that a chair or a table is now consumed as rapidly as a dress and a dress used up almost as quickly as food. The industrial revolution has replaced all workmanship with labor, and the result has been that the things of the modern world have become labor products whose natural fate is to be consumed, instead of work products which are there to be used (Arendt, 1958, p. 124).

These developments in industrial manufacture, and consumption – the 'depreciation of all worldly things, which is the hallmark of the waste economy in which we now live' – has unleashed a hypertrophic cycle of violence against nature (Arendt, 1958, pp. 252–253).[9] The increasing sophistication and indispensability of our technology exacerbates this movement, as, for example, minerals are extracted from toxic mines at terrible cost to produce devices whose obsolescence is planned.[10] Our *vita activa* is predicated on machines that are themselves consumers of fossil fuel. Fuel extraction epitomizes the ecological violence Arendt associates with fabrication, enacted within consumption's processual paradigm.

Our expanding, accelerating cycle of production and consumption has unleashed forces beyond our control; we 'act into nature,' setting off 'new unprecedented processes whose outcome remains uncertain and unpredictable' (Arendt, 1958, p. 231; Voice, 2013). As science and technology proceed in 'acting in the mode of making,' the violence of fabrication is multiplied (p. 238; Belcher & Schmidt, 2021). The quantitative growth of ecological violence induces a qualitative shift in its phenomenal character, from finite/teleological to processual – and, thus, comparable to violence in the political realm.

The developments characteristic of the Anthropocene receive an elliptical but overtly critical treatment in *The Human Condition*, which braids together technical, economic, and sociopolitical developments to problematize violent instrumentality as a mode of relation to nature. The churning consumption of worldly objects enacts wanton violence against nature and world. By this light, instrumental violence is disclosed as a condition of worldliness, and thus politics, but its limitation is posed as a crucial political question – even before the issue of violence against human beings is introduced.

Labor: Violence and the Realm of Necessity

Situated at the ground of worldliness and fabrication, violence also has complex associations with the condition of life and the activity of labor. Expositions of this theme have often been focused on the adequacy of the 'social' as an analytic category; for a summary of this conversation, see Klein (2014). However, emphasizing the phenomenology of violence casts these issues in a somewhat different light: the experience of violence, rather than its exercise, is of primary relevance to the human being as laborer.

In *On Revolution*, Arendt elaborates her assertion from *The Human Condition* that subjection to the force of bodily necessity is homologous to violence. Recall, 'necessity' is multivalent, referring to the forces of biological life and history, as well as their tangled interplay in revolutionary theory and practice. At the nodal point of this complex necessity, where these forces are conjoined, Arendt finds the raw problem of poverty. Not without irony, she frames it in terms of 'the social question,' a nineteenth-century euphemism for the contemporary dilemmas of material inequality.[11] That delicate phrase is at odds with the experience of poverty, which Arendt identifies as bodily necessity rendered coercive by the fact of its going unmet:

> Poverty is more than deprivation, it is a state of constant want and acute misery whose ignominy consists in its dehumanizing force; poverty is abject because it puts men under the absolute dictate of their bodies, that is, under the absolute dictate of necessity as all men know it from their most intimate experience and outside all speculations (1963, p. 50).[12]

Controversially, she claims that acting out of this state of duress is fatal to freedom. However, in *On Revolution*, Arendt also begins to develop the Marxian claim 'that poverty itself is a *political not a natural phenomenon*, the result of violence and violation rather than scarcity' (p. 53, italics added; see Gündoğdu, 2015, p. 68).[13] This argument can be clarified in terms drawn from *The Human Condition*: the young Marx developed a 'political account' of why the superabundance of labor power and human fertility fail to counter the force of bodily necessity, naming violence as the means by which the natural necessity of embodied life (an inexorable but discrete aspect of the human condition) is alleviated for some and experienced as a dehumanizing force by others. In 'unmasking' poverty as human-made violence, Arendt asserts, Marx's innovation was to critique socioeconomic conditions in political terms, effectively spurring action in response (1963, p. 54).

Arendt prefaces her discussion of this politicization of the economy with an allusion to 'the many authentic and original discoveries made by Marx' – as in *The Human Condition*, her treatment of his thought is subtly ambiguous.[14] However, her judgment of his legacy is not. In *On Revolution*, Arendt emphasizes the effective reversal of Marx's original discovery through the economization of politics in his late work and in the governmentality of the U.S.S.R., expressing overt contempt for the development of the link between political violence and natural necessity in Marxist theory and practice.

Arendt also questions Marx's emphasis on class conflict and his 'model of explanation' for poverty, which she identifies as 'the ancient institution of slavery, where clearly a "ruling class" ...had possessed itself of the means with which to force a subject class to bear life's toil and burden for it' (1963, p. 52). She explains her skepticism as a concern for the 'historical sciences,' suggesting that Marx anachronistically reads the structural features of a slave economy, 'where a "class" of masters actually rules over a substratum of laborers,' onto the historically distinct social form of capitalism. She, therefore, questions the utility of this account beyond 'the early stages of capitalism, when poverty on an unprecedented scale was the result of expropriation by force' (1963, p. 52).

However, there are good reasons to press at this juncture. Poverty is a socioeconomic relation whereby 'some' come to perpetually occupy (or struggle to avoid) a condition of abject necessity (Arendt, 1963, p. 52; 1958, p. 88, p. 255; 1973, pp. 123–124). It remains for us to think through how violence subtends the 'social question' of poverty, a relation that Arendt sometimes acknowledges but often elides.

From a historical perspective, violence is understood to be an efficient cause of what Arendt terms our 'laborers' society' (1958, p. 126). Onur Ulas Ince (2016) has demonstrated Arendt's oblique yet consistent concern with 'expropriation' or 'primitive accumulation' as an event that 'stand[s] at the threshold of the modern age' (Arendt, 1958, p. 248), 'when poverty on an unprecedented scale was the result of expropriation by force' (1963, p. 52). A sympathetic reader of Luxemburg, she had analyzed the link between capital and colonial imperialism in *Origins* and maintained that the phenomenon of expropriation is a cyclical requirement of capital in accord with its process logic (1958, p. 255; 1972, pp. 211–212; 1973, p. 148).[15] This line of thought indicates that expropriative violence is best understood not merely as a cause of wealth accumulation, but also as its structuring condition.

In the passages on Marx in *On Revolution,* though, Arendt avoids mentioning that slavery was a modern as well as ancient institution that fed the development of capital until the late nineteenth century. When she briefly addresses the 'primordial crime upon which the fabric of American society rested' a few pages later (1963, p. 61), she intimates that slavery dampened 'the social question' but draws no direct connection to her prior discussion of the same topic.[16] The coordinated violence by which slavery was maintained is not addressed, obscuring some of the most trenchant insights that stand to be drawn from her analysis.

The Politics of Domination

Arendt asserts in *On Revolution* that slavery was Marx's explanatory model for the relation of violence, politics, and bodily necessity (1963, p. 53). More light can be shed here by continuing to read that passage against *The Human Condition*'s analytic of labor and fabrication; there, blunting the force of necessity by easing the toil of labor is identified as the basic purpose of all human-made tools. Slavery is the violent 'fabrication' of a human tool whereby a person is forcibly appropriated as material and cast as an *instrumentum vocale* (1958, pp. 121–122). In a relation of domination predicated on violent compulsion, slaves are used as instruments, enabling slaveholders to 'master' their own bodily necessity. The processual compulsion to bodily activity is diminished, acquiring a more 'objective,' less coercive character. We might also consider slavery's importance for the development of industrial capital in this light, as work in the mode of labor and use in the mode of consumption were facilitated by the violent displacement of irreducible labor onto a dominated class.[17]

Slavery's extreme mode of domination reveals how violence and power can function in tandem. In *On Violence*, Arendt contends that the organized violence of the system of slavery would be impossible if it did not rest on a political structure. Even multiplied by instruments, the individual slaveholder's strength could not establish or maintain the relation without the political organization of the class: 'Single men without others to support them never have enough power to use violence successfully' (1969, pp. 50–51; see 1958, p. 200; Ince, 2016). The systematic application of means-ends reasoning to other human beings is conditioned by power.[18] In essence, 'Everything depends on the power behind the violence' (1969, p. 49).

It would, thus, be a mistake to think that power – and by extension, freedom – is somehow pure in Arendt's conception. Read alongside her analysis of Marx's 'discovery' of violent expropriation, this analysis of slavery highlights the tendency of the powerful, acting freely in concert with one another, to use violent means to further ends that are both private and collective. Again, acknowledging that exclusionary political power can scaffold the maintenance of a violent socioeconomic system foregrounds the importance of violence as a political question. Here, the 'boomerang effect' whereby the instrumental violence of a dominating power recoils upon the body politic, must be borne in mind (Arendt, 1969, pp. 53, 81; 1973, pt. II; Mantena, 2010). On the other hand, these analyses indicate that 'guarding' a political realm from the force of necessity does not require, *ipso facto*, the deployment of violence. For, if poverty is rooted in political arrangements, these arrangements are neither natural nor necessary.

This returns us to Arendt's engagement with Marx in *On Revolution*, where she cautiously endorses a twofold link between violence and necessity. First, as instrumental to the mastery of bodily urgency, interpersonal violence is 'a function or surface phenomenon of an underlying and overruling necessity' (1963, p. 55). Tentatively, we might broaden this idea to include the artificial 'necessity' of economic processes. Second, for those subject to it, expropriative and dominative violence engenders abject necessity; a case where 'the past is never dead, it's not even past' (Arendt, 2003[1975], p. 270, quoting Faulkner), instrumentality structures political exclusion and inegalitarian socioeconomic forms. The historical and phenomenological analysis of the relation between labor and violence reveal the 'social question' to be political, not only in its potential expression (Honig,

1995; Zerilli, 2005; Myers, 2013) or institutional mediation (Klein, 2014) but also at its root (Ince, 2016).

Conversely, Arendt disputes the notion, attributed to the late Marx and his interpreters, that necessity can 'be simply reduced to and completely absorbed by violence and violation' (1963, p. 55). This qualification pertains to every entangled usage of the term 'necessity.' As the force of bodily urgency, the experience of necessity *in extremis* feels like violence but is not reducible to it. Although the drive to master necessity motivates the foundation and maintenance of oppressive social arrangements, the our beholdenness to bodily necessity is not predicated on them, but rather is the condition of life itself; thus, their violent overthrow cannot guarantee freedom from this condition. Finally, most crucially for Arendt's critique of Marx, the laws of historical necessity do not determine the success of violent means toward that end; the force of history moves according to a subtler calculus, its momentum and course contingent upon the turn of human events (1963, p. 104; 1958, pp. 129–135; 1969, p. 56).

From a phenomenological perspective, violence structures poverty insofar as the condition of living 'hand to mouth,' subject to the immediate demands of necessity, is adjacent to the experience of violence. In the same violent movement that initiated the process of accumulation, the ironically 'liberated' free laborer is made subject to 'their daily needs and wants, the force… more compelling than violence' (Arendt, 1963, p. 53). Arendt indicates how this precarity exacerbates the plurality-shattering leveling effect that animates so many of her political anxieties. Although Arendt rejects the simple model of class exploitation *qua* immediate rule by violence, her account leaves ample room for consideration of how 'the social question' is structured by the legacy of dispossessive violence, and by the quasi-violent experience of physical necessity poverty threatens to induce.

Action: Violence and political instrumentality

While the violence of slavery is motivated by desire for mastery of the condition of life, violence also enters the public realm through the desire to master politics itself. In this most widely known dimension of Arendt's theorization of violence, the means-end logic of fabrication is applied to human affairs. Like life, action has a process character, an inherent unpredictability that frustrates the possibility of objective accomplishment. Arendt emphasizes the longstanding discomfort with this phenomenon evident in the western tradition of political thought, and reason's traditional efforts to substitute making for action (1958, pp. 226–230).

Where political action takes on the aspect of fabrication, violence enters politics under the banner of reckoning means and ends. Awareness of how violence stops processes to procure material for the realization of ends clarifies how common, and yet disastrous, this logic has been (1958, pp. 188 n.14, 228). Modernity intensified this tendency through the 'conviction that man can know only what he makes, that his allegedly higher capacities depend on making and that he, therefore, is primarily *homo faber*' – the persona who self-presents as lord and master – 'and not *animal rationale*' (pp. 144, 293–298).

Violence, 'which has always played an important role in political schemes and thinking based on an interpretation of action in terms of making,' was emphasized as the predominant means by which human affairs are 'made' and was glorified as such – especially in revolutionary politics (Arendt, 1958, p. 228; 1969, p. 48). Even when this is not the case, when the instrumentality of violence is qualified by platitudes of its appropriate restraint, all interpretations of 'the realm of human affairs as a sphere of making' imply violence because they cannot actualize the principle of their own limitation: 'As long as we believe that we deal with ends and means in the political realm, we shall not be able to prevent anybody's using all means to pursue recognized ends' (p. 229). This claim lies at the heart of Arendt's critique of political philosophy.

In the words of Beatrice Hanssen, Arendt understands violence and power as related, but in a 'nondialectical and asymmetrical relationship' (2001, p. 58). The nondialectical nature of the relationship indicates that the contradictions of one do not necessarily give rise to (or seek reconciliation through) the other (Arendt, 1969, p. 56). Its asymmetry means that violence and power are variable in their proportions and do not increase or diminish in tandem. In short, although they often appear together (p. 52), violence and power are not essential to one another.

In *On Violence*, Arendt significantly shifts the emphasis of her typology of activity as presented in *The Human Condition* by positing violence as a form of action, however, 'marginal' (1969, p. 80; cf. 1958, pp. 180–181). This classification highlights how, while violence does not generate power or constitute a proper politics, violence against human beings is not 'natural'; it is quasi-political, because it belongs to the realm of human affairs (1969, p. 82).

Like the free action that generates power, interpersonal violence is a response to plurality, the human condition of equality in difference. Plurality must be actively and imaginatively taken up in relation to others (Zerilli, 2005, p. 145); violence is the absolute enactment of its refusal. As instrumentality, violence in human affairs treats the plurality of human beings as an obstacle to the accomplishment of ends, rather than as the grounds of free action in concert; in doing so, it simultaneously denies and overrules plurality by the application of a leveling force that reduces persons to bodies.

The act of violence inverts the self-revelation achieved in free action (Arendt, 1958, pp. 175–181). Rendering the other object, the agent not only effaces their own individuality but reveals themselves only as a 'what,' that is, as a perpetrator of violence. In effect, the political collective that uses violent means acts as a single agent. This is largely a function of the fact that violence is pure deed, incapable of speech. The objective, instrumental relation constitutes no common 'inter-est' and fosters no mutually acknowledged world. One is 'for or against' rather than 'together with' others – in political terms, it is a non-relation (Arendt, 1958, p. 180). The combination of muteness and dissolution of worldly interest give the act of violence its inherent meaninglessness: meaning can only be sought *post facto*, in a context where the story can be told and heard.

For these reasons, Arendt calls violence anti-political action (1969, p. 64). As action, violence initiates processes, but these tend to involve continual and reciprocal acts in its own mute, instrumental image: 'The practice of violence, like all action, changes the world, but the most probable change is a more violent world' (pp. 80, 82; 1958, p. 323). By shattering its world and severing its web of relations, violence can destroy power. It cannot substitute for power, cannot produce power, because while power holds people together, violence can only hold them in place (1958, p. 202; 1969, p. 53). Nevertheless, Arendt clearly states that violent action can be justified by immediate goals and even serve, in the case of revolution, as a conduit to political foundation (Arendt, 1969, pp. 63–64; Finlay, 2009). At stake in her strong conceptual distinction between violent and free action is the assertion of a political principle. By refusing to locate violence at the ground of political life, Arendt posits a crucial and unambiguous conceptual backstop to the chain of means-ends reasoning that would normalize its use (1958, p. 154).

This is the force of her distinction between the justification of violence and its legitimation. Violence can be justified with respect to immediate goals ('the danger is not only clear but also present') and under these circumstances is a rational course of action (1969, pp. 52, 66). But violence can never be legitimate; as a strategic approach to life in common, it can only refer to an uncertain future end (1969, p. 52). Power, on the other hand, is self-legitimating in that it constitutes its own ground, which is just the manifest free action in concert of plural individuals. Taking up Benjamin's understanding of violence as instrumentality and of speech as the sphere of nonviolent agreement, she departs from his conclusions, holding out as an alternative hope, not the messianic violence of the divine miracle, but the miraculous human capacities to begin something new and to forgive in light of what has come before.

Violence as the Question of Politics

Arendt recognized ephemerality, vulnerability, and their frustrations as inherent to a free politics, and understood the western tradition of political thought to have masked and evaded them by valuing fabrication over action. The technical intensification of government bureaucracy, she deduced, fostered the progressive elevation of the political status of violence. It is an Arendtian truism that the temptation to violence increases as power is lost (1969, p. 54). When the relational basis for negotiating community interests through reciprocal initiative diminishes, common questions are more likely to be determined by instrumental means. The idea of human obstacles to or materials for political ends, and the ruin upon ruin of this reality, explain the centrality of violence in Arendt's conceptual framework.

'Realist' accounts that conflate politics and violence do not confront the challenge of Arendt's critique – the potential for 'murderous consequences' when political violence is legitimized by the positing of an equivalence between them (1958, p. 229). Moreover, her association of necessity (and privacy) with violence has the status of a historical observation, not an ontological absolute: 'neither violence nor power is a natural phenomenon' (1969, p. 82). The use of domination to master necessity is a contingent political arrangement. It follows that other arrangements are possible – that blunting the force of necessity to facilitate freedom's exercise might be accomplished by means other than violence.[19]

However, the resources that Arendt offers for understanding violence and politics and imagining their disentanglement must be taken up with a clear-eyed view to the historical legacy of their imbrication, of how politics has upheld violence—a challenge Arendt herself was often unable to meet (Norton, 1995; Gines, 2014; Owens, 2017). Patriarchy, slaveholding in Athens and the Americas and contemporary schemes of racialized political exclusion rely on forms of governmental relationality that are legible as 'properly' political, insofar as they rest on institutionalized relational networks of mutual acknowledgment and coaction among the dominators. The problems posed by the legacies of political violence are sharpened by the tendency to anti-Black racism in Arendt's own work. While the surrounding issues are denser in their implications than has usually been acknowledged (LeSure, 2020), the problematic of political exclusion is figured, *in nuce*, by Arendt's failures to recognize Black action and its identification with violence in her work (1969, pp.18–19, 21–22, 94–95; 1972, , pp. 202; 1973, pp. 193–194, 203, 209–210: see Norton, 1995, p. 249 n.4; Moten, 2018, ch. 2). In her own terms, it is a failure of comprehension: a refusal to examine and bear consciously the burden which history has placed on us; avoidance of 'the unpremeditated, attentive facing up to, and resistance of reality – whatever it may be' (1973, p. viii). With a view to history, and to what 'Arendt cannot see,' her idea of politics can appear to be a cruelly optimistic paradox, a practice to be refused (Berlant, 2011; Moten, 2018, p. 78).

In her reading of the contradictions in Marx's utopian ideal, Arendt writes,

> Such fundamental and flagrant contradictions rarely occur in second-rate writers, in whom they can be discounted. In the work of great authors they lead into the very center of their work and are the most important clue to a true understanding of their problems and new insights (2006, p. 25).

This is an apt description of Arendt's treatment of Blackness and violence. Her insights into power and the potential in her paradigm of politics as anti-violence are discordant with her failure to adequately acknowledge the order of violent exclusion structured by anti-Black politics, or the glory of the Black political agents who confronted it. This contradiction in Arendt's work directs us to political judgment as the locus of democratic politics' stubbornest challenges as well as its singular potential; it is upon judgment that the claim to free action depends (Zerilli, 2016, p. 190). The shared practice of judgment brings a common world into being as such, through the correction and enlargement of our partial perspectives by the perspectives of others; through this process in speech, political differences appear 'as politically relevant 'objects' for judgment, matters of common concern' (pp. 8–9).

The legacy of politics' intimacy with violence is a 'common' world scarred and structured by violence and exclusion. From within the impasse of a tragic history, sustaining a democratic sense of the political as a promise worth keeping may depend on whether and how those scars and structures can be effectively rendered objects of political judgment – on the possibility of acknowledging this legacy and reckoning with it as a matter of common concern. This process is not an end in itself: it can only foster an anti-violent politics insofar as it constitutes the effective grounds of future-oriented, nonviolent action, not premised on the democratic sacrifice of racially subordinated groups (Hooker, 2016). Politics, then, requires consideration of when action stands to open a space where *archê* is anti-violence, and when, because action maintains a space where *archê* perpetuates violence, it must be refused or resisted. These ethical and strategic decisions require 'perspectival mobility' in the judgment that precedes and follows upon (or refuses) political agency (Shulman, 2021).

However, even the keenest judgment cannot insure against the unpredictable effects of what we do. This reality exceeds the political, encompassing all realms of life—including the decision to act or to refuse. Perhaps all too well-aware of this, Arendt appeals to love of the world, the miracle of forgiveness, and courage. If politics is not to be relinquished to violence, the inspiration to imagine, enlarge, and furnish the space of their distinction must be drawn from these wellsprings of democratic promise.

Conclusions

It may be inevitable, that politics will be continually beleaguered by the question of violence. In maintaining a distinction between instrumental violence and political power, though, we render the political judgment of violence possible; the meaningfulness of this distinction is what enables recognition of how violence corrodes the freedom and plurality of politics. Attending to the comprehensive development of Arendt's critique of violence shows how these corrosive effects transpire beyond the realm of action, revealing the political relevance of violence in every domain of human activity.

Regarding labor, we cannot understand the use of violence in a political community without accounting for the concrete, often unacknowledged sociopolitical arrangements by which necessity is managed. As ministration to physical necessity, labor is irreducible. The will to eliminate concern for bodily necessity engenders a willed misrecognition of human beings as *instrumentum vocale*, continuous with the nature they are used to master; the fault lines of formal political exclusion tend to run along the lines of Arendtian labor, not 'work' in ordinary language terms. Arendt's analysis helps explain why such relations remain fixed despite stunning gains in technical capacity, shedding light on gender oppression and its intersectional nuance, chattel slavery and its afterlives, and the hypocrisies of immigration policy.

Thinking with and against Arendt, we might term this phenomenon 'labor domination,' a notion which incorporates the racialized and gendered legacies of political violence, the conversion of manufacture ('work') into labor, and the uneven political inclusion of the working class.[20] Considering the 'social question' in this light suggests that rather than essentialize the violent exclusion of bare life (Agamben, 1995), we should seek the root of political violence in the implacable need to care for and maintain it. From this angle, the Arendtian political concern is not that laboring bodies must be excluded from a pure public realm, or that political actors require violent liberation from bodily concerns in order to act freely (Gines, 2014, Chap .6).[21] Rather, what must be acknowledged and publicly confronted is how the power born of political association is a temptation to violence, and how the legacy of that violence persists in the social and political order.

Violence against nature demands public acknowledgment along the same lines. As a condition for the fabrication of the world as a built environment, such violence is pre-political. However, its reality is occluded by the techne of global industry, the elevation of necessity as a locus of concern (Smith's 'necessaries and conveniences') and the process logic of the 'waste-economy' (Arendt, 1958, p. 134).[22] Insensibility to the violence of fabrication and the corresponding lack of respect for the durability of goods are aspects of earth and world alienation. Violence against the natural environment is at the point of crisis, and its visibility as a matter of common concern is a political problem of the highest order. To 'see' the violence of mass consumer production would demand that we re-see durable goods and the built environment as ends, rather than fodder for the cycle of consumption and development.

Bringing Arendtian violence into the foreground reveals the continuity between human domination and ecological devastation: respectively, they are mis- and overapplications of an instrumental mode of relationality that, although irreducible given the human condition of worldliness, must be limited by political means. As manifest in contemporary social and ecological crises, Arendt's analysis subtly but certainly links these phenomena to the violence of capital accumulation, past and present, and the process logic of boundless growth by which it operates. She maintains that notwithstanding the conditions of worldliness and embodied life, our modalities of fabrication and labor are not natural forces or processes, but rather products of collective human agency, bound up with the past use of instrumental violence.

On this basis, the means by which we manage our bodily needs and fabricate our physical world must be understood in their political articulations; they demand an adequately political response. Political claims about labor domination and ecological violence require the recovery of violence as a social fact and the discovery and acknowledgment of our positions with respect to it (Zerilli, 2005). The apolitical, bureaucratic form of administrative governmentality that characterizes the Arendtian social (McClure, 2007; Owens, 2012) – legible as the biopolitical administration of needs (Braun, 2007; Duarte, 2005) – poses a stubborn barrier to the adequate politicization of contemporary violence. This, I argue, is the crucial relevance of Arendt's critique of the 'social' to the questions at hand.

Acknowledging violence as a public fact enables and encourages care for the world (Myers, 2013). This ethical and institutional task will require a higher regard for the labor of maintenance (Denis & Pontille, 2022), in and through associative political action. Arendt's 'The Crisis in Culture' recuperates a Roman concept of culture that 'indicates an attitude of loving care and stands in sharp contrast to all efforts to subject nature to the domination of man' (2006[1961], p. 208; Bowring, 2014; Whiteside, 1998). As a political principle, this notion of culture as cultivation and caretaking holds potential to curb the violence of world consumption, so often today mistaken for freedom.

Acknowledgments

For their thoughtful and enormously helpful comments on previous drafts, I gratefully acknowledge Amit Anshumali, Victoria Gross, Cate Fugazzola, John M. McCallum, Mary Elena Wilhoit, Patchen Markell, George Shulman, Linda M.G. Zerilli, and Rose Owen, as well as two anonymous reviewers and the editors at *CPT*.

About the Author

Dawn Herrera is a research scholar at the Oregon Institute for Creative Research. Her current research is on the genealogy of the nation-state in Michel Foucault's Collège de France lectures. She holds a Ph.D. from the University of Chicago's Committee on Social Thought.

Notes

1. For a critique of several of these positions and a Foucauldian argument that violence is external to politics, see Oksala (2012).
2. My analysis of instrumental violence leaves aside the particulars of its enactment. For insight regarding the gratuity of violence in pursuit of its ends, see Adriana Cavarero's *Horrorism* (2009).
3. Annabel Herzog (2017) locates the question of violence in a different phenomenological context, positing that Arendt's public–private distinction and other important conceptual divisions are organized by their relation to violence: 'Her categories appear in the process of distinguishing themselves from violence' (p. 177).
4. *On Violence* describes force more narrowly than *The Human Condition,* which seems to identify *any* immediate compulsion as force: if strength is a capacity, force describes a certain mode of its enactment. There, the account of life in terms of force reads as almost vitalist, in the vein of Bergson or (Arendt's) Nietzsche. While her opposition to that value orientation is unambiguous, life force can still be understood as basic to Arendt's phenomenology and to the question of violence in her work.
5. Apropos Arendt's caveat that these phenomenal distinctions are not pure descriptions of lived reality, strength does not seem wholly irrelevant to life or politics. Regarding biological life and the activity of labor it conditions, the definition of strength and the way it encounters violence (1958, p. 203) capture something of the individual's capacity to bear up against the force of necessity. More controversially, strength is also relevant to action. Although Arendt describes at length how the power of action-in-concert threatens the strong, strength of character is, arguably, of a piece with public excellence or virtue; while these qualities always sit in uneasy tension with equality in the public realm, it would seem odd to associate the capacity for *arché* and *prattein* with individual weakness.
6. Herzog (2017) shows how Arendt's concept of violence responds to Martin Heidegger's 'The Question Concerning Technology.' For Heidegger, 'instrumentality' signifies the reifying framework of order that tends toward the concealment of Being; paradoxically, it also holds forth the revelatory (and, thus, redemptive) power of art. The danger of instrumentality, and its association with reification, emerges from this implicit conversation. For Arendt, Herzog argues, the danger is not to *Sein* but to *Mitsein*—coexistence, rather than Being is concealed by the instrumental frame.
7. In this analysis, we see the conceptual loss entailed by the restriction of the portrayal of force from *The Human Condition* to *On Violence*. In the paradigm of *On Violence*, where force is a wholly impersonal phenomenon, there is no language to account for instances of impersonal abuse without the use of implements.
8. This idea runs counter to the affective charge and irrationality we associate with interpersonal violence. Here, the need for post hoc justification is telling; where violence takes the form of a 'senseless' outburst, it is a means to the end of affective release, which presumably could have been accomplished by other means. When violence would seem to function as its own end, it is really a means to the pleasure of the perpetrator. Arendt's assertion in 'Auschwitz on Trial' (1966) that 'sadism is basically sexual' is pertinent here. In any case, the enactment of violence is frequently nested in other structures of domination, which entail the instrumental logics discussed below. Thanks to Tori Gross for drawing my attention to this point.
9. This assessment of the vicissitudes of industrial production dovetails with Arendtian political critiques of the growing instability of the human world as a background for action (Markell, 2014).
10. Thea Riofrancos (2020) elucidates the violence of extractivism in Ecuador and the radical politics that opposes it.
11. On the framing and temporality of 'the social question' see Case (2016).
12. Arendt paraphrases Demosthenes: 'Poverty forces the free man to act like a slave' (1958, p. 64).

13. Note the contrast with Hobbes, for whom scarcity and violence are the natural, pre- and apolitical conditions of human life.
14. CF the introduction to the 'Labor' chapter of *The Human Condition*, which prefaces the critical reading of Marx with an oblique but respectful homage. See Howard (2020) for a helpful reappraisal of Arendt's engagement with Marx and of her work as a contribution to political economy.
15. See Hannah Arendt, 'Rosa Luxemburg: 1871–1919' in *Men in Dark Times* (1970); Ince (2018).
16. Arendt's disregard of the role of violent dispossession of indigenous land is a major oversight here. On the recursive logic of 'dispossession' in this context, see Nichols (2018).
17. See Eric Williams, *Capitalism and Slavery* (1994 [1944]); Sven Beckert, *Empire of Cotton* (2014). While the particulars of the 'New History of Capitalism' have been hotly contested, to maintain that the advance of capital was abetted by the provision of raw material by slave labor should not be a controversial claim.
18. Also reading Arendt against Marx, Ince (2016) comes to a similar conclusion by a different route.
19. For generative provocations on this topic, see Graeber and Wengrow, *The Dawn of Everything* (London: Allen Lane, 2021).
20. Unhappily, this intervention sits at odds with Isabella Bakker's (2007) proposal to distinguish work from labor on the grounds of alienation; I hope our perspectives will eventually be brought into conversation.
21. See Arendt's glowing assessment of the potentiality of the 'political labor movement' (1958, pp. 215–219).
22. For a depiction of industrial violence, see *Koyaanisqatsi* (1982).

References

Agamben, G. (1995) *Homo Sacer: Sovereign Power and Bare Life*. Translated by D.H. Roazen. Stanford, CA: Stanford University Press.
Arendt, H. (1958) *The Human Condition*. University of Chicago Press.
Arendt, H. (1963) *On Revolution*. New York: Viking.
Arendt, H. (1969) *On Violence*. New York: Harcourt.
Arendt, H. (1970) *Men in Dark Times*. San Diego: Harcourt, Brace.
Arendt, H. (1972) *Crises of the Republic*. San Diego: Harcourt, Brace.
Arendt, H. (1973) *The Origins of Totalitarianism*. Boston: Houghton Mifflin Harcourt.
Arendt, H. (2002) Karl Marx and the Tradition of Western Political Thought. *Social Research: An International Quarterly* 69(2) 273–319. https://doi.org/10.1353/sor.2002.0059
Arendt, H. (2003 [1966]) Auschwitz on Trial. In J. Kohn (ed.). *Responsibility and Judgment*. New York: Schocken, pp. 227–256.
Arendt, H. (2003 [1975]) Home to Roost. In J. Kohn (ed.) *Responsibility and Judgment*. New York: Schocken, pp. 257–275.
Arendt, H. (2006 [1961]) *Between Past and Future*. New York: Penguin.
Ashcroft, C. (2021) *Violence and Power in the Thought of Hannah Arendt*. Philadelphia: University of Pennsylvania.
Bakker, I. (2007) Social Reproduction and the Constitution of a Gendered Political Economy. *New Political Economy* 12(4): 541–556.
Beckert, S. (2014) *Empire of Cotton: A Global History*. New York: Knopf.

Belcher, O. and Schmidt, J.J. (2021) Being Earthbound: Arendt, Process and Alienation in the Anthropocene. *Environment and Planning D: Society and Space* 39(1): 103–120.

Benjamin, W. (2019) Critique of Violence. In P. Demetz (ed.) *Reflections: Essays, Aphorisms, Autobiographical Writings*. Translated by E. Jephcott. New York: Schocken, pp. 291–316.

Berlant, L. (2011) *Cruel Optimism*. Durham: Duke University Press.

Birmingham, P. (2010) On Violence, Politics and the Law. *Journal of Speculative Philosophy* 24(1): 1–20.

Bowring, F. (2014) Arendt after Marx: Rethinking the Dualism of Nature and World. *Rethinking Marxism* 26(2): 278–290.

Braun, K. (2007) Biopolitics and Temporality in Arendt and Foucault. *Time & Society* 16(1): 5–23.

Breen, K. (2007) Violence and power. *Philosophy & Social Criticism* 33(3) 343–372. https://doi.org/10.1177/0191453707076143

Cannavò, P.F. (2014) Hannah Arendt: Place, World and Earthly Nature. In Lane and Cannavò (eds.) *Engaging Nature: Environmentalism and the Political Theory Canon*. Cambridge, MA: The MIT Press, pp. 253-269.

Case, H. (2016) The "Social Question", 1820–1920. *Modern Intellectual History* 13(3): 747–775.

Cavarero, A. (2009) *Horrorism: Naming Contemporary Violence*. Translated by W. McCuaig. New York: Columbia University Press.

Denis, J. and Pontille, D. (2022) *Le Soin des Choses: Politiques de la maintenance*. Paris: La Découverte.

Duarte, A. (2005) Biopolitics and the Dissemination of Violence: The Arendtian Critique of the Present. *HannahArendt. Net* 1(1): 1–15.

Duong, K. (2022) Violence: Introduction to the Special Issue. *New Political Science*. https://doi.org/10.1080/07393148.2022.2031024.

Finlay, C.J. (2009) Hannah Arendt's Critique of Violence. *Thesis Eleven* 97(1): 26–45.

Frazer, E. and Hutchings, K. (2008) On Politics and Violence: Arendt Contra Fanon. *Contemporary Political Theory* 7(1): 90–108.

Gines, K.T. (2014) *Hannah Arendt and the Negro Question*. Bloomington: Indiana University Press.

Graeber, D. and Wengrow, D. (2021) *The Dawn of Everything*. New York: Farrar, Straus, and Giroux.

Hanssen, B. (2001) *Critique of Violence: Between Poststructuralism and Critical Theory*. London: Routledge.

Gündoğdu, A. (2015) *Rightlessness in an Age of Rights: Hannah Arendt and the Contemporary Struggles of Migrants*. Oxford: Oxford University Press.

Herzog, A. (2017) The Concept of Violence in the Work of Hannah Arendt. *Continental Philosophy Review* 50(2): 165–179.

Honig, B. (1995) Introduction: The Arendt Question in Feminism. In B. Honig (ed.) *Feminist Interpretations of Hannah Arendt*. University Park: Penn State Press, pp. 1–16.

Hooker, J. (2016) Black Lives Matter and the Paradoxes of U.S. Black Politics: From Democratic Sacrifice to Democratic Repair. *Political Theory* 44(4): 448–469.

Howard, M. (2020) Hannah Arendt's Contribution to a Critique of Political Economy. *New German Critique* 47 (2 (140)): 45–80.

Hyvönen, A.-E. (2016) Invisible Streams: Process-Thinking in Arendt. *European Journal of Social Theory* 19(4): 538–555.

Hyvönen, A.-E. (2020) Labor as Action: The Human Condition in the Anthropocene. *Research in Phenomenology* 50(2): 240–260.

Ince, O.U. (2016) Bringing the Economy Back In: Hannah Arendt, Karl Marx, and the Politics of Capitalism. *Journal of Politics* 78(2): 411–426.

Ince, O.U. (2018) Between Equal Rights: Primitive Accumulation and Capital's Violence. *Political Theory* 46(6): 885–914.

Klein, S. (2014) "Fit to Enter the World": Hannah Arendt on Politics, Economics, and the Welfare State. *American Political Science Review* 108(4): 856–869.

LeSure, A. (2020) The White Mob, (In) Equality Before the Law, and Racial Common Sense: A Critical Race Reading of the Negro Question in "Reflections on Little Rock"'. *Political Theory*, 0090591720943211.

Markell, P. (2006) The Rule of the People: Arendt, Archê, and Democracy. *American Political Science Review* 100(1): 1–14.

Markell, P. (2011) Arendt's Work: On the Architecture of the Human Condition. *College Literature* 38(1): 15–44.

Markell, P. (2014) The Moment Has Passed: Power after Arendt. In R. Coles, M. Reinhardt, and G Shulman (eds.) *Radical Future Pasts: Untimely Political Theory*. Louisville, KY: University of Kentucky Press: pp. 113-143.

Markell, P. (2015) Anonymous Glory. *European Journal of Political Theory* 16(1): 77–99.

Mantena, K. (2010) Genealogies of Catastrophe: Arendt on the Logic and Legacy of Imperialism. In S. Benhabib (ed.) *Politics in Dark Times: Encounters with Hannah Arendt*. Cambridge: Cambridge University Press, pp. 83–112.

McClure, K. M. (2007) The Social Question Again. *Graduate Faculty Philosophy Journal* 28(1) 85–113. https://doi.org/10.5840/gfpj200728120

Moten, F. (2018) *The Universal Machine*. Vol. 3. Durham: Duke University Press.

Myers, E. (2013) *Worldly Ethics: Democratic Politics and Care for the World*. Durham: Duke University Press.

Nichols, R. (2018) Theft Is Property! The Recursive Logic of Dispossession. *Political Theory* 46(1): 3–28.

Norton, A. (1995) Heart of Darkness: Africa and African Americans in the Writings of Hannah Arendt. In B. Honig (ed.) *Feminist Interpretations of Hannah Arendt*. University Park: Pennsylvania State University Press, pp. 247–261.

Oksala, J. (2012) *Foucault, Politics and Violence*. Evanston, IL: Northwestern University Press.

Owens, P. (2012) Human Security and the Rise of the Social. *Review of International Studies* 38(3): 547–567.

Owens, P. (2017) Racism in the Theory Canon: Hannah Arendt and 'the One Great Crime in Which America Was Never Involved'. *Millennium: Journal of International Studies* 45(3) 403–424. https://doi.org/10.1177/0305829817695880

Reggio, G. (Dir.) (1982) *Koyaanisqatsi*.

Riofrancos, T. (2020) *Resource Radicals*. Durham: Duke University Press.

Shulman, G. (2021) Fred Moten's Refusals and Consents: The Politics of Fugitivity. *Political Theory* 49(2): 272–313.

Swift, S. (2013) Hannah Arendt, Violence and Vitality. *European Journal of Social Theory* 16(3): 357–376.

Voice, P. (2013) Consuming the World: Hannah Arendt on Politics and the Environment. *Journal of International Political Theory* 9(2): 178–193.

Whiteside, K.H. (1994) Hannah Arendt and Ecological Politics. *Environmental Ethics* 16(4): 339–358.

Whiteside, K.H. (1998) Worldliness and Respect for Nature: An Ecological Appreciation of Hannah Arendt's Conception of Culture. *Environmental Values* 7(1): 25–40.

Williams, E. (1994) *Capitalism and Slavery*. Chapel Hill: UNC Press Books.

Zerilli, L. (2005) *Feminism and the Abyss of Freedom*. Chicago: University of Chicago Press.

Zerilli, L. (2016) *A Democratic Theory of Judgment*. Chicago: University of Chicago Press.

Publisher's Note Springer Nature remains neutral with regard to jurisdictional claims in published maps and institutional affiliations.

Springer Nature or its licensor (e.g. a society or other partner) holds exclusive rights to this article under a publishing agreement with the author(s) or other rightsholder(s); author self-archiving of the accepted manuscript version of this article is solely governed by the terms of such publishing agreement and applicable law.

Epilogue: On Retraining the Senses

Karen Zivi

In "Conclusion 1" of *Living a Feminist Life*, Sara Ahmed describes what she calls her "Killjoy Survival Kit," that depository of books, objects, tools, and people, among other things, that sustain her in the face of the often exhausting, sometimes joyous, never-ending struggle against the forms of intersectional gender injustice meted out by white heteropatriarchy. Every feminist, Ahmed suggests, should have such a kit containing "those things that are necessary for your survival" (Ahmed, 2017, p. 236). That might include books that uplift and inspire, objects that remind you of work done and call you back to work that is unfinished, tools that can be used to dismantle and others to rebuild, and even feelings like anger and frustration or the adamant refusal to be grateful for the mostly symbolic gains that traffic under the sign of "progress" (Ahmed, 2017, pp. 235–249). This Collexion of articles, Critical Exchanges, and reviews published in *Contemporary Political Theory* between 2019 and 2023 has now been added to mine.

Time, Ahmed explains, is another key element of any feminist survival kit. Time to "pause," "breathe," "slow down" (Ahmed, 2017, p. 242). I cannot remember when I last took the time to read an entire issue of a journal, let alone two curated Conversations. And I'm so glad I did. The contributions in these volumes took me on an intellectual and emotional journey, allowing me to visit the generative and risky feminism of earlier days while also speaking directly to some of the most compelling and complicated issues of the day. And I am thankful that Terrell Carver, who writes as Editor here, that *CPT* allows conversations to emerge rather than be contrived, took the time to pull these

---

K. Zivi (✉)
Grand Valley State University, Allendale, MI, USA
e-mail: zivik@gvsu.edu

specific works together for us. Emergent conversations can be difficult to recognize, particularly in journals devoted to the terrain of political theory broadly understood. They are difficult to recognize, given the attention deficit disorder that is, for so many of us, brought on by the digitization and proliferation of journals in the field, as well as by the information overload that results from a 24-hour news cycle and the reach of social media.

The contributions that make up this Collexion provide something of an antidote to the despair that fills much of what passes as news these days. They remind us that feminists have creatively and courageously taken on seemingly insurmountable challenges in the past, continue to do so today, and have no intention of giving up as we face the future. Reading these contributions felt like being in the audience of an amazing panel of scholars—some dear friends, others strangers, some who are there at the start and stay until the end, others who come and go at different times, and all of whom show great respect and deep appreciation for what the other thinks, even when they disagree profoundly. In this Collexion, scholars—not all of whom identify explicitly as feminists—push each other to clarify ideas, raise pointed criticisms, offer heartfelt and deeply grounded compliments, and think together, sometimes directly but often indirectly, about what it means to understand and do politics with a deep commitment to goals.

I cannot do justice to all the synergies that I see between the contributions or identify all the exciting conversations emerging from these pages. Nor can I celebrate the valuable insights that each and every author has to offer. Instead, I want to highlight a specific conversation that I see developing in these pages and some of the lessons and exhortations it has for readers. This is the conversation about what it means for feminist scholarship and activism to take intersectionality seriously. A conversation that calls on feminists to reckon with the whiteness and heteronormativity that still resides at the core of a good part of our scholarship and activism.

This conversation, to be sure, is a continuation of one that has always been central to the project of feminist political theory—asking questions about who or what counts as an object or subject of politics, about who counts as a political theorist, and about what counts as political theorizing. But in the conversation that I find developing in these pages, the questions are turned back on feminism itself. Just as feminists have long demanded that non-feminist political theorists see politics in places and practices that have long been "assumed to be unpolitical" (Maxwell in Maxwell et al., 2019, p. 644, ch. 4 here), the contributions ask feminists to take stock of our own commitment to this project, calling on us to acknowledge and confront our own blind spots and occlusions. In so doing, these readings remind us that there is a feminist theory canon of sorts, a specific archive of thinkers, texts, issues, and analytic lenses that is both a manifestation of power and a mode of governance that has very real material and psychological effects. This archive is, at best, incomplete and ripe for thinking anew about emancipatory politics. At worst, it is imbricated in, and in some cases, benefits from, the continued subordination of those already marginalized on the basis of, for example, race, sexuality, class, and indigeneity.

To shed light on this conversation, and to address the shortcomings it exposes, I turn to Lauren Berlant's concept of an "esthetic education," introduced in the Critical Exchange on their work appearing here in Conversation II "Feminist Lives, Desires, Futures." The exchange celebrates the legacy of a scholar who was deeply committed to exploring the experiences of subaltern subjects and showing how their very strategies for survival might serve as a resource for all who are frustrated by the limited gains made by drawing on traditional ways of thinking and doing politics. As Ali Aslam suggests, Berlant's work locates a capacity for building new worlds and new relationships in an esthetic education, a practice that involves retraining the senses, unlearning old habits, and creating new ones, so that we can see "what lies hidden in plain sight" (Aslam in Galloway et al., 2023, p. 124, ch. 16 here). And what lies in plain sight, many of the contributions to this Collexion suggest, is feminism's tendency to obfuscate and, at times, willfully disregard, the experiences and contributions of women of color and queer feminists in the interest of some form of gender progress. Retraining our senses is necessary both to see and rectify the facts and costs of this practice of marginalization.

The process of retraining our senses begins with seeing and hearing in a manner that is more attentive to the voices of those whom feminists have cast aside. Shateema Threadcraft's engagement with Bonnie Honig's work on agonism is both an example of this, and also an exhortation to do the work of retraining the senses. As her contribution suggests, feminists, even those deeply committed to unsettling the forms and structures of power that oppress women, and recognizing the remainders and exclusions that dominant forms of political practices produce, often overlook the extent to which feminist theory and politics is guilty of the same. Threadcraft illuminates and explores the way feminists and feminism relegate the suffering and the political work of black women to the margins, or misread it when it is seen. We see this, Threadcraft suggests, in the blindness to the intersections of race, class, and gender which has long been a part of efforts to advance gender equality in the workplace. But we can think here, too, of the way that efforts to secure reproductive rights, which focus primarily on abortion access and individual privacy, have rendered concerns about the right to have children, or about the economic barriers to accessing reproductive care, of secondary importance.

A retraining of our senses also allows us to see the marginalization of black women's experience and political activity in the way that Toni Morrison's work is, at best, tangential to the discipline of political theory. As the contributors to the Critical Exchange on her work, appearing here in Conversation!: Feminist Classics, Genres, Contestations," make abundantly clear, Morrison may write in a different genre, but her fiction takes on concerns that are clearly political. Her work explores, for example, the role that race plays in determining "whose lives matter and whose don't" (Zamalin in Zamalin et al., 2020, p. 707, ch. 6 here), and illuminates the fact that violence is disproportionately directed toward black people and members of other "populations considered not quite human" (Winters in Zamalin et al., 2020, p. 709, ch. 6 here). Her fiction can thus speak to the crises of our time, "rising nationalism, authoritarianism, violence, racism, and far-right extremism" perhaps better than more traditional political theory can (Zamalin in Zamalin et al., 2020, p. 707, ch. 6 here). But it can only do this if it has a more prominent place in a feminist theory archive, and that requires us to read and understand her work in new ways.

Of course, it is not just the suffering of women color that is often written out of the history and consciousness of dominant strands of feminist theory and practice. The experiences and work of queer feminists also ends up in the remainder bins. Lorna Bracewell's contributions to Conversation II make this clear, whether in her retelling of the history of the "Sex Wars" of the 1980s or in her analysis of the SlutWalks of the early twenty-first century. In the former, Bracewell argues that feminists' embrace of liberal conceptions of harm and freedom have obscured the race and class dynamics associated with pornography and have left a more radical and intersectional vision of sexual freedom advanced by feminists of color and queer feminists on a dusty shelf. Bracewell finds a similar tendency in the way SlutWalks relies on individualistic conceptions of harm that then look to the criminal legal system and the carceral state for redress (Bracewell, 2020, ch. 11 here).

As Elena Gambino puts it in her review of Bracewell's work, a feminism interested in advancing sexual freedom will not be able to "adequately conceptualize the range of harms" (Gambino, 2022, p. 98, ch. 12 here) or the "intersectional realities" (Gambino, 2022, p. 101, ch. 12 here) of people's lives if it continues to embrace traditional liberal political strategies and visions of freedom. That may mean, as Federica Gregoratto's review of Amia Srinivasan's *The Right to Sex* suggests, recognizing that "the law and the judicial system are not the right medium for solving the most controversial problems faced by feminism today—especially from the perspectives of women of color, or of queer and non-cis persons" (Gregoratto, 2023, p. 64, ch. 15 here).

As these examples show, retraining our senses to take responsibility for the way that whiteness and heteronormativity work within feminism requires seeing the suffering and the work of marginalized populations. Indeed, it requires centering different voices. But this is not simply about replacing one set of exemplars with another, or substituting one vision of freedom with another. The esthetic education that is a retraining of the senses must also recognize the reality that there are "differential stakes" for those who are differently embodied. Centering new voices requires acknowledging what Threadcraft describes as the "problematic division of democratic labor in a world of remainder and sacrifice" (Threadcraft, in Maxwell et al., 2019, p. 655, ch. 4 here). It requires recognizing, for example, that relying on the state to address the harms of sexual violence means something radically different for marginalized populations than it does for white middle-class heterosexual women. Indeed, while practices of political resistance may be exhausting for everyone, they are only deadly for some (Threadcraft, in Maxell et al., 2019, p. 654, ch. 4 here).

Given this reality, retraining our senses will likely entail understanding practices of resistance in new ways and seeing them in new places. As Aslam reminds us, "When subjects can no longer see themselves in the story of which they aspire to be a part—because they realize it did not include people like them or it remains persistently and exhaustingly out of reach—they must invent something else to survive, to connect with others, or to find themselves" (Aslam in Galloway et al., 2019, p. 122, ch. 16 here). Such political inventions become visible in Saidiya Hartmann's depiction of the daily survival of ordinary black women, as Danielle Hanley's review of the work illuminates (Hanley, 2021, ch. 8 here).

And these inventions are present in Morrison's portraits of black women engaged in modes of resistance that reject the expectations and standards of the white world. This refusal to participate in conventional political practices often appears as illegible to the unretrained eye and ear even when it is done by white feminist actors. This, I take it, is part of what Ani Chen suggests in her discussion of Simone de Beauvoir's *Les bouches inutiles* (Chen, 2023, ch. 2 here). What seems at first as a failure of political resistance on the part of women whose plaintive voices go unheard, can be recognized as a refusal to be heard on terms that reproduce patriarchal forms of power when one's senses are retrained. This, it seems, is what the Yugolsavian Women in Black do as well. As Sara Murphy explains in her review of Athena Athanassiou's work, their silent public vigils "challenge what it can mean to appear in public space, to engage in the life of the polis" (Murphy, 2019, p. 8, ch. 9 here).

As the above examples suggest, an esthetic education is not just about seeing and hearing anew. It is also about thinking and doing things differently. Several of the contributions to this Collexion suggest that one place where feminism dearly needs this retraining of the senses is with respect to its understanding of, and investment in, the supposed promise of American democracy. Feminism, whether it embraces more traditionally liberal or more explicitly agonistic understandings of freedom, or similarly with practices of political resistance, must grapple seriously with the racial violence on which American democracy is built and the anti-blackness that continues to haunt it. As the Critical Exchange on Morrison reminds us, "the American 'dream' of democratic egalitarianism" rests upon and perpetuates racial violence and class exploitation (Olson in Zamalin et al., 2020, p. 715, ch. 6 here), and to the extent that feminism embraces traditional American conceptions of progress and freedom, it is complicit in this violence.

How, then, does feminism avoid becoming "a master's tool" (Ahmad, 2019, p. 125, ch. 18 here)? One way is to acknowledge the problematic nature of the feminist canon and to rethink it, to acknowledge the way its embrace of a vision of progress is complicit in the erasure and obfuscation of racial violence, for example. This is already happening with respect to the work of Hannah Arendt as Dawn Herrera's contribution in Conversation II illustrates. Herrera reminds us that Arendt, a thinker central to much contemporary feminist scholarship, failed "to adequately acknowledge the order of violent exclusion structured by anti-Black politics, or the glory of Black political agents who confronted it" (Herrera, 2023, pp. 16–17, ch. 19 here). And any feminism that ignores this part of Arendt's work perpetuates the problem.

Bonnie Honig shows us what it might look like to rethink one's engagement with Arendt in her response to the interlocutors of the Critical Exchange, appearing here in Conversation I, on the "agonistic turn" in political theory. Were she to write *Political Theory and the Displacement of Politics* today, she would make abundantly clear that "Arendt's silence on the genocidal displacements of indigenous peoples and her erasure of the impact of slavery's legacy on the American republic are enabled by her rather unagonistic embrace of the new, and this is supported by her signing on to the myth of an immigrant America, one of the carriers of the idea of natality as an "In the beginning" rebirth or new start" (Honig in Maxwell et al., 2019, p. 667, ch. 4 here). Had she reckoned with this part of Arendt early on, Honig admits, she would have spent far more time thinking through the intersections of race and gender, as she has done in subsequent work.

The contributions to this Collexion propose a variety of other ways feminists can avoid becoming a master's tool, in the varied meanings of the term. Some thinkers, like Bracewell, call on feminists to be far more wary of their engagement with state institutions, particularly those implicated in the criminal legal system, for redress of gender injustice and harm that than they currently are. While others, like Cristina Beltrán, caution against ceding the power of the state to the far-right in a move to embrace unconventional and agonistic political practices. As the dismantling of abortion rights and the rise of authoritarianism prove, feminism does so at its own peril. In the realm of theory, feminists who have retrained their senses might commit to building new relations of care and community rooted in "bold, transformative, and adamantly anti-carceral visions of sexual freedom" (Bracewell, 2020, p. 98, ch. 11 here). Or it might "think of freedom in collective terms" (Gregoratto in Gregorrato et al., 2023, p. 66, ch. 15 here), adopting "canny electoral strategies to win power for those who will do right by those betrayed by today's faux-populism" (Honig in Maxwell et al., 2019, p. 664, ch. 4 here), while also embracing and encouraging strategies of survival, when needed, which refuse to be legible in conventional political terms.

As the contributions to this Collexion suggest, whatever new ways of seeing, thinking, and doing result from a retraining of our senses, an intersectional feminist theory and activism capable of understanding and responding to the challenges of the twenty-first century must be willing to live with the feeling of being unsettled and willing to let go of deeply ingrained fantasies of pure justice and equality, of happiness and reconciliation. This is what Hagar Kotef's provocative reading of *Frozen* reminds us. A feminism willing to acknowledge and address the way it perpetuates forms of racial violence and queer oppression is one that is committed to "engaging rather than displacing remainders" (Kotef in Galloway et al., 2023, p. 645, ch. 16 here), one that does not fear "refusing the logic of closure," to borrow Cristina Beltrán's words (Beltrán in Maxwell et al., 2019, p. 649, ch. 4 here). Such a feminism may not be easy to create or sustain, but, as the contributions to this Collexions illustrate, feminist theory and practice is filled with examples of sorority and solidarity, creativity and courage, resilience and resistance, which can inspire and sustain us while still calling us to account.

Reference

Ahmed, S. (2017). *Living a feminist life*. Duke University Press.

Printed in the United States
by Baker & Taylor Publisher Services